SHARE

A New Model for Social Work

By Siobhan Maclean, Jo Finch and Prospera Tedam

Illustrated by Harry Venning

> **We would like to dedicate this book to the memory of two incredible people, Connor Sparrowhawk and Jo Cox. Jo was an inspirational woman who spent much of her time attempting to bring communities together. She recognised the commonalities rather than the differences amongst us.... Connor was an inspirational young man who died because of the indifference of professionals. Both are referred to in this book and both have had a significant impact on the development of the SHARE model.**

ISBN: 978-1-912130-70-2

First published 2018

This is the perfect bound version of the book.
A spiral bound version is also available.

A catalogue record for this book will be available from The British Library.

© *Kirwin Maclean Associates Ltd, 4 Mesnes Green, Lichfield, Staffs, WS14 9AB.*

© *Individual Stakeholder Voices: Copyright remains with author.*

All Rights Reserved.

No Reproduction, copy or transmission of this publication may be made without written permission.

No paragraph of this publication may be reproduced, or transmitted save with written permission or in accordance with the provision of the Copyright, Designs and Patents Act 1988.

Any person who does any unauthorised act in relation to this publication may be liable to criminal prosecution and civil claims for damages.

Design work by Steve Bailey of Accent Commercial Resources.
Printed by 4edge Limited, Hockley, Essex

Contents

    Introducing the authors 7
    Meet the illustrator 11
    Meet the stakeholders 11
    Introducing the reader 12

Chapter 1: Introducing the SHARE Model 13
    The components 13
    Sensory aspects of SHARE 14
    Emotional context of SHARE 16
    Stakeholders 16
    Different dimensions 17
    Connecting components and dimensions 17
    Research 18
    Why now? 18
    The scope of this book 19

Chapter 2: The Development of the Model 21
    Why the word share? 21
    More in common 22
    Share in contemporary practice 23
    The digital share 27
    Is sharing, caring? 31
    Information sharing 31
    Knowledge sharing 34
    Reciprocity 36
    Reciprocity in social work training 37
    Sharing and wellbeing 40
    Sharing and kindness 40
    Sharing and belonging 41
    Othering 42
    Complexity and reflexivity 44
    Values and anti-oppressive practice 46
    Hopeful social work 48

Chapter 3: Social Work Theory 51
    Theories, models, methods and approaches 51
    Using SHARE to understand the difference between theories,
    models and approaches 53
    Hopeful approach 55
    Strengths based approach 57
    Restorative approach 61
    Restorative questions 61
    The importance of WITH 62
    Relational approach 63
    The 4Ps 64
    Systemic approach 69
    Holistic approach 71

Chapter 4: Adult Learning Theory 73
    Approaches to adult learning 74
    Behaviourist approach 75
    Social learning theory 76
    Situated learning theory 77
    Cognitive approach 78
    Humanist approach 79
    Experiential learning 80
    Learning styles 81
    Social pedagogy 84
    Digitalisation in social work: impact on learning 85
    SHARE in adult learning 92

Chapter 5: Seeing 95
    Observational skills 95
    Seeing things differently 97
    Observation as a research method 100
    The use of direct observation in practice education 101
    Informal observation and Formal observation 103
    Observation in social work practice 104
    Hawthorne effect 104
    Multi-sensorality 104
    Visual thinking 107
    Examples of visual thinking in social work 108
    Social Work in 40 Objects 108
    Experiencing the Social Work World 110
    Creative arts in social work 113
    The journey model for practice education 116
    The use of visual thinking in this book 118
    Visual representation as a mechanism of oppression 119
    The concept of vision 120
    Supervision in social work 121
    Intervision 123
    Acknowledging what we don't see 124
    Invisibilisation 124
    Colourblindness 126
    Normalisation 127
    Connecting components: A seen child is not a safe child 129
    Who do we see? 130

Chapter 6: **Hearing** 133
 Hearing and listening 133
 Being a 'good listener' 134
 Empathic listening 134
 Active listening 135
 What is hearing about? 137
 Barriers to hearing 139
 Organisational barriers 147
 SHARE: holistic listening 148
 What we hear in social work: the use of language 148
 What we hear in social work: the place of humour 151
 What we hear in social work: the importance of feedback 154
 A final word about SHARE in feedback 159
 Conversational practice 161
 Conversations: the five Cs 164
 The importance of having a voice 167
 Speaking up as social workers 171
 Whistle-blowing 174

Chapter 7: **Action** 177
 SHARE: the centrality of action 177
 What? Why? How? 178
 What is social work? 179
 Thinking about the history of social work 180
 Social work role models 183
 The politics of social work 187
 Social work as a human rights profession 190
 Getting down to the WHY question: why am I a social worker? 192
 How do we do social work? 193
 Managerialism in social work 195
 Radical social work 196
 Social work has the X Factor: Praxis 198
 Activism 200
 Boot Out Austerity 204
 Days of action 206
 World Social Work Day 206
 Adult PSW Network activities 207
 Stress and burnout in social work 209
 Forms of stress 209
 Professional resilience 211
 Acts of self-care in social work 214

Chapter 8: **Reading** 217
 The importance of reading 217
 What do we read in social work? 222
 What we read in social work: Literature 222
 What we read in social work: Case files 223
 What we read in social work: The press 226
 Barriers to reading 231
 Clinical barriers to reading 232
 Attitudinal barriers 235
 Organisational barriers 239

        Recording in social work practice 240
        Recording: employer focus 241
        Recording: the 'wh' questions 242
        What to record 243
        Why record 247
        When to record 249
        Where to record 249
        Who will read the record 250
        The which question 251
        How to record 251
        Using the SHARE Model in recording 252

Chapter 9:   **Evaluation** **255**
        What is evaluation? 255
        Reflective practice 256
        Stages of reflection 256
        Spaces of reflection 257
        SHARE in reflection 258
        Emotional intelligence and social work 259
        Emotions and evaluation frameworks 260
        Turning knowledge into understanding 261
        Evaluation in contemporary practice 264
        Witchcraft labelling 264
        Modern day slavery 265
        Death making 266
        Connecting Components: Looking Deeper 269
        Critical thinking 270
        Analytical skills 272
        The A-Z of evaluation 276

Chapter 10:   **Applications of the SHARE model** **279**
        Assessment in social work practice 281
        Exploring the service user's share 284
        Risk assessment and defensible decision making 286
        Collaborative working 288
        Continual Professional Development 290
        Assessed and Supported Year in Employment 293
        Induction for new staff and students 299
        Supervision 302
        Designing and delivering teaching sessions / training 306
        Planning placement learning 309
        Assessing a student in practice 313
        The A-Z of the SHARE model 316

Chapter 11:   **Conclusion** **319**

        References 322

Introducing the authors

Between us, we have almost 70 years of social work experience, which spans working in different areas of practice; delivering and using services; working in different counties, countries and continents; direct practice, teaching and research.

This book is very much jointly authored. We have not named individual chapters as being written by one or the other of us, because it is very much a joint development. At times, however, we have shared our own research or practice experience. These contributions are referred to as individual shares within the main text.

Here, we provide a little information about ourselves to provide the context of our individual share in the development of this exciting new model for social work practice and education.

Siobhan Maclean

I qualified as a social worker aged 22 with a degree in social work and a CQSW (the professional qualification of the day). I have now been a social worker for more than half of my life. If you cut me in half it would say social worker all the way through. Social work is not just what I do, but who I am.

I have worked in a variety of social work settings in both the statutory and voluntary sectors. I have been a practice educator for many years and really enjoy working with students. In 2013 I had a major stroke. This has impacted on my understanding of social work in many ways as I will share in this book. Since that time, I have not been a direct case holder, although I still support other social workers in discussing their work directly. I also still work as an offsite practice educator.

I was privileged to hold the position of Honorary Secretary of the International Federation of Social Workers (European Region) for a number of years. I learnt a great deal from this role, gaining an international perspective on our profession and am keen to further develop the international links which I have.

I have written a number of books for students and for social workers and I undertake a great deal of training. Largely my writing and my training falls into the areas of social work theory and critical reflection which is where my passions lie.

I believe strongly in the importance of creativity in social work. Now more than ever, social workers need to be creative. They need to be supported in creative workplaces by creative managers and they need to have creative models to support their practice.

I am also a mother to two wonderful young women.

Jo Finch

I qualified as a social worker aged 25, with an MSc in Social Policy and Social Work Studies and a Diploma in Social Work (DipSW), the qualification that came after the CQSW in the UK. Prior to undertaking my social work qualification, I worked in a council in the South of England, in what was termed then a 'residential unit', with adults with learning disabilities, a number of whom had recently been released from long stay learning disability 'hospitals'. This was the very start of care in the community, with residents living in ordinary houses in the community. Whilst young, and somewhat idealistic, I saw first-hand the patronising and disablist attitudes that some care staff held. I fought hard for the residents to live age appropriate lives, not be treated like children, and make full use all the facilities in the community, like any other citizen. Whilst at times, it felt like we were banging our heads on a wall, we had some notable successes. I then decided to travel to India and I was involved in voluntary work with a charity in Mumbai, before beginning my social work training.

As a qualified social worker, I have worked in a number of London Boroughs in children and family settings, and also worked in the voluntary sector in different roles. My journey into teaching social work was rather unplanned and I have now been a social work educator for 15 years. I have taught a wide range of modules over those 15 years, but now mostly focus on teaching social policy and research methodology. I have a strong identity as a social worker, recognising of course, I am not in direct social work practice, other than in an advisory role as a school governor responsible for safeguarding in two schools in East London. I have been concerned to see a rather anti-academic stance emerge in social work, and remind people that both the field and the academy are vital in training the social workers of the future. Social work is after all, as the International Federation of Social Workers reminds us, a practical and academic pursuit.

Life is busy, but in my limited spare time, I am a book lover. I read a wide variety of fiction books and I can't possibly go to sleep unless I have read at least five pages of a book. I am the mother of two boys, both of whom play football and I can often be found on winter Sunday mornings, shivering on some wind-swept football field!!

Prospera Tedam

I qualified as a social worker in 1996 at 24 years of age from the University of Ghana. My undergraduate thesis was exploring FGM in the area of Ghana where I come from. Following graduation, I worked on a number of projects funded by UNICEF in the area of integrating refugees who were fleeing war in Liberia. The work was both challenging and rewarding and I remember my supervisor providing me with updates while in public transport on our journey to the hosting centres to assess clients for eligibility for our services and support.

In 1998, I embarked on an MA in International Development at Leeds University where I developed my understanding of concepts such as inequality, marginalisation and poverty. I researched women's health and the implications for development in Ghana with the view of returning to Ghana to lead on the Women Refugee Project. However, marriage changed the 'plan' and I remained in the UK with my husband and have had various employment as a social worker in both the statutory and voluntary sectors.

I joined the Open University in 2004 as a part-time Associate Lecturer on the practice modules and thoroughly enjoyed working with students and decided to become a full time social work academic from 2006. That said, I continued to offer practice expertise wherever possible and chaired a fostering panel for an Independent Fostering Agency, taking on consultancy work around safeguarding BME children and also chaired the board of trustees of AFRUCA (Africans Unite Against Child Abuse). I was instrumental in enabling AFRUCA to provide placements for social work students and offered supervision to social work staff.

Between 2007 and 2009, I studied for the MA in Child Care Law and Practice at Keele University and taught on a range of undergraduate and post-graduate modules at the University of Northampton

I am always willing to support any projects and ideas that enhance social work practice and developed the MANDELA model for building relationships between practice educators and their students.

Currently, I am the Lead academic for Practice Quality at Anglia Ruskin University. I am delighted to be collaborating with Siobhan and Jo on this exciting and much needed model for social work practice.

Meet the Illustrator
Harry Venning

Harry Venning is an award winning cartoonist, comedy writer and performer based in Brighton.

The current UK Art Trust Strip Cartoonist Of The Year, Harry's cartoons have appeared in publications as diverse as Mathematics Today, The Radio Times, Music Teacher and The Stage. For twenty-one years he has provided The Guardian with the weekly strip cartoon Clare In The Community, based upon the misadventures of an empathy free social worker. In 2004 he developed Clare In The Community into a successful BBC Radio 4 sitcom starring Sally Philipps, which has recently been recommissioned for a twelfth series.

Harry says: When I am not at a desk writing or drawing, I tour my cartoon workshop 'Release Your Inner Cartoonist' around schools, theatres, arts centres and festivals.

I also work as a graphic visualiser, providing live cartoons to illustrate talks and speeches at conferences, festivals and team building events.

I have a wife called Geri, a daughter called Minnie, a cat called Petal and a bald patch.

Meet the stakeholders

A wide range of people have contributed to this book in the form of 'stakeholder voices'. We are immensely grateful to each of the contributors who will introduce themselves as they appear. They have generously given their time to share their stories and experiences. Without their voices, this book would not have been possible. In some situations, we asked people to contribute their thoughts in certain areas, in others we asked people what they wanted to share. The voices are not ours, we do not necessarily agree with everything that is shared, but we are seeking to engage in a conversion about this new model for social work practice and we are delighted that so many people have responded to our requests.

Introducing the reader

Social work is all about self-awareness. We have written this book in the hope that it will be useful to a wide range of stakeholders in social work. We invite you here to think about how you would like to introduce yourself. Who are you? What is your interest in social work? What do you want to get from this book? We have given you some space here to begin to introduce yourself. This may sound strange but this is the start of developing a clear sense of self which is so important in social work. Indeed, with the impact of austerity and the widespread cuts that social workers are seeing in their everyday practice, then often the only resource a social worker has to fall back on is themselves. You must know and be familiar with the tools of your trade, and in fact **you** are the tools of your trade.

Developing your 'share' as you read the book, will help you to frame your own understanding of the model (it will also be good for your CPD).

Chapter 1: INTRODUCING THE SHARE MODEL

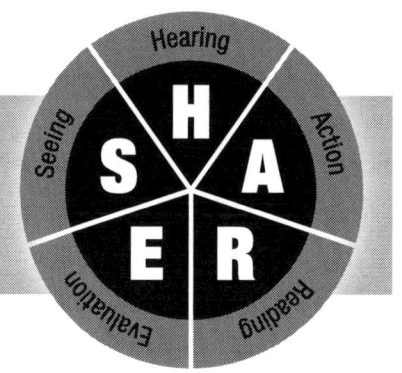

We are proud to be able to share a new model of practice for social work in this book. In recent years, we have come together to discuss our work and our experiences, and we have begun to recognise that as three very different women with diverse experiences, we share a number of things in common. As part of our common understanding about contemporary social work, we wanted to develop a new model for social work which would have applications to both direct practice and to social work education.

This chapter provides a brief introduction to the model and its individual but ultimately interconnecting components.

The components

At its heart, the SHARE model is straightforward, but that does not mean it lacks sophistication. As we go on to discuss, SHARE is a model that is rich in theory and research; based around a reflexive approach, it promotes in-depth critical reflection and analysis. The model is based around five key components which make up the acronym SHARE.

S — Seeing
H — Hearing
A — Action
R — Reading
E — Evaluation

In social work, models provide a framework for intervention. Essentially, they are about what we 'do'. Each of the individual aspects of the SHARE model is about 'doing'. In fact, each component of the model is a relatively uncomplicated thing that we all do on a daily basis. SHARE brings the five components together to create a holistic model building on the value of the interconnections between each individual component. The word SHARE is not accidental, it has been specifically chosen for a number of reasons - which we explore in Chapter 2.

Sensory aspects of SHARE

The SHARE model builds on aspects of human senses. This partly relates to the humanistic stance of the model; it is based on human capabilities (much like social work) so computers, assistive technology and robots cannot do it.

Humans have five traditionally recognised senses:

- Sight (vision)
- Hearing (audition)
- Taste (gustation)
- Smell (olfaction)
- Touch (somatosensation)

Increasingly, spatial awareness is also being referred to as a sense, although for many years the 'sixth sense' has been used to describe extrasensory perception (ESP). The use of the human senses in social work is receiving more attention in contemporary literature. Lisa Morriss has undertaken a great deal of work in this area and she explains the value of the senses in the first stakeholder voice.

We have been excited by the increased acknowledgement of the value of sensory practice in social work and have drawn on this in the development of the SHARE model. The SHARE model draws explicitly on the two senses of seeing and hearing. However, we see the model as multi-sensory in that smell, touch and taste are embodied within the connections.

What we want to be very clear about is that the seeing and hearing aspects of the model are about much more than the physicality of sight and hearing. These components are about drawing on the fullest range of senses as we clarify in Chapters 5 and 6.

In recent years there has been an increasing awareness of the importance of the human senses in social work, as our first stakeholder voice from Lisa discusses. At the same time there has been an increasing interest in the use of the senses in learning and education. In fact, Doyle and Zakrajsek (2013) assert that the way in which senses work in co-operation with each other is being increasingly recognised in education, arguing that when two or more senses are used together then learning is more effective and memory is boosted. The SHARE model is multi-sensory and as such we hope that it will support the development of both social work practice and social work education as each of the components is inter-connected.

STAKEHOLDER VOICE: LISA MORRISS

Lisa Morriss is a Lecturer in Social Work at the University of Birmingham. She qualified as a social worker in 1995 and worked in Community Mental Health teams for over 10 years.

Social work practice takes place in affective and atmospheric encounters; both in the office and on home visits. Social work is sensory work (Morriss, 2017). Sensory ethnography is an interdisciplinary critical methodology which - unlike a classic observational approach - situates ethnography as a reflexive and experiential process in which the researcher closely attends to the senses throughout the research process. Thus, there is a deep resonance between sensory ethnography and social work. To illustrate, here is an extract from an adoptive parent, F, talking about links to their child's past:

> *R, at three, she came with a tiny little white, like Snoopy dog and that was from, that was from birth mother era and that has a cigarette burn on it, the same as she has a cigarette burn, she has, um, and then she paid no attention to it whatsoever. You know, they accumulate so many toys and things. I've always kept that in her room but it's hidden at the back of the pile. (Brown et al., 2014 p.179)*

The Snoopy dog has a visceral quality: the size, colour, and the cigarette burn in the fur invoke a multisensorial response. F appears to distance themselves from their child's past life by referring to the 'birth mother era'. S/he makes a physical connection between the toy and the little girl: both share a cigarette burn inflicted in this former life. The Snoopy dog is a powerful symbol of a time when F's daughter lived with her birth family; a time when she was either intentionally or accidentally harmed. F cannot simply throw this toy away as it is a direct connection with their daughter's history; at the same time, the material presence of this toy is seemingly unbearable. Moreover, although the child may pay no attention to the Snoopy dog at the moment, there is also a sense of an anticipated future when she may wish to reconnect with her past. To manage this ambivalence, F keeps the toy in the daughter's bedroom, but it is deliberately hidden at the back of the pile of other toys. The Snoopy dog is there but not there; secret but discoverable; connected to the past but also to a possible future. Thus, sensory ethnography is a means of exploring such unspoken, felt or sensed elements of everyday experiences (Pink, 2015). Social work practice is a deeply embodied, sensory and mobile experience and by attending to the sensory, social work researchers can evoke this lived experience in their accounts.

© Lisa Morriss

Emotional context of SHARE

We recognise the vital importance of emotions in social work and feel that the emotional context of practice is often missing from academic and theoretical discussions about practice. We have debated whether the E of SHARE should relate specifically to emotions but have concluded that the evaluation component of the model is vital. We hope that when the model is used, emotions will be fully explored as part of the evaluation component. Certainly, the emotional context of practice is considered in Chapter 9 where we explore evaluation in more detail.

Human emotions are often expressed through sensory means and what we experience through our senses certainly impacts on feelings. We therefore see the SHARE model as encompassing the emotional context of practice, which is regularly demonstrated in the stakeholder voices throughout this book.

Stakeholders

We come from the position that certain people in our professional world hold significantly more power than others and that often only a few privileged stakeholders are consulted about the development of social work policy and new approaches to practice. We recognise that there are many stakeholders in social work and want to ensure that our model is inclusive of everyone with an interest in social work.

Building on the ideas of Tony Morrison (2005) and his inclusion of four key stakeholders in an integrated model of supervision, we recognise a wider range of stakeholders, as:

- Service users and their families
- Social workers
- Students
- Practice educators
- Managers
- Employers
- Higher Education Institutions (Universities and Colleges)
- Lecturers
- Other professionals
- The general public
- Politicians and civil servants

Our view is that everyone should have a stake in the provision of good quality social work. Our observations over the years suggest that whilst there have been a number of very positive developments, for example, the involvement of experts by experience (sometimes referred to as service users and carers) in social work programmes, there remains a need for a more participatory and broader approach in considerations of what is, and should be 'good' social work practice. We remain concerned, that we continue to see practice, as well as social work literature which creates a distinct 'us and them' approach to the development of social work. Our hope is that the SHARE model can be used in a way which recognises that we all have a stake in the development and practice of our profession.

The model proposes that each individual SHARE component should be considered from the perspective of all the stakeholders involved in any situation being considered. As such, we have included the full range of 'stakeholder voices' throughout this book, to explore diverse experiences of social work. We feel it is important that the very development and writing of this book, should be congruent with the SHARE model and the values that underpin our approach. Of course, each of the different stakeholders identified has a different level of interest in the various aspects of social work policy, practice and education covered in this book.

We have included 43 stakeholder voices in this book. One of the things that is really interesting about the different stakeholder voices is that they each have a different style and tone. Some, for example link their voice to academic references, therefore connecting their voice to that of others. Other voices draw essentially on their own personal experience. This in itself demonstrates the different perspectives of each stakeholder. Our aim here is to present a variety of 'voices' and not privilege a particular voice over another. To that end, stakeholders were given a very open brief, to write about what was important to them. We have placed the stakeholder voices into the chapters that we think they most complement, but one aspect of the stakeholder voices is that they each demonstrate the ways in which the five components of the SHARE model interconnect, so they could just as easily fit into one of the other chapters.

Different dimensions

Bringing the components of the model and the key stakeholders together creates a range of different dimensions. The SHARE model is about not just what you see, hear, do, read and how you evaluate this, but it is also about how all the other stakeholders evaluate what they see, hear, do and read. Different stakeholders will inevitably see different things in the same situation and may hear what is said differently. This is clearly illustrated in the stakeholder voices included throughout this book, where a range of stakeholders share their very different perspectives. As you explore the different aspects of the SHARE model in this book, it is important to acknowledge that it is a model which promotes the recognition of the whole, in light of the parts. So, everything should be considered from the perspective of each stakeholder involved in any given situation.

Connecting components and dimensions in a dynamic, non-linear manner

The most important aspect of the SHARE model is that it should not be used in a linear way. It is dynamic in that it recognises the connections between each component. For example, what we read may well impact on what we see and hear in a situation. What a person does may well be influenced by what they have taken (evaluated) from what they have seen and heard. The components do not need to be taken in any particular order.

It is also inevitable that in some situations or at key times, it may be more important or useful to focus on one component; or because of various priorities, there may be clearer and more obvious connections between two or three of the components than others. There are also interconnections between what each stakeholder sees and how this relates, or not, to what other stakeholders identify.

Thus, within SHARE, the connections are of equal importance to the individual components. The processes and the shifts and changes in the connections, are an important way to fully take account of the complexities of peoples' lives, their interactions with a range of professionals as well as wider societal interactions with people and institutions. We are therefore somewhat suspicious of linear models, which in our view, are overly simplistic, prescriptive and do not adequately portray the complexities of human lives.

Research

The development of the SHARE model has been influenced by research in two main ways. Our own research experiences have taught us much about holistic anti-oppressive approaches to social work and what we sadly see as the growing divide between social work practice and social work education. We come from a position which embraces the International Federation of Social Worker's definition of social work, namely that social work is both a practice based profession and an academic discipline. To that end, we value and embrace the contribution that research makes in social work policy and practice, and actively seek to promote research mindedness. Practice that is not informed through reference to theory and research, is in our view, dangerous practice. The model thus draws on a wide range of research relevant to social work practice and education and to that end, we have included messages from research in each chapter.

Why now?

As we have documented earlier, we have over 70 years of social work practice and education experience behind us, working in different counties, countries and continents. We felt that the time was right to develop something new and innovative. We have some frustrations with existing models of social work which are to some extent outdated and reinforce a particular view of the world. We feel very privileged indeed that many different stakeholders have shared with us some of the current movements and happenings related to contemporary practice which truly challenge many of these outdated (often linear) models.

There is also an overt political motivation, linked to our concerns about how social work services, in England at least, are being shaped along very neoliberal lines. We also wanted to overtly acknowledge that the many hundreds if not thousands of social workers and practice educators we have worked with over the years, come from increasingly diverse backgrounds in terms of countries of origin, age, gender, sexuality, disability and class. We remain concerned about the narrowing of diversity of students on some newer approaches to social work education. The SHARE model was thus developed with an explicit acknowledgement of the increasingly globalised world we all live in.

We also feel, that social work in England, has to some extent lost its way. The time it seemed, was right to develop something new: something underpinned by research, theory, social work values as well as practice experience, and, perhaps most importantly, something which recognises the vital importance of all stakeholder voices. We also wanted to develop something that could have relevance and applicability beyond the UK, so the model is adaptable to social work policies and practices in other countries, and indeed, we also feel that the model could be applied to a wide range of comparator professions, for example youth work, social care, nursing and many other allied health professions.

The scope of this book

This introductory chapter has just given you a brief overview of the model and provided a 'flavour' of the values that underpin the model. The next chapter discusses the development of the model, as this is the first step in understanding SHARE and being able to use it in practice. Chapters 3 and 4 explain the theories which have influenced the development of the SHARE model and Chapters 5 to 9, provide an account of each of the components of the model, highlighting some key aspects of each component. Whilst each component is individually valuable it is vital to recognise that the strength of the SHARE model lies in the relationships between the components. We therefore conclude in Chapter 10 with some examples of the application of the model.

Key points

- The time is right for a new model for social work practice.
- The basic premise of the SHARE model is straightforward, but there is complexity in the interconnections between the parts.
- The model has an extended range of applicability.
- SHARE seeks to include all stakeholders.

Reflective Questions

What does the word share mean to you?

In what ways is social work sensory work?

In what ways is social work emotional work?

What do you do to ensure you are in touch with your senses and emotions?

The development of the SHARE model has been very organic and we have drawn on a range of voices. We very much want you to be a part of the development of this new model for social work. To this effect we have included a range of doodle pages in the book which we would encourage you to use to develop your share. Take a photo of the pages you doodle on, tweet it, get involved with the wider social work community as the model develops. These pages may also be useful to you as CPD evidence. If you are a student take these pages to supervision. Use this book in any way that works for you.

My Share

What am I thinking?

What am I feeling?

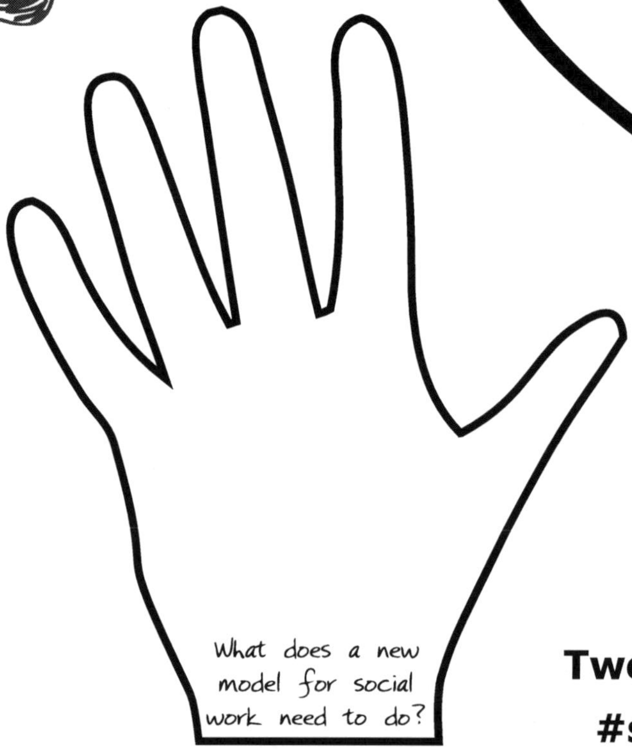

What does a new model for social work need to do?

Tweet your responses #socialworkSHARE

Chapter 2: THE DEVELOPMENT OF THE MODEL

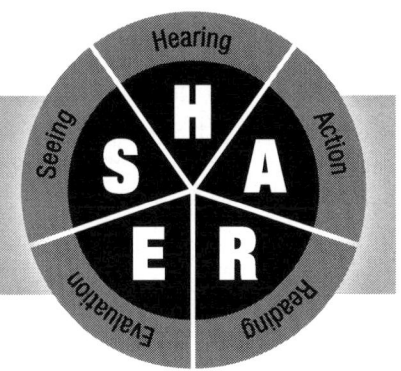

A number of key ideas have influenced us in the development of the SHARE model. This chapter will explore the way that the model was developed and provide some background to our rationale. We begin with an exploration of the word share.

Why the word share?

The word share is used in a range of ways - each of which has influenced the development of our model.

Sharing is about both giving and receiving. Early years professionals often concentrate on helping children learn how to share, and parents encourage their children to share from an early age - for example, sharing toys and sharing attention. This focus on sharing from an early age is culturally universal and is considered important across the lifespan, through adolescence and into adulthood. Indeed, in some societies sharing is essential for survival and a focus on individualism is frowned upon. We wanted to develop a model for social work which came from this perspective, namely a global and collective view of the word, and one that challenged, what we see as an individualised focus which is, in our view, impacting negatively and divisively on contemporary social work policy and practice in the UK. Indeed, we want to acknowledge here the influence of neoliberalism, which impacts on service users lives in adverse ways, and sets the agenda for the development of social policies, legislation and in turn, social work policy and practice. Whilst neoliberal governments are something we have to live with in the West, we want to instead emphasise the innate human good in sharing something. We also feel that the whole concept of sharing has very obvious resonance with social work values.

More in common

Sharing is also about what we have in common. Whilst a recognition and celebration of diversity is important for all of us, we work on the basis that we all share a common humanity. Whilst there are ways in which each and every individual is unique there are also many ways in which we share similarities and in some basic (biological) ways we are all the same.

Jo Cox was an MP for just 13 months when she was murdered in 2016. In her maiden speech (June 2015) she outlined the diversity of her constituency stating, *"We are far more united and have far more in common than that which divides us."* We hope that the SHARE model will encourage people to concentrate more on what we have in common than on what divides us.

In addition to a common humanity, we also believe in the importance of a common profession. Whilst social workers are employed in a range of different settings and contexts, we all share a framework of values and ethics, and, all work within the international definition of our profession:

"Social work is a practice-based profession and an academic discipline that promotes social change and development, social cohesion, and the empowerment and liberation of people. Principles of social justice, human rights, collective responsibility and respect for diversities are central to social work. Underpinned by theories of social work, social sciences, humanities and indigenous knowledge, social work engages people and structures to address life challenges and enhance wellbeing."

(International Federation of Social Workers 2014)

In England, we see a significant move away from a common profession approach to social work. So that, for example, children's and adult's social work seems to be becoming more and more specialist with the two 'strands' often taking different directions. We feel strongly about the importance of 'one profession'. Children live with adults and social workers need to understand issues across the lifespan. We hope that the SHARE model demonstrates what all social workers share in terms of their practice experiences and skills. The presentations and discussions at the recent Joint Conference for Principal Social Workers illustrated the importance of a shared profession (Wright and Pearson 2017). Ruth Stark, President of the International Federation of Social Workers has suggested that *"social workers need to be able to identify with a global profession in the way that lawyers or health professionals do."* (Schraer 2014). We agree that a sense of belonging to a global profession is vital for social workers and hope that the SHARE model can be used to highlight what social workers around the world have in common.

The international definition of social work points to central themes around the idea of sharing. Every member of society has something to contribute to their own lives and the lives of others. Social workers become involved in people's lives with the aim of understanding their situation and supporting them to regain control. Service users share the stories of how they got to where they are, and rely on social workers to use their professional knowledge and skills to assist them. The theme of 'collective responsibility' is very much in line with the ethos of the SHARE model. Being collectively responsible means that people will, in many ways, contribute to the overall outcomes of a community or society. It implies that people share in the positives and negatives and the challenges and opportunities. It minimises the potential to apportion blame to any one group of people, family or individual.

Share in contemporary practice

The word share comes from the Middle English word 'shear' which denotes the cutting or division of land. A share is therefore about the division of a resource. Social workers are involved in decisions about the sharing of resources, and are often asked by society to operationalise the division of resources in ways which they themselves may not agree with. Traditionally, social work has engaged with people who have not had an equal share when things have been divided. With the impact of the austerity era we believe that this situation is getting worse. The divide is getting wider and will continue to do so. We wanted to develop a model which recognises the inequality in society and comes from an anti-oppressive stance.

We don't all get an equal share of the cake

KEY MESSAGES FROM RESEARCH: POVERTY

In 2014, 6.5% of the UK population were in persistent poverty, equivalent to approximately 3.9 million people (Office for National Statistics 2016).

28% of those in poverty in the UK are disabled (3.9 million people) while a further 20% of people in poverty (2.7 million) live in a household with a disabled person (New Policy Institute, 2017).

30% of Britain's children are now classified poor (around 4 million children) (Butler, 2017).

67% of poor children are from working families (Butler, 2017).

Poverty is higher amongst ethnic minority groups than the white majority population in Scotland (Kelly, 2016).

Children from the poorest areas of the UK are up to two years behind their classmates when they sit their GCSEs. The attainment gap between 'persistently' poor children and non-disadvantaged peers has widened in the past decade (Andrews, Robinson and Hutchinson 2017).

In the UK, the number of households accepted as homeless and the number of households in temporary accommodation have both increased for five years in a row. Evictions by landlords are near a ten year high (Tinson et al, 2016).

In the business world, the word share has a very different connotation. Shares which are based on the principles of sharing in the profit and losses of a business are sold on the stock market. The current political climate is based on a neoliberal ideology which celebrates wealth creation and accumulation, and promotes an individualistic society. In this context, the worth of people is often valued in light of stocks and shares.

Currently, business models are being applied to the profession and to social work education in a variety of ways. We hope that the SHARE model can be used to reposition social work more explicitly with its foundations of social justice and human rights.

People are people, not commodities

KEY MESSAGES FROM RESEARCH: STOCKS AND SHARES

The National Audit Office (2013) identified that the four biggest outsourcing companies in the UK receive around £34billion per year to run a variety of public services in the UK. This figure is growing.

ATOS is a French based multi-National company. It received £700 million for UK public sector delivery in the NHS, Home Office and Welsh Government in 2012 (National Audit Office 2013).

ATOS was responsible for capability assessments in relation to benefits. 40% of the decisions made by ATOS assessors were overturned on appeal (We Own It 2017).

Serco received £1.8billion from the UK Government to deliver services in health, education, welfare support etc. (National Audit Office 2013). Serco is a multi-national company but 60% of its income relates to UK Government contracts.

In a 2014 survey (Survation 2014) 21% of the public trusted outsourcing companies; 69% felt they were motivated by profit maximisation; 22% felt they were motivated by providing the best service; 16% think there is adequate regulation of private outsourcing companies running public services.

In 2016 the UK Government spent £477million keeping 2,500 people with learning disabilities in hospital: more than half of them in the private sector (Brown and Hatton 2017).

In 2017 G4S sold its children's care home business for £11million (Jozwiak 2017).

The digital share

Digitally, the word share is used to describe giving people access to online content - particularly in relation to social media. Many social media settings have a 'share' option. Phrases 'file-sharing' software and 'video-sharing' sites are in common usage. Whilst we recognise the many benefits that social media can bring to our profession, we have been concerned by some of the things that we have seen posted and shared, which in our view perpetuate oppressive stereotypes about people who may use social work services.

There has long been a negative narrative of social work within the wider press which focuses on alleged failings in the profession, most notably when children known to social services die at the hands of their parents or carers (Finch and Schaub, 2015). Indeed, we discuss this in more detail in Chapter 7. The emergence, however, of a destructive narrative within social media, sadly some of which is propagated by some misguided individuals within the profession itself, rather than by journalists with limited understanding of our role, is even more alarming. We hope that the SHARE model will address some of the negative stereotypes of our profession and re-orientate social work to a more egalitarian relationship-focused position.

STAKEHOLDER VOICE
WARREN BELCHER

Warren is an advanced practitioner / social worker working in an adult's service. @ermate

Social work has become very much part of my own identity; it's a big part of my life and a part I have chosen to express like many others on social media. Writing blogs has enabled me to connect with people who either work or experience social work in some form.

My opening statement for a blog I wrote for World Social Work Day held in March 2017 attempted to identify what social work means to me:

> *Social work is and always will be about people, about the complexities of relationships, environments, the human condition, oppression, abuse by people towards other people, opportunity, empowerment, identity, human rights and enabling choice and control over one's own life. My social work role enables to me focus on citizens whose lives require this support and understanding. I help with practical support to get things done and to help maintain or prevent poor situations developing outside of people's own choices and control.*

I have also written personal accounts about adult safeguarding, the challenges of social work process, practice education and the use of social media by social workers.

Writing down my own thoughts and feelings enables me to think about a profession I am immensely privileged to be part of and I hope has encouraged debate and thinking with others. I believe social work has a responsibility to reflect and think about what it actually is and where necessary to identify what works well and what is difficult. These thoughts can feel deeply personal and more private for some. If you do share your thoughts about social work via social media it's important to be mindful that your contribution can also be influential. Social work must be truthful to itself; it must identify the positives but also not be afraid to frame the challenges in order to work towards solutions together. I have learnt through blogging and by my own social media comments that my own contribution is just a snapshot, a moment of comment and not necessarily a basis for anything else than what the reader wants it to be.

Public comments made by social workers are very visible, so such comment should be used to create a balance and to be accountable to both ourselves and to others. Public confidence must be based upon our profession's ability to retain our values with careful yet honest balanced reflection. It is very easy for comments on social media to create confirmation bias or bandwagon effects leading to uncomfortable content. I try my best to write balanced blogs and make reasonable comments but it's not necessarily easy. What is possible is not to create a situation, which can spiral quickly; it should always be possible not to cause individual distress for anyone concerned. Social media can cause defensive positions where original points can get lost within the process of negative and deeply personal language and argument. Social work is about people, so we must demonstrate to the public that we can converse appropriately with each other even within challenging debates and frustrations concerning our practice or conditions of practice.

When social work related topics are played out on wider social media platforms it naturally places social work under the microscope and I welcome this, as social work needs to be visible in order to be valued. However what social workers think they are looking at under such a microscope can be at risk of being viewed very differently by citizens and by influencers. The actual process of social work away from social media will always be based upon research, theories, skills, methods and of course politics. Social media enables commentators from all different areas to come together for respectful and stimulated debate to both embrace and challenge social work accordingly. However, it will always be our own experiences including our relationships with each other, which will impact on citizens and the communities we support. So, let's keep blogging and discussing together, but with kindness and mindfulness because everyone matters, even when we might think differently.

© Warren Belcher

So as discussed by Warren, there is a further element to digital sharing that needs exploration as it can be a 'double edged sword'. It is clear that technology can be used positively to connect people who might not meet in real life. We all use social media and have enjoyed the on-line connections we have made not only with social work academics, practitioners, users and carers but also people from a wide range of backgrounds, countries and professions; many of whom we have been able to approach about contributing to this book. We have enjoyed reading social work blogs that explore areas of practice we might not be so familiar with and also reading blogs from people outside of the profession which can be informative in a range of ways. Such blogs used well, can serve to breakdown some of the stereotypes and misunderstandings between various groups of people. Indeed, the use of social media in terms of knowledge sharing can be really positive.

The use of technology has become part and parcel of everyday life, which many of us could not do without. In the writing of this book, we have used online document sharing techniques as well as group texts to discuss and share our emerging ideas. However, we need to remember that many people cannot make use of the technology that most of us take for granted and are therefore excluded. For example, we note the use of online forms for many government departments which effectively exclude those who do not have internet access at home or cannot use computers. There is a scene in the film 'I-Daniel Blake', where we see the lead character struggle to use an online form and the member of staff from the employment office, is castigated for supporting him to use the computer. This illustrates the way that many people are being 'left behind' in the use of technology.

We feel that everyone with an interest in social work should watch this film.

A further concern we have relates to those who use social media in destructive ways. For example, perpetuating on-line abuse and trolling. We note how women in the public eye are particularly vulnerable to online abuse and trolling. We recall the example in 2013, when Caroline Criado-Perez, campaigned to get the face of Jane Austen on the back of a £10 note. The online abuse and threats she received were shocking and resulted in her being advised by the police to leave her home (Philipson, 2013).

Regulatory bodies require practitioners to conduct themselves appropriately on social media and as we said at the outset of this section, we have been concerned at instances where we feel some peoples' use of social media has not accorded with regulatory requirements and serve instead to perpetuate stereotypes about users of social work and health services. Unlike a conversation in real life, messages on social media are there in perpetuity for lots of people to see. Therefore 'sharing' by registered social workers has to be done within clear ethical and professional boundaries both online and in real life in our day to day interactions with users of social work services and other professionals.

During the final stages of writing of this book, the HCPC (which regulates social workers in England as well as other professional groups) has published new guidance on the use of social media by regulated professionals. This guidance discusses what professionals need to do in order to use social media safely, and demonstrates the benefits of social media use. Using the SHARE model to guide use of social media can be helpful, and we would encourage you to think this through on the following page.

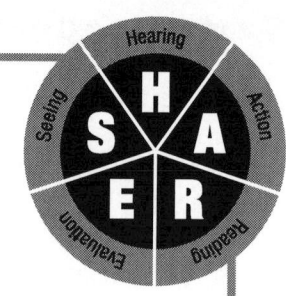

 SEE: What do I see on social media? For example, what do I see about how social work is portrayed? What might people see about me through my use of social media? (How might they view me as a result?)

 HEAR: What do I hear about social media? Is it always negative?

 ACT: What sort of things do I share? How do my professional values impact on who I 'friend' or follow or what I post? How do I respond when I see something that concerns or angers me on social media?

 READ: What do I like reading on social media?

 EVALUATE: What are my overall impressions on the use of social media? What are the main benefits? What are the potential pitfalls?

What social media do I use?

Why do I use this social media?

How do I use it?

To what extent am I conversant with regulatory guidance with regard to social media?

What are my employer's requirements with regards to the use of social media?

30

Is sharing, caring?

If you do a quick google of the word share, very quickly you will come across the phrase 'sharing is caring'. Whilst this may be somewhat of a cliché we do feel strongly that we need to emphasise the importance of empathy and compassion in social work. We acknowledge that the word care has negative associations implying dependency and frailty. For example, the Social Platform (2010:1) recognised that:

> "The disability movement challenged the term 'care' replacing it with 'right to support'. For many disabled activists, the very concept of 'care' embodies an oppressive history in which the practices of paid (particularly professional) and unpaid carers have maintained disabled and older people in a position of unwanted dependency, at worst abused, segregated and stripped of their dignity, at best patronised and protected from exercising any agency over their lives. Instead care needs are reinterpreted as having choice and control as the strategies for the empowerment of disabled people".

We come from the position that the links between 'share' and 'care' reflect our view that everyone should have choice and control over their own lives and that life is about interdependency. No one person is an island. We are all reliant on others to some extent. For example, the three of us use public transport regularly and as such we are all reliant on train drivers and other public transport workers. We are however called passengers or travellers rather than service users. Rather than reinforcing any individual's dependency we must begin to recognise that everyone has a dependency on others. We are all interdependent on one another. Dominelli (2017) recognises that all citizens are interdependent and interconnected in some way. We hope that the SHARE model will promote an interconnectedness which can realign power differentials and work as a counter weight to the neoliberal promotion, and indeed, celebration of individualism and competition, which in our view, is damaging, rather than liberating.

Information sharing

Social workers are used to the phrase information-sharing which is regularly used in relation to collaborative working, particularly where there are safeguarding concerns. Indeed, there is a range of national policy guidance covering the importance of information sharing in social work.

The BASW code of Ethics states that *"Social workers should ensure the sharing of information is subject to ethical requirements in respect of privacy and confidentiality across agencies and professions, and within a multi-purpose agency"* (BASW 2012a). What we know however is that information sharing across agencies is a real challenge to ensure we manage the balance between upholding the rights of privacy of individuals and families, set against the legal duties to safeguard and protect.

There have been notable lapses in information sharing, as recognised in a range of serious case reviews and public inquiries into child deaths (see for example, Blom-Cooper, 1995; Laming, 2003; Bichard report, 2004). We also note concerns about poor information sharing in terms of adult services. SCIE (2010) remind us that accurate recording and information sharing safeguards children, families and individuals as well as ourselves.

An interesting and controversial view about the value of information sharing between agencies can be found in the work of French urban Sociologist Jacques Donzelot. In his 1977 book, 'The Policing of Families'. He claims that early intervention and information sharing across services, can serve instead to blur the line between the assistential and the penal and so does not help families at all. Of course, this is a controversial view but nonetheless raises the spectre of how families might feel, when and if agencies share information.

There is clear guidance about information sharing in relation to social work practice. For example, in 2004 a Practitioners Guide to Information Sharing was developed for professionals working with children and young people, the Government revised this guidance and extended it to cover professionals working with adult service users in 2008. It was republished in 2015 (HM Government 2015). The focus of the guidance is on sharing information legally and appropriately. The guidance contains the seven 'Golden Rules' for information sharing, which we would summarise as follows:

1. Remember that the Data Protection Act is not a barrier to sharing information but provides a framework to ensure that personal information about living persons is shared appropriately.

2. Be open and honest with the person (and / or their family where appropriate) from the outset about why, what, how and with whom information will, or could be shared, and seek their agreement, unless it is unsafe or inappropriate to do so.

3. Seek advice if you are in any doubt, without disclosing the identity of the person where possible.

4. Share with consent where appropriate and, where possible, respect the wishes of those who do not consent to share confidential information. You may still share information without consent if, in your judgement, that lack of consent can be overridden in the public interest. You will need to base your judgement on the facts of the case.

5. Consider safety and wellbeing. Base your information sharing decisions on considerations of the safety and wellbeing of the person and others who may be affected by their actions.

6. Necessary, proportionate, relevant, accurate, timely and secure. Ensure that the information you share is necessary for the purpose for which you are sharing it, is shared only with those people who need to have it, is accurate and up-to-date, is shared in a timely fashion, and is shared securely.

7. Keep a record of your decision and the reasons for it – whether it is to share information or not. If you decide to share, then record what you have shared, with whom and for what purpose.

KEY MESSAGES FROM RESEARCH: INFORMATION SHARING

Richardson and Asthana (2006) identified a typography of patterns of inter-agency information sharing within health and social care agencies. Such interactions included, ideal, over-open, over-cautious and chaotic and were dependent on organisational culture around inter-professional information sharing but also how professionals related with one another.

Steven Hoskin, who had learning difficulties, and was known to a range of services, was tortured and brutally murdered by several people in 2006. The Serious Case Review, conducted by Cornwall Adult Protection Committee found that many agencies failed to share information about his vulnerability and requests for help (Flynn, 2007).

Research undertaken by the Social Care Institute for Excellence (SCIE) in an analysis of 38 Serious Case Reviews (SCRs), found that schools were reluctant to share information in child protection processes because of a range of perceived barriers, including not wanting to damage relationships with families (SCIE, 2016).

In 2015, a 17-week year old baby died whilst co sleeping with his parents and subsequently overheating. There were many concerns about the parents and agencies were criticised about poor information sharing (NSPCC, 2016).

In 2014, a 7-week year old baby 'Thomas' was admitted to a Devon hospital with a non-accidental head injury. The SCR report, amongst other things, recommended a review of communication systems across agencies (NSPCC, 2016).

Two thirds of local authorities have no arrangements for sharing information with the Police when a child is reported missing, meaning that the police lack crucial knowledge about the child's life (Chetwynd and Pona 2017).

Children's Society research indicates that a lack of information sharing between professionals impacts on risk assessments in relation to missing and vulnerable children (Chetwynd and Pona 2017).

As it can be seen, information sharing is really important and is often cited in Public Inquiries and Serious Case Reviews as a factor in what went wrong, with a recognition that many organisations IT systems are not compatible. This also needs be set against the very real concerns about public surveillance and loss of privacy, plus the legal requirements about information sharing.

Knowledge sharing

Generally, social workers do recognise the value of information sharing. However, what we are not always so good at is recognising the value of sharing knowledge and practice wisdom with other social workers. The SHARE model recognises the value of social workers sharing their knowledge and experience to develop the profession. It also recognises the importance of other key stakeholders sharing their experiences and knowledge to ensure that the profession develops in a holistic way which takes into account the lived experiences of all stakeholders. No voice should be lost as we seek to find a new, more shared, understanding of our profession.

The International Federation of Social Workers recognises the vital importance of social workers sharing knowledge and insights in a range of ways (IFSW, 2014). Shennan (2017) highlights the importance of social workers having conversations with one another and with key stakeholders to share knowledge to ensure that the profession remains relevant in the modern world, this links with the contemporary focus on conversational practice (see page 161.)

STAKEHOLDER VOICE — GUY SHENNAN

Guy Shennan uses solution-focused ideas in social work - and is the Chair of the British Association of Social Workers.

Knowledge is social!

A couple of years ago I was captivated by a presentation by Niels Barkholt, the Vice-President of the Danish Association of Social Workers, called Knowledge Sharing in Social Work. Its central message was a simple one - social workers need to talk with each other. We have lots of knowledge, but this can't always find its way into practice, especially when 'pushed' towards us by the powers that be. It is found in books, policies and procedures, but just reading these is not enough. For knowledge is social, and we have to talk with each other for it to affect our practice.

Listening to all this took me back over twenty years, to the beginnings of my discovery of solution-focused practice. I was working with a family where the constant fighting between two brothers was driving their single mother to distraction. I was feeling stuck, and ready to try something new. I had recently bought a book called A Brief Guide to Brief Therapy (Cade and O'Hanlon, 1993), and was especially attracted to a chapter called 'Exceptions, Solutions and the Future Focus', again, drawn to the simplicity of the ideas I found there. I learned that the idea of exceptions was that, whatever problem a person has, there are always times when it doesn't happen, or happens with less intensity, or with less frequency. And it could be useful to focus on the exception times and not just on the problem. This seemed to make sense!

Having read this, the next time I saw the family I asked the boys if they could think of a time when something had happened which might have made them fall out with each other, but where they had managed not to fight, and done something else instead. They could, or at least one of them could, and he told me of a time. I remember smiling wanly while frantically trying to remember what the book said to do next. Unable to, all I could think to do was to say, "Great, keep it up!", thinking this must sound a little lame.

Reading a book was not enough, and it was only after attending a course on solution-focused brief therapy that I was really able to utilise the skills of this approach in my work. And the most essential aspect of this course, and all the training I have done since, was the practice opportunities it afforded, coupled with the reflections on practice that one can engage in during a course. I had a safe (enough) space to have a go at asking a question ("Can you think of a time when...?"), listening to the answer, and then following up that answer with another question ("How did you manage to do that?"), and then another ("What difference did that make?")

We should create reflective spaces outside of training courses too, where by talking with each other we can develop our knowledge and allow it to find its way into our practice. For knowledge is social!

© Guy Shennan

We have explored, therefore, some different connotations of the word 'share' and 'sharing' but in summary, it largely concerns the act of 'giving' or 'dividing up resources'. We now change direction slightly and explore the notion of reciprocity, which goes further than the giving out, of a share of something.

Reciprocity

Reciprocity refers to the practice of exchanging things with others for mutual benefit and is often used in terms of privileges granted by one country or perhaps an organisation to another, or indeed *"a mutual exchange of privileges"* (Merriam-Webster online dictionary 2017a). Being 'reciprocal' therefore implies something that might be *"shared, felt, or shown by both sides"* (Merriam-Webster online dictionary 2017b).

Thompson (2016) argues that reciprocity is an important theme for social workers to hold on to, particularly those working with older people. She suggests that the idea of being able to give as well as to receive is of importance for social workers and their service users and that the concept is both a sociological and psychological one.

Uehara (1995) suggests that the give and take relationships that exist between citizens can be unequal, consequently not all reciprocal relationships are beneficial. We have noted that relationships within social work education which may be described as 'reciprocal' are often unequal in terms of give and take. For example, social workers often go into Universities to provide guest lectures for students with limited reciprocity for them as a practitioner. This is a particularly alarming issue for service users who become involved in supporting social work programmes.

Reciprocity is clearly an important ideal for social workers themselves. At the International Federation of Social Workers European Conference in Iceland (2017) the 530 participants from 47 countries were asked for three key words which described their idea of social work: the concept of reciprocity consistently appeared - through words like togetherness, partnership and sharing.

Thorolfsdottir (2107) asserts that reciprocity is one of the key factors in international social work and all human services work with vulnerable people. It is, however, important that social workers recognise that reciprocity does not always equate to an equal relationship particularly when working with service users from a range of diverse backgrounds. Indeed, SHARE affords us the opportunity to understand why there is inequality in society and which groups bear the brunt of an unequal society. A reciprocal relationship should be a fair one particularly in terms of service users and social workers. Note the overarching factor here is fair, not equal because much as we would all wish to live in an equal society, we acknowledge that this is far more difficult to achieve than we can comprehend.

Reciprocity in social work training

When the degree in social work was introduced in England in 2003 and in Wales, Northern Ireland and Scotland in 2004, a key requirement was to have service users, carers and experts-by-experience involved in all aspects of a social work programme (DH, 2002). The legal requirement to have service user involvement, originally stemmed from Part IV, Sections 63-66 of the Care Standards Act (2000). This Act also set out the regulatory requirements for social work students and practitioners, the protection of title and registration, and laid out the legal basis for the setting up of the four regional Care Councils (Finch, 2010). The Care Act (2000) has now been superseded by the Health and Social Care Act (2012) which in effect paved the way for the Health Care Professions Council (HCPC) (prior to this known as the Health Professions Council) to replace the General Social Care Council as the regulator of social work in England. It is positive to note the HCPC's continued focus on service user involvement in social work and the other professions it regulates (Anka and Taylor, 2016). There are plans for a new regulator for social workers in England and we hope that they will continue to extend on this area.

In terms of the means to support service user involvement, a payment was made available so universities and higher education institutions could pay service users and carers for their time and input onto a programme. We recall some of the issues around payment, not least in the concern that it might adversely impact on those service users who were in receipt of benefits and indeed this is highlighted in research (Social Care Institute for Excellence, 2009). We felt the same payment to all universities was potentially unfair given the differing numbers of students on every course. We also recall discussions taking place about going beyond tokenism in our approaches to how service users would be involved on the social work programmes we either worked with or were associated with, and that meant, at the very least, paying a rate similar to associate lecturers.

So, it has become commonplace, not least in that it is mandatory, for social work programmes to have service users and carers involved in all aspects of the programme, from course design and validation, initial entry onto a programme, assessment, course management and practice assessment panels. We note that internationally, it is not always a requirement to have the input of those who use social work services on social work programmes. Indeed, the North American regulatory body, the Council on Social Work Education, in its Education policy and Accreditation standards does not make a reference to service users and carers involvement in social work education, nor make it a requirement to achieve accreditation of the programme (Council on Social Work Education, 2013).

A central principle of the development of the SHARE model, and indeed in the writing of this book, is to engage with, and involve a wide variety of services users, carers and experts-by-experience and it seems to us now, common-sense and obvious, that people who have been impacted by social workers, both positively, negatively or indifferently, are involved in the training of would be social workers. The question remains however about how far universities give something back to the many hundreds of people, including service users, carers and practitioners who are involved in the training of future social workers. To what extent is the relationship reciprocal?

KEY MESSAGES FROM RESEARCH: SERVICE USER INVOLVEMENT IN SOCIAL WORK EDUCATION

- Despite the limitations of the funding, Social Care Institute for Excellence (2009) reports that there was evidence of good practice of service user involvement, but it remained "patchy" (2009:vi).

- Not all service user organisations are involved in social work education and the individuals and organisations who are involved, would like more involvement (Social Care Institute for Excellence 2009).

- Wallcraft et al (2012) found that service user involvement on post-qualifying (CPD) programmes was very weak.

- The involvement of service users, carers and experts-by-experience in the assessment of social work students remains under-developed (Anka and Taylor 2016).

- Finch (2016) found that on practice assessment panels, service user voices often got drowned out by social work tutors and at times, service users and carers participation felt tokenistic.

- Chambers and Hickey (date unknown) found that service user involvement in programmes requiring HCPC registration, other than social work, was beneficial to students in challenging their assumptions and stereotypes. The same research found that involvement made service users feel valued.

- 20 members of staff in a Faculty of Health stated that they wanted to develop the involvement of users and carers in the delivery of their teaching, but they identified three key barriers around a lack of leadership and direction in this area, poor links and networks and organisational and cultural barriers (Gutteridge and Dobbins 2010).

As it can be seen, some progress has clearly been made, and we are pleased to note that service user involvement is now the norm, not the exception. There is, however, clearly more work to do. We know from our work with social work students over the years, that service user and carer input is really valued by students. In the share below Jo discusses a powerful and educative experience of service user involvement.

Jo Shares

I recall a mental health service user coming to talk to us as social work students. This was prior to the mandatory requirement to include service users and I think, though I am not 100% certain, this person was the only user of social work services we met on the taught element of the course.

The man talked eloquently and powerfully about his experiences of being involved in the mental health system. He didn't pull any punches and said it as it was, which was incredibly educational. He said, *"social workers will never be my friend"* referring to the power of what was then called Approved Social Workers (ASWs) and now Approved Mental Health Professionals (AMHPS) and their power to detain people under the Mental Health Act (1983). He spoke movingly about the impact of his mental health diagnosis on him and the effect of the powerful anti-psychotic drugs he had been compelled to take which had caused physical disabilities. He spoke of the abuse he suffered from his neighbours, who thought him 'weird' and 'odd' and had accused him of being a paedophile. He talked of his support network, which was a group of people with mental ill health who advocated for each other when, in his words, *"one was out to lunch"*. Those therefore that were 'in lunch' worked to support those who were 'out to lunch'. Whilst this description of 'in or out to lunch' does not accord with a professional discourse, it nonetheless revealed a vivid image. I still remember this phrase after twenty years and I would like to thank that man who came and spoke to us very naive, inexperienced and idealistic social work students.

I realised what courage it takes to talk frankly and openly about difficult and painful experiences to a group of strangers. In that one-hour session, however, we learnt about the impact of living with mental ill health, not least the shame, stigma and discrimination, as well as the day to day realities and the effects of the medication. We also learnt about alternative user led discourses of mental ill health, including the adverse impact of sectioning. This man willingly 'shared' his experiences in the hope of informing would be social workers and in the hope of reciprocity, better understanding and practice from social workers in the future.

Sharing and wellbeing

The five ways to wellbeing, developed by the Centre for Wellbeing at the New Economics Foundation (NEF) provides the main framework for understanding and promoting wellbeing in contemporary social work in the UK. The five ways to achieve wellbeing, are based on a range of research (Aked et al 2014) and can be summarised as follows:

Connect: People need to connect with those around them - with family, friends, colleagues and neighbours.

Be active: Research indicates that exercising makes people feel good. The advice in the model is that people need to find some physical activity which they enjoy and which matches their level of mobility and fitness.

Take notice: It is important to be curious. People should *"catch sight of the beautiful. Remark on the unusual. Notice the changing seasons. Savour the moment"* (Aked et al 2014). This illustrates the importance of reflection and mindfulness.

Keep learning: Learning new things will make you more confident and can be fun.

Give: The fifth way to wellbeing recognises the importance of kindness. It suggests that you do something nice for a friend, or a stranger; thank someone; smile etc. Seeing yourself, and your happiness, linked to the wider community is satisfying and creates connections with the people around you.

These five ways to wellbeing demonstrate the importance of sharing. Whilst sharing is not explicitly used as a word in the five ways model, it makes clear that we need to connect (share) with other people and that we should give (share) to promote our own and others wellbeing. Wellbeing is such a central aspect of social work practice, both in terms of the social work role in supporting service users to develop their wellbeing and in relation to social workers needing to take care of their own wellbeing.

Sharing and kindness

Sharing is widely viewed as an act of kindness. Kindness and sharing have been seen as interconnected virtues for centuries and in many ways such virtues were the foundations of early social justice movements. One of the negative side effects of moving towards the professionalisation of social work appears to have been a move away from fundamental virtues such as kindness and sharing.

Ballatt and Campling (2011) argue the importance of 'rescuing' kindness within the culture of health care provision and refer to the need for 'intelligent kindness' to challenge proceduralised practice and provision.

Ferguson's research into social work practice consistently illustrates the kindness of social workers, but still he argues that social work operates within a 'deficit culture' where social workers do not recognise the value of their kindness (Ferguson 2017a). We hope that the SHARE model will provide a language and a model to help us recognise the importance of kindness and sharing in social work.

Sharing and belonging

Everyone wants to belong because it is a valued part of human existence. The SHARE model promotes sharing and working with others in a way that takes account of individual and collective values, strengths, limitations and aspirations. We know that people feel isolated and marginalised when they do not feel they belong, for example, it can be difficult for some children to feel a part of a family or a group due to complexities around early attachment and / or other difficult circumstances (Howe, 2011). Marvin's stakeholder voice below, discusses the issue of belonging.

STAKEHOLDER VOICE — MARVIN CAMPBELL

Marvin Campbell spent most of his life in care, living across many foster families and children's homes. He now works directly with young people in a children's home while supporting local authorities and providers to improve their services.

I think a sense of belonging is so important, we all want to feel a part of something and we all deserve to feel a part of a family. Having so many different placements, you don't feel like you belong, just the child in care. You spend your life watching other children, their families and sometimes you just long for that normality. The worst times were Christmas or the annual holidays, often I would feel so out of place or sent on respite elsewhere while the carers had a break.

A seed is implanted in our very existence and nurtured throughout our childhood and adolescence, usually without any conscious thought. It's a sense of belonging, embedded through the unconditional love and support of our parents and wider family. The understanding, empathy and unrivalled commitment of those closest to us which instils in us the confidence and resilience to navigate the world. I often use the analogy of growing flowers; you find one spot of soil, continuously nurturing the flower bed, removing any weeds, providing sufficient water and sunlight to ensure the flower blossoms. This same principle applies to us all. Without a safe, loving and nurturing environment how can we grow and withstand the challenges life throws at us? For many children in care, that sense of belonging, to anything other than the 'Looked-after-Child' is usually beaten out of us.

© Marvin Campbell

Marginalisation, isolation and exclusion can leave people at risk of further difficulties and complications arising from a lack of networks and weak social connections. People need to feel a sense of belonging to some group or network to enhance their wellbeing.

Othering

The word othering is increasingly being used to describe the process of marginalization where an individual or group of people become seen as 'not one of us'. Spivak (1985) originally coined the phrase 'othering' since when it has grown in prominence amongst a number of academic disciplines. Jensen (2011) notes that othering also draws on a range of philosophical traditions. Othering is a really important concept as it's not just about the labelling of the 'other' but the process of othering itself, which serves to reinforce one's own sense of identity, dominance, superiority and power over that other. Crucially, there is a de-humanisation of that other, which as history has shown us, in its extreme form, can lead to genocide. The concept of othering has been particularly influential in the academic exploration of post colonialism (see for example Said, 1994, 2003) and women's rights (see for example, De Beauvoir, 1972) and is now applied and studied in respect of other minority groups. We can certainly see the process of othering, in terms of the right-wing media's response to immigrants arriving in unsafe boats from Africa and Syria.

Essentially, othering cuts right across the concepts that we have discussed of belonging, interconnectedness and reciprocity. When someone is 'othered' they are viewed as different to 'the rest of us.' Othering is often done in very subtle ways but key aspects of it include people being seen as part of distinct groups, with those who hold power deciding who the 'other' groups are.

We have become concerned by what we see as a growing acceptance of othering within the social work profession. In recent years, we have seen less and less questioning of 'othering' processes and in some circumstances social work has become a key mechanism of 'othering'. This book includes various examples of 'othering,' many of them drawn from the experiences highlighted in stakeholder voices.

In what ways might I 'other'?

Am I 'othered'?

Prospera Shares

A common area of exclusion and othering in social work and in daily living is in relation to names. When people refer to my name as 'strange' or 'interesting', I am rarely amused! I could never imagine myself referring to the name 'Jane' using similar language. In a recent conversation with Black African students, many shared similar experiences. They reported that they appreciated lecturers and service users asking for confirmation of the pronunciation of their names as this demonstrated respect. One student reported that their practice educator had asked them what crime they had committed to deserve their name. The inference here being that the student's name represents some sort of punishment, is unattractive or difficult. Your name is a key aspect of your identity and treating a name with respect is the first step in treating a person with respect.

We hope that the SHARE model will support social workers to explore the process of othering and to challenge this as they consider each person's 'share' in any given situation. This involves looking at each component of the model from the perspective of every stakeholder.

Essentially sharing is about creating a relationship which challenges othering and any move towards a culture of us and them:

A social worker shouldn't need to look closely to see that 'they' are 'us' and 'we' are 'them'.

Complexity and reflexivity: Social work has the X Factor!

Social work is more than complicated. It is complex.

Complexity theory is a recent idea, taken from scientific fields it originally comes out of experimental mathematics and chaos theory. Ideas around complexity theory are still developing and are seen as providing the basis of science for the future (Johnson 2011). Essentially, complexity theory seeks to understand, predict and control complex situations, starting from the basic premise that complexity in itself is difficult to define.

One aspect of complexity theory which may be useful to social work is the recognition that something can be complicated but not complex. For example, a task which has many stages is complicated - but if the stages are followed through in order then the task can be reliably completed. It is complicated but not complex. Where there are many interconnections (some of which may not appear to be initially related) which are all competing for limited resources then something becomes complex rather than complicated. Linear thinking sees something as complicated, whilst systemic thinking recognises that something is complex. Recent developments in social work which link social work processes with technology try to break social work down into a series of tasks to be followed, with subsequent data being gathered. This breaking down of social work into a series of tasks fails to recognise the significant complexity of much of the work that social workers do.

"People say social care isn't Rocket Science. I say it's a lot more complicated than that."

(Beresford 2017)

Charles Dickens said that *"a very little key will open a very heavy door"* (Dickens 1859). We are not denying the complexity of contemporary social work practice, but we believe that social work is often able to locate the key to situations - finding the simplicity in the complex. We are confident that SHARE can provide a model to cut through some of the complexities of practice, hopefully providing that small key to open a potentially very large door.

De Bono (2015) is clear that *"simplicity is not easy"* we acknowledge the truth of this, but feel that simplicity is important in terms of people from a range of backgrounds coming together to develop a shared understanding. Leahy (2012) includes 'simple' as one of his top ten words for management, asserting that a commitment to simplicity is vitally important in good leadership although he recognises that this is often frowned on.

We have spent a great deal of time supporting students and social workers in developing their skills in reflective practice and critical thinking. We have noted significant confusion in terms of an understanding of reflexivity. Reflexivity is drawn from research - it is about more than being reflective. Reflexivity puts the worker at the heart of the reflection. It recognises interconnectedness and circularity and is about the relationships between people and parts (Houston 2015). We hope that the SHARE model will encourage people to recognise the complexity of social work practice and the interconnectedness between different aspects of a situation, whilst providing a simple framework for the consideration of this complexity. Essentially, we see SHARE as a reflexive model for practice, as such we have included various reflections on contemporary social work themes and news events throughout this book.

Siobhan Shares

I find that often people lack clarity around the differences between reflection and reflexivity. When working with students and practitioners to help them understand the concept of reflexivity, I ask them what they 'see' in the word reflexivity. If people are used to alternative therapies and spa treatments, they quickly 'see' the word reflexology. This can really help by giving a visual association to help deepen understanding of reflexivity.

Reflexology is based on the theory that different points of the feet or lower legs link with different parts of the body. So, if you went to a reflexologist with a headache they may touch your big toe! On the face of it the two things don't interconnect. That gives a clear idea about reflexivity. It is all about how different aspects of a situation which do not immediately appear to be related might actually be interconnected. A good professional should be able to 'see' this interconnectivity even where it is not obvious to others.

In the word reflexivity the letter I is at the centre, illustrating the way that reflexivity helps the individual to place themselves at the very centre of their reflections. (What impact did I have on this situation and what impact did it have on me?)

But I've got a headache....!!!

Values and anti-oppressive practice

We come from an anti-oppressive, values-informed perspective and as such hope that this provides the foundations of the SHARE model.

For many years, the word share has been used within literature which explores the oppression of particular groups within society. For example, Aline Helg used the concept of sharing to explore Black history in 'Our Rightful Share: The Afro-Cuban struggle for Equality' (Helg 1995).

The Brazilian educator Paulo Freire is well known for his writing on empowerment. His book 'The Pedagogy of the Oppressed' (first published in English in 1970) is seen as a seminal text. Freire saw empowerment as being created rather than being 'given'. The concept of sharing underpinned his work. For example, he viewed one of the key aspects of empowerment as learning being shared between individuals. Freire also promoted the importance of a shared critical consciousness.

An understanding of power and empowerment is vital in terms of the values of social work and working in an anti-oppressive way. We have observed and explored power dynamics in a range of ways through our careers and are committed to working in a power-informed manner. Our understanding of power and the major impact of power in social work has significantly influenced us in the development of the SHARE model. We like to take a 'belt and braces' approach to social work values - meaning that we address values issues as integral to every aspect of our work, but we also pick out specific issues to aid in critical reflection on our work and we have tried to reflect this in our writing.

Research by Nzira (2010) found that families from BME backgrounds were less likely to 'share' their concerns with people in authority especially social workers. The view that, culturally, issues of concern remain within the family is one that has been found to perpetuate abuse and maltreatment. How then can the SHARE model be used to work effectively with service users from diverse backgrounds? The idea of collectivism, according to Hofstede (2001:225) refers to

> "a society in which people from birth onwards are integrated into strong, cohesive in-groups, which throughout people's lifetime continue to protect them in exchange for unquestioning loyalty. Members of 'we'- group societies make a clear distinction between themselves and those who are not in their group - or clan".

This notion of collectivism may in part provide the rationale for why some people from BME backgrounds may consider 'sharing' information with social workers and other professionals as undermining their loyalty. In developing the SHARE model we recognise the need to revisit the principles of collectivism to ensure that the model is relevant for work with diverse people.

As has already been mentioned, Uehara (1995) cautions against viewing sharing and reciprocity as being fair and equal. The suggestion made is that some people give more than they receive and vice versa. This is very much in line with the sentiments of the SHARE model and the need to ensure that social workers consider the circumstances in which they work with families, individuals and groups is as fair as possible. As three women seeking to live and work from an anti-oppressive standpoint our experiences on a range of levels have influenced the development of the model. For example, at the time of writing, we are concerned about the thousands of refugee children languishing in unclear and unsafe situations. The UK government had pledged support to reintegrate many of these children however there appears to have been a change of commitment. In relation to refugee children, the SHARE model provides a framework for further consideration, as follows:

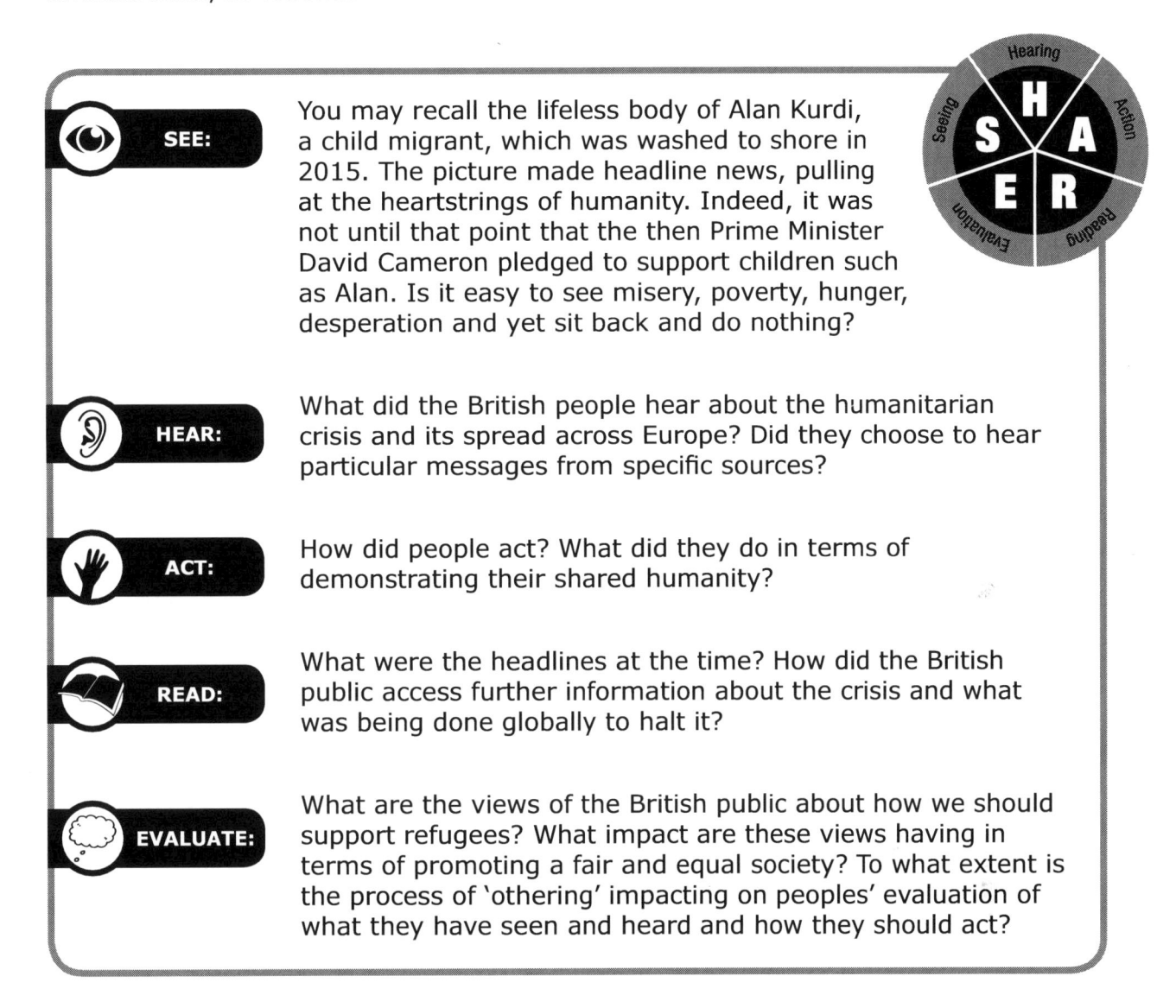

SEE: You may recall the lifeless body of Alan Kurdi, a child migrant, which was washed to shore in 2015. The picture made headline news, pulling at the heartstrings of humanity. Indeed, it was not until that point that the then Prime Minister David Cameron pledged to support children such as Alan. Is it easy to see misery, poverty, hunger, desperation and yet sit back and do nothing?

HEAR: What did the British people hear about the humanitarian crisis and its spread across Europe? Did they choose to hear particular messages from specific sources?

ACT: How did people act? What did they do in terms of demonstrating their shared humanity?

READ: What were the headlines at the time? How did the British public access further information about the crisis and what was being done globally to halt it?

EVALUATE: What are the views of the British public about how we should support refugees? What impact are these views having in terms of promoting a fair and equal society? To what extent is the process of 'othering' impacting on peoples' evaluation of what they have seen and heard and how they should act?

This application of the SHARE model to a contemporary issue begins to demonstrate one of the ways that the model can be used. We also note that whilst this is a continuing issue with many people fleeing war travelling across the sea in very unsafe boats, it has become so common-place that we don't see it on the news every day. Often 'shares' change and we need to revisit them on a regular basis to consider how things have changed – perhaps as a result of political priorities.

Hopeful social work

We have used the word hope a number of times in this chapter. This reflects our commitment to hopeful approaches in practice. Social workers who recognise the intrinsic value of hopefulness in social work are more effective (Clark and Hoffler 2014) and more resilient (Grant and Kinman 2015). Stanford (2011) also asserts that hopeful approaches help practitioners to maintain a focus on ethics, particularly during times of resource scarcity.

According to Clark (2012) there are two types of hope:

Personal hope: which is embedded in a wider social context. A range of issues can impact on personal hopefulness - such as family, culture and personal experiences. Personal hopefulness can be strengthened by effective social networks and diminished by neglect, abuse and trauma.

Professional hope: this is embedded in the professional value base and a belief in the possibility of change. Professional hopefulness can be strengthened by effective communities of practice and diminished by bureaucratic practice.

Clark (2017) outlines some key essentials of hopeful practice for social workers. She argues that social workers have an obligation to bring hope to their practice, especially as we live in a 'hope challenged' world.

One of the key aspects of hope in social work is the importance of sharing an understanding of hope and what that might mean to each individual. Since everyone should be given the opportunity to decide what to hope for. We believe that aspects of the blame culture that has built up around contemporary social work have led to the profession becoming hope-challenged and we wanted to develop a model which could bring some element of hope back into a shared understanding of practice. Indeed, an important and intrinsic social work value is the belief that all people have the capacity to change and develop, and within this we can see the importance of hope. As Clark (2017) argues there is always something to hope for and everyone has the right to hope. There is no such thing as false hope, there can be false reassurances, but never false hope because hope does not require certainty.

The development of the SHARE model reflects our professional hopefulness that it is possible for everyone to have an equal share in society.

There is a significant focus on strengths based approaches to assessment in contemporary practice. This is often described as taking a glass half full rather than glass half empty approach. We prefer to see the glass as refillable.

Whether you see the glass as half empty or half full, it is always refillable.

So, as we have described, a number of basic values underpin the SHARE model. We hope that as we have started to demonstrate in this chapter the way that the model can be used to reflect on a number of social work issues, in order to develop a more reflexive approach to practice.

Key Points

- The SHARE model is based around key components which spell out the word share. The word share does not come out of the components by accident - the use of the word is an integral aspect of the model.
- The word share is associated with key virtues and concepts such as kindness, belonging, wellbeing, caring and reciprocity. These are core aspects of good social work practice.
- Social media and the digital world is having a significant impact on social work and this needs to be acknowledged within contemporary theory and practice.
- People are interconnected in society. Developing a deeper understanding of the SHARE model requires an understanding of the complex interconnections between the individual components.
- People do not get an equal share in society. The SHARE model recognises this and builds on anti-oppressive foundations.

Reflective Questions

At the end of Chapter 1 we asked what the word share meant to you: what are the similarities and differences between the way you understand the word and the way that we have explored it?

In what ways does the fact that we don't all get an equal share in society impact on you and your work?

In what ways do you see or hear othering in your work? What action can you take in response?

In the next chapter we move on to consider the social work theory which has influenced us in the development of the SHARE model. In considering your own 'share', think through the following prompts.

My Share

In terms of social work theory:

I have always……

I have never……

I would like to…..

On a scale of 1-10, 1 being totally confused, 10 being entirely confident how would you score yourself in terms of:

My understanding of social work theory

My use of social work theory

My understanding of the difference between a theory, a model, a method and an approach

What would it take to move you up the scale?

Chapter 3: SOCIAL WORK THEORY

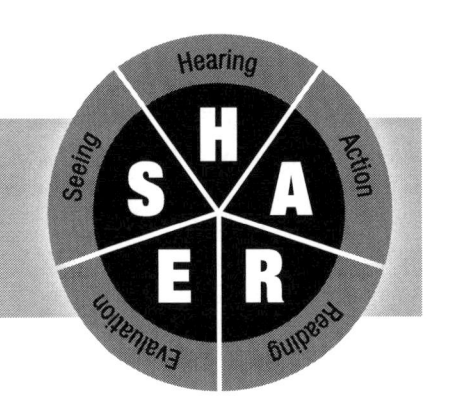

Many social workers take an eclectic approach to practice, drawing on a range of theories and models to inform their understanding and their practice. We share this approach. This chapter will highlight that a range of approaches, theories and models have impacted on our development of the SHARE model. The chapter will start with an explanation of the difference between theories, models, methods and approaches.

Theories, models, methods and approaches

We have noted a distinct lack of clarity about the difference between theories, models, methods and approaches in the social work community. Very often they are all lumped together in teaching, or in the literature, under the heading theory, which ironically is exactly what we have done in entitling this chapter. In some ways whether something is a theory, a model, a method or an approach is merely semantics, but actually, understanding the differences can be really helpful in aiding social workers to be more theory-informed in their practice.

In science, a theory is said to:

1. Describe (what is happening?)
2. Explain (why is it happening?)
3. Predict (what is likely to happen next?)
4. Control and bring about change (how can I change what will happen, to produce a different outcome?)

In many ways, this can be applied to social work pretty effectively, although we would change the first word in the final phrase from control to intervene. We acknowledge that very often in contemporary social work practice there is an element of control to the social work role, but for the purposes of developing a more egalitarian stance in practice the phrase 'intervene and bring about change' is more comfortable for us and recognises also that not everyone would choose to have social work intervention.

With this change to the final phrase, these four points could be used to describe the social work role: in an assessment, we seek to describe what is happening for someone and try to explain why the situation came about, and where there is any element of risk we look to predict what might happen next. Then we look towards planning with the individual or family group what can be done to bring about change. As such, these four points are often used to explain why a social worker is always using theory in their practice even if they are not able to confidently name it (sometimes we use theory unconsciously or tacitly).

We see the four points as helpful in clarifying the difference, in social work, between a theory and a model. Essentially a theory helps us to do the first three points. It helps us to describe, explain and predict. It does not help us however, to intervene and bring about change - it informs our intervention but it does not structure it. A model on the other hand does not help us to describe, explain or predict but it does help us to intervene and bring about change. In short, a theory informs our 'thinking' and a model informs our 'doing.'

An approach brings together theories and models - an approach is a way to describe our overall way of working. If a theory is about thinking and a model is about doing then an approach is about 'being.' Our approach describes the way we like to go about something. Social workers develop their own approach to practice over time. Some employers adopt a particular approach to practice and the social worker may find it difficult if this is not complimentary to their own approach. Some approaches work well together, but others clash.

This leaves us with the concept of a method. How does a method differ from a model? We view a method as a specific tool or a particular technique. Generally, a method puts a particular model into practice. The method describes the particular way of putting the model into practice. In many ways methods are about specific applications. We have tried to provide some specific methods to implement the SHARE model within this book. A number of examples are provided in each chapter as the book develops. For example, the theory as music method (which follows) is drawn out of the SHARE model. Finally, Chapter 10 provides some specific methods for application in particular areas of social work.

Approach: Overall way of working

Theory: Way of understanding a situation

Model: How to intervene in a situation

Method: Specific 'tool' for practice

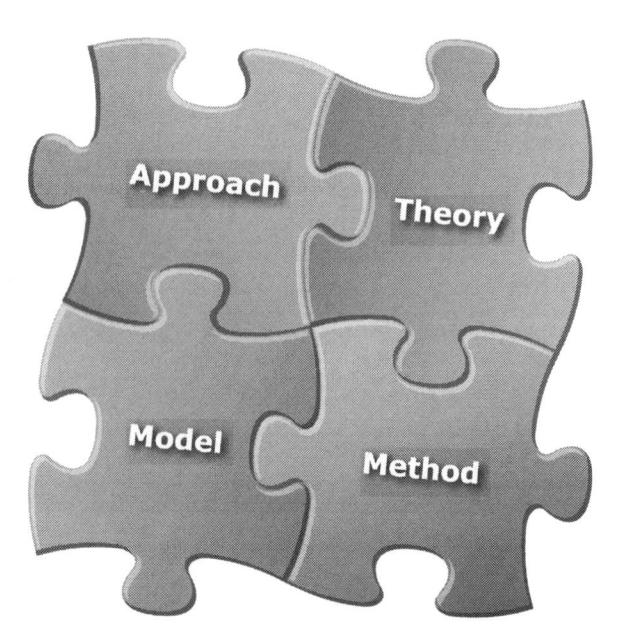

Using SHARE to understand the difference between theories, models and approaches

Drawing directly from the SHARE model we try to use a range of ways to help students and practitioners to recognise the difference between theories, models and approaches to enhance their practice. This entails drawing on the practitioner reading about the difference (as you have just done) and then seeing it differently and drawing on hearing experiences. This use of the Seeing, Hearing and Reading components mean that the student or practitioner can Evaluate their learning so that they can become more theory informed in their Action.

One SHARE method we use in this area is to help people make associations between theories and music (Maclean 2015). This draws on the analogy that theory provides the soundtrack to social work practice. The genre of music you like to listen to is your approach (punk, country and western, classical, 80s pop...) your choice of music says something about you and your approach to life. Some people are avid fans of one particular style of music and this impacts on their whole identity - the way they dress, the things they do, the places they go etc. Whereas other people like some easy listening and have an eclectic musical taste, they are happy to listen to whatever is popular at the time.

Each 'approach' (or genre of music) contains a number of theories and models (artists and bands and their records). Some artists are accepted within more than one genre because they may have developed a fusion style or because some genres are actually quite closely related (just like approaches in social work).

Drawing on the Hearing component of SHARE to think about theory as music can be very helpful. For example:

- ♪ Think about contemporary listening to music - most people have play-lists. They probably have a different set of play-lists for different activities and different moods: a play-list for the gym, another for chilling out, one for a rainy day etc. In social work, very often people draw on just a few favourite theories that they play over and over again. Actually, we need to draw on a range of theory play-lists to suit the situation and the preferences of the people involved.

- ♪ Using the associations between music and theory can help students and those new to a particular theory to explore the ideas behind the theories. Association also helps us to remember the theory.

- ♪ Songs are very often covered by different artists and the most popular songs might have a significant number of cover versions. This is just the same for theory in social work, you can often tell when someone qualified by who they think developed certain theories, because they may be more familiar with the cover version than the original.

♫ Music often provides a background rather than being the main focus of what is happening. Often people will say that they haven't thought about a particular song for some time, but when it comes on the radio for example, they can sing along immediately. That is much like the way that we can often take theory for granted in our practice; using it as an unconscious background to our work.

♫ We can sometimes hum along to a tune, or we know a few key lyrics (the catchy ones) but we don't know the whole song, or we might not remember who sang it, rarely will we know who wrote it. That's much like theory. We often know some of the headlines of the theory, but little of the detail.

I take more of an eclectic approach.

SHARE is a model for practice. It supports action and is about how practitioners should work. As we come from an eclectic stance then we feel that the SHARE model could be used as part of a range of different approaches, which we will outline in the remainder of this chapter.

- A practitioner may adopt one of a number of approaches
- A practitioner's choice of theory will impact on how they understand a situation
- The SHARE model can be used as part of a social worker's intervention
- A range of methods can be employed as part of the SHARE model

Hopeful approach

We have already highlighted that we take a very hopeful approach to practice (see page 48) and that our commitment to hopeful social work has influenced the development of the SHARE model in a range of ways.

Hopeful social work is growing in popularity in the UK. Certainly, the concept of hope is important in a number of social work theories and models. For example, hope is a key element in the recovery model in mental health and the importance of hope is recognised in addressing learned helplessness. However, it is in America where hopeful approaches to social work have a high profile. Clark and Hoffler (2014) argue that social workers can lay claim to be the 'profession of hope'. They describe social workers as the holders of hope for individuals and in many ways for society as a whole. They argue that, in fact, social workers should dispense hope in the way that doctors might dispense medication or a judge might dispense justice.

A hopeful social work approach involves:

- A positive, optimistic outlook
- Understanding the reality of oppression and how people might communicate their experiences of this
- A belief in the possibility of change
- Commitment to relationships
- Supporting people to feel a sense of 'belonging'
- An awareness of the dynamic nature of hope
- An ability to imagine a different way of doing things
- Skills in supporting people to develop goals and look to the future

Essentially, a hopeful approach is about adopting a particular set of positive attitudes and then communicating these through your practice. Grant and Kinman (2015) highlight the importance of social workers adopting a hopeful optimistic outlook in order to become more resilient practitioners. The links between the lessening of hope and burnout are well evidenced (Schwartz, Tiamiyu and Dwyer 2007).

There can be a negative aspect in terms of 'hope' however that is important to acknowledge and address in practice. Your hope for example, that someone will change, either in a professional or indeed a personal context, can result in not wanting to acknowledge the limited change that has been made. Hope in someone, can be experienced as an investment in someone and of course, when one invests, it can be difficult to acknowledge the 'investment' has not paid off in the way we would ideally like. This phenomenon is more widely known as the rule of optimism, a phrase originally coined by Dingwall et al (1983) and taken up by Blom-Cooper (1985) in his Public Inquiry report into the death of Jasmine Beckford, a young child known to Social Services in the London Borough of Brent, who was tragically killed by her step-father. Essentially, this term refers to the process where, as in this case, social workers were too optimistic and focused on strengths at the expense of the very real risks factors. In over-optimism, practitioners do more than just focus on the perceived positives or strengths, but actually over estimate them.

The saying *"however long the night, the dawn will break"* an African proverb which is also likely to have versions in other cultures, is an example of the extent to which hopefulness exists on a daily basis for many people. It is this hopefulness which encourages people to persevere in spite of the many areas of difficulty and distress impacting on their lives. Whilst this proverb may ring true for many, it could also lead to non-action on the part of some people. This is because, taken literally, we (as people) did not have to do anything for dawn to arrive. It is not within our gift to speed up the appearance of dawn or daybreak. Hopeful practice must go hand in hand with proactive practice.

Social work is always about a fine balance

It is important, therefore that social workers recognise the difficult balance between hopefulness and over-optimism. At times, there is a very fine balance. However, hopefulness in practice (albeit realistic hopefulness) is vitally important. In fact, people who have faced challenge and oppression often refer to the importance of hope in terms of creating resilience and strength. Sometimes people describe hope being the only thing they have left in a situation. This photograph is of part of a mural in the Shankhill area of Belfast. Entitled 'Women's Voices Matter' the mural depicts a patchwork quilt created by women living in the area. The importance of hope and the link this has to people being (and feeling) 'heard' is powerfully illustrated.

The SHARE model comes from a hopeful stance and we would encourage everyone using the model to share their hopefulness with others as a key aspect of effective social work. Indeed, Friere (1994) highlights the vital importance of sharing an understanding of hope as a key part of working in an anti-oppressive way.

The importance of hope was highlighted in the General Election campaign of 2017, with the call for people to 'Vote for Hope' taking a central place in the campaign.

The fact that many more young people became engaged in politics during this time is often attributed to the focus on hope.

Strengths based approach

Sometimes referred to as an asset based approach, the strengths based approach came about partly as a reaction against two features of traditional social work and the provision of health and social care.

1. An increasing medical classification and diagnosis of individuals leading to labelling of large sections of society. This labelling is negative and has a deterministic theme (eg: you had a traumatic childhood therefore you will be a terrible parent and your children will end up in care).

2. Assessments of needs have always been weighted towards listing people's deficits, vulnerabilities and negative past experiences. In the current environment where demand for services is increasing but the resources available have declined or, at best, barely increased, then there is an increased focus and heightening of service users' lack of capability and risks.

In both of these suggestions, there is a structural or bureaucratic bias against recognising people's strengths, abilities and resilience.

Although very much in the limelight at present, the strengths based approach is nothing new. Right back in 1996 Saleebey generated the following comparison of a professional pathologising approach against a strengths based one:

To me, a strengths based approach is about....

Pathology	Strengths
Person is defined as a 'case'; symptoms add up to a diagnosis.	Person is defined as unique; traits, talents, resources add up to strengths.
Intervention is problem focused.	Intervention is possibility focused.
Service user accounts are filtered by a professional to aid the generation of a diagnosis.	Personal accounts are the essential route to knowing and appreciating the person.
Professional is sceptical of personal stories and explanations.	Professional knows the person from the inside out.
Childhood trauma is the precursor or predictor of adult dysfunction.	Childhood trauma is not predictive; it may weaken or strengthen the individual.
Professional devises treatment or care plan.	Focus is aspirations of individual, family or community.
Professional is the expert on service user's life.	Individual, family or community are the experts.
Possibilities for choice, control, commitment and personal development are limited by label, diagnosis or condition.	Possibilities for choice, control, commitment and personal development are open.
Professionals' knowledge, skills and connections are principal resources for service user.	The strength, capacities and adaptive skills of the individual, family or community are the principal resources.
Support is centred on reducing the effects of symptoms and the negative effects of emotions or relationships.	Support is focused on getting on with one's life, affirming and developing values and commitments and making or finding membership in a community.

More recently, a strengths based approach has been described as a conceptual framework including the three key components of:

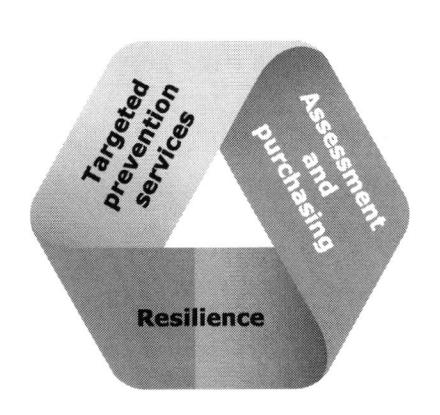

1. Resilience

Individual resilience needs to be considered, with specific consideration given to:
- Personal resources.
- Networks of support.
- Community resources.

2. Targeted prevention services

Interventions are delivered once certain trigger points are reached. All interventions need to be focused on creating and re-creating resilient individuals.

3. Assessment and purchasing

Assessments and processes / systems should be slimmed down.

(TLAP 2017)

In January 2017 a round-table event was hosted by Lyn Romeo, the Chief Social Worker for adults (England) and the Social Care Insitute for Excellence. The event explored what a strengths based approach means for people, concluding:

> "A strengths-based social work approach to working with adults is not yet a fully formed set of ideas and the evidence base for some more recent models is still emerging. However, strengths-based practice is not a new concept and reflects the core principles at the heart of the social work profession. The approach sees everyone including the most vulnerable and those with long-term needs as citizens who also have rights and responsibilities, skills and expertise." (Department of Health 2017:6)

Strengths based practice complements many of the concepts which have influenced our development of the SHARE model, such that many of the approaches discussed in this chapter share common threads. For example, Pattoni (2012) asserts that a strengths based approach:
- Values the capacity, skills, knowledge, connections and potential in individuals and communities.
- Requires practitioners to work in collaboration, helping people to do things for themselves. In this way, people can become co-producers of support not passive consumers of support.
- Enhances wellbeing.
- Promotes self esteem.
- Creates a climate of optimism, hope and possibility.
- Promotes better outcomes.
- Supports relationships-based practice.
- Provides a more satisfying approach for practitioners.

We are very committed to a strengths based approach to social work practice, as is illustrated throughout this book. We see the SHARE Model as a key part of being strengths based in practice, as many of the direct applications covered in Chapter 10 demonstrate. In fact, strengths based perspectives are very often linked with many of the basic aspects behind the development of the SHARE model, covered in Chapter 2. For example, the Social Care Institute for Excellence assert that

> "Strengths-based practice is a collaborative process between the person supported by services and those supporting them, allowing them to work together to determine an outcome that draws on the person's strengths and assets. As such, it concerns itself principally with the quality of the relationship that develops between those providing and those being supported, as well as the elements that the person seeking support brings to the process. Working in a collaborative way promotes the opportunity for individuals to be co-producers of services and support rather than solely consumers of those services" (SCIE 2017).

This links into the ideas of collectivity and reciprocity which we covered in Chapter 2. We hope that practitioners using the SHARE model will find it supportive in building on a strengths based approach in their practice.

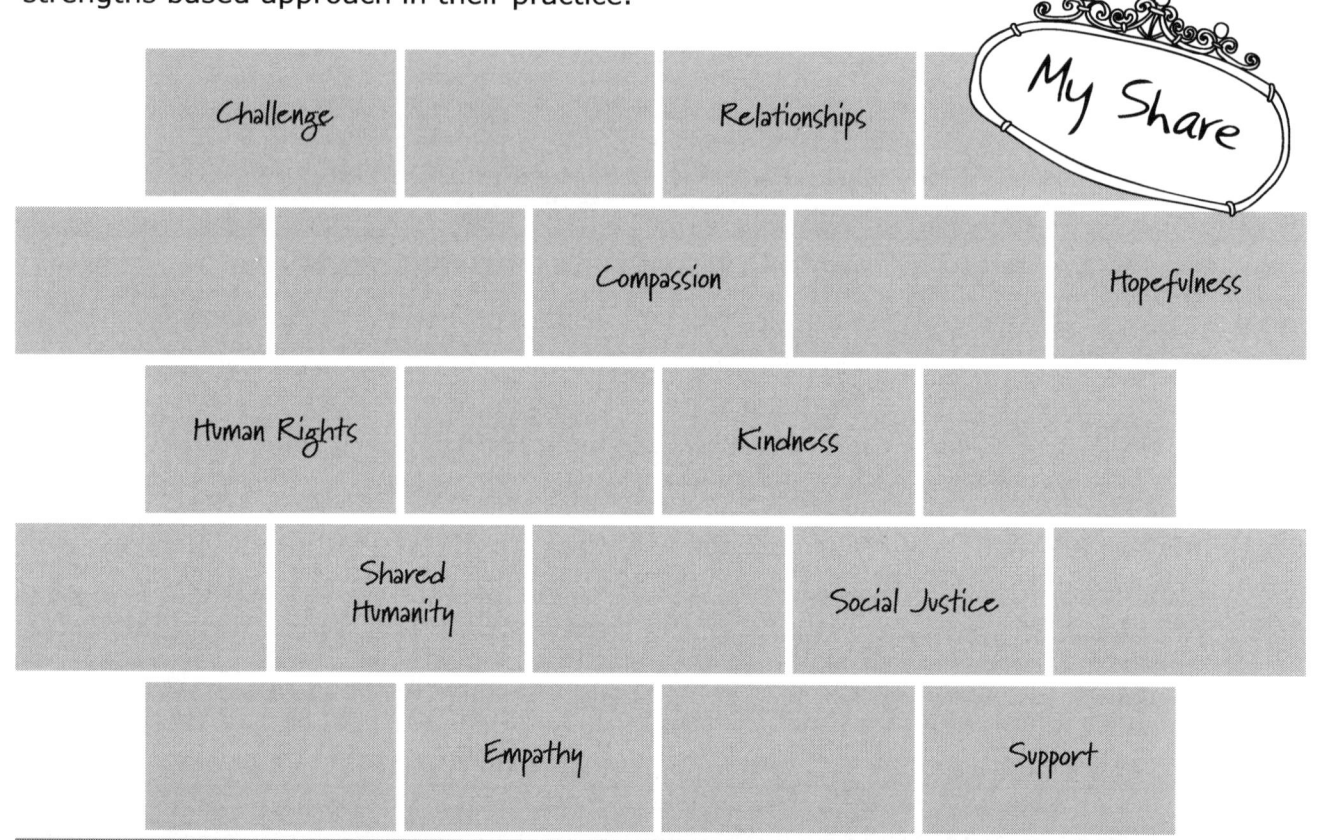

Challenge   *Relationships*   *My Share*

Compassion   *Hopefulness*

Human Rights   *Kindness*

Shared Humanity   *Social Justice*

Empathy   *Support*

The SHARE model builds on a strengths based approach to social work

Add some words for yourself...

Restorative approach

Restorative practice is described as a specific social science which explores how social capital can be developed. It seeks to achieve social discipline through participatory learning and decision making (Wachtel 2016). Restorative practice is having a significant impact in education, criminal justice, organisational management and, increasingly, social work. The increasing popularity of restorative practice in social work has become clear in the UK in recent years, with a number of local authorities now adopting the approach across all local authority services or all services for children and young people.

The restorative approach is based on the importance of relationships. It is built on a continuum of methods which range from formal methods such as circles and restorative meetings, to informal practice which focuses on the vital importance of relationships in creating change.

Examples of restorative practice methods

Circles: Circle time has been popular in schools for a long time, but is becoming increasingly popular in organisational leadership.

Family Group Conferences: Originally this was seen as a method to empower families. Increasingly however, the process of FGC is being seen as part of a restorative approach. In the US for example, FGC was reframed as Family Group Decision Making.

These methods are about working collaboratively with people - with all key stakeholders involved in decision making.

Restorative questions

Restorative questions are based around Borton's (1970) model of reflection and analysis (What? So what? Now what?) They are designed to support a person to reflect on a situation and analyse what might have happened. These questions can be useful to social workers both in terms of gathering information from people they work with and in terms of reflecting on an incident they have been involved with.

WHAT: What happened? What were you thinking? What were you feeling?
These questions help to explore each individual's perspective.

SO WHAT: Who has been affected? What is the impact on them and on you? How do you feel now?
These questions help to identify the way that thoughts and feelings influence behaviours.

NOW WHAT: What needs to happen? What does that look like? What and who can help you?
These questions help to identify solutions from different perspectives.

Restorative questions draw on What? How? Who? When? and Where? but do not include a consideration of why? It is important to recognise that social workers need to maintain the why dimension to questioning, particularly in terms of reflexivity. However, restorative questions can be helpful in exploring situations with people in a non-threatening way.

One key aspect of the restorative approach is the social discipline window (Wachtel 2016). This has wide application across a range of settings:

	SUPPORT LOW	SUPPORT HIGH
CHALLENGE HIGH	**TO** Punitive Authoritarian	**WITH** Restorative Authoritative
CHALLENGE LOW	**NOT** Neglectful Irresponsible	**FOR** Permissive Paternalistic

The social discipline window is based around the two aspects of challenge and support, creating four domains. The restorative domain draws on high support along with high challenge to work with people collaboratively. Doing things *to* people is authoritarian, falling into the punitive domain, whilst doing things *for* people (without involving the person fully) is paternalistic, falling into the permissive domain.

The importance of WITH

'With' is the most important aspect of a restorative approach. This is about working with people in a way which offers high levels of support but also high challenge. Working with people involves creating, developing, sustaining and repairing relationships. According to Lloyd (2016) working with people is not a tool, or model but a way of being.

The word share is often followed by the word with. People don't generally share *to* or share *for* but they very often share *with*. We see the SHARE model as a way of embedding the idea of working with people, building on a restorative approach.

TO WITH FOR

Relational approach

Relationships between service users and social workers have been traditionally viewed as central to social work, in other words relationships have always been seen as at the heart of social work. The recognition of the importance of relationships between professionals and service users, has become enmeshed in social work legislation and guidance which often places a duty on organisations or social workers, for example, to work in 'partnership' with service users. Unfortunately, such mandates may serve only to proceduralise or, trivialise relationships, or reduce them to a legal mandate. Relationships which are mandated may be viewed as tokenistic and are not reflective of the huge power differentials that are associated with social work roles and tasks. Indeed, this point was raised earlier when we discussed the reciprocity aspects of relationships - for example in respect of service users being 'involved' in social work programmes in a mandatory and therefore tokenistic way with the power and control remaining with university staff.

Almost fifteen years ago, Trevithick (2003) raised a concern that the centrality and importance of relationships appeared to be declining in social work practice. We have noted that despite the growing rhetoric around the importance of relationships in social work in the last few years, relationships between service users and social workers seem to be conceptualised in more conflictual and problematic ways. One of the most recent ways we seen this manifestation of conflictual relationships in action has been some memes posted on social media, which in our view, portray service users in particularly hostile or discriminatory ways. Indeed, this was one of our motivations to develop a more respectful model of social work practice. There are however other manifestations of such 'under-the-surface hostilities' towards service users and this concerns the use of military metaphors in social work practice, not least the oft used phrase 'frontline practice'.

Beckett (2003) for example, explored metaphor in the language used by social workers in children and family settings. In particular he noted the abundance of military metaphors in use, namely, strategy, duty officer, intake and the frontline to name but a few. Such militarisation of social work practice was also seen in a Canadian study, where Newberry-Keroluk, (2014) suggested newly qualified social workers should resist military metaphors in social work, such as soldiers, social work as an 'Arena of war' (2014:54) and 'hitting the ground running' (ibid) which serves to construct service users within neoliberal lines, namely they are the enemy, or the 'other', as discussed earlier. This serves to create a 'them and us' situation that we are so concerned about. The SHARE model therefore promotes a relationship-based approach to social work but emphasises the reciprocity of relationships, and attempts to move away from the social worker as expert model.

The use of military metaphors in practice does not help in relationship development

The 4Ps

Social pedagogy offers a great deal to social workers in terms of developing a relationship-based approach to practice. Relationship-based practice calls for the worker to have a well-developed sense of self. Bengtsson et al (2008) identify that pedagogues need to be aware of three different aspects of the self in developing relationships, which have become known as the 3Ps. We would summarise these as follows:

The private pedagogue: The person who is known to friends and family. The private pedagogue should not be in any familial / kin relationship with a service user. The private pedagogue is the pedagogue outside of work.

The personal pedagogue: The person within the professional setting. The personal pedagogue offers aspects of their own self to the person they are working with. Social pedagogues have to put aspects of their personal selves into relationships so service users can relate to them.

The professional pedagogue: The professional pedagogue is that aspect of practice which enables the social pedagogue to keep on offering contact even if this is being refused. A professional reflection on practice enables social pedagogues to evaluate the progress they have seen with people.

We have found the 3P framework helpful in our own practice and have developed the idea to consider what practitioners should share with people as part of a relationships-based approach. We have added a fourth P to the framework, and present our way of using the framework in practice as follows:

We all have 4Ps to our 'self':

Our private self: This is shared only with our close family members and intimate partners.

Our personal self: This is shared outside of work, with friends and family.

Our professional self: This is the self that we share at work.

Our public self: This is shared with everyone. It relates to what everyone sees. It would also include our use of social media platforms.

We find the 4Ps helpful in considering the development of relationships in social work practice and the importance of boundaries in practice. Every social worker should consider themselves in relation to the 4Ps. By all means share aspects of the personal P with people. For example, in developing conversations with service users, you might share information about yourself ("I have a dog…" "I prefer tea to coffee…" etc), but don't share parts of the private P. Larissa's stakeholder contribution highlights the importance of professionals considering aspects of the boundaries to their relationships using the 4Ps.

STAKEHOLDER VOICE — LARISSA

Larissa is mum to two teenage daughters, she is also a lunchtime supervisor.

I was invited to attend a family group with my daughters. I say invited, because that's how it was described to me. I didn't feel able to say no, so it wasn't really an invitation. I reckon if I'd said no that I would have been judged as lacking commitment or something similar. So, we went. The group sessions were actually OK. We generally had a bit of time together with other families at the start then we would separate out into a kids' group and a parents' group. We'd talk about things and then we would all come back together to eat a meal and do something together like play a game or do some making stuff. Actually, we got quite a bit from it as a family.

There were three staff at the sessions. One would be with the kids and one with the adults and one would get stuff ready and then all three of them would be involved at the end when we all came together. Different ones did different things each week so we pretty much got to know the three of them. They were really different. One was really cold, you know, she never said anything about herself at all. If we asked her if she had kids she would refuse to answer and say stuff like 'this isn't about me...', another one was more friendly like and would say a bit of stuff about himself and he said he had found being a parent to teenagers difficult, you know that kind of stuff. Not a lot but I felt like we could relate. The other one, well she talked all the time about herself. What she was going through with a divorce, where she had been on her holidays, how her kids were going away with their dad, you know everything. To be honest I got a bit fed up hearing about her problems. I was thinking 'hang on a minute I thought this was about helping me with my girls.'

© Larissa

It is clear how important relationship-based practice, and specifically, boundaried relationships is to each of us, because we each wrote our 'share' in this chapter around this area. We did so individually and when we came together we wondered if we should amend our 'shares' but decided they were about what we felt was important and that in fact, it clarified the importance of relationship-based practice for us.

There is a complicated balance to be struck between being personable, and making relationships and meaningful links and connections with service users and other colleagues, whilst at the same time, not overburdening service users or other professionals with our own concerns and stresses. In other words, the task of a social worker, as well as other professionals, should be to help contain the anxieties and preoccupations of those we work with. Therefore, professionals need to contain their own emotional state and anxieties. Jo shares below an example of when this doesn't happen and how it can leave one feeling.

It's that fine balance again!

Jo Shares

A few years ago, I had to have a biopsy on a lump. I was told to ring a specialist nurse after two weeks to get the results, in other words was the lump benign or was there something to worry about. Of course, I was really worried, and frightened myself by looking online at medical websites. After the two weeks, I then tried to make contact with the nurse which wasn't easy. When I did make contact, I was advised to ring back in a week as the results were not yet in. I then tried to make contact and left messages with the nurse's colleagues and on her answer-phone. Long story short, the nurse made contact with me one evening and her presentation over the phone was stressed, she seemed tired and a little cross; she commented that I had seemed anxious so whilst she had more people to contact who had been waiting longer than me, she thought she would ring me first. This made me feel as if my anxiety was unfounded and that I was a burden. I then felt guilty about this poor nurse, working in the evening, and who clearly was stressed and overwhelmed. I then went into social work mode and started rescuing the nurse, sympathising with how busy she was! Of course, on reflection, it was perfectly reasonable I was anxious as I was waiting to see if I the lump was cancerous and she should have helped contain my anxiety, not the other way around.

The 4P model as discussed earlier, can therefore be a really useful reflective tool for thinking about what we share, as well as how we present - indeed we should consider 'presentation' as a culmination of the 4Ps. Professional presentation therefore, links very readily to notions of professional values, and how we present can too often reveal values that are not in accordance with social work values. Indeed, as Siobhan shares:

Siobhan Shares

I once worked alongside a social worker who was very particular about her appearance. One of the things she liked and was very interested in was handbags. She took delight in having the latest designer handbag, which invariably cost a fortune. I often wondered how service users felt when she arrived at their home carrying a handbag that cost more money than their whole family had to live on for a month.

One day I heard this particular social worker in the office talking about taking a service user's parents to a meeting in her car. I was appalled by her conversation about how she had put plastic on the seats to make sure that they didn't get dirty, whilst making disparaging comments about the parents' personal hygiene. Whilst in itself this was terrible what was worse was the way that other social workers joined in with the conversation, making widely negative comments about service users. I did intervene as you can imagine. I asked everyone in the office to imagine how they would feel if offered a lift by someone who then put plastic bags and paper on the seats to protect the car from them. What does this kind of behaviour do for the development of relationships with service users?

The very heart of our practice is about how we demonstrate a shared humanity with the people we work with. I have always been aware of what I wear to work and how I am viewed by others, but ever since that conversation I have been even more conscious of the way that I present myself.

My Share

How do I demonstrate a shared humanity with the people I work with?

Prospera Shares

The 4Ps aptly describe the personalities I have within my personal family life, my career and my private life. These also reflect the various roles I occupy in relation the various people and groups I belong to. I am 'mum' to two sons, 'auntie Pros' to many more children and young people within my wider networks.

I become 'Prospera' to my work colleagues and 'Dr Tedam' to students. Interestingly, during my time as a children and families practitioner, a Nigerian parent insisted on her children calling me 'auntie'. I politely advised her that this was inappropriate especially as her children would call other (non-black) social workers by their first names. On reflection now, I wonder whether I would have been more accepting of the 'auntie' title if it had been fairly applied to all the professionals working with the family and not just me. From a professional perspective, the way you are addressed is an important indicator of the relationship and titles like 'auntie' are likely to blur the boundaries.

Relationships are perhaps the most important aspect of good social work practice and there is certainly a renewed interest in the importance of relationship-based practice, which O'Connor 2017:14) understands as:

> *"An attempt to reclaim social work from the imperatives of managerialism and ensuing proceduralised, risk adverse approaches to practice."*

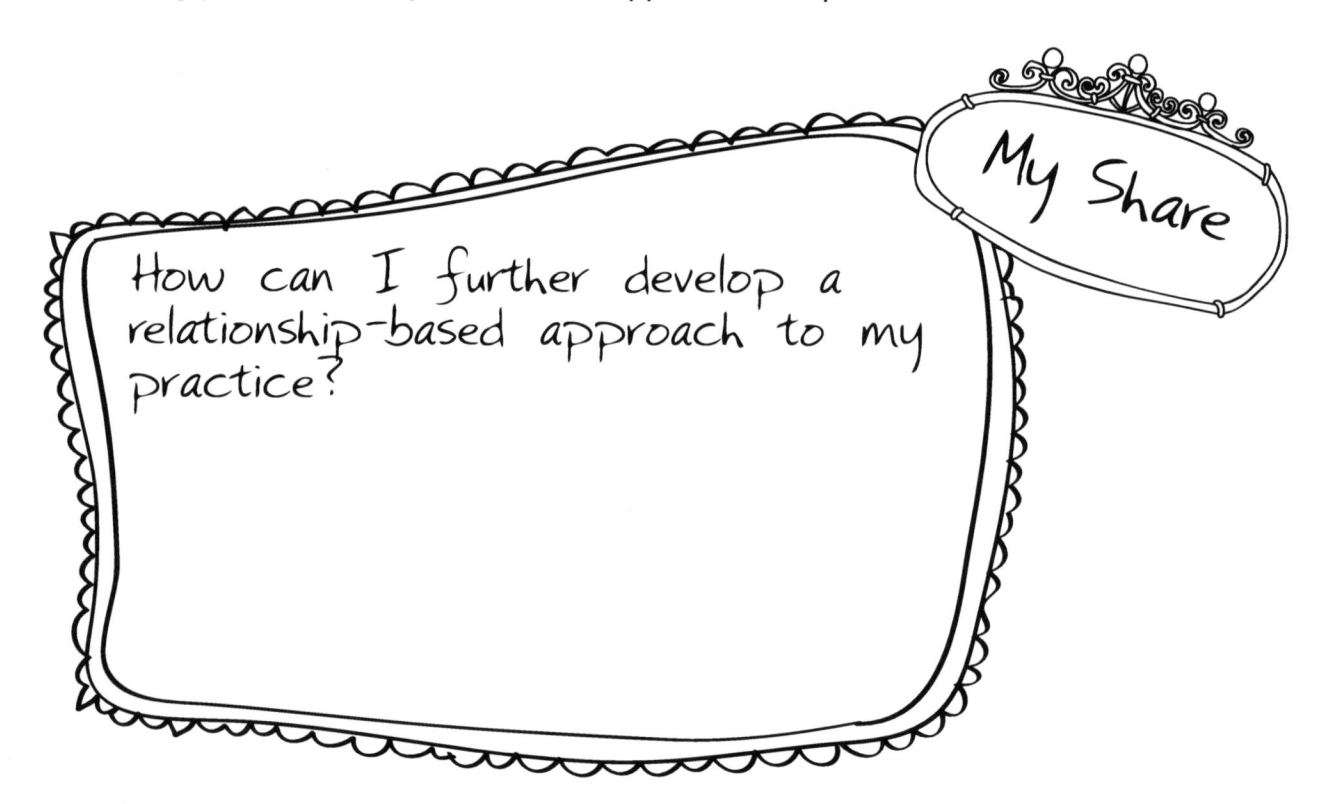

My Share

How can I further develop a relationship-based approach to my practice?

Systemic approach

Systems theory has a long history in social work. In their work on systems theory Pincus and Minahan (1973) suggested that society and people operate within three systems (informal, formal and public). Since that time many writers have developed systems thinking further, building on the complexity of our understanding. For example, Bronfenbrenner (1994) defined five interconnecting systems: microsystems; mesosystems; exosystems; macrosystems and chronosystems. The theory and the thinking around systems has developed to such an extent that it is now generally viewed as an approach.

Like much of the social work knowledge base, at the heart of the systems approach is a straightforward claim. One of the key starting points is that no person is an island. Everyone has contact with other people. Some of the people are family, some friends and others are people who represent an organisation. The relationships we have with all these people and organisations form a web (or system) around us. The system around us should sustain us and enrich us. There should be a sense of harmony, balance or smooth working in our system. The relationships and interconnections that we have with others are very rarely linear (that is we don't always see people in the same order, and some of the people we know may also have relationships with each other.) Recognising these simple concepts at the heart of systems thinking can aid an understanding of the systemic approach.

Students often find it useful to think about systems in a visual way - perhaps as a machine made up of a number of cogs. If the cogs are all running smoothly then the machine operates well. However, if one cog is missing or out of place then the whole machine can, very quickly, come to a grinding halt.

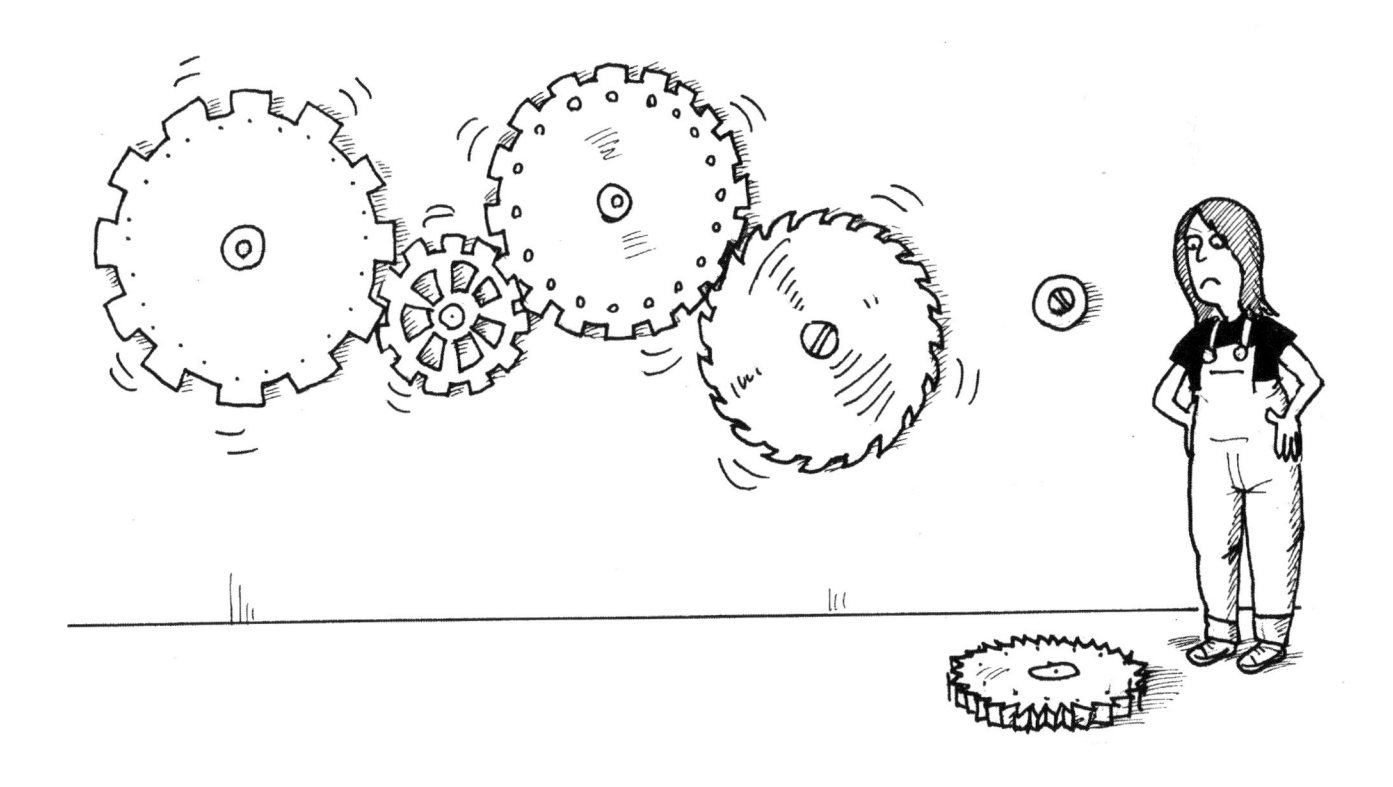

The Social Care Institute for Excellence has long suggested that systemic thinking is relevant to social work because:

- It describes and explains the recurring patterns of behaviour found in families, groups and organisations.
- It concentrates on the relationship between the parts rather than parts in isolation.
- Linear thinking, a straightforward cause and effect approach, is a common approach to analysing problems. Systemic thinking, however, offers a different perspective. It suggests there are multiple causes and effects involved and recognises that we are actively involved as a part of the problem and its solutions.

(Social Care Institute for Excellence 2004:18)

We consider the SHARE model to be systemic in that it breaks down the 'whole' into the component parts of seeing, hearing, action, reading and evaluation. Each of these is a vital cog in the social work 'machine' and if one is missing then the social work machine will be faulty. The interconnections between the different cogs may operate differently at different times, making the machine more complex than it may seem at first. The inter-relationships between the cogs is vital but at times each cog may need to be taken out and looked at more closely to ensure that it is playing its full part in the way that the machine operates.

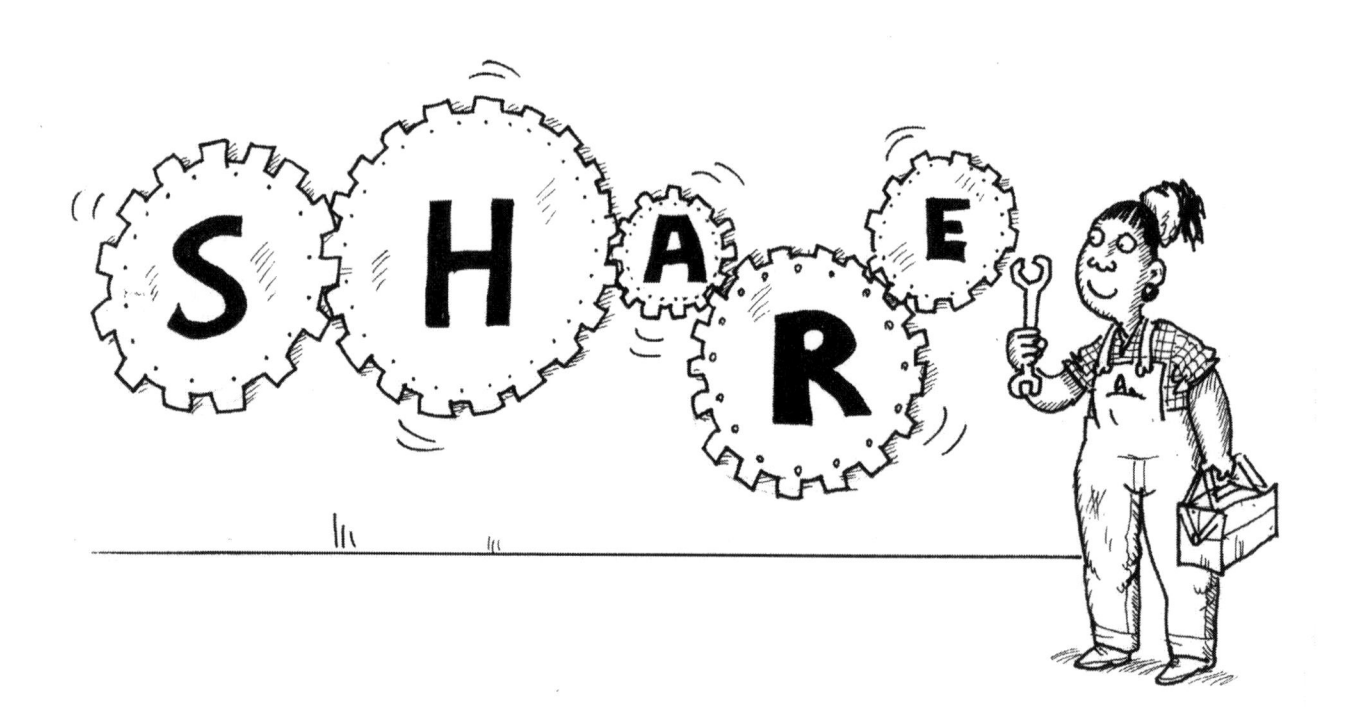

Holistic approach

A holistic approach is referred to very often in social work - both in practice and in social work education. For example, the implementation of a holistic approach to the assessment of students gained a high profile following the recommendations of the social work reform board, with the then College of Social Work developing a number of papers exploring the context and practice of holistic assessment in social work practice (College of Social Work 2012).

Practitioners and students alike often refer to taking a holistic approach, or describe working holistically but there is little clarity or depth of discussion in social work literature about what this really means. The idea of holistic social work though is being discussed in more detail with the growth of interest in spirituality in social work.

Taking a holistic approach is generally seen as working in way which looks at the whole picture - considering all aspects of person's life and their situation. The phrase holistic health care is seen as describing an integrated approach which treats the whole person, not just focusing on disease. In the assessment of social work practice, holistic assessment is often seen as being about moving from the partial to the contextual and understanding the inter-relationships between the individual, the local and the structural (Doel et al 2002).

The lack of depth of discussion around holistic social work means that there is a danger that a practitioner working from a holistic perspective takes a generalised overview of a situation, possibly missing some key elements. We believe that the most important aspect of holistic practice is seeing the whole in the light of the individual parts The SHARE model provides a practitioner with a framework to ensure that all the parts are considered in coming to an understanding of the whole.

**Holistic practice is not just about 'seeing the bigger picture'.
It is also about recognising the intricacies in the picture itself.**

Key learning points

- Theory is essential in social work practice.
- Any model for social work practice should position itself within approaches to social work.
- The SHARE model can be positioned within a number of different approaches: it is hopeful, strengths based, restorative, relational, systemic and holistic.
- There are a number of similarities between different approaches to social work.
- The SHARE model can be used to help aid understanding in any area. In this chapter, we have used the Hearing and Seeing elements to support an understanding of the essential difference between a theory, model, method and approach.
- Social work practice that is atheoretical and entirely focussed on skills is potentially dangerous.

Reflective Questions

How do you understand the difference between a theory, a model, a method and an approach? Has this changed since you explored your share on page 50?

In what ways do you draw on a hopeful approach to practice? What are the challenges to this?

How do you adopt a relationships-based approach to your practice? What are the challenges to this?

When using a model in practice is it important to understand the approach it is drawn from? Why?

Chapter 4: ADULT LEARNING THEORY

One of the reasons we began to develop the SHARE model was our concern about the increasing divide between social work education and practice. This divide, perceived or real, between the academy and the field is perhaps not so new. Brandon and Davies in 1979, in their research on practice learning, noted tensions, most notably around power and decision making. Finch (2010 and 2017) also notes more recent frustrations and tensions between the field and the academy. The gap between social work education and practice is not unique to social work in the UK. In fact, the International Federation of Social Workers has recently established an Education Commission with the expressed aim of *"closing the gap between social work education and practice"* (IFSW 2017a). The statement about the establishment of the Commission states that *"IFSW members and social work educators have together raised concerns over a long time about the relevance and consistency between education programmes and practice policies and requirements. This has resulted in many countries recognising that social workers leave the profession within five years of completing their training"* (IFSW 2017a).

The SHARE model aims at bridging this growing gap, by emphasising what is shared between social work education and social work practice, acknowledging that there is always a continuum of learning and development, and that both the field and the academy have a stake in social work education and practice. It is important to recognise that we all want the same thing, to promote good social work practice and improved experiences for the people who social workers work with.

In Chapter 3 we explored the social work theory which has influenced the development of the SHARE model. In recognising the importance of building on what is shared between social practice and social work education we have also found a range of adult learning theory useful in developing the SHARE model. This chapter will explore how the SHARE model has a place within adult learning theory.

Approaches to adult learning

In Chapter 3 we explored how theories, models and approaches fit together to create the whole picture. In terms of adult learning theory there are three main approaches, which we will explore in this chapter:

- Behaviourist approach
- Cognitive approach
- Humanist approach

In exploring these approaches, we will consider the influence that each has in terms of application to social work education. We will conclude by exploring the impact that our understanding of these main approaches to adult learning has had on the development of the SHARE model.

In Chapter 3 we explored the differences between theories, models and approaches. As a quick reminder, in this area we see the differences as:

Approach: Your overall way of looking at adult learning.

Theory: How you understand a learner.

Model: How you support the learner to learn.

Method: Specific technique you use to 'teach' or to help facilitate learning.

As a model SHARE can be used to think about how you might support a learner to learn. This might be in terms of formal learning, for example with a practice educator helping a student to learn but likewise it may be about informal learning. Social workers can support people to learn in a whole range of ways, for example we may support parents to develop their parenting skills, we might support a person to learn or relearn social skills or improve their daily living experiences. Social work is about facilitating change and this is often promoted by helping people to learn and develop. The use of the SHARE model in terms of learning should not therefore be sidelined to something that is for practice educators and trainers, but rather something that every one of us can do.

Behaviourist approach

This approach is based on the idea that learners respond to external factors - such as stimulus in their environment or role models. The idea being that a good facilitator of learning will consider the learning environment and will provide lots of opportunities for learning to be practiced and repeated.

A behaviourist approach to adult learning focuses on learning as a change in a person's behaviour. Initially developed by Skinner (1973), the belief is that behaviour is intrinsically linked to consequences. A behaviourist approach to learning therefore emphasises the importance of setting learning objectives and matching learning opportunities to those objectives to ensure that the objectives are met. How the person will know (through external factors) that the learning objective has been met is also considered as important. The idea is that a learner will repeat desired behaviours as a result of positive consequences - for example, if positive feedback follows the behaviour. The 'rewards' in behaviourist approaches are seen as external to the learner. Burns (1995) noted that many competency based training programmes were based on the basic aspects of behaviourism. However, he argued that whilst it may be a useful theory in relation to repetitive tasks and work skills which require a great deal of practice, higher levels of learning are not involved.

In social work, there has been a move away from a competence based approach, towards a consideration of capabilities, which takes a more holistic approach (Finch, 2010). However, practice learning plans and programmes like the Assessed and Supported Year in Employment (in England) still emphasise the importance of setting learning objectives and having measurable targets. The behaviourist approach is therefore still very influential in UK social work education and training.

The two main theories drawn from the behaviourist approach which are used in social work education and indeed social work practice are social learning theory and situated learning theory, which are covered across the next few pages.

A behaviourist approach is influential in our lives in a wide range of ways. For example, the use of rewards for desired behaviours is drawn from a behaviourist approach to learning.

Social learning theory

One of the principal writers of social learning is Bandura (1977). Like so many theories, this is just describing a common life event. Social learning describes the way that we engage in a behaviour because we have seen another person engage in the behaviour and that other person benefited from the behaviour (or they avoided something unpleasant happening to them). Social learning is more likely to be successful if the role model has status or standing with the learner and the new behaviour can be rewarded. Arguably, much of what we learn is through role modelling. This is most apparent in a parent / child relationship but there are lots of other examples. Many teenagers and young adults learn social skills from their peers through social learning. Many adults have learned skills through watching others succeed at the task (in relation to computer skills, it is often their child!)

It can be useful to draw on social learning when considering leadership in social work. Social workers often act as role models to others. For example, social care staff observe the way that social workers communicate with service users and they may well draw on their observations and model their own communication and responses to service users on these. Parents who need to develop their parenting skills may well model their responses to their children and other professionals based on the way they see social workers respond. The power of social learning in enabling change and acting in a leadership capacity should not be under-estimated. Being clear about the way that you may be a role model for others is vital at every stage of a social work career.

Prospera Shares

In 2012, I was working with a student of African heritage who expressed some difficulty with grasping social learning theory and I decided to use what I considered to be a familiar case scenario to facilitate her understanding. I used the example of a young girl in Africa learning to collect water as a vehicle to bringing Bandura's social learning theory to life. I explained the four conditions which make learning from others possible using the example of a girl learning to collect water. The four conditions are attention, retention, reproduction and motivation (Bandura, 1977).

Attention

The collection of water is often a gendered role and so young girls begin by accompanying their mothers to the stream and simply walking alongside them and watching how this water is collected, raised to the head and then balanced for the duration of the journey back home.

Retention

The young girl needs to retain and remember the strategies used to collect water, the shortest and safest route home and how and where to deposit the water collected. Usually, water is collected into a basin or bucket.

Reproduction

This stage involves the young girl attempting this process on her own, with initial supervision by an older female member of the family. The young girl works out what size to begin with and gradually works her way to using a large size basin or bucket which can take 60-100 litres of water. The goal at this stage is not to spill the water on her way home.

Motivation

The young girl must be motivated to learn the art of collecting water. The wider family expect this of her and the reward can be verbal praise and encouragement, not only by the immediate family, but also by peers in school and surrounding villages.

(Tedam, 2012)

This was my attempt to use what I perceived to be a culturally appropriate scenario to enhance my teaching and facilitate my students understanding of social learning theory.

Situated learning theory

The whole concept of practice learning in social work is based on the idea of situated learning theory – a term coined by Lave in the 1980s. He argues that learning needs to take place in the context and culture in which the activity ordinarily occurs (where it is situated). Social interaction is an essential aspect of situated learning. Learners need to become involved in a 'community of practice'. As the learner moves from the edge of this community to its centre, they become more active and engaged in their learning. Lave and Wenger (1990) call this process 'legitimate peripheral participation.' They carried out an analysis of situated learning in five different settings. In all five cases, they found that learners had a gradual acquisition of knowledge and skills as they learnt from 'experts' in the context of everyday activities. Others have further developed the concept of situated learning. For example, Brown, Collins and Duguid (1989) emphasised the idea of 'cognitive apprenticeship'.

Social work has long valued the importance of situated learning, building on the vital importance of practice learning for social work students. In England, a significant amount of work is underway to develop an apprenticeship in social work. The 'trailblazer group' developing this is hoping that the first entry to the apprenticeship programme will be around the point of publication of this book.

The vital importance of communities of practice is becoming more widely recognised in social work. Increasingly, teams working around an individual are being referred to as a community of practice. For example, a team around the child approach can be seen as creating a community of practice to support the child and their family. Communities of practice should have:

- A set of shared values
- A shared goal
- A shared commitment to working together to achieve the goal
- Individual skills and attributes which can be brought together and shared to create the community of practice.

Situated learning theory uses the concept of sharing in many ways (as can be seen in the bullet points above) and we have drawn on the importance of situated learning in a range of ways when using the SHARE model in terms of social work learning and development.

Situated learning theory can also help us to consider supporting others to learn in a range of ways. For example, to what extent are parenting groups which take place away from the actual practice of being a 'parent' going to help people learn? Surely support to develop parenting skills should take place in the home environment in the busy hustle and bustle of being a parent?

Cognitive approach

Whilst a behaviourist approach focuses on factors external to the learner and stresses the importance of the learning environment and the learning facilitator, a cognitive approach emphasises the role of the learner's 'active mind' in the learning experience. As such, it links quite closely with the importance of reflection in learning which is widely recognised in social work.

The modern-day origins of critical reflection in professional practice are seen as lying with John Dewey, whose book 'How we Think' was first published in 1910. This introduced ideas about states of thinking and began to identify some of the links between reflection and learning.

Perhaps now, Schön (1984) is the most widely referred to academic in relation to reflective practice, since his book 'The Reflective Practitioner' is seen as a seminal text. In fact, Schön's University thesis focused on Dewey's ideas about thinking and many commentators agree that the work of Dewey significantly impacted on the ideas later developed by Schön, Kolb, Boud and others, such that many of the threads in current models of reflective practice can be traced back to Dewey's early work.

Dewey believed that the most important aspect of learning involves 'learning to think' or 'reflective thought.' He also identified the importance of critical thinking which is a phrase now commonly used in both social work education and practice. To Dewey, the purpose of thought is attaining a state of equilibrium, enabling an individual to solve problems and to prepare them for further inquiry (Dewey 1933).

Humanist approach

Humanist learning developed from the work of Carl Rogers (1980) this is sometimes referred to as facilitative learning. Opposing behaviourist approaches which see learning as a consequence of extrinsic (external) rewards, humanists argue that learning is a result of intrinsic (internal) rewards. The approach is based on the belief that people have a natural eagerness to learn and that people will learn in order to meet their needs for self actualisation.

A number of specific theories are drawn out of the humanistic approach. Perhaps most oft referred to is the work of Malcolm Knowles (1978) who argued that most adult teaching has consisted of teaching adults as if they were children. He asserted that adults are different from children as learners in three critical ways:

1. In terms of their self-concept. Whereas a child first sees themselves as a completely dependent personality, the adult has developed a concept of themselves which values a certain degree of autonomy. Adults have a need to be perceived as self-directing. The deepest need an adult has is to be treated as an adult, to be treated as a self-directing person, to be treated with respect.

2. In terms of their experience. Whereas a child defines his or her self-identity by reference to their family, school and community, adults usually define themselves in terms of their experiences. Self-identity is derived from what we have done. Accordingly, adults are very conscious of the worth of our experience and wherever we find people devaluing our experience, not paying attention to it, not incorporating it in the education plan, we feel rejected as people.

3. In terms of their time perspective. Whereas in most aspects of life, a child's time perspective is one of immediacy they find it hard to postpone the satisfaction of present desires, an adult is more accustomed to postponing immediate satisfactions. However, in regard to learning, the time perspectives of children and adults is reversed. Children become used to learning things that will not have immediate application, but will be accumulated into a reservoir of knowledge and skills that will be useful in adult life an adult's perspective in regard to learning is likely to be one of immediate application. According to Knowles the reason an adult enters into education is to be able to better deal with some life problem about which they feel inadequate now.

Knowles refers to the approach of teaching children as pedagogy and says that the teaching of adults should be based on a different approach which he calls andragogy. Andragogy should take account of the differences outlined above.

Experiential learning

As we discussed in Chapter 3, theories and models may well sit comfortably into more than one approach. We identified, for example, that the SHARE model can be used as part of a range of different approaches to social work. This also goes for the learning theory which is perhaps the most widely referred to in social work education, experiential learning theory, which in many ways draws from all three of the main approaches to adult learning.

This theory is sometimes misinterpreted as simply saying that people learn through experience. To some extent this is true but experiential learning theory asserts that it's not enough for people to have an experience - they will not learn from this unless they spend some time reflecting on the experience.

Perhaps the most well-known writer in terms of experiential learning is Kolb (1984). Kolb sees learning as a dynamic process, in which people are able to construct their own learning through the following cycle of learning:

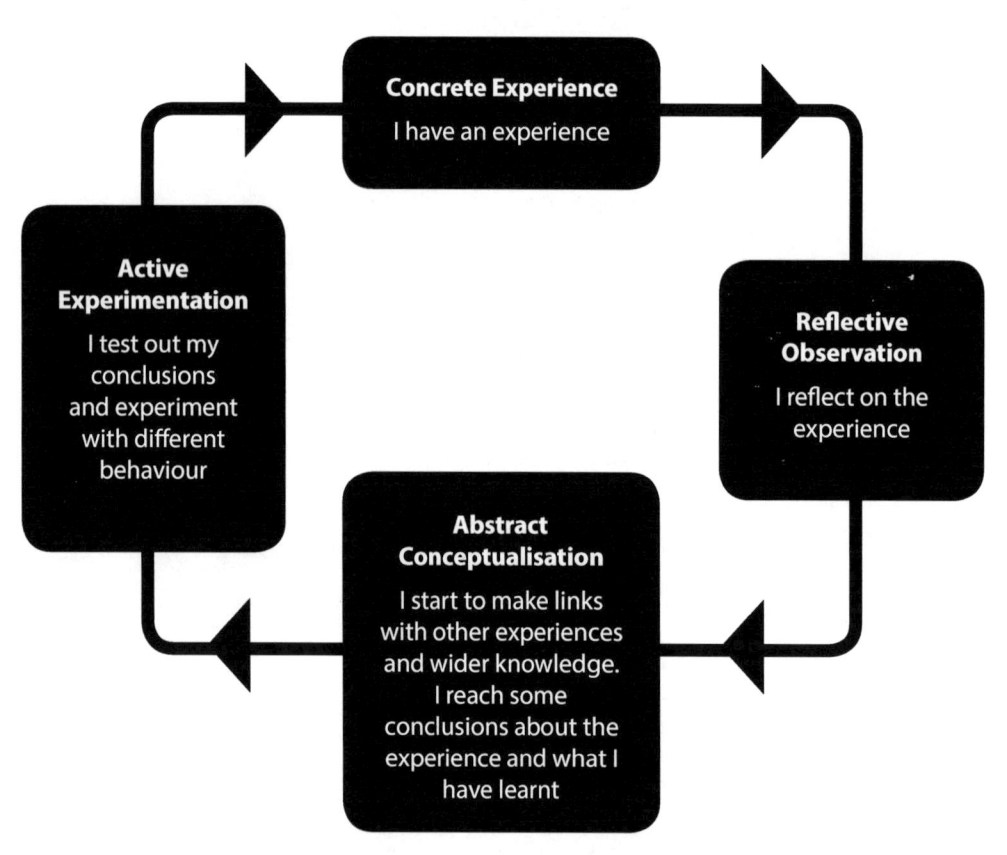

```
                    Concrete Experience
                    I have an experience

   Active                                      Reflective
   Experimentation                             Observation
   I test out my                               I reflect on the
   conclusions                                 experience
   and experiment
   with different
   behaviour

                    Abstract
                    Conceptualisation
                    I start to make links
                    with other experiences
                    and wider knowledge.
                    I reach some
                    conclusions about the
                    experience and what I
                    have learnt
```

Really Kolb draws on aspects of all three approaches to adult learning in that he recognises the importance of adults constructing their own learning based on their experiences and their evaluation of this learning.

Kolb's (1984) experiential learning cycle has been used to develop a range of ideas around learning styles. Specifically, Kolb's theory leads to a learning styles inventory which categorises learning into two distinct processes, firstly how to how to approach a task by either watching or doing it, and secondly, our emotional responses to it, either thinking or feeling. The learning styles identified are referred to as diverging, accommodating, converging and assimilating.

Learning styles

Most social workers will recall being asked to complete a learning styles questionnaire at some point during their qualifying training. Additionally, when social workers undertake practice education training, they are taught about learning styles, often with reference to the various learning styles inventories (LSIs). Indeed, new practice educators are often required to use such inventories to identify their own 'style' of learning. Some of these are perhaps familiar to you.

In our experience, the two most popular learning styles questionnaires used in social work practice learning are Honey and Mumford's (1982) learning style inventory, which identifies learners as reflector, pragmatist, theorist or activist and the VAK model (Visual, Auditory, Kinaesthetic) which was devised in the 1920s; also known as VARK (Visual, Auditory, Reading and Kinaesthetic) and VAKT (Visual, Auditory, Kinaesthetic and Tactile) (Barbe, Swassing and Milone 1979).

Jo Shares

I recall undertaking the Honey and Mumford (1982) learning style inventory whilst undertaking the Practice Teaching Award in 1999. There were a series of multiple choice questions to answer, then we plotted our answers onto a grid and watched as the ticks grew or not in the various columns (reflector, pragmatist, theorist, activist). I recall at the time thinking that this seemed a very blunt tool, and the multiple choice answers did not precisely match my answer I would have given so I knew I was only approximating. My preferred learning style came out strongly as a reflector, with very few 'ticks' for the activist. I wondered what this meant for my social work practice and what this meant in terms of me as a learner. Did it mean for example, that I was too focused on reflecting at the expense of the doing? Did it mean I wasn't a good social worker if I was low on 'activist'?

My Share

If you've ever completed a learning styles questionnaire what did it identify? What did it mean to you?

Much of the theory surrounding learning styles has been criticised. For example, Busch (2016) refers to a number of myths developed from neuroscience that have permeated teachers' understanding – using the word 'neuromyths'. He refers to the 'learning styles myth' that learning styles should be followed up by matching learning activities to the student's identified learning style. Despite the distinct lack of evidence to back up this claim, research has identified that 93% of teachers in the UK believed that the need to link learning activities to learning styles was scientifically true (Dekker, Lee Howard-Jones and Jolles 2012).

Allen (2017) reports that there is no scientific evidence to support claims that individuals have preferred learning styles and claims that matching learning styles to learning needs is 'bunk'. Further, an open letter to the Guardian newspaper by Bruce Hood, Chair of Bristol University's Developmental Psychology in Society Department urges schools and teachers to stop wasting their time and resources on this *"long running pedagogical fad"* (Guardian, 2017).

Yet the power of the notion that people have distinct learning styles remains and indeed, in England the Practice Educator Professional Standards require a practice educator to 'Discuss and take into account individuals' learning styles...' (Domain B:4). As trainers of social workers on practice educator programmes, we encourage participants to think about different ways of learning, and also introduce ideas about differentiation in terms of learning, not least that students all have different starting points when commencing their placements. Practice educators continue to explore in their essays, the importance of thinking about students individual learning styles, as well as their unique or distinct approaches to learning, so the theory behind learning styles remains influential.

More recently there has been a move towards the use of the phrase 'learning preferences' rather than learning styles – as this recognises that a variety of factors influence peoples' learning experiences. A brief search of the literature however, reveals, that this might be a semantic rather than substantive shift, as there is still heavy reliance on learning styles approaches to categorise the ways in which people prefer to learn. Specifically, what is not considered in these debates, are issues around culture and ethnicity, as well as gender and disability, which we believe have a significant impact on peoples' experiences of learning, and so influence how they might learn.

It is vitally important to recognise that many things impact on an individual's learning. One of the issues which impacts on learning is the fact that not everyone has an equal share within educational systems, and inequalities within education start from an early age. The following research shows too starkly that within social work education itself, differential outcomes are a reality, which given the values social work espouses, is a great concern. What does this say therefore, about social work with those in discriminated groups?

It is important then to reflect on our assumptions about learning, and our own 'share' (what do we see, hear and read in relation to social work education? How do we evaluate this? and what impact does that have on our actions?) How people learn is clearly very individual and complex and internal and external factors are both significant.

KEY MESSAGES FROM RESEARCH: DIVERSITY IN SOCIAL WORK EDUCATION

- Hussein et al (2008) and Moriarty et al (2009) found that female students of Black African origin, students with disabilities and men were at the greatest risk of failure on social work programmes.

- Hussein et al (2008) and Moriarty et al (2009) found that progression for black and ethnic minority social work students was slower (i.e. more repeated modules) than for other groups.

- Students from Black and minority ethnic groups and students from lower socio-economic groups achieve a disproportionately lower-classification of degrees, (Mountford-Zimdars et al, 2015).

- Hillen (2013) and Fairtlough et al (2014) found that Black and minority ethnic students took longer to complete their social work degrees and were over represented in fails, particularly placement fails.

- There are fewer BME students on social work fast track programmes compared with university based programmes (Maxwell et al, 2016).

- Zuchowski et al (2013) found that in Australia, many Aboriginal or Strait Island social work students experienced racism on placement.

- Whilst numbers of Black and ethnic minority students are increasing on all programmes in universities in the UK, attainment and progression rates are poorer compared to their white peers (Lenkeit et al, 2015; HEFCE, 2016).

Social pedagogy

Social Pedagogy is widely practised across Europe, particularly in Denmark, France, Italy, Germany and the Netherlands and is a field of growing interest in the UK. The word pedagogy is off putting to some people, it is derived from the Greek pais (child) and agein (to lead, to bring up) (ThemPra 2009) but is about a great deal more than bringing up children.

Social pedagogy is about educating people (children and adults) in a way which recognises their role as active learners, so that they can take a full and healthy role in a diverse society. There are key issues within social pedagogy around the valuing of diversity, inclusion and opportunity as the social pedagogue seeks to provide opportunities and learning for those excluded or disadvantaged within society. Social pedagogy draws on approaches to learning which recognise learners as active partners in the process.

Social pedagogy is a holistic, reflective approach which has the importance of relationships at its heart. The concept of sharing is vital in social pedagogy; for example, service users and professionals are seen as inhabiting the same life space, not as existing in separate hierarchical domains (Stevens 2010). In many ways, social pedagogy could be used as a way to describe what we seek to do as practitioners in supporting people to grow and facilitate change in a wide range of ways.

Many of the ideas around social pedagogy have influenced the development of the SHARE model and as such we will introduce aspects of the links between social pedagogy and SHARE throughout this book. For example, the 3Ps which we referred to in Chapter 3 are drawn from social pedagogy.

Siobhan Shares

I trained as a practice educator (then called practice teacher) fairly early in my career. I remember feeling that the adult learning theory I had covered as part of the course was really useful to me in my social work practice. At that time, I was working in mental health and I found an understanding of adult learning theory really useful in supporting people with recovery planning. When I later moved to work in children's safeguarding I reflected on how much I was drawing on adult learning theory in my work with parents. I suppose this highlighted even more a feeling that the 'divide' between social work practice and social work education was a real problem for practice.

It was only later when I started to do some work across Europe that I became aware of social pedagogy. I found this fascinating as it seemed to bring together social work skills and my feelings about the usefulness of an educative approach in practice.

Digitalisation in social work: impact on learning

There is an increasing recognition of the way that social work has been slow to adapt to the digital age and a number of practitioners and academics are working to explore this digitalisation in both social work education and practice. For example, Amanda Taylor has done a great deal of work to progress thinking in this area. She asserts that *"Digitalisation and its relationship to social work is multi-layered, fluid and complex, and as such must be understood in context."* (Taylor 2017:870). In our experience the theory behind adult learning in social work has not yet widely addressed issues of digitalisation and so we wanted to give some acknowledgement to the importance of technology in this chapter. In the following stakeholder voice Jon gives some advice about the impact of technology in learning.

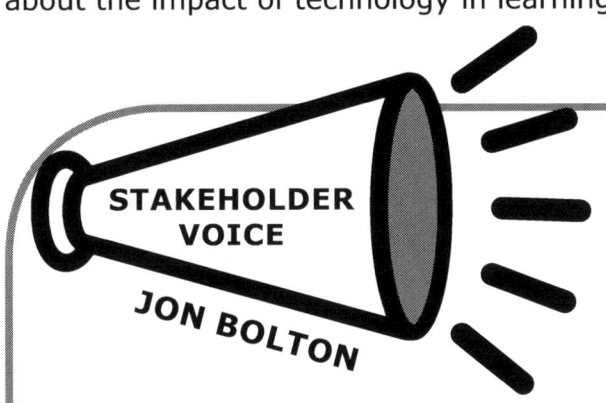

STAKEHOLDER VOICE — JON BOLTON

Jon is a qualified social worker with over 20 years' experience in a variety of practice settings. He is now a consultant and trainer - and also a Social Work Practice Tutor for the University of Dundee. He was previously a senior social work manager and also a Workforce Development Adviser for the SSSC, the social service regulator and workforce development agency in Scotland.

"The next generation of social services will rely on a backbone of new technology and confident, IT-savvy social care and health specialists."

I smiled as I recently read through my undergraduate dissertation. It was written 20 years ago and was about the internet, and its implications on social work practice. Yes, I was a geek even back then! So much has changed since I wrote it... but there were things that I wrote that are still topical today.

Technology is now very pervasive and impacts on all areas of our lives. It is more available than ever before, and gets better and (usually) cheaper as time progresses.

Advancements in technology have exponentially changed not only the ways in which we experience the world, but also completely revolutionised – in a relatively short span of time – how we work and learn. Just in the past few years, the expectation of connectivity has become ubiquitous in nearly every aspect of our daily lives.

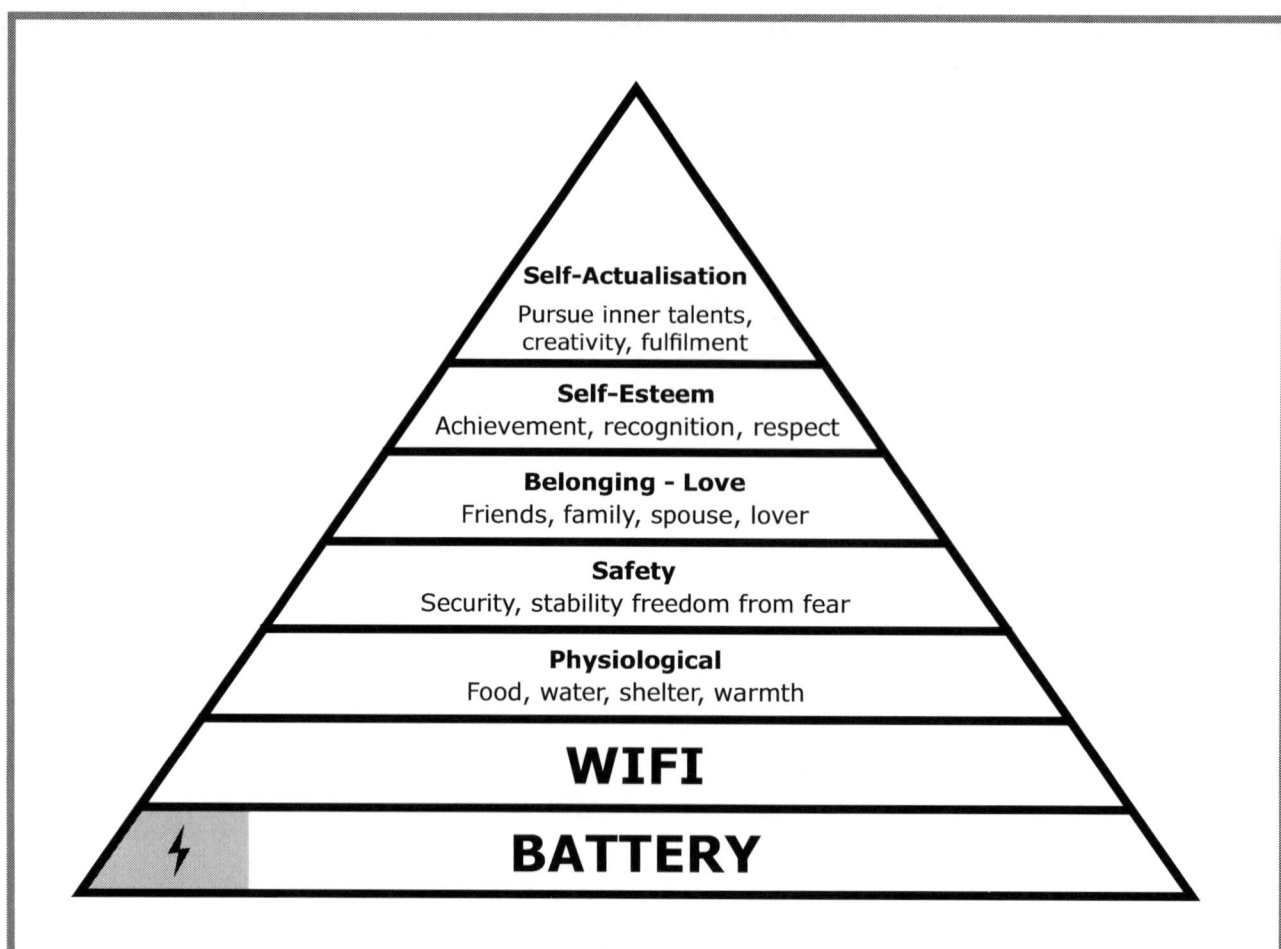

```
          Self-Actualisation
          Pursue inner talents,
          creativity, fulfilment
        ─────────────────────────
          Self-Esteem
          Achievement, recognition, respect
        ─────────────────────────
          Belonging - Love
          Friends, family, spouse, lover
        ─────────────────────────
          Safety
          Security, stability freedom from fear
        ─────────────────────────
          Physiological
          Food, water, shelter, warmth
        ─────────────────────────
                  WIFI
        ─────────────────────────
          ⚡        BATTERY
```

Adapted from Maslow 3.0, Morten Øverbye - https://twitter.com/morten/status/503519307402600449

Smartphones, tablets and even watches now have considerably more power than the computers that put humans on the moon. Information is flowing in all directions, constantly. We live in an "always on" society, where information is readily available at our fingertips.

So how do we as social workers harness that technology and what is its impact on learning?

I could write a whole book on this topic - there's LOTS to think about - but for now, I'm going to introduce* just four areas:

- Technology in learning
- Technology in practice
- Making sense of information
- Social media

*I deliberately chose the word 'introduce' – space does not permit any great depth on any of these areas. If your interest is piqued, there are lots of resources that will be useful:

Technology in learning

There are many potential benefits of technology relevant to the social services workforce. Some are obvious – convenience and flexibility – but others are less obvious, such as the immediacy of feedback leading to speedier remediation, and the ability to reference material in supporting decision making.

Technology permits increased creativity and innovation, greater ownership of learning by learners, real world problem solving and the development of complex ideas and knowledge transfer. It allows 'just in time' reinforcement and reminders – great for knowledge about policies and service delivery, compliance updates and performance support.

Recommended Resources:

Social Work Theory: Your Critical Friend (Kirwin Maclean Associates)

This interactive app is about social work theories and critically reflective practice. Content is regularly updated and is designed to appeal to users at various stages of their social work career - for example, information is provided on reflective supervision in social work.

https://itunes.apple.com/gb/app/social-work-theory-your-critical-friend/id1169559980?mt=8

ScOPTbox (Scottish Organisation for Practice Teaching)

ScOPTbox contains resources to support social work practice learning and also provides individual spaces to be used by practice educators in supporting their students. These spaces can be used for discussion, revision tools, assessment, evaluation, interactive case studies, reflective journals... and much more! Although ScOPTbox has been developed by the Scottish Organisation for Practice Teaching, much of the content is applicable across geographical boundaries and professional disciplines.

www.practicelearning.info

The LearningWheel: A model of digital pedagogy (Deborah Kellsey and Amanda Taylor, 2016)

LearningWheel is a rich resource generated by practitioners for practitioners offering suggestions to digital what, why and how questions. They are a simple graphic device to help bridge the gap between traditional teaching methods and contemporary digital learning content and resources. They guide people through digital technologies by linking platforms, apps and web content to learning delivery. The wheels help you to gain knowledge and competency, from building confidence and understanding around digital technologies through to the application of technologies within your own areas.

http://www.criticalpublishing.com/the-learning-wheel

Technology in practice

We need to know about technology in how we relate to and support service users. It's crucial for us to understand online safety, not only to give us as adults the knowledge to keep children and young people safe, but also to help us equip them with the skills and the resilience to recognise and address risk... but how can we protect and safeguard children and young people, if we don't have a clear understanding ourselves of the available technologies and the potential risks? The same goes for vulnerable adults and many other groups.

For example, social workers involved with fostering and adoptive families can feel deskilled and uncertain about how best to support and advise foster carers, adopters, children and their birth families when contact arrangements are undermined if informal approaches are made by young people and their birth families online.

We also need to understand the relevance of technology to the development of services.

Recommended Resources:

Digital working, learning and information sharing (Skills for Care)

www.skillsforcare.org.uk/Topics/Digital-skills/Digital-working.aspx

The future for personalisation? Service users, carers and digital engagement (IRISS, 2011)

http://comment.iriss.org.uk/content/digital-engagement.html

Learning Zone (Scottish Social Services Council)

http://learningzone.workforcesolutions.sssc.uk.com

Core digital skills for social care (Skills for Care)

A guide to help you understand why people in social care need core digital skills and to identify what they are.

http://www.skillsforcare.org.uk/Documents/Topics/Digital-working/Core-digital-skills-in-social-care.pdf

Making sense of information

How do we make sense of information, specifically in terms of fact-checking? Social workers need to apply theory to practice, evaluate information, use the best evidence in practice, and use different approaches and perspectives that fit the particular problem presented. But how we check that it's the right information?

The Open University (2014) suggests that information literacy is knowing when and why you need information, where to find it, and how to evaluate, use and communicate it – and digital literacy goes beyond this to encompass communication, collaboration and teamwork, social awareness in the digital environment, understanding of e-safety and creation of new information. Both digital and information literacy are underpinned by critical thinking and evaluation.

Actually, Belshaw (2011) argues that digital literacy should actually be plural – ie. literacies (he suggests 8), and that those digital literacies are context-dependent.

Recommended Resources:

23 Digital capabilities to support practice and learning in social services (SSSC)

http://23digital.sssc.uk.com

Confidence Through Evidence Toolkit (IRISS)

A toolkit with four steps designed to help you Acquire, Assess, Adapt and Apply evidence in your practice.

http://toolkit.iriss.org.uk/

Information Literacy Interactive Tutorial (IRISS)

A tutorial which will provide you with an understanding of information literacy in six simple steps: Question, Sources, Find, Evaluate, Combine, and Share and Apply

http://content.iriss.org.uk/informationliteracy/

Finding Evidence to Inform Your Practice: A Guide for Social Workers (SSKS)

An interactive PDF to help you find evidence quickly and effectively.

http://www.ssks.org.uk/media/178910/ssks-interactive-pdf.pdf

Managing knowledge to improve social care (SCIE)

An e-learning programme that sets out to help front line social workers gain a basic understanding of the principles and practice of knowledge management, as well as organise and manage their knowledge and information as effectively as possible.

http://www.scie.org.uk/publications/elearning/knowledgemanagement/

Evidence Informed Practice (Skills for Care)

A video explaining how research evidence can be used in decision-making

https://vimeo.com/117171646

Social Media

While the technology and the tools might be relatively new, the concept of social networking has been around much longer than the internet or even mass communication. People are naturally social creatures. That's what makes social media such a powerful concept. Social media channels allow human beings to sort themselves into groups and factions seamlessly, and maintain intimate relationships at greater distances than ever before.

The number of social networking tools is many and varied, and many are already being used by professionals in the social services workforce to network, collaborate and learn. By their very nature, these resources are highly engaging and if used appropriately offer innovative opportunities for service improvement.

Our digital identities matter, but we need to consider how we manage our digital identities. What we post, share, say, upload, snap, and tweet represents our digital identity. It's our online presence. In recent years there has been an increase in the number of Fitness to Practise cases as a result of inappropriate behaviour relating to social networking sites and digital communications. Students have been discontinued from their programme and practitioners dismissed from employment. Taylor (2016) suggests that social work practitioners are navigating unchartered waters when it comes to practice in a digital world, where the boundaries between digital knowledge, skill and ethics are not explicitly understood in terms of appropriateness and professionalism.

Recommended Resources:

The Social Work Social Media App (Tarsem Singh Cooner)

This app offers a way to explore some of the ethical issues of using social media in social work. The aim of the app is to encourage discussion and debate.

https://sites.google.com/site/socialworksocialmedia/

Social Media in Social Work Education (Joanne Westwood, Editor)

This book discusses social media activities and how they can contribute to student learning, and social work practice. The contributors, all innovators in the use of social media, introduce the landscape and discuss how social media activities have begun to impact on both social work education and on practice.

http://www.criticalpublishing.com/social-media-in-social-work-education

Grow your personal learning network (IRISS)

Growing your personal learning network is all about making the most of the web to grow who you know and what you know and will give you tools to do things faster and more effectively. Learning, sharing and connecting are even more important in new world of health and social care integration. We've got to be savvy about how we work - and the web can help!

https://courses.iriss.org.uk

And finally...

There are many reasons to implement digital learning tools for students, practitioners, managers and educators. However, the prospect can seem intimidating: Where do I start? What will work best? How much will it cost?

Just because digital technology is all around and irrevocably changing learning and social work practice, it doesn't necessarily mean that everyone is comfortable using it in the different contexts of their life. We need to be aware that people have different motivation, attitudes, skills and confidence about accessing and using the technology. People need enough time to learn about and practice using new technologies.

© Jon Bolton

My Share

What digital resources do I use?

How do I use digital tools to assist in learning?

How can I expand on this use?

SHARE in adult learning

AS we cover in Chapter 2 considerable thought was given around the choice of the word share. As three women involved in various aspects of student journeys in social work education we recognise that learning is a shared experience. We learn as much from students as they learn from us. It is widely recognised that learning is always enhanced when undertaken on a partnership basis (Williams and Rutter 2015).

As part of our hope that the SHARE model bridges the growing divide between social work education and social work practice, we have drawn on the way that social work theory and adult learning theory shares some basic premises and we have tried to build on this in developing the model. For example, we recognise the importance of being strengths based and hopeful in working with students. We recognise the vital importance of relationships to support learning and reflection in practice. Finally, we hope to take a holistic approach to social work learning in a way which draws on aspects of all three of the main approaches to adult learning, underpinned by an anti-oppressive stance.

SHARE can be used as a specific model for adult learning. For example, think through what does the learner see, hear, do and read? and how do they evaluate their learning? It can also be used as a model to assess learning - with the assessor considering what they have seen the learner do, what they have read of the learner's work, what they have heard both from and about the learner and how they evaluate this. Specific examples of using SHARE to design and develop training, to support induction for new staff and students and to both support and assess new workers are covered in Chapter 10 and in relation to practice education we provide specific examples of how SHARE can be used to plan placement learning and to assess a student.

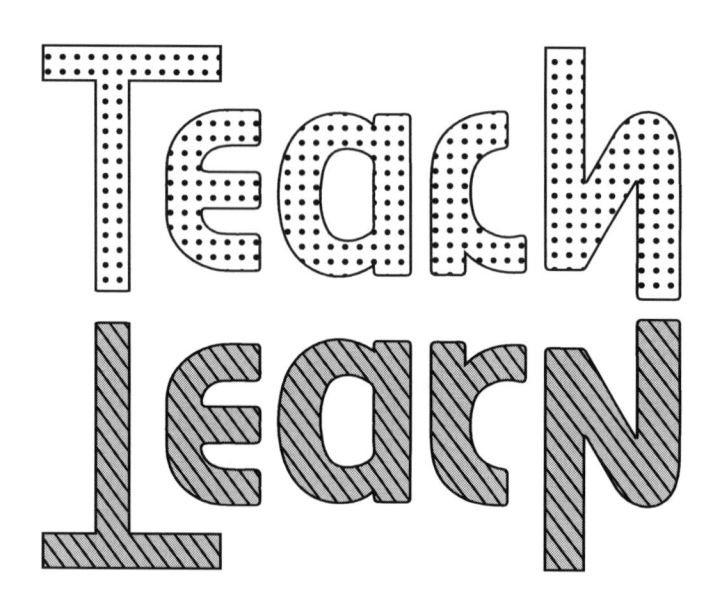

Teach
learn

Reflection is always important but look what it does for those who teach.

Key points

- There is a divide between social work practice and social work education. we fear that this divide is growing and hope that the SHARE model can be used to help bridge the gap.
- We have drawn on theory from both social work practice and from adult learning in developing the SHARE model.
- Just as the SHARE model can be positioned within a number of different social work approaches, it can also be aligned with the main approaches to adult learning.
- Adult learning theory can be useful in practice and social work theory can be useful in understanding learning.
- Social pedagogy is a growing field of interest in the UK and this has much to offer social workers.
- The SHARE model can be used to support adult learning in a range of ways.

Reflective Questions

To what extent do you see a gap between social work practice and social work education?

What impact does this have on social workers and the people who social workers seek to support?

Do you draw on theories of adult learning in your practice:

    If so, how?

    If not, why not?

My Share

How do I learn?

How do I support others to learn?

What could I do differently after reading this chapter?

Chapter 5: SEEING

The first component of the SHARE Model is seeing. This component includes a range of issues; observational skills, visual thinking and the whole concept of vision. Each of these will be explored in turn in this chapter. This component of the model should also be used to explore what is not seen, and the chapter will conclude with this aspect of the first component.

Observational skills

"You can observe a lot by watching" (Berra 2008). This quote from an American baseball player in the 60's in response to a reporter's question, sums up the process very well. There is of course more to it than that, but in essence he is correct; observation is pretty much about watching. Watching is essentially a natural human activity that requires little thought or analysis. However, in social work this 'natural activity' needs to be carefully considered, because it is possible to 'watch' without actually seeing.

The importance of observational skills in social work practice cannot be underestimated. Munro (2011) asserted that social workers need to have well developed observational skills. Indeed Islam (2011) places observational skills at the very start of her list of the top five skills in a social worker's tool-kit. However, O'Loughlin and O'Loughlin (2014) believe that although observation is central to social work, little consideration is given to the complexities and demands of observation. Rogers et al (2017) recognise that observational skills are often taken for granted, even though they really need to be practised and developed.

Indeed, on many social work programmes in the UK, students will be taught how to observe and they may be required to write an assignment on the experience. Observing people in their homes or in another key setting will enable a social worker to go beyond listening to someone, enabling true 'hearing' by really 'seeing' the person. It can help us to really understand how people live and experience their environment, as well as being a useful way of exploring contradictions between what is said and what is seen.

Siobhan Shares

As a fairly new practice educator, many years ago, I undertook a direct observation of a student social worker who was placed on a Community Mental Health Team. The observation was of a home visit. As I observed the interactions, I noticed an area in the room which I can only describe as a sort of 'shrine' there were a number of candles, some photos and a framed set of footprints and hand-prints. I reflected that the service user had probably experienced a stillbirth.

After the observation, I asked the student about the shrine and what she knew about how the stillbirth had impacted on the service user's mental health. The student looked puzzled. She knew nothing about the still birth and had never noticed the 'shrine' despite making many visits to the service user's home.

I had always assumed that observing surroundings when on a home visit would be something that everyone would do, but from this observation and the subsequent feedback session I learnt the importance of students being supported to develop their observational skills.

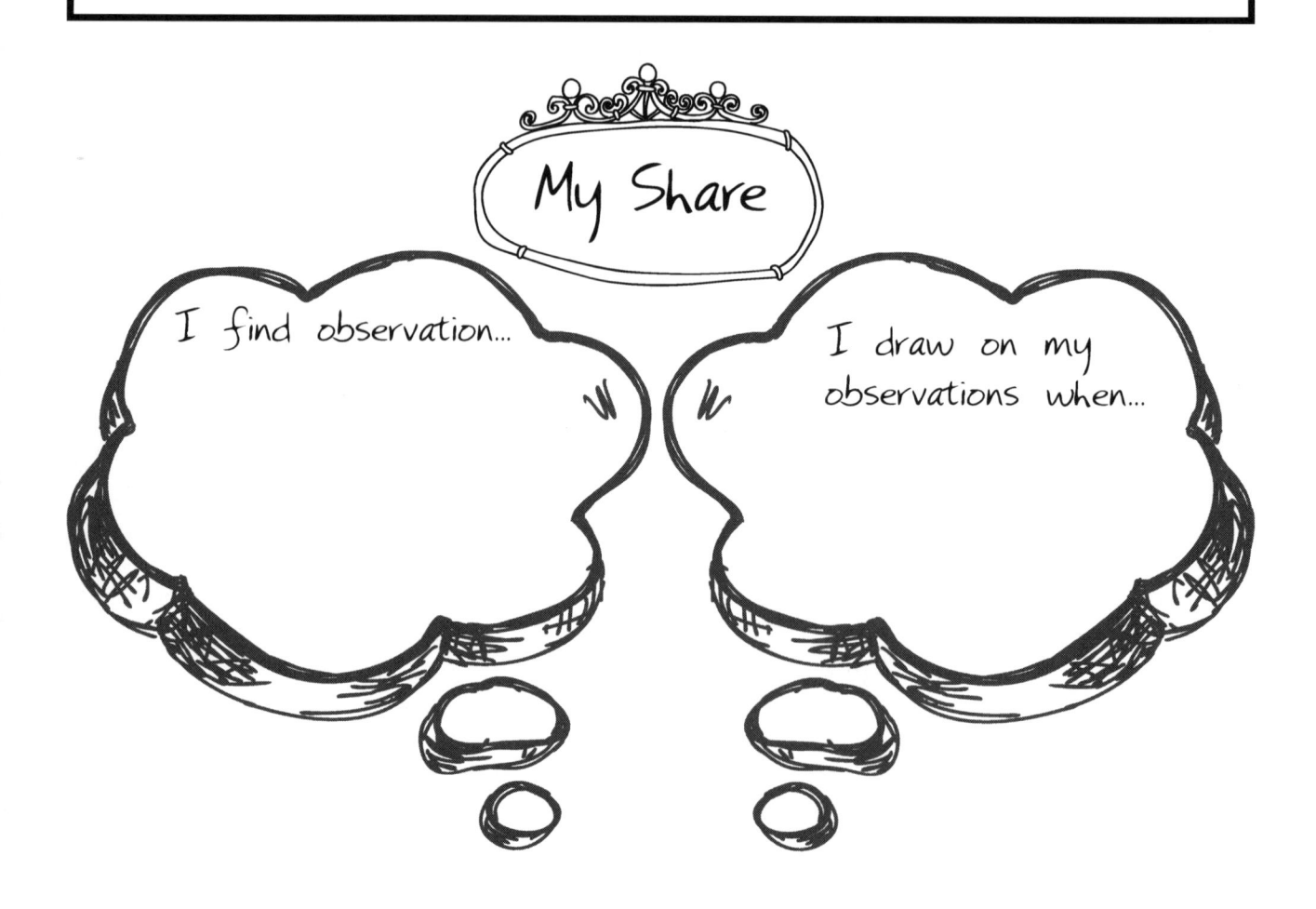

My Share

I find observation...

I draw on my observations when...

Seeing things differently

What we see is often informed by a range of factors; culture, gender, race, ethnicity, age, disability and a host of other variables. There is an old phrase often attributed to Anais Nin,

> "We don't see things as they are, we see them as we are."

Take this picture, for example. Do you see a tree? Or do you see the outline of two faces? In just the way that everyone will see a different image first in this picture, with the second one coming to them when it's pointed out by others, every professional will see situations differently.

Since we all see things differently, our observations are always open to perceptual errors. Being aware of this and checking out the meaning of our observations in a range of ways is important. The SHARE model can help with this, for example:

- Share your observations: It is helpful to share exactly what you see with anyone else involved. This can help to clarify whether they have seen the same thing or whether they have the same interpretation of what you have seen. For example, voice what you see to a service user - they might be able to clarify how they see something.

- Share your conclusions from your observations with other professionals and check out if they see things differently to you.

- Share your thoughts with colleagues: If you have seen something which puzzles you, or which disturbs you then find the time to discuss this with your supervisor or team colleagues.

- Set your observations against the other elements of the SHARE model - for example is what you are seeing congruent with what you hear and read? Or are the different components of the model highlighting conflicting information?

My Share

How do I check out what I see?

STAKEHOLDER VOICE: BRIDGET CAFFREY

Bridget Caffrey is a Senior Lecturer at the University of Chester.

For the last two years, I have been the module leader for BA students Readiness to Practice module at the University of Chester. The first year BA students do not go on placement, but we invite in service users, both young people and adults to work with the students to teach core skills including communication and assessment skills. The involvement of service users in this module for students to practice their skills with and learn from is invaluable. However, I am conscious that there is more complexity to social work home visits and assessments than we were teaching in class, even with service users present. I acknowledged and wanted to address specifically, the need to develop the students' skills of observation.

I therefore introduced the skills lab to our module this year; this can be set up to resemble a home, complete with furniture and life size manikins, who can, if required communicate verbally. The technician set up the lab as a bedsit with two young female tenants (manikins) and a young baby (manikin). He added pieces of home living to the flat, including take away food wrappings, post and nappies. I gave the students a referral for one of the young women and her 6-month-old baby, and explained they were to undertake a home visit. They went into the bedsit (lab) in small groups and had 15 minutes to observe the scene.

They were allowed to move around but could not ask questions about the scene. Those that did move around (not all did) observed final reminder / debt collection correspondence and a possibility of illicit drug use. There were objects which contradicted the referral information, for example, signs a male may be cohabiting. After 15 minutes, the group left. Once all groups had visited the bedsit, we discussed in class.

The discussion included exploring what was seen: students picked up on different things allowing a discussion of why this might be so and how accurate memories are? Possible interpretations of the scene were considered, including assumptions students made. The students also discussed what, following their observations, they needed to know and how they might go about gathering this information. Finally, the students addressed how to record what they saw. The depth and breadth of learning available from one brief visual exercise was significant.

Some students struggled with aspects of the exercise; they wanted to ask questions and some focused on how realistic the manikins were. I have reflected on how to improve the explanation of the purpose of the exercise to the students beforehand. I also recognise that the exercise can be improved. I recall home visits I undertook as a social worker and recognise what has been described by Ferguson as the 'complex and hidden practices' of social work home visits. He points out that social work is a deeply embodied, sensory and mobile experience (Morriss, 2017). Nothing will fully convey that experience to students at a University, but an exercise such as this can help prepare them. So, next time, I will ensure that the bedsit impacts on other senses as well as visual; smells of damp walls and the noise of a TV and electronic game may also greet the students.

© Bridget Caffrey

Like any new skill, the more we practice 'noticing' the easier it becomes. Of course in the busy world of qualified practice, we do not have the luxury of simply observing, but need to engage with individuals whilst simultaneously observing people and environments.

So, drawing on observational skills is an important aspect of the SHARE model. However, the information drawn from observation, must be placed into context by drawing on the other components of the model, as Prospera's share demonstrates:

Prospera Shares

In my days as a Principal Social Worker, I often challenged practitioners who reported that the absence of toys in a home meant a child or children had little or no stimulation. Social Workers and particularly Family Support Workers often worked on the assumption that the presence of toys or play equipment automatically meant children were being stimulated within the home. I found that social workers were working on a simple tick-box approach to what they 'saw' in the home without always considering what and how the toys may be being used. I impressed upon practitioners the need to draw on the other components of the SHARE model, for example, by asking questions about stimulation, which might result in a discussion around how parents and carers stimulate their children within the home.

Observation as a research method

Students often find modules on research methodology problematic and once they have completed their dissertations they lose sight of their learning around research, not always seeing it as relevant to practice. However, many of the methods which we use in social work have their roots in research methodology. The origins of observation in social work lie in research, where observation is a method used within qualitative research. Quantitative research gathers data in numerical form, whereas qualitative research gathers more descriptive data. Qualitative research is commonly used in the social sciences where the researcher seeks to understand the 'why and how' of aspects of human behaviour rather than simply the 'what'. Qualitative approaches to research draw on a variety of methods, including participant observation and direct observation.

Participant observation	Direct observation
This requires the researcher to become an active participant in the activity or culture being observed. This method usually requires weeks or months in order for the researcher to be accepted as part of the culture, enabling accurate findings to emerge.	This differs from participant observation in that the researcher is not part of the event taking place. The researcher is able to adopt a detached view of the event although this in itself can potentially impact on the findings of such research as the researcher is likely to influence the interaction being observed.

Direct observation has long been seen as a useful method in research, particularly in relation to social sciences (Jersild and Meigs 1939). Whilst social work students often report finding research modules difficult and unrelated to practice, social workers are in fact researchers in the community (Gauci and Kent 2015). Effectively when social workers are undertaking an assessment they are researching the situation that the service user is in. When a practice educator is assessing a social work student on placement then they are researching the quality of the student's practice. As a consequence drawing on observations - both formal and informal is vital in completing a sound evidence based assessment. So being a researcher is in many ways another 'hat' for a social worker to wear.

A social worker needs to wear a number of hats and draw on a range of skills, being research minded is important.

The use of direct observation in practice education

Requirements for direct observations of practice in social work education and training are relatively new. Indeed, according to Danbury (1994: 100) in the fairly recent past, *"direct observation was not considered to be viable, as it was a firmly held belief that the relationship between student and client would be damaged, possibly irreparably"*. The use of direct observation was only formally introduced to social work training through 'Paper 30' in 1991. At a similar time, requirements for practice educators to be observed as part of their assessment was introduced. It seems impossible now that professional practice could ever have been assessed without practice being directly observed as a key part of that assessment. According to Skills for Care (2013a) the emphasis on the ongoing assessment of even the most experienced workers means that the process of directly observing practice will continue to be a key feature of social work education and continuous professional development.

During 2016 Skills for Care undertook a project designed to improve the use of direct observation in assessing social work practice. The project involved a small group of employers and universities working together to explore a new approach to direct observation in practice. Part of this project researched and developed the facility for the secure storage of video of observational evidence and processes and protocols to support direct observations of newly qualified social workers in practice. The resources are being further developed as this book goes to publication. Mary Keating of Skills for Care outlines the project in the following stakeholder voice:

STAKEHOLDER VOICE — MARY KEATING

Mary Keating is a Project Manager and a member of the Skills for Care team responsible for developing and implementing the revised ASYE for adult social work.

The direct observation by an assessor of a social worker's practice is the 'optimal method of assessing professional skills because it is closest to 'real practice' '[1] This was one of the conclusions of a scoping report conducted by Research in Practice into practice observation methods. This assessment method directly engages with the complexity and subtlety of the social work task and the performance of the practitioner in relation to this.

The use of direct observation of students, and more recently that of NQSWs, has been used as an assessment tool for 16 years. A trawl of the literature would suggest that there is still plenty of scope for more research into the conduct of the process and the outcomes but there is enough evidence to suggest some broad parameters.

Based on the experience of nationally moderating the assessments of Newly Qualified Social Workers undertaking the ASYE in adult services, in 2015 Skills for Care decided that the time was right for improving the guidance and the assessment process. Reviewing the assessments of direct observations had indicated a lack of consistency in the way that the direct observations were conducted and recorded. If direct observations are a crucial element in the assessment of social work professional capability then we needed to do something to improve the quality and consistency of this.

Based on the research evidence we concentrated on the following areas:

- Developing more standardised assessment criteria
- Structuring a post observation reflection
- Identifying the knowledge and skills needed by assessors for observation

These three developments were in the context of developing a process to video direct practice and at the same time to ensure that this data was kept completely safe.

As the social work role is so complex then this assessment cannot be one dimensional, and based on one viewpoint. The new guidance brings together the standardised observation data collected by the assessor - 'raw data', together with a reflective interpretation by the social worker that is designed to test the ability to conceptualise practice and to be able to learn from a review of this practice. These two, together with feedback, from the Person in need of Care and Support provide a triangulated perspective for the assessment.

It won't come as a surprise to realise that a central component of any good assessment are the skills of the assessor. What are the knowledge and skills required by assessors in order to carry out good observations? There is of course overlap with other aspects of assessment but what are the specific skills for observation? It was difficult to find any reference to these but based on information available we developed initial learning outcomes. Central to the development of these was the issue of Observer Bias.

We all have biases the important thing is recognising and finding ways to deal with them and be able to work across differences. In the direct observation, the assessor is the 'Observer', they need to leave behind their roles of supervisor or manager and put on one side what they already know about the student or the social worker. Easier said than done? We have tackled this area by offering new learning outcomes and training ideas for assessors. The standardised assessment criteria also helps by structuring the observation and in this way standardising and making it more 'fair'.

The video will help this process because it is not only the social worker who can use it as a learning tool it is also one for the assessor. Reviewing the video, the assessor can check the accuracy of their observation skills and learn from the process. As we progressed with the project it became apparent that the skills we were identifying are not just applicable to the assessor role they are core skills for every social worker in their everyday practice. For this reason, we have recommended that the NQSW receives a similar training package.

Skills for Care will continue reviewing and refining the guidance. Video is used by most professional groups to test practice, but it is new to social work and currently daunting for social workers and assessors. Our work will test out the feasibility of using video and provide evidence that will seek to convince the profession of the enormous benefits that can come from this for learning and for improving the quality of social work practice.

[1] Research in Practice, Evidence Scope regarding the use of practice observation as part of the assessment of social work practice. July 2015

© Mary Keating

Informal observation

In research methodology, informal observation is referred to as 'free' or unstructured observation. Informal observations are basically observations of events or behaviour which are unplanned and unstructured. Informal observations of practice are often used in social work. For example, students on placement are being observed all the time - during their interaction with other members of the team, in team meetings or simply in the office environment on a day-to-day basis. This informal observation will perhaps consider the student's interpersonal skills, whether they are respectful to others or whether they communicate effectively by telephone.

Formal observation

Although informal observation occurs on an ongoing basis, formal observation will include a planning stage and should result in formal feedback. Formal observations of practice are generally used to inform an assessment of capability in social work practice. As such, the use of formal observations in social work is similar to the use of formal observation as a research method. The observer is essentially 'researching' the quality of practice being observed.

Based on their work with trainee teachers, Weade and Evertson (1991) identified an 'observation continuum'. They contrasted everyday informal observation that occurs subconsciously with formal observation which is used for the purpose of assessment. They suggested that data collected from the informal observation is absorbed by the assessor even if it is not used explicitly in the assessment process, concluding that the process of observation does not just move through a continuum but provides a feedback loop with information from the formal and informal observations interacting together to inform the full picture (Le Riche 1998). Whilst Le Riche, Weade and Evertson were writing about observation as part of the assessment of professional practice their conclusions have direct application to social work practice, in that social workers often draw on both formal and informal observations.

Observation in social work practice

Observation is drawn on in a range of ways in social work practice. For example, social workers very often draw on their informal observations during home visits and meetings. The importance of this is being more widely recognised in social work education, as Bridget's stakeholder voice (see page 98) illustrates.

More formal observation is also used in social work practice - particularly in relation to children and families work where relationships between birth parents and looked after children are often observed as part of a supervisory process. Such observations are usually formally written up and form parts of records about service users, often being shared in decision making arenas such as courts.

Hawthorne Effect

Practitioners should always be mindful of the 'Hawthorne Effect' when observing anything. This was first described by Rothlisberger and Dickson in 1939. They used this phrase following a study carried out in the 1930s at the Hawthorne Works, an electrical engineering company near Chicago. The study attempted to assess whether workers' productivity was influenced by light levels in the workplace. A number of years later, researchers recognised that the data generated from the study suggested that productivity increased while the research was being carried out and slumped when it had been concluded. The conclusion being that individuals modify their behaviour simply as a reaction to being observed.

It is really important that practitioners take the Hawthorne effect into account when they are undertaking observations. Also, the fact that we all see things differently is very important. So, when you are undertaking an observation - whether that be of a service user or student make sure that you consider these issues and set the findings of the observation against the other components of the SHARE model.

We all do strange things when we are being observed!

Multi-sensoriality

It is very important to be clear that in the SHARE model the seeing component addresses much more than the physicality of seeing. In many ways, 'seeing' is about the drawing together of the sensory experience for all stakeholders. In primary school teaching the word observation is used to describe the process of children gathering information drawing all five senses - touching, seeing, hearing, smelling and tasting. Ellen's stakeholder voice recognises that seeing is not just about what you see with your eyes but what you sense - feel and touch.

STAKEHOLDER VOICE
ELLEN ANDERSON

Ellen qualified as a social worker in 2011 and has been employed at North Staffordshire YMCA since then.

My role is to support women who have lost their children to the care system. In their desperation to mother a child, they become pregnant again. Without a supportive partner, or the care of a loving family, the outcome is the same and their pregnancies result in empty arms.

Being visually impaired, or, 'as blind as a bat' as I prefer to describe it, my journey both through university to employment has not been an easy one. I am constantly battling against my own insecurities of not feeling good enough, demons that are always standing at the door of my subconscious waiting for the opportunity to oppress me. As a disabled person, it may be forgiveable to settle into society's assumptions and to follow the stereotypical line of least resistance, an opinion too often shared by those I support. For me every day just getting to work presents a new challenge, every step a step of faith, not knowing for sure whether I will reach my destination. When reflecting on my own fears, I can empathise with those I support. Though our situations may differ, our anxieties run parallel. I can comprehend what it feels like to experience isolation, vulnerability and the lack of control over aspects of one's own life. I share their fear of being judged, a battle I often feel ill-equipped to fight. When feeling like this I have to take charge of myself and remind myself of the goals I strive to achieve; a message that I hope permeates through to those I support.

I am aware that it may sometimes appear that I exuberate confidence in an attempt to hide my anxieties, determined to fill the void that blindness creates, engendering a sense of unwelcome pity. Once disclosed my badge sports disabled and broken, the case files of those I support painting tacit labels of their own.

Within social work there is always a battle to balance care with control. Social workers are often tasked with enforcing guidelines when working with families especially those tangled in child protection proceedings. Their passion may often be misinterpreted as obnoxious and difficult as they desperately fight for their children, against the organisation that advocates a compassionate service. I too experience a personal fight of my own as I urgently fight against adversity and hidden discrimination. I have learned to temper my response when in meetings irrespective of the presence of my guide dog, introductions are omitted as it is assumed I already know who is in the room. I can empathise when service users make known their disapproval when presented with assessments written in an unfamiliar language, littered with acronyms and abbreviations, evoking a sense of inferiority. When presented with printed material which is of no use to me, serving only to rob me of my confidence and my skills. In these situations, I use humour as a vehicle to disguise my injured pride and hide my frustration. It is in such situations that I find myself questioning the impact of the Equality Act. With amusement, I have detected humour when reading their assessments to me service users foster an air of power, a single protest against corporate control.

Taking the above into consideration, how do I weave what I have learned into the fabric of my practice? Firstly, I urge those I support to look beyond their circumstances. I will always be without sight and how I handle this will determine how others view me. For example, I have to acknowledge that the lack of sight limits what I do but, I will not allow it to stop me from achieving my goals. I am a person with a disability, not a disabled person. I encourage those I work with to acknowledge their circumstances however, in acknowledging them does not mean they have to surrender to them.

I have found that my disability has acted as a gateway into the way I work with people. A social worker may be depicted as one that has power, however, due to my disability, when I visit a person at their home, the power balance is reversed as I ask to be guided to a seat. This small demonstration of vulnerability helps to stabilise the pendulum of power versus' control.

The ethos running through social work is to adopt a non-judgemental attitude. I believe that being without sight may place me at an advantage in this area as I cannot judge a person from their appearance, which so often the sighted may do subconsciously. It may also be argued that being without sight offers me a greater opportunity to explore a person's hidden emotions. I am unable to pick up on body language often a visual sign telling the professional that they are treading on forbidden ground. Finally, when speaking with people I try to encourage them to embrace challenges as invariably opportunities are concealed inside challenges. It is better to go through the test than to miss out on an opportunity. Very often we surprise ourselves if determined enough. Social work may be the change agent but it is up to the individual to embrace the chance to change situations. I will always be blind and although my lack of sight is frustrating the choice is that I do what I can with what I have or let the lack of sight blind me from striving for my goals.

© Ellen Anderson

Visual thinking

Visual thinking is also referred to as spatial learning or pictorial thinking. The idea is that some people are more likely to see things pictorially, they will have visual memories and may like the use of analogies to understand something new. If you need to find a place for the first time which of the following direction styles would you like?

Verbal	Visual
Turn left in 500 yards then drive for a mile. Take the third right, then go left half a mile furtherr, then you will come to a roundabout, where you should take the second exit...	Turn left just after the pub. Keep going until you see a big house painted white, turn right there, then go right at the church...

Think about when you need to put together flat pack furniture or something similar. The instructions always come with both words and pictures. Which do you look at first?

In our experience of teaching and training, many social workers are pictorial thinkers, but this is not recognised in practice. You can't go to court with a picture and present this as your recommendation!

Further, in our experience, both as parents and as educators, we see the most recent generations, known as Generation Y, Generation Z or the Millennials, as more pictorial in their thinking style (most researchers and commentators use birth years ranging from the early 1980s to the early 2000s).

This pictorial thinking style is not always addressed in social work education and training, but there is great value to the use of visual thinking in social work, as the following examples illustrate:

I've coloured it in really nicely!

Examples of visual thinking in contemporary social work

There is an increasing recognition of the value of visual thinking in social work and in reflective practice more widely. We have chosen a few examples which really illustrate the value that visual thinking can bring, as we cover in the next few pages:

Social Work in 40 Objects

The Social Work in 40 Objects blog instigated by Mark Doel illustrates the way that visual thinking has much to offer our way of understanding the world. The contested nature of the profession and the value of using objects and visual thinking to portray this

A picture can paint a thousand words

is clearly illustrated in the book which came out of the project (Doel 2017). Indeed, the nature of social work, the exploration of who we are and what we do is perhaps more fully explored and more widely illustrated in this very visual book than in many verbal accounts. The use of visual imagery and thinking really attracts the reader and prompts a different way of thinking about the profession.

In the blog Mark invited social workers to suggest an object which might, to them, represent social work. Social workers from 24 countries across five continents suggested objects.

One of the 'objects' was **Eyes**, proposed by Reineth Prinsloo, Associate professor at the University of Pretoria in South Africa. Reineth writes:

"For me, eyes equal social work! As a social worker I observe harsh circumstances, I see sadness, despair, anger, conflict: I see all that in people's eyes. I convey empathy; I look for opportunities; my eyes show determination in the face of discrimination.

What I see helps me engage; what they see gives hope."

In our work, we have used Mark's prompt on training sessions, in group supervision and in seminars. Students and social workers have enjoyed putting a range of ideas together, helping them to discuss their understanding and experiences of social work in creative ways, as the following selection of photographs illustrate.

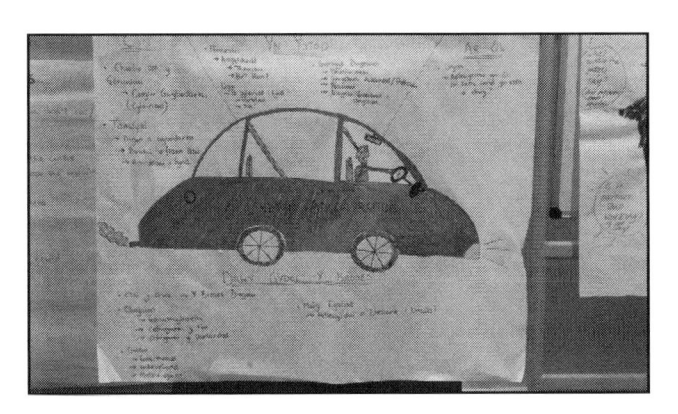

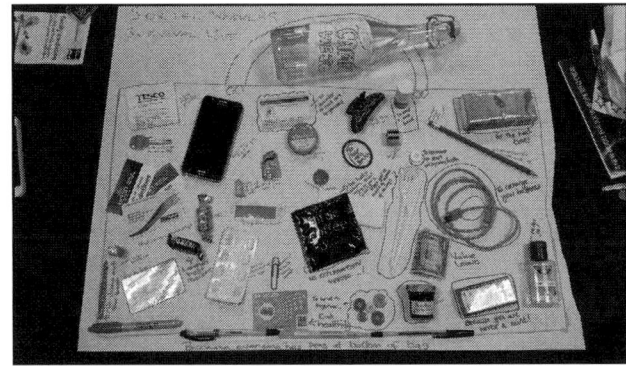

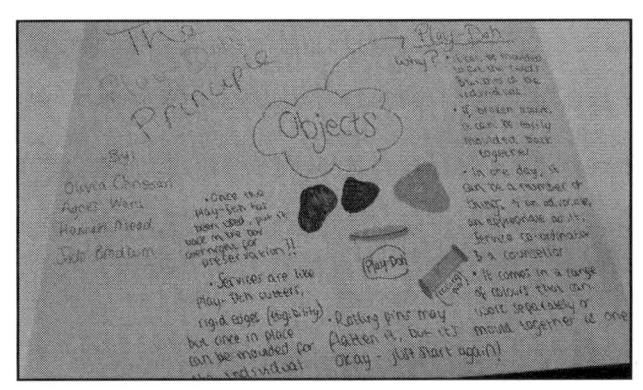

Social work as... a car, the contents of a bag, a tree or playdough.

My Share

What object would I choose to represent social work?

109

Experiencing the Social Work World

Siobhan has had the privilege of seeing this art exhibition first hand and would recommend it to anyone who has the opportunity to see it. Jadwiga Leigh and Lisa Morriss (whose stakeholder voice is included in Chapter 1) have written about the project for inclusion in SHARE as follows:

Jadwiga Leigh is a Lecturer in Social Work at Sheffield University. She qualified as a social worker in 2005 and has always worked in child protection. Lisa Morriss is a Lecturer in Social Work at the University of Birmingham. She qualified as a social worker in 1995 and worked in Community Mental Health teams for over 10 years. Jadwiga and Lisa met at Salford University during their doctoral studies and bonded over a shared interest in social work identity and in the use of visual methodologies. They are the co-founders of Experiencing the Social Work World.

Experiencing the Social Work World is an arts-based research project devised by two registered social workers, Jadwiga Leigh and Lisa Morriss. The aim of our project was to give statutory social workers the opportunity to create artwork which represents their lived experiences of 'being a social worker'. Silenced by confidentiality, social workers are often unable to report on the positive work that they do; or discuss the struggles and challenges they face in trying to do their work. When their voices are heard, it is often distorted through channels such as the media which favour a negative 'damned if you do, damned if you don't' narrative. We wanted to give social workers a voice to tell their stories of how it feels to be a social worker in this current climate in order to raise public awareness about some of the issues social workers face. We chose to use an arts-based approach as we felt that if people see and hear how social workers feel, they are more likely to apprehend the stories being told.

After gaining ethical approval, we ran a day-long workshop with eight social work participants. The morning sessions were led by our visual methods practitioner, Matt Morriss. Matt demonstrated how to work with mono printing, wire work and clay and the social workers tried each of these materials in turn. After lunch, the social workers each created a final artwork using the materials of their choice. Some of them chose to combine two of the materials to create their work. We thought that our social workers, being so used to working closely with less creative modes of expression such as the Integrated Children's System, might struggle at first to convey their feelings through art. We were wrong. They embraced every medium with such passion and energy; and rather than producing one final piece of artwork, many of our participants produced three.

Once the social workers had completed their work, we interviewed them in order to gain an in-depth understanding of their story and the artwork that they produced. Through doing this, a powerful narrative emerged which explained how certain organisational issues and public perceptions of social work deeply affected participants' identity and their practice. Rather than talk about one experience in particular, participants talked about their lived experiences since qualification. All of the interviews were very moving as it became immediately apparent that all our social workers deeply valued and appreciated working with children, adults, and their families. However, in many cases it became clear that actually accomplishing this part of their work was extremely difficult because of a large number of barriers which those outside of the social work profession are largely unaware.

Finally, we curated an exhibition of the artwork produced by the social workers at the People's History Museum in Manchester, UK. By seeing the artwork, reading participants' narratives and hearing the emotive content of their interviews (voiced by actors), visitors to the exhibition gained an understanding of what 'being' a social worker means and what 'doing' social work entails. Through this sensory and affective approach, we aimed to engage the public and in turn challenge current dominant stereotypes about social work. We held two events at which we invited 'Annie' from Surviving Safeguarding and Kathryn Littlewood, author of 'Cultivating Mad Cow' to speak about their experiences. Finally, during the exhibition, we held an arts-workshop with people who had experienced social work services. We received an overwhelmingly positive response from visitors to the exhibition. We have been invited to exhibit the artwork at other venues and are currently writing articles about the project. Further details of forthcoming exhibitions can be found on our project website:

https://experiencingthesocialworkworld.com

We are really fortunate that two of the social workers involved in the project have a allowed us to share their work in this book. Here, Sheila who was qualified for one year shares her systems model whilst on page 237 Demi shares her work.

Systems model

This is my systems model. The little bowling ball in the middle is the child or the young person and then the systems around the child are there as support. In my world that's much more of a depiction of how I would like to work and like to manage my cases.

It is quite an oppressive look because we're looking in and making all those decisions and my intention was for it to be a bit more of a protective thing not a controlling thing. But I suppose families may see it as a control thing. We are not always wanted. I get that.

Jo Shares

I am very much a 'pictorial person', and so I often use diagrams, pictures or colourful tables, to help me understand theories or complex and often abstract, concepts. I make liberal use of these in my teaching, recognising of course, that my pictures or diagrams might not make sense to every student present in the room. My aim in this is to break down excluding academic barriers, and share academic knowledge, particularly around research methodology in an accessible and non-threatening way, but certainly not in a simplistic way. Of course, when writing, we all need to convert those pictures and diagrams into a narrative that conforms to the accepted standards.

The pictures below, for example, aim to help students go beyond the quantitative versus qualitative debate and to see all research as on a 'spectrum' (Bryman, 1988) rather than as two opposing (dichotomous) approaches.

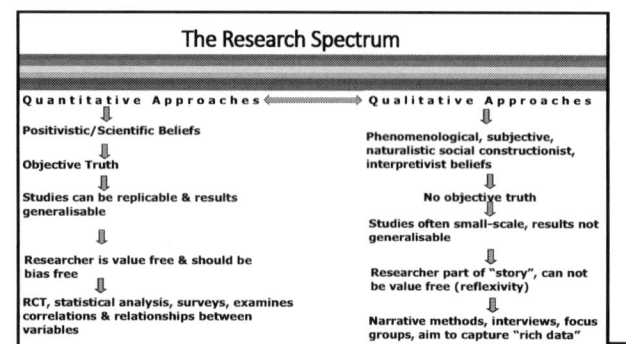

I also use pictures to try and explain some of the philosophical differences inherent in quantitative and qualitative approaches, which I appreciate might not work for everyone!

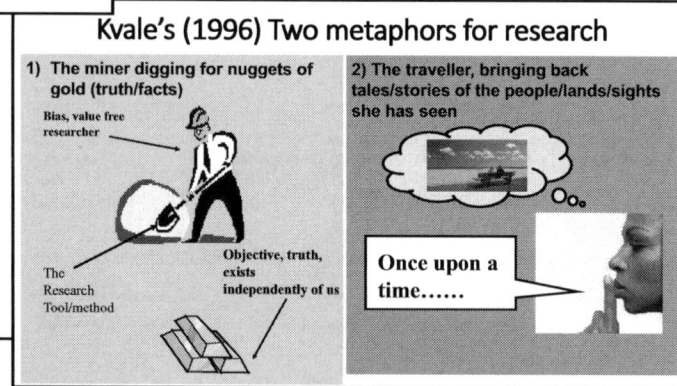

The Research Spectrum

Quantitative Approaches ⟷ Qualitative Approaches

Positivistic/Scientific Beliefs → **Phenomenological, subjective, naturalistic social constructionist, interpretivist beliefs**

Objective Truth → **No objective truth**

Studies can be replicable & results generalisable → **Studies often small-scale, results not generalisable**

Researcher is value free & should be bias free → **Researcher part of "story", can not be value free (reflexivity)**

RCT, statistical analysis, surveys, examines correlations & relationships between variables → **Narrative methods, interviews, focus groups, aim to capture "rich data"**

Kvale's (1996) Two metaphors for research

1) The miner digging for nuggets of gold (truth/facts)
   - Bias, value free researcher
   - The Research Tool/method
   - Objective, truth, exists independently of us

2) The traveller, bringing back tales/stories of the people/lands/sights she has seen
   - Once upon a time......

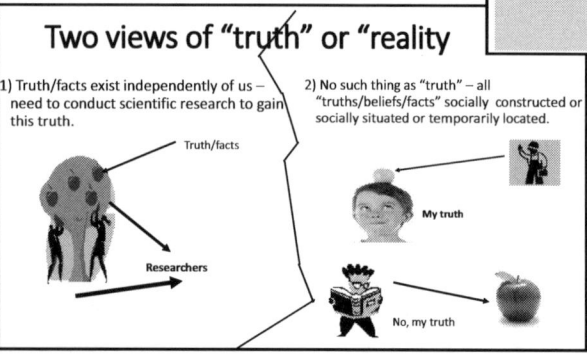

Two views of "truth" or "reality"

1) Truth/facts exist independently of us – need to conduct scientific research to gain this truth.
   - Truth/facts
   - Researchers

2) No such thing as "truth" – all "truths/beliefs/facts" socially constructed or socially situated or temporarily located.
   - My truth
   - No, my truth

© Jo Finch

Creative arts in social work

Social workers have long recognised the value of the creative arts. In the Global social work community, some countries view the relationship between social work and the creative arts as more important than others. In the UK the use of the creative arts in mental health social work and in social workers working in palliative care is increasing (Turner and Rowe 2013; Hartley and Payne 2008).

Thinking visually and using creative arts techniques can be very helpful in promoting creativity in practice. Creativity, critical reflection and analysis are closely related as is recognised in the Professional Capabilities Framework for social work in England.

We have found that visual and creative arts based thinking has great potential to support the development of self-awareness and to promote change. Helping people to see something differently can help in changing attitudes and in motivating them to move forward.

We have found at times, however, that there can be resistance to utilising creative methods in social work teaching and training. Some of the resistance, we feel, may stem from negative experiences of using creative techniques and methods in schools, where messages such as 'you are not good at art' continue to impact on people. For some, such approaches may be deemed not 'academic enough.' Indeed, one of us was criticised by an academic for breaking complex things down, through the use of the very negative term, 'dumbing down'.

Creative social work can grow out of the use of the creative arts

KEY MESSAGES FROM RESEARCH: CREATIVE ARTS IN SOCIAL WORK

- Significantly, there is a growing body of research which indicates that creativity and engaging in the creative arts enhances mindfulness which in turn improves reflection and problem-solving skills (see for example Ostafin and Kassman 2012).

- Using creative arts in professional training can promote more compassionate and empathic humanistic practice (Le Navenec and Bridges 2005).

- The use of the liberal arts is effective in promoting reflection in social work (Fook et al 2016).

- The creative arts are useful in promoting leadership in social work (Hafford-Letchfield et al 2014).

- A study in America, used observing art, to help develop nursing students clinical observation skills. The study found that those who attended the arts programme, developed better clinical observation diagnosis skills (Pellico et al, 2005).

- Lucas and Greany (2000) found that creative methods can help develop students reflexivity, teamwork, communication, resilience and problem solving.

- Mcaughan et al (2013) explored the benefits of using arts based techniques for social work students placed in a voluntary agency set up to support people with adults experiencing emotional or psychological distress. Crucially, the arts activities helped students develop skills in relationships-based practice.

STAKEHOLDER VOICE
NICOLE DAVIES

Nicole is an independent educator of social work practice and a visiting lecturer in social work.

I had attended training on use of visual analogies to represent complex ideas in social work training - for example stimulating students' reflection on their social work practice by comparing the process to baking a cake - what ingredients do you need, how do you know when the cake is done etc? It's a really exciting way of getting students to engage in more in-depth reflection, especially if provided with a range of art materials and if doing the exercise as a group endeavour, seeing different perspectives on what sort of (practice) cake should be produced.

All too often service users are excluded from this reflective process, yet applying the key principles of SHARE it's vital that social workers include in their reflection the perspective of the person being assessed and seek feedback on what they want from their interaction with social workers?

I took what I'd learnt from the training and suggested to two students on their first placement that they utilised art materials at their agency (a day centre for adults with long standing poor mental health and substance dependence) to draw a poster entitled 'Social Work is…' and mentioned the baking analogy idea. At the next supervision the students were keen to show me their work. They had not only developed the poster together, but more importantly done it with a service user attending the centre. She had given them a totally different insight into what she wanted from them. The painting was in two halves, overall entitled 'Social Work is a Piece of Cake'. The students had painted a large slice of pink cake, deep, many layered and with icing. They both saw their practice as the icing - noting that students had more time than an employed worker to go that extra mile, for example feeling that the clients were likely to be chaotic and forget to keep appointments, the students phoned a day ahead to remind the person, and again on the morning. They felt this enhanced the social work cake.

The service user had noted on her half of the painting that the cake was overdone, sickly sweet, and not what she needed at all. What the students saw as useful appointment reminders the service user perceived as bothersome, patronising and unnecessary - 'over egging the cake'. The students learnt that however well meaning, not everyone would appreciate their 'keen and attentive' calls - they could not assume everyone was disorganised or lacked a diary, and they learnt to simply ask the client whether they would like a reminder of their appointment or not, and in what format.

© Nicole Davies

The journey model for practice education

The journey model (Maclean 2016) proposes that placement planning draws on the concept of a student undertaking a journey. The journey analogy is used a great deal in terms of both social work and adult learning and is sometimes therefore overused in practice learning (Stone and Harbin 2016). However, providing specific visual ideas around the journey (therefore 'sharing' the travels) has worked well for social work practice education, and as the use of the model has spread into the ASYE (in England the Assessed and Supported Year in Employment) and into CPD (Maclean 2017) the value of this particular visual tool for exploring learning and development has become clear.

The model takes a visual approach drawing on the analogy of a journey. It draws on Lester's (1999) assertion that a competence based approach to the assessment of learners is like the learner following a map, whereas a capabilities approach introduces the idea that the learner is the map maker. In the journey model, the student is supported to recognise the destination they need to reach, but they decide on the best route for them. The model empowers the student to consider their starting point and to plan their route with guidance from the practice educator (as a more experienced traveller).

Supervision provides a passport for the journey (since you can't get very far without it). The student considers what they are bringing in their bags, and what they would like to experience along the way. Postcards provide a very visual method of reflection, with the student bringing a postcard to the beginning of each supervision session to discuss where they feel they are on the journey. At times, the journey is shared and at other times, when the student feels more confident, they travel alone checking in with others along the way and keeping a clear travel journal.

The use of postcards is a very practical application of the journey model.

STAKEHOLDER VOICE
SANDI OWEN

Sandi is a final year social work student.

On starting my first placement my practice educator introduced the journey model and we discussed how it could give a good idea of my progress from the beginning to the end of placement. My practice educator gave me a suitcase filled with postcards and we agreed that one or two should be chosen to bring to supervision. These postcards were to be used to reflect on my own thoughts and feelings, just as I would do when on holiday. Although I did consider that when on holiday we do try to pick the nicest postcard to show where we have been as no one wants to see the horrible side of a holiday or trip.

However, after initial discussions I found myself thinking of my journey since starting the social work degree. In the beginning, I will pack my suitcase with the knowledge and skills I already have using them to draw on when dealing with diverse situations. However, along the way I will collect and pack more into this suitcase then move onto the next destination. Everything I learn along the way is a learning experience, just like when you travel. When on holiday, I like to meet new people, experience different cultures and foods and take in the beautiful scenery. However, sometimes when going abroad it can be difficult to see how people have to survive through poverty and discrimination. And the scenery may not be as expected. This has been no different to my placement journey.

By choosing a relevant postcard I was able to use it as a visual aid to describe my thoughts and feelings, where I was and am now. I found choosing a weekly postcard helped me to reflect honestly. I have been able to express my feelings and emotions through a wide range of depictions. Postcards are a good idea as people could find it difficult to describe what has been happening. For me looking at pictures was useful; I felt that the postcards were able to represent my feelings and learning at that point in the journey. In addition, the postcards gave me a platform from which to discuss any issues and by sharing the postcard at the start of each supervision, I felt my practice educator was able prompt discussion and in some circumstances she helped me to see things differently. The journey model has assisted me to recognise how full my suitcase is becoming. Before packing the placement experience, I have been able to explore my emotions through the postcards and put them into perspective ensuring I am moving forward safely.

© Sandi Owen

The use of visual thinking in this book

Since visual thinking is a key part of the SHARE model, we have included various visual images in this book. We have drawn on photographic images, visual design work, and illustrations drawn by Harry Venning (well known in the social work world for his years of work on Clare in the Community).

Why is it that books for children have lots of vibrant illustrations but books for adults are just full of words? Academic books sometimes introduce figures and diagrams, but are still predominantly made up of pages full of words. Does that in some ways stifle creativity? The visual thinking element of the SHARE model is about promoting creativity and adding a different dimension to thinking, both about practice and about learning.

STAKEHOLDER VOICE — HARRY VENNING

Harry is a cartoonist. He has provided The Guardian with the strip 'Clare In The Community' for over twenty years. He has illustrated many social work publications and more recently has been 'live cartooning' at social work conferences and AGMs.

There is almost always humour to be found in social work. I can remember a chill running down my spine when I found myself live illustrating a lecture on death, loss and bereavement. The very real prospect of me failing to produce a single cartoon over thirty five minutes loomed up before me. But it turned out to be such a rich vein of material that my pen hardly stopped scrawling and, more importantly, everybody present seemed amused and appreciative of the images I produced.

Far worse than the twin topics of death and bereavement is a lecture that comprises a lot of statistics. I'm afraid statistics are both impossible to draw and inherently unexciting. To do my job I require imagery from a lecture and so does an audience, if they are going to stay awake and engaged.

Sometimes, instead of humour, I will use pathos to get a point across. Cartoons can be powerful as well as funny, and it is amazing to find just how much emotion can be expressed in a few black lines. In twenty years I have had a handful of complaints about the content of my cartoons, but overwhelmingly the response has been a positive one. My one rule is never to make fun of the client / service user but focus instead upon the absurdities of social work itself, such as the office politics, practices and language.

© Harry Venning

Visual representation as a mechanism of oppression

There are many mechanisms of oppression in contemporary society. One key mechanism of oppression lies around the visual representation of certain groups of people, which stereotypes these groups. For example, in advertising and television programmes certain groups of people are stereotyped or ignored. Karin Kihlberg, manager at the Museum of Brands has identified six stereotypes of women in advertising, which she argues have not changed considerably during history. She argues that women are stereotyped in adverts as:

- Domestic obsessive (unnaturally energised by domestic issues, often cleaning)
- Selfless nurturer (self-sacrificing subsuming own needs for others)
- Sex object (one-dimensional desirability targeted at men)
- Unattainable goddess (aspirational unattainable ideal targeted at women)
- Fraught juggler (busy working mum with too much to do)
- Bit part (supporting actor for the male protagonists)

(Kemp 2007).

Chadborn (2017) highlights research by IDEA (Improving Dementia Education and Awareness) which investigated the images running alongside newspaper stories on dementia. This research identified that these were largely stock images which portrayed suffering, strife, pity - and little else. The power of this imagery and the way that it invokes fear and dread was acknowledged in the research. This research led to a range of action planned to challenge the identified stereotyping in visual imagery. For example, campaigns such as #nomorewrinklyhands! on twitter has had a fairly high profile in challenging visual stereotyping of older people.

So, in using visual imagery as part of the SHARE model we would urge social workers and educators to be very aware of social imagery as a potential means of oppression.

The concept of vision

Covey's seven habits of highly effective people (Covey, 1999) highlight the importance of developing a clear vision. Covey argues that one of the main habits of success is to begin with the end in mind - to be clear about where you want to go. Vision is used as a word to describe both developing an idea of the end goals and helping to communicate these to those involved, supporting other people to get to the identified goals. In many ways, this is what social work is all about - supporting people to develop their own vision for where they want to be and then helping them to identify how they can get there.

On the peace murals is Belfast the following quote appears, which really illustrates what the concept of vision is all about.

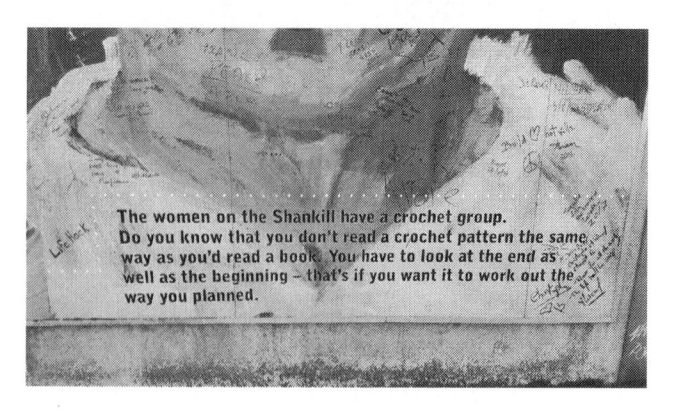

The women on the Shankill have a crochet group. Do you know that you don't read a crochet pattern the same way as you'd read a book. You have to look at the end as well as the beginning – that's if you want it to work out the way you planned.

Visions often focus on longer term goals. The British Association of Social Workers published a document called 'Our 2020 Vision' containing the proposed aims of the organisation for the five-year period 2015-2020. In this sense visions are about long-term goals which set out where we want to be, and what things will look like when we arrive.

The concept of vision is particularly important in the literature around leadership. Key reports around organisational policy and practice recognise the vital importance of organisations having leaders who develop and communicate a clear vision (for example see MacLeod and Clarke 2009). So, social work leaders need to develop a clear vision and communicate this widely to ensure that people are working collaboratively towards the shared vision.

However, this concept of vision is not just important for organisational leadership. The Professional Capabilities Framework in England introduced the idea that social workers need to see themselves as leaders at every level of their career, with the inclusion of a domain on professional leadership at every level of progression. Indeed, the American Association of Social workers describe social work as 'leadership in the community' (NASW 2010). Social workers should work with service users to develop a vision for the future. What does that child, adult or family want in the future - what are their aspirations, how do they imagine their future? All of this is about supporting the development of a vision. Social workers can support people to work towards their vision in a range of ways, but it is this development of a shared vision and support to work towards this vision that is a key aspect of empowerment in social work practice.

Visions and aspirations can be individual or shared, and people can be inspired by them. In 1963 Martin Luther King had a 'dream' which was shared by many and he has been referred to as a 'moral visionary' (Roberts et al. 2008).

Supervision in social work

It might seem strange to find this subtitle part way through this chapter. What does supervision have to do with 'seeing'? In truth, the fact that we have placed a short discussion about supervision at the centre of this chapter on the first component of the SHARE model is no accident: we see supervision as central to both good social work practice and effective social work education, and the idea of seeing is closely related to supervision, with the word supervision being derived from two Latin words:

> Super - which means over
>
> Videre - which means to watch or to see

Literally taken then, the word supervision means 'overseeing'. The roots of contemporary social work supervision lie in the growth of charitable social organisations in Europe and North America. These organisations engaged volunteer 'visitors' who were 'overseen' by a nominated 'overseer'. In the very early part of the 20th Century as casework practice became more common the beginnings of more developed approaches to supervision took root. The first books on supervision began to appear more than a hundred years ago - for example, 'Supervision and Education in Charity' by Jeffrey Bracket was published in 1904.

Munson (2002) argued that the form and structure of supervision remained fairly constant from the nineteenth century. However, some practitioners argue that managerialist approaches in contemporary social work have led to a regression to earlier forms of simple overseeing. Kadushin and Harkness (2002) refer to the concept of 'Snoopervision' where the purpose and nature of professional supervision has been misunderstood, perhaps on the basis of a misunderstanding of the concept. Supervision must be about more than simply 'overseeing' performance if it is to have any value.

Supervision rather than 'snoopervision' is about much more than the simple overseeing of practice.

The idea of vision is also relevant to supervision in that good quality supervision helps the supervisee to clarify their 'vision' for future practice and supports them in reaching the vision.

We feel strongly that good quality reflective, emotionally supportive supervision is one of the cornerstones of good social work practice. Social work supervisors and practitioners need a shared understanding of the importance of supervision, and we should all seek to improve the quality of both the supervision we receive and the supervision we might provide. The SHARE model can provide a useful framework for both evaluating the current quality of supervision and for improving supervision (see pages 302 - 305).

KEY MESSAGES FROM RESEARCH: SUPERVISION

Kadushin (1992) explored supervisees perspectives of their supervisors in a large-scale study in the United States. Supervisees rated their supervisor's strengths as practice expertise and relationships skills within the supervisor relationship, but in terms of shortcomings, the study found that supervisors were perceived as reluctant to exercise managerial authority, were hesitant to advocate for staff and did not give enough time to supervision.

A survey by the Social Work Task Force in England in 2009 found that access to supervision was variable across the country and supervisees felt it tended to be process driven and case management oriented at the expense of reflection and emotional support (Department for Children, Families and Schools, 2009).

Research by the American National Association of Social Workers (Social Work Policy Institute 2011) identified that supervision rated as one of the top three factors impacting on job efficacy (the other two were caseload size and manageable paperwork).

Supervision specifically enhances the development of evidence based practice and cultural competence (Social Work Policy Institute 2011).

In research by the British Association of Social Workers (2011) 62% of respondents stated that their personal development was not adequately addressed in their supervision, whilst 70% felt that the emotional issues arising from their work was not addressed.

In a systematic review of research on supervision in child welfare settings, Carpenter et al (2013) found that supervision was associated with worker satisfaction, self-efficacy and lower stress but that there was no high-quality research to evidence that supervision produced better outcomes for service users.

Intervision

If supervision is about 'watching over' then intervision is 'watching between' (Romeo 2017). Intervision groups have a long history in continental Europe (van der Haar 2007) and are becoming increasingly popular in the UK context (Fairtlough 2017). In the UK intervision still remains more popular in other professions such as medicine and therapy (Klimek and Atkinson 2016) but there is a growing recognition of the value of intervision in social work.

Intervision describes the process of a group of professionals coming together to discuss situations which they are finding emotionally challenging. The discussion groups promote critical peer reflection based around in depth compassionate listening and exchanges which recognise the emotional context of the practice. Intervision is based around a mutually supportive exchange and challenge between professionals who are equal. There is no hierarchy, although sessions should be chaired and recorded to support learning, these roles are shared and rotated.

We see the idea of intervision as supporting social workers to develop a vision for their practice through reflexivity. As such we see it as fully complimenting the SHARE model, which can be used to good effect within intervision, through each professional bringing a 'share' to intervision (something that they have seen, heard, done, read or something relating to their evaluations of practice).

According to Kennedy (2000) a critical component of intervision is the mutual respect that is garnered and sustained through the shared interest in supporting and developing each member's skills, expertise and competence. In order to achieve this, it is important that group sizes are kept to a minimum (six to ten people) and that they speak to the diversity of practitioner, skill and background. This will ensure that participants feel supported and that their opinions and ideas are heard.

Staempli, Fairtlough and Royes (forthcoming) examine and evaluate the development of intervision on the social work programme at their University. They identify the need for some ground rules which need to be understood and accepted by group members from the outset. These ground rules outline for example, roles and responsibilities, timings for case presentation and discussion with and without the presenter and also the summary of learning achieved by participants / peers.

Intervision mirrors the components of SHARE in that intervision assists peers to see each other as peers in learning, to hear particular case presentations, to discuss their feelings, thoughts and learning and to review the information provided by the presenter to evaluate their learning at the end of the session. Intervision develops and enhances social workers presentation skills which peers and participants can learn from and mirror. There is a level of self-management involved in intervision and the group operates as a peer learning group, minimising the opportunities for hierarchy and the misuse of power. Indeed, intervision is all about share(d) learning.

Acknowledging what we don't see

Values and anti-oppressive practice link with every component of the SHARE model. In relation to seeing, there is a very well-known phrase 'it must be seen to be believed'. In fact, we feel that this phrase could be reversed 'it must be believed to be seen'. As such, the 'seeing' component of SHARE is as much about recognising what we don't see as what we do see. In terms of social work there are two key processes that can help us to understand what we are failing to see, invisibilisation and normalisation.

Invisibilisation

Social imagery has long been recognised as one of the main mechanisms of oppression (Wolfensberger 1983). The dynamics and relevance of social imagery should not be under-estimated, even though this is often belittled and minimised by reference to the term 'political correctness'. Generally, people using this term are not devalued people who are affected by social imagery and oppression more generally. As one of the main mechanisms of oppression, social imagery feeds into the processes of stereotyping and labelling.

Invisibilisation is the process of devaluation in which various groups of people are not represented in social imagery. Media images are noted for focusing on the dominant, more powerful groups in society and by doing so they have ignored other groups (invisibilising them). Older people, people with disabilities and people who are poor are significantly under-represented in the media. Where they are visible, then often stereotypes are reinforced through the imagery.

Contemporary thinking around invisibilisation also draws on the way that society is structured so that people are effectively invisibilised, which leads to devaluation and powerlessness. For example, the rise in the number of people who are on zero-hours contracts means that these workers are invisible (not seen) in terms of employment rights and statistics.

The number of social workers (particularly those who are newly qualified) who are on short term contracts could be seen in terms of their invisibilisation from the profession. Often these workers are 'invisible' from workforce planning and processes and workforce development. They may not be given the opportunity to undertake the ASYE for example.

The process of invisibilisation is well explained by Hinson and Healey (2003:5), who explain:

"When those who have the power to name and to socially construct reality choose not to see you or hear you…. when someone with the authority, of a teacher, say, describes the world and you are not in it, there is a moment of psychic disequilibrium, as if you looked in the mirror and saw nothing. It takes some strength of soul - and not just individual strength but collective understanding - to resist this void, this non-being, into which you are thrust, and to stand up, demanding to be seen and heard."

People can be invisibilised in a range of ways

STAKEHOLDER VOICE
BOB WILLIAMS-FINDLAY

Bob Williams-Findlay is joint coordinator of Disabled People Against Cuts West Midlands

The experience of being in segregated schools and a residential college meant that my peer groups were other disabled people and the only non-disabled people I talked to the majority of the time were either teachers or support staff. I wasn't required to question let alone think about what it meant to be 'disabled' because there was no need, the reality as I saw it then, was right there before my eyes. Contrast this experience with moving to a small village where the only disabled person I knew was a person with MS who resented me being a guest in his home. I felt socially inadequate and naïve when I entered the world of the non-disabled or the 'land of the normal' (sic). Until I left college I was only periodically exposed to a public gaze and looks of disapproval. Nevertheless, it made me feel self-conscious of my difference when subjected to these looks, the finger pointing and strangers laughing at me in the street.

A paradox is said to be a statement that apparently contradicts itself and yet might be true. Having been in a segregated environment, my world had been quite 'normal', until I had to consider what lay beyond it; the world of 'normal persons'. Once on the outside of the 'disabled' world, which had appeared 'normal', I was confronted by the world of 'normal persons' and, subsequently, found myself to be 'disabled'. There was of course no rehabilitation scheme to assist me to make the transition into the alien world of 'normal persons' or offer me advice on living within a disabling society. One of the consequences of being subjected to the public gaze is that disabled people become public property; to be prodded, poked or interrogated. Did I internalise how public attention made me feel; did this influence my coping strategies when dealing with social relationships; did it assist in altering my identities, sense of self and individuality?

I believe the identities I have both now and especially in the early 1970s, have been shaped by societal attitudes through this public gaze. This has had huge implications for how I and other disabled people go about making sense of 'the self' and our individuality. Looking back I'm not exactly sure how I saw myself because I accepted that my body was affected by cerebral palsy which impacted upon my functional ability, but this doesn't really reveal very much about my own self-perception in terms of how I actually saw myself. I made a distinction between having a body restricted in function and the societal opinion of me as being flawed or abnormal. In my opinion, this distinction between accepting impairment reality and rejecting negative stereotyping is further complicated by the fact that I, like so many other disabled people, rarely saw people like me within newspapers, books, films or on TV. It is my view that outside of standard stereotyping, disabled people are largely invisible. It's hard to make sense of who and what you are if you are denied.

© Bob Williams-Findlay

Colourblindness

The view is offered by Fryberg (2010) that in terms of race and ethnicity, the 'colourblind' approach is both harmful and discriminatory. The concept of colourblindness has been used in many instances to justify racism and racial discrimination. When for example social workers or other professionals argue that they see the person before the colour / race, it can be problematic. This is because colourblind approaches invalidate the unique experiences of black and ethnic minority people alongside rejecting their cultural heritage.

We need to acknowledge that we see 'race' otherwise how can we purport to actively engage in discourses about race and racism? To ignore it is to deny it and this can lead to some BME people feeling 'invisible' in their places of work or study. Guo (2013) coined the phrase the 'triple glass effect' to refer to the multiple layers of barriers affecting immigrants into Canada. He argues that at the fore of the exclusionary barriers is the glass gate which prevents entry into employment. If immigrants manage to break through this glass gate, they are confronted with the glass door which restricts employments into highly regarded professional jobs. Finally, the glass ceiling prevents progression once in these jobs, resulting in large numbers of ethnic minority people in Canada holding lower paid jobs regardless of their qualifications and expertise. Recognising the salience of race and racialised discourse in social work is an important aspect of anti-oppressive practice and 'seeing'.

Writing about transnationally adopted children in Sweden, Tigervall and Hubinette (2010:489) conclude that *"non-white bodies of adoptees are constantly made significant in their everyday lives in interactions with the white Swedish majority population"*. When it came to identifying with Sweden and Swedishness, all adoptees in the study identified themselves as being Swedes, but, as adults, they were well aware that their skin colour disqualified them from becoming 'fully' and 'truly' Swedish, in spite of the fact that most of them not only had been socialised as white majority Swedes but also had grown up in, and belonged to, the middle and upper classes of Swedish society.

The idea of colourblindness is very popular. According to an MTV funded research report (David Binder Research and MTV 2014), the millennial generation believe that colourblindness is an aspirational goal that will help society to eliminate racism:

- 73% believe never considering race would improve society.
- 68% believe focusing on race prevents society from becoming colourblind.

The dangers of this approach have however been highlighted very recently, perhaps most significantly, criticisms of the slow response to concerns about child sexual exploitation have highlighted concerns about practitioners adopting a colourblind approach (Bingham 2013).

This discussion about colourblindness holds value for the SHARE model in that it challenges social workers to 'see' race and not ignore it as though it is irrelevant. The model further encourages us to listen to the experiences and narratives of service users, carers, students and various stakeholders which will inform our future intervention and work with them. The action part of the model can be used when social workers actively work to make people from diverse background feel comfortable and listened to. It can also be used to actively challenge racism and racial stereotyping of minority people.

Normalisation

Normalisation is another process that impacts on what we do not see. Normalisation refers to situations where something has become so 'normal' to us, so much a part of our everyday existence, that we fail to see its relevance or meaning. For example, social workers see poverty on a daily basis, so much so that they may fail to see the effects of poverty because they have come to 'normalise' it.

Backwith (2015) explains this normalisation of poverty by social workers:

> "In child protection, for instance, the toxic trio of drug abuse, domestic violence and mental health problems is often compounded by poverty, but this and other social factors do not get the attention they merit from professionals. In the current context, this poverty-blindness is not hard to understand: social workers are caught between cuts in services and tighter eligibility on one hand, and growing hardship and social exclusion on the other. Faced with grinding privation every day, social workers can feel powerless to effect meaningful change."

This cartoon was drawn by Harry Venning at the Conference of the Child Welfare Inequalities Project held at Kings College London on the 28th February 2017. It quickly became incredibly popular on social media and at subsequent conference events.

Concepts such as 'poverty-informed practice' (Parkes 2015) and 'trauma-informed practice' (Steele and Malchiodi 2012) have developed as a way of highlighting in practice what social workers may fail to see as part of the normalisation of everyday experiences in social work. It is vitally important that social workers keep their own practice under review, reflecting on what they may be failing to see.

KEY MESSAGES FROM RESEARCH: INVISIBILISATION

- Menzies-Lyth (1959) observational study of a London teaching hospital, noted that nurses stopped seeing the patients as individuals people, but as their diagnosis or illness, 'the kidney in bed 5'.

- Rustin's (2005) article, analysing key incidents in Victoria Climbie's short life, suggests that professionals in Victoria's care, stopped 'seeing her', because of various defences against anxieties that were in operation to protect the workers from Victoria's acute mental pain.

- The Francis Inquiry into Mid Staffordshire NHS Foundation Trust found that staff had become so used to the conditions that they work in that they 'simply do not see what is happening' (Francis 2013, Department of Health 2015).

- Ferguson (2016) focuses on how children become invisible in child protection social work. He describes the ways in which the organisational culture, limited time for direct work and inadequate support affect social workers' preparation for, and experience of, home visits, with consequences for their interactions with children. Ferguson suggests that the emotional demands and complexity of working with angry and resistant parents and family members can leave social workers unable to contain their own emotions, to think clearly and keep the 'child in mind'. The very demands of child protection work can act to obscure children and make them invisible.

- Craig (2013) found that race has become invisibilised from public policy in England. This began in the final term of the New Labour Government, but developed considerably during the coalition Government.

Connecting components: A seen child is not a safe child

One of the key aspects of the SHARE model is the need to connect the five components. Sometimes initiatives in social work push the focus into one area - often at the expense of others. So, for example, there is significant focus on the importance of social workers seeing children in relation to safeguarding. However, simply seeing a child is not protection against harm. Haringey Local Safeguarding Children Board (2017) highlights the fact that every child who has been subject to a serious case review over the last 40 years was 'seen' by a professional within days (even hours) of their death. A 'seen' child, therefore, is not necessarily a safe child. Further, Serious Case Reviews have regularly highlighted the fact that professionals have failed to fully take account of the child's world, for example see Staffordshire Safeguarding Children Board 2017.

The importance of taking a sensory view to understand the child's world is becoming more widely acknowledged. For example, Ferguson (2017b) asserts the importance of not only seeing a child's world, but also hearing and touching a child's lived experiences on home visits.

It is vital to take full consideration of the experiences of children and young people. They may not be able to 'tell' you about how things in their world are, perhaps because of their young age, a lack of vocabulary to describe what is happening, normalising certain experiences etc. In order to truly understand the child's experiences think about 'their' SHARE, and make sure that you can answer all of the following questions with confidence:

Explore the child's world by considering:

SEE:
Who and what does the child see?
How do they view this?
What impact does this have on the child?

HEAR:
What does the child hear?
How often?
What impact does this have on the child?

ACT:
What does the child do?
How does the child behave?
How is this behaviour viewed by the people around them?

READ:
What does the child read?
Does what is written about the child really reflect their world and their experiences?

EVALUATE:
How does the child evaluate all of their experiences?
How do you know?

Who do we see?

When working with individuals it is vital that social workers take a person-centred perspective, really 'seeing' the person as a unique individual. When social workers are busy they may well fail to see the person behind the 'case'. It is vital to recognise that social work is about people not 'cases.'

The famous poem 'Look Closer, See Me' (as opposite) illustrates the way that a person's unique identity and life story can be lost. This poem appears in many places without attribution. However, it is thought to have been written in the 1960s by Phyliss McCormack, a nurse working in Montrose.

Do you always see the person behind the 'case'?

My Share

What gets in the way of 'seeing' the individual I am working with?

How might I address these barriers?

How can I show the service user that I really 'see' them?

What do you see nurses
What do you see?
A crabbit old woman
Not very wise
Uncertain of habit
With far-away eyes
Who dribbles her food
And makes no reply
When you say in a loud voice
"I do wish you'd try"
Who seems not to notice
the things that you do
And forever is losing
a stocking or shoe
Who unresisting or not
Lets you do as you will
With bathing and feeding
The long day to fill
Is that what you're thinking
Is that what you see
Then open your eyes nurse
You're not looking at me
I'll tell you who I am
As I sit here so still
As I use at your bidding
As I eat at your will
I'm a small child of ten
With father and mother
Brothers and sisters who
Love one another
Young girl of sixteen
With wings on her feet
Dreaming that soon now
A lover she'll meet
A bride soon at twenty
My heart gives a leap
Remembering the vows
That I promised to keep
At twenty-five now
I have young of my own
Who need me to build
A secure happy home

A Young woman of thirty
My young now grow fast
Bound to each other
With ties that should last
Now grown will soon be gone
But my man stays beside me
To see I don't mourn
At fifty once more
Babies play round my knee
Again we know children
My loved one and me
Dark days are upon me
My husband is dead
I look to the future
I shudder with dread
For my young are all busy
Rearing young of their own
And I think of the years
And the love I have known
I'm an old woman now
And nature is cruel
Tis her jest to make
Old age look like a fool
The body it crumbles
Grace and vigour depart
There is now a stone
Where once was a heart
But inside this old carcass
A young girl still dwells
And now and again
My battered heart swells
I remember the joys
I remember the pain
And I'm loving and living
Life over again
I think of the years
All too few-gone too fast
And accept the stark fact
That nothing can last
So open your eyes nurses
Open and see
Not a crabbit old woman

Look closer - see ME

Key points

- Seeing is the first component of the SHARE model.
- It is important to remember that the seeing component is not simply about the physicality of seeing, but rather it addresses a whole host of issues in relation to the use of a holistic approach in practice.
- Each component can be used to consider a number of issues and as such 'seeing' can be used to reflect on observation in social work, visual thinking and what we do and don't see in our practice.
- One element of the 'seeing' component is the importance of vision in social work. Good supervision can support social workers to clarify their vision for practice.
- Sometimes social workers do not 'see' what is really in front of them and this can be seen as a 'failure' and blamed on individual social workers without consideration of issues such as invisibilisation and normalisation.
- A number of complexities impact on what we might 'see' or 'not see' in practice. The SHARE model can be used to explore these complexities by considering the interconnecting components of the model.

Reflective Questions

When you think about social work what do you see?

What do you see in your practice?

What might others see in you?

What stands out the most for you from this chapter? Why is that?

How might you be able to improve your practice in relation to the seeing component?

Chapter 6: HEARING

The second element of the SHARE Model is hearing. We begin this chapter with a consideration of hearing and listening and the complexities of this in social work practice; we explore the barriers to hearing which social workers often encounter. We then move on to consider what we might hear in social work and here address issues of the use of language, the place of humour and the importance of feedback. We conclude the chapter by looking at conversational practice, the importance of everyone having a voice, and speaking up as social workers.

As stated in Chapter 1, we acknowledge that many people have hearing impairments, which clearly affect what they might be able to physically hear, but this component is not just about the physicality of hearing, in very much the same way that the seeing component is about so much more than the physicality of sight.

Hearing and listening

Hearing and listening are two different things. You can 'hear' without meaning to, for example, by overhearing something, but listening requires purpose, commitment, attention and an effort to understand what is being communicated. It is also possible to listen without actually hearing, since fully hearing what someone is saying can be really difficult. So, the link between hearing and listening is really complex. This chapter begins by looking at the connections between listening and hearing.

Listening is not merely a skill. It is a rich metaphor for the helping relationship itself – indeed for all relationships (Cree 2011). A recognition of the intrinsic links between listening and relationships is embedded into most social care and childcare qualification structures. For example, the diplomas in health and social care refer to communication and relationships throughout the qualification requirements (Maclean and Harrison 2014).

> **Listening is always more important than talking: 'We have two ears and one mouth so that we can listen twice as much as we speak.' (Epictelous)**

An academic review of listening, reveals two key themes of active listening and empathic listening, both of which are vital in social work practice.

Being a 'good listener'

We often hear this phrase, but there is not always a clarity about what being a 'good listener' means. It is certainly a quality which is valued both by those providing and those using social work services and social workers often pride themselves on being a 'good listener'. Listening is of key importance in helping people feel valued and ensuring that their preferences and choices are recognised, as such it is a vital aspect of our shared humanity. The importance of listening and the links this has to power has long been recognised (Drakeford 1967).

In many ways, the skill of listening illustrates the way that the different components of the SHARE model interconnect. Empathic listening in itself connects hearing and seeing, as this kind of listening is about not just what you hear but also what you see. Active listening links the 'action' component since active listening is not just about hearing what is said, but also indicating to the other person through actions that we have heard it.

Empathic listening

Empathic listening is described as listening which enables the listener to really understand the speaker's' world. It's a kind of 'being with' a person, getting alongside them to develop an understanding of the person and their world (Cree 2011:156.)

Tolan (2017) highlights the importance of empathic holistic relationships in social work practice, describing this type of relationship as one where the practitioner is able to see the whole world as the other person sees it and is wholly accepting of that world. The foundation of such relationships is empathic listening - not only through traditional listening to 'words' but also through the use of observational skills. The following poem which was written by a person with learning disabilities illustrates this very effectively:

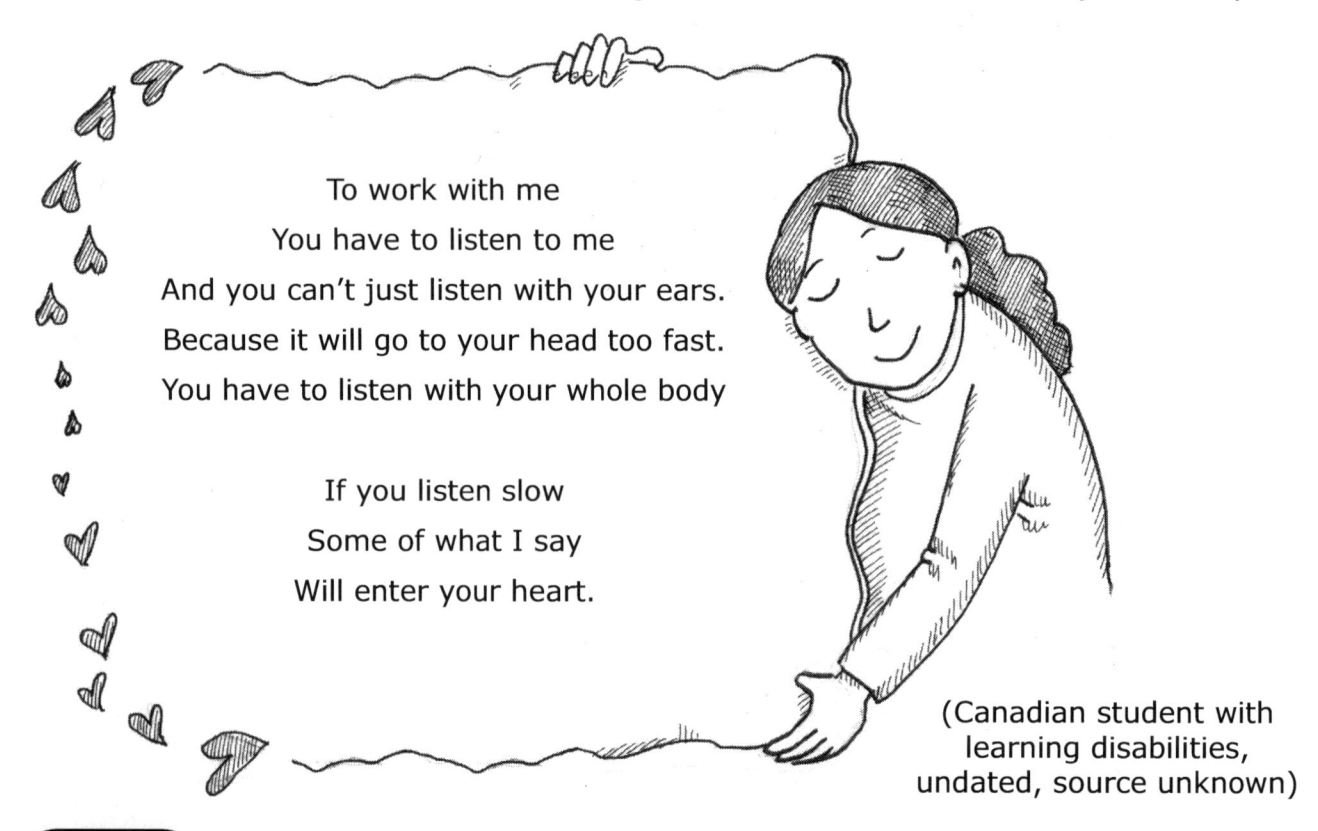

> To work with me
> You have to listen to me
> And you can't just listen with your ears.
> Because it will go to your head too fast.
> You have to listen with your whole body
>
> If you listen slow
> Some of what I say
> Will enter your heart.

(Canadian student with learning disabilities, undated, source unknown)

Active listening

Active listening is an inter-personal skill which is often described as a key social work skill (Moss 2017). Active listening involves demonstrating to the 'speaker' that you are listening, it is not enough to have heard what someone has said; you need to show the person that you have heard them, through your actions.

Active listening is a really difficult skill and although some people are undoubtedly better than others at listening, everyone can work to develop their skills further. Sometimes when considering listening skills, it is worth revisiting core literature. Egan's work around 'micro-skills' in counselling; particularly the SOLER model (2002) can be helpful in considering active listening. Egan believes that basic nonverbal skills improve active listening, and developed the SOLER model around:

- **S**it squarely in relation to the service user - this is said to demonstrate that you are ready to listen.

- **O**pen position - open body language indicates more attentive listening. This means not folding arms etc.

- **L**ean slightly towards the service user - this is said to encourage the speaker as it shows you are interested in what the person has to say.

- **E**ye contact - maintain good eye contact and encourage the 'speaker' to maintain eye contact. This can create a human connection and more empathic listening.

- **R**elax - it is important to be relaxed and to sit still without fidgeting to demonstrate attentive listening.

This of course applies to all means of communication and receiving information (hearing or making sense of) and is certainly important when communicating with someone with a hearing impairment who will need to see you lip reading and / or signed to. This is also a useful model in terms of considering skill development in active listening. However, it is important to recognise that cultural difference impacts on communication and Egan's model was developed based on North American culture. In some cultures, for example, eye contact can be seen as threatening or rude.

It is also vital to remember that using the SOLER model is only the very beginning of listening. It might demonstrate attentiveness to the person 'speaking' but it doesn't mean that you will really hear what is being said. In fact, if you are focusing too much on whether you are sitting fully squarely, whether you are holding eye contact well enough etc... then you may not allow yourself the space to truly hear what is being said.

Active listening is often understood differently by different stakeholders. For example, McLeod (2008) illustrates the way that a social worker may believe that they are actively listening to a child, because they are nodding and making affirmative noises and therefore actively showing that they are listening. However, the child may have a very different view, believing that they have not been heard, because nothing changes and what they want to happen doesn't come about. Active listening is therefore about much more than the kind of 'micro-skills' referred to by Egan, listening must be linked to action; if you really hear what a person is saying then this should be demonstrated to them through your actions.

Jo Shares

An interesting assessment task I have often been involved in as an assessor, are 'service user interviews'. This is where actors play the role of a service user and the students need to respond. The actor has a brief and students are given some, but not extensive information about the 'service user' coming to see them. The interviews are timed (usually 10 minutes) and the students are assessed by a social work lecturer, social work practitioner and a service user, carer or expert by experience. Amongst other things, they are assessed on how good their communication skills are. As discussed in the previous chapter, the Hawthorne effect can often come into play here and of course students will be highly nervous. The important task however is that students reflect accurately on their overall performance, in discussions after the event. What I have noticed over several years of being the assessor in these 'interviews' is that social work students find it hard to really 'listen' to the service user as it seems to us, that they leap too fast into problem solving. Observing the actor in such situations, I note their frustration, and disengagement in the 'interview'. It seems at times, that some students cannot bear the pain the actor portrays and problem solving may be a 'defence against anxiety'. In the more successful interviews, we note the students talk less, show excellent active listening skills, ask clarifying questions when appropriate and comment in a timely and accurate way on the actor's emotional (and often unsaid) presentation.

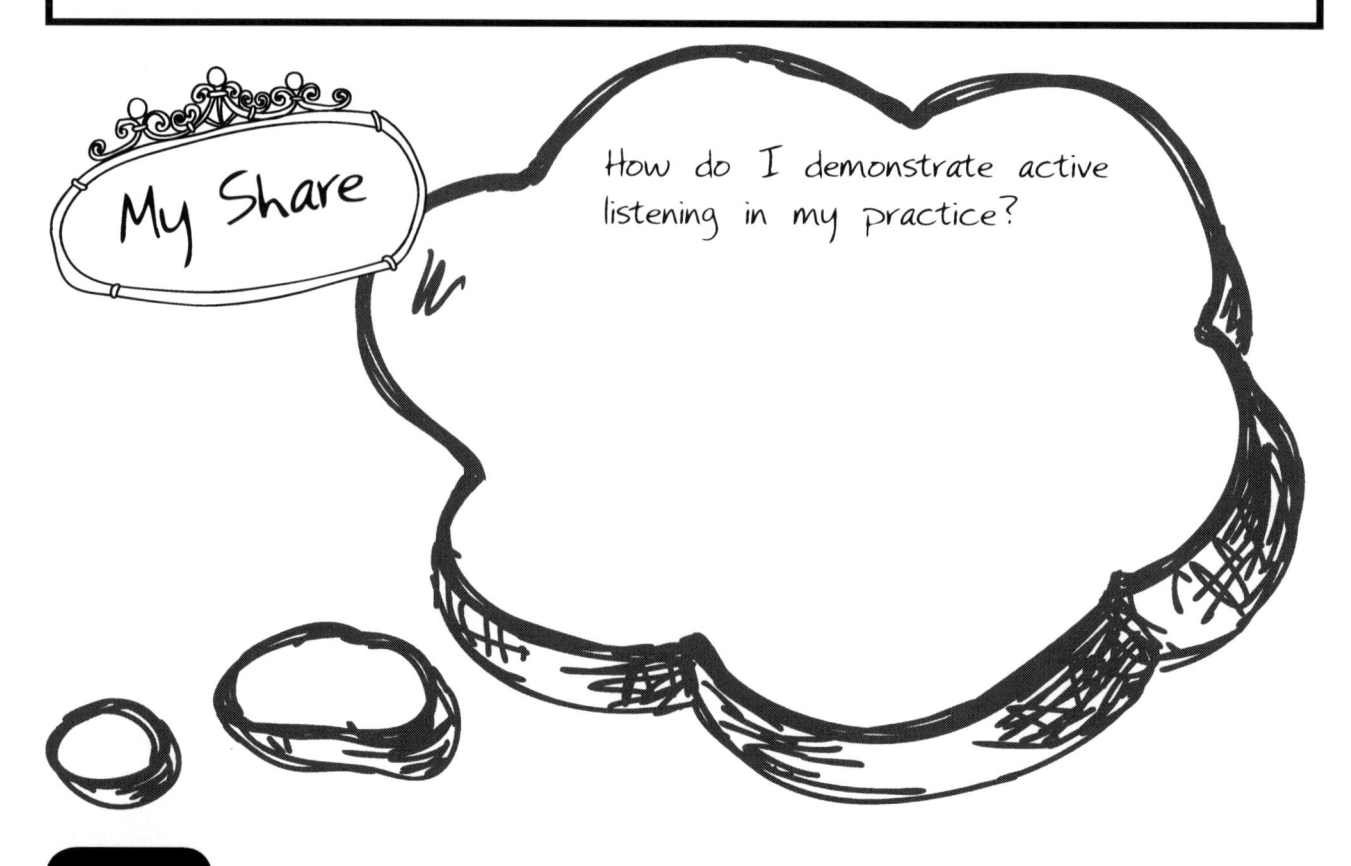

My Share

How do I demonstrate active listening in my practice?

What is hearing about?

Hearing, and therefore communication, is about far more than words so we need to listen to far more than words. To hear effectively we need to listen to what a person is saying AND:

How the person is speaking: 'It's not what you say, it's the way that you say it' is a phrase in common usage and it is undoubtedly true that you can tell a great deal from the way someone speaks. This can relate to:

Speed: The speed someone talks at is significant and may well indicate their emotional state. For example, if someone is speaking quickly they may be excited or anxious.

Tone: People are often not aware of the tone of their own voice. However, tone has a real impact on what people hear.

Volume: How loud or softly we speak has a significant impact on communication. For example, loud speech can be indicative of anger or aggression and yet social workers very often raise their voice when talking to service users: how is this interpreted?

Register: The register of speech refers to how formal or informal it is. A person's register can indicate the way that they view the involvement of social workers and their perceptions of power.

It is important of course not to make assumptions based on the way that someone is speaking, and you must check this out. Sharing how you have interpreted the way a person is speaking is important. So, for example, you might say to someone "it sounds to me as though you are very sad about that." This gives the speaker the opportunity to agree or disagree with your conclusions; ensuring that you are more likely to truly hear what they are saying and the speaker is more likely to feel heard.

The way that someone speaks can say a great deal which we don't always fully recognise. When Siobhan met with Ellen (see page 105) to discuss the development of SHARE, she was struck by the way that Ellen described asking service users to read reports aloud to her, this enabled Ellen to 'hear' how the person felt about what was written and the author of the report. Ellen described the way that service users would use a different voice for the different contributors to the reports and the way that the tone, speed, volume and register they used said a great deal to Ellen about the service user's experiences of the system.

A person's body language: Observe the whole person, but be aware that body language can be inaccurately interpreted in a range of ways. For example, if someone is smiling, you might assume that they are happy, but sometimes people smile when they are anxious or because they think that smiling is the social expectation on them. Again, it can be helpful to describe what you are seeing and how you are evaluating that to clarify communication and ensure that the person is really 'heard'.

A person's behaviour: Some behaviours such as crying and aggression can communicate a great deal. However, you need to listen to the 'whole person' to be clear exactly what the behaviour is communicating. For example, people can cry tears of either joy or sadness. Sometimes a person's behaviour is too readily labelled as 'challenging' or 'difficult' without any real attempt to hear the person being made.

STAKEHOLDER VOICE
VICTORIA HART

Victoria is an adult social worker with an interest in mental health.

First, we listen and then we hear. We can only learn when we hear what people are saying to us. Being in a room when someone is talking is not the same as hearing what they are saying. Often, it's not just the words that are being said but the ways they are being said. Someone might tell us that they are managing fine but the wavering tone will lead to further, gentle questions allowing them to feel safe enough to share additional concerns. Someone might shout and rage at us but we need to hear what's behind the anger and what has contributed to the rage. We need to know what is being said and we need to hear through the anger and the rage or through the despondency and indifference.

The skill of hearing what is said but also what isn't said is core to assessing and understanding situations as a social worker and being able to provide support, services, interventions or lack of intervention in the lives of others.

We also hear stories. As a social worker with older people, I heard many stories of lives which made me pause and consider. I heard the stories of asylum and war, of families reuniting and being pulled apart by circumstance, tragedy and happy fortune. People are inherently interesting. Everyone has a story whatever their age and whatever their circumstance. When we hear the stories people have, we see who people are behind the 'caseload' and behind the 'file'. It is by hearing what people say and how people tell their stories that we learn from everyone who comes into contact with a social worker and we learn how to serve better.

Sometimes we hear sadness and sometimes we hear hope. Often, we hear pain and distress. By hearing, we can also make the first steps to distributing power. We all need to be heard. Everyone needs to be heard. As social workers, we have the privilege of being in the position to hear when people can feel most powerless and disenfranchised. We can change that by hearing and responding to what we hear.

© Victoria Hart

Victoria's stakeholder voice puts this really well: First we listen then we hear. However, there are a number of barriers to hearing which impact on social work practice:

Barriers to hearing

Barriers to hearing, and indeed to communication more generally, can be categorised in terms of:

- Environmental barriers
- Clinical barriers
- Emotional barriers
- Attitudinal barriers
- Bureaucratic barriers
- Cultural barriers
- Organisational barriers

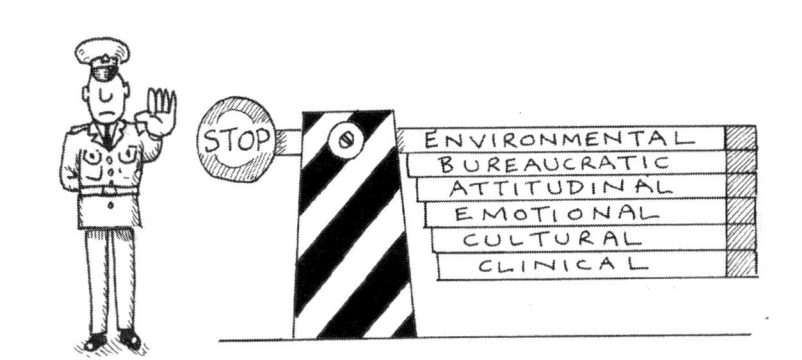

Many of the stakeholder voices that we have received, illustrate these barriers from different perspectives. We have therefore elected to consider each potential barrier in turn although we recognise as we conclude this section that the barriers often compound each other to create a host of barriers working together to prevent people being heard.

My Share: What gets in the way of me hearing others?

Social workers take a person-in-environment position, recognising the vital importance of environments. We know, for example, that people behave differently in different environments. Every social worker works in many different environments, so that a social worker might be in a range of different homes, formal settings such as courts, institutional environments such as schools and hospitals, as well as their own office base in any given week. The barriers that these environments can create in terms of hearing are potentially vast and we cannot cover these in detail in this chapter. However, we would encourage all social workers to think about the impact of the environment in terms of communication, hearing and relationships. Maxine's stakeholder voice illustrates the impact of hearing on her views towards social work involvement and addresses an issue that workers may not often think about.

STAKEHOLDER VOICE — MAXINE

Maxine is mother to two children who are currently living with a foster carer.

I see my children and spend time with them in what the social workers call 'supervised contact'. There are lots of things that I find difficult with this from the environment to how intrusive it feels. One thing though stays in my mind so much. You know how there are certain sounds that go through people? Well I have a new sound that will forever, to me, be associated with social work. The woman who 'supervises' the time that I spend with my children has really long lavishly painted nails. She has a tablet and she sits in the corner tapping away at it through the whole time that I am playing with my children. Tip tip tip tap. Those bloody fingernails on the screen. I can feel myself becoming more and more anxious the quicker the tip tap goes. We can see that she is there. I wish that we didn't have to hear her as well.

© Maxine

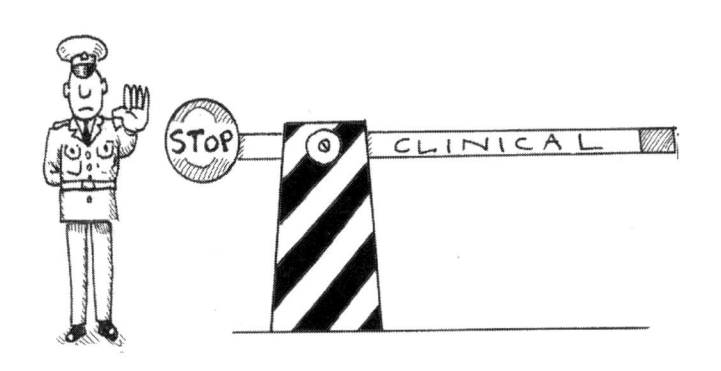

Clinical barriers is a term used to describe situations where people might have an impairment which can impact on their communication. So, where a person has a hearing impairment, for example, this can create a barrier to hearing. It is vital to recognise though that rarely do the most significant barriers lie with an impairment; more likely the barriers to hearing created by an impairment come from peoples' responses, attitudes or lack of skill in effective communication.

STAKEHOLDER VOICE — MARK DOEL

Mark is a social work writer. He was a community social worker for twenty years and he has always had a hearing impairment.

Many people might assume that a hearing loss would make life as a social worker difficult, especially in my special field of practice, groupwork. Certainly, working in an open plan office and trying to hear people in distress on the phone has been challenging. However, as I have reflected on my hearing impairment, I have begun to realise that it has given me certain strengths. I think it has made me much more aware of non-verbal communications, better attuned to subtle gesture and conscious of context. My audiologist was amazed that I so enjoyed theatre, assuming that I wouldn't be able to hear much of what was said; but poor hearing has nurtured a tolerance of ambiguity and developed an openness to different interpretations of what might be going on in any particular situation.

I've learned that listening is not dependent on hearing, and that it is more about being attentive and wanting to understand another person. When precision is important, the practice I have in asking people to repeat themselves is also useful. It's helped me to understand when precision is significant and when it is not.

In groups I am aware that there may be other people who have hearing difficulties but might not feel able to declare them. It is important to let people reposition themselves if necessary (more people rely on an element of lip-reading than we know).

My childhood hearing loss was undiagnosed. Indeed, it was a social worker for the deaf (as he was known) who first helped me to an awareness that I had an impairment. Since then, age-related loss has worsened my loss further, though it is not sufficient to make me 'deaf' and so I cannot claim to be a member of that community, which I know to be a very strong one. I feel myself at the boundary. Am I becoming deaf? I was very moved by a production of the play, Tribes, in which these issues of cross-over between different social groups (tribes) is powerfully explored in relation to deafness.

Finally, I am intrigued by the difference between the aids we have to help us see and those to help us hear. Glasses have become items of fashion; hearing aids most definitey not. Why is that? We don't call glasses 'seeing aids' so I've coined 'oracles' to describe my hearing aids. I'm just waiting for some bright young entrepreneur to produce some outrageously garish oracles that I can wear with pride - and maybe pick up Radio 4 at the same time!

© Mark Doel

Emotions regularly impact on peoples' ability to 'hear'. Think about how difficult it is to hear what is going on around you when you are distressed.

A range of emotions can impact on hearing, so for example we know that:

- People may be reluctant to engage in a conversation or to listen to someone when they are embarrassed about the content of the discussion.
- Where people are anxious this can have a significant impact on their ability to hear what is being said.
- People who are shocked or angry may find it difficult to listen to someone else.

However, emotions which may be considered to be more positive can also act as a barrier to hearing. So, for example, if you are excited about something you may well find it difficult to concentrate effectively to hear what is being said.

There is very often a chicken and egg situation in relation to emotions and hearing which can create barriers in a range of ways. For example, stress levels impact on a person's ability to really hear what is being said whilst what we hear in social work can impact on stress levels. Which comes first: the chicken or the egg? This is clearly demonstrated in the following stakeholder voice from Sass:

STAKEHOLDER VOICE
SASS BOUCHER

Sass Boucher MSc BA(Hons) MBACP is a registered Counsellor, Psychotherapist and writes and trains on how we can use SelfCare to balance the impact of working with clients who have experienced trauma. Her research is 'Looking Through a Lens of Terribleness' A Thematic Analysis of the Experience of Practitioners, Social Workers, Counsellors and Specialist Domestic Abuse practitioners'.

Work based stress is identified in literature as an area of concern for practitioners listening to service users' trauma. Concepts such as compassion fatigue, vicarious trauma secondary trauma and burnout are also discussed in the literature as ways in which practitioners may be affected by their work. So, listening, the very core of work with service users can actually have the potential to harm us.

McNab (as cited in Tehrani, 2010) suggests that "*Trauma is contagious; when anyone comes into contact with it, they risk a piercing impact leaving them infected and vulnerable*" (p283). When we are working with those who have experienced trauma, we are often listening to service users who have experienced fear, terror, physical violence and emotional abuse. We may even be in the home where it happened. We listen to their experiences, sometimes in great detail, if we're taking notes, producing reports or going to court. This is likely to impact on us both professionally and personally.

Research suggests that work based stress is high in social care and health, being aware of professional trauma and fatigue, my collective way to describe all of the concepts that may affect us, is essential if we are to try and manage this. So how might we make a difference by listening to the listener?

Peer support, peer supervision or informal supervision ran through most of the participant's dialogue in my project around what they felt was valuable useful good support. "The best types of support were informal supervision with a colleague, maybe in the car going on a joint visit," suggested one participant. They also stressed that "if you don't have that peer group for support in your office . . .you can roll back your chair and think 'Oh my god!'"

There was however a concern that "peer support is going to get less and less as people get more and more stretched, tighter deadlines, larger caseloads and more responsibility." The importance of practitioners making time for each other was consistently highlighted with one practitioner suggesting "no one else can understand the job and the pressures unless they've been there".

Kapoulitsas and Corcoran (2014) discuss similar results under the heading 'Debriefing with Colleagues' 'bouncing ideas off colleagues, not being judged, using co-workers as sounding boards and research sharing were all phrases used to describe the idea of valuable peer support' (Kapoulitsas 2014, p11).

Christenson and Kline (2000) suggest that group supervision has always been used widely in counselling circles. My participants felt that this could also be useful in other professions, 'It can provide an ideal arena where you can learn and develop as professionals,' feel heard understood and valued.

Conversely it was recognised 'participation anxiety' as a phenomenon could inhibit the process working effectively. One participant discussed her anxiety at attending such sessions until she realised that they could be a valuable arena to share experiences with other staff, reflect on cases and share knowledge.

'Shut off, unable to deal with hearing anymore stuff, not able to do my role,' were the words from one of my participants, succinctly describing the long-term impact of listening to those experiencing trauma without appropriate and effective support. The good news is that hearing this trauma can be buffered by listening to each other as professionals, in the same way we might listen to service users. Respectfully non-judgmentally honestly and empathically.

© Sass Boucher

The barriers created by attitudes and bias are perhaps the most concerning when we see them in social work practice. Where people have negative attitudes towards the person they are listening to, then the quality of 'hearing' will certainly suffer, but attitudinal barriers go much further than this.

Morris (2017) highlighted statements made by social workers about certain areas of deprivation. For example, she quotes a social worker as saying, 'you hear that they are a family from that road and you just think 'urgh'.' This exemplifies the way that attitudes can have an impact on the way that a social worker might approach working with a particular family simply on the basis of what they have heard.

Prejudice, lack of respect and arrogance create significant barriers to communication and to hearing in particular. The barriers created by such attitudes are often referred to by professionals in relation to the service users they are working with ("he's got a real attitude problem in terms of authority figures"), but it is important to recognise that such attitudinal barriers to hearing often lie with professionals.

Social workers need to take a whole system approach to understanding the barriers that can be created by attitudes:

- What is the ethos, atmosphere or culture of the organisation?
- How do individual practitioners reinforce that or cut across it in their own communication style?

Prospera Shares

Understanding attitudes and bias in relation to communication is particularly important. I have developed a particular interest in attitudes about accents. My research with students from Black African backgrounds has identified accents as potential barriers to communication and relationship building. Research by Harrison and Ip (2013) suggests that in any communication, there is a joint responsibility by both parties (speaker and listener) to ensure they understand what is being discussed. For many black African students their experience was of the listener simply responding 'I don't understand your accent' and in another example, of the listener putting the phone down on the speaker due to what they described as a difficult accent.

Montgomery (2008) has commented that pronunciation by some people can be perceived as 'pleasant' and 'correct' while others become stigmatised as 'ugly', or 'incorrect'. Research also suggests that some accents (such as the French and Italian accents) are regarded as more pleasant than African accents.

A personal strategy I utilise when working with linguistic and accent difference is to first engage in a general conversation to 'tune' my ears to pronunciation and accent. This enables me to progress the discussion without undermining the working relationship. Using this strategy means the listener takes active responsibility for understanding what is being discussed.

In developing awareness about how different accents can predispose social judgements and contribute to recognition of social stratification, I find a discussion with students about the stereotypes associated with particular accents a useful warm-up exercise.

My Share

How do people respond to my accent? Why?

There are a range of bureaucratic layers in social work, many of which create barriers to hearing for practitioners.

Morrison (2016) identified a body of research (for example Broadhurst et al, 2010; Munro, 2010, 2011) illustrating how the systems in social work can have a negative impact on how effectively social workers hear children and young people. The factors identified include heavy caseloads, high levels of staff turnover and a preoccupation with bureaucratic, administrative and technical aspects of the contemporary social work role.

Ruch (2013) explored the practice of six social workers in relation to communication with children. Social workers described:

- Children did not communicate in the linear way that formal assessments, thresholds, evidence gathering or procedures require, which created a mismatch between the demands of the social work role and practicing genuine hearing.

- Feeling that they were forced to withdraw from cases before they felt their work was done, leading to feelings of anxiety and stress on the part of the worker.

- Feeling distressed by the content of what children said and feeling unable to share this because of concerns that emotion may be treated as a sign of 'weakness or professional inadequacy' rather than professional sensitivity and attunement to the child's circumstances.

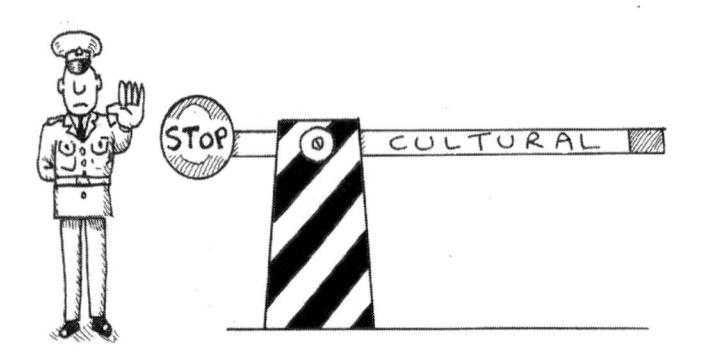

A very significant barrier to hearing relates to a lack of cultural competence in listening. Cultural competence has been defined as the combination of knowledge, attitudes and skills necessary for care providers to deal effectively with cultural and ethnic diversity (Betancourt 2006).

The models of communication taught on social work training, such as the SOLER model (see page 135) often come from a very North American base and the inherent lack of cultural awareness within these is recognised by the American National Association of Social Workers (NASW 2017).

Culturally competent listening may mean using an interpreter to facilitate communication and this is not a skill that should be undervalued. When communication involves more than one person, active listening may become difficult and culturally competent listening, even more elusive. Lum (2007) has suggested that listening to marginalised people is one of the most important aspects of culturally competent practice.

Victoria Climbie's aunt, Kaoau, and indeed Victoria herself were first language French speakers having come from Cote d'Ivoire through France to the UK. The Laming Inquiry concluded that there was miscommunication and poor communication arising from the fact that no interpreters were used. This left the social worker limited ability to 'speak' directly with Victoria. Victoria's voice was never 'heard'.

The need for language interpreters in social care is one that has been written about extensively, however it is recognised that as part of the ongoing austerity cuts in the United Kingdom, fewer services offer language interpreters as the emphasis is on enabling and empowering 'foreign' people to learn English. It is acknowledged that this process of learning English is not a quick fix and that ultimately service users will take some time to become proficient speakers of English. What will happen in the interim? This responsibilisation of people whose first language is not English does not create a fair society in that there are many places in the UK where access to English language courses are very limited.

Organisational barriers

We end this consideration of the main barriers to hearing with an exploration of organisational barriers. The barriers created within organisations are multifaceted and exploring them demonstrates how all the barriers to hearing which we have covered so far can compound each other within a powerful organisation to actively prevent listening and hearing in a range of ways. For example, the Francis Report into Mid Staffordshire NHS Foundation Trust identified a fundamental lack of listening (Francis 2013).

Whilst health professionals very often focus on 'clinical' barriers to communication (effectively 'blaming' individual patients and their impairments or medical conditions) often there is an interplay of barriers with all the other barriers identified in this chapter so far, impacting on the organisational culture. For example, in exploring listening in the NHS, Williams (2013) identified a number of issues which we have categorised in terms of the barriers we have considered so far:

Environmental barriers: around immediate barriers such as a lack of privacy for discussions in hospital, to wider organisational environment issues.

Emotional barriers: around clinicians having 'fear and anxieties' (p6) which impacted on their ability to really hear what patients had to say.

Attitudinal barriers: where medicine is seen as something that doctors 'do to' patients (p4) and patients should be listening to doctors.

Bureaucratic barriers: such as a focus on political priorities and financial pressures (p5).

The Department of Health (2015) has acknowledged the way that the barriers to listening are compounded and systemic in the NHS asserting that *"a strong patient voice is only heard when the system is listening"* and committing to work towards a changed culture in the NHS.

SHARE: Holistic listening

Whilst the literature refers to empathic listening and active listening, the SHARE model encourages 'holistic listening'. This kind of listening recognises the interplay between the different components of the SHARE model - considering what we see, hear and do when we are listening, along with how we evaluate what we hear. It also acknowledges everyones' 'share' in terms of hearing: how do we enable other people to really 'hear' us? Is our communication clear and power sensitive? Finally, it recognises the barriers to hearing and seeks to work in ways which address each of these barriers and the compounding nature of these.

What we hear in social work: the use of language

In 1926 the French writer Antoine de Saint-Exupery famously said, *"language is the source of most misunderstandings."* Good social workers recognise the vital importance of language in clear communication and they are well aware of the way that language (particularly what we commonly refer to as jargon) can be used to exclude people.

We have noted that there is a culture of academic language which can be excluding and can render some writing inaccessible. Thompson (2010) refers to this as 'academic code', recognising that social work theory, for example, can be expressed using a language that 'excludes people who are not members of a certain club'. This can leave students concerned about their abilities to understand key concepts in social work. Often defence around this academic style of writing refers to the need for improved intellectualism in social work and the danger of 'over simplifying' concepts. However, social workers do not 'over simplify' the issues they discuss with service users and yet they seek to meet the challenge of communicating clearly in a way which does not de-personalise and does not exclude.

Terry Leahy who was the CEO of Tesco for 14 years, highlights the fact that this move towards a complex language is not specific to social work, suggesting that *"our culture tends to instill in us a sense that complex understanding of life is a sign of intelligence. We look up to people who use long words, jargon and sophisticated terms, perhaps in the hope that they have the answers to all these hideously complex challenges we face"* (Leahy 2012: 207).

We have a commitment to making the knowledge base accessible. If social workers can barely understand the language used around a theory or approach then what does this mean for service users? Service users have the right to understand the theories which social workers are using to analyse their situations. We have therefore sought to ensure that we use accessible language in introducing the SHARE model.

We are also aware that language is used in a way which creates an 'us and them' divide. Language which is used to describe people who share particular characteristics is often a key part of the 'othering' process. Indeed, we note the work of French Philosopher Michael Foucault, who explored how some discourses of language and knowledge acquire the status of truth and therefore become powerful and dominant explanatory narratives, whereas other discourses are subjugated and marginalised, i.e. become 'the other' (Foucault, 1972). That said, the work of Foucault is extremely challenging and can be excluding in itself but his ideas about why some knowledge is privileged over others, and how language (what he calls discourse) replicates inequalities, is important nonetheless.

Stories of Jargon in social work

Social workers (and other professionals) use a range of jargon in their practice, sometimes not even recognising this as jargon. Often this jargon is nonsensical outside of the profession - being made up of abbreviations. A couple of stories that we are aware of, illustrate the humorous side of the use of jargon, but do be aware that the use of such jargon and abbreviations can be dangerous in practice.

A social worker who had recently moved from youth justice to hospital social work read a referral which said the 85 year old man concerned was TWOC. She was surprised to read that this man had been 'joyriding' (taking a vehicle without consent). When she got to the ward and asked the staff about this, she learnt that in this context TWOC meant 'trial without catheter'.

A service user wondered why his garden wasn't being maintained when it was clear on the support plan he had that it would be. What was written on his plan was 'mow' he was receiving help with meals (MOW = meals on wheels).

Siobhan was surprised when asking social workers where they worked to hear a number of people working on a 'riot team'. She didn't realise that there was so much civil unrest in the area - until she asked a little more and discovered that they worked on the referral intake online team. Imagine hearing that you have been referred to the RIOT team!

When the DipSW changed to the degree in social work there was an initial move away from the word placement to the term practice learning opportunity. At a pre-placement meeting Siobhan was 'told off' by a tutor for referring to a placement rather than a practice learning opportunity. By the mid placement meeting the tutor was referring to a plop! (Shorthand for Practice Learning Opportunity).

Jo once had a post in the voluntary sector working as a Children's Outreach Worker. The children she worked with referred to her constantly as the 'Cow', much to the concern of their parents who thought it was a comment about Jo's practice. In another animal related situation, when Jo first went to work as a lecturer in social work, she kept wondering why people were referring to Sows, (female pigs). She learnt eventually it meant 'Scheme of Work', in other words, a timetable of the sessions to be covered in the module.

Whilst these above examples are of course, lightweight and humorous examples of social work jargon and acronyms, we return to the point made earlier, about how professional jargon can unintentionally create othering, for anyone outside of that profession, and indeed how it can serve to exclude and oppress others. We can see this very starkly in Siobhan's SHARE.

Siobhan Shares

I was admitted to hospital shortly before having a stroke. When I was admitted, the nurse told me that she would 'assess' me. My experience of being assessed was that she asked me a series of questions, ticking boxes on the form she held on a clipboard. She got about halfway down the page and asked me "and can you feed yourself?" I said "No" and she looked up at me for the first time, saying "I don't think you understand the question"... When I explained that I could eat but that I would not be "feeding myself" she tutted and moved on. I became known as a non-compliant patient!

When I had the stroke and I needed assistance to eat my meals, I can't describe how it felt to hear staff talking about "the feeders" and asking who was "feeding her" today. Think about the word 'feeding'. What image do you see? What you see is likely to relate to either babies or animals - hence demonstrating the way that language infantilises or dehumanises people. The use of this kind of language (I no longer had a napkin or serviette - it became a 'bib') was so disempowering and reinforced the dependency that I had on others for essential needs in a way which stripped me of my dignity.

Perhaps what upset me the most though was hearing social workers coming onto the ward asking questions like "Can you feed yourself? ... do you mobilise independently?" these are not only closed questions but they immediately create a sense of 'othering'. Social workers must de-construct this othering and use the same language in their assessments as they use for themselves. If you feed yourself your meals then by all means ask others if they can feed themselves - but I very much doubt that you do!

When I have spoken to people about this they have suggested that it is important to use language like feeding to show what help people need - but that's nonsense. There were a number of us on the ward who needed help to eat; we all needed different types of help and at different stages of our recovery the help we needed differed, but it was always referred to as 'feeding'. What happens when that kind of language is used is that bank staff come along and simply load the fork and put it to the person's mouth - whether that is the kind of assistance they need or not. It is something that is done to people.

What we hear in social work: the place of humour

Humour is considered a vital component of humanity. We often hear about people with a good sense of humour, as a positive attribute. As we have said earlier, one of our concerns has been the use of social media by social work professionals who have perpetuated myths about users of social work services, and indeed, other social work stakeholders, in negative and damaging ways. An excuse given, is that this is just 'letting off steam', or indeed, just 'being funny' or an attempt at humour. Where someone tries to challenge this, it is then described as having 'no sense of humour' or 'political correctness'. So, whilst humour is important, it is also crucial that it is done appropriately and does not cause offence. Realistically, however, what one person perceives as humorous may not be the case for others.

In relation to the SHARE model we may consider when might be a good time to inject a bit of humour into a situation or circumstance. This will involve seeing / viewing the situation to aim for maximum appropriateness. We listen for cues to use humour- so for example are we using humour to mitigate stress, to calm a difficult situation or simply as a conversation starter? We may consider how people respond to our humour (act) and then we should make sure to evaluate how the 'joke' might be seen and heard by others.

Whilst the use of what is sometimes referred to as 'gallows humour' (Sullivan, 2002; Dessau, 2012) in social work may be acceptable in a social work office, we really must give consideration to the ethics around the use of humour on social media and sharing this. Whilst it may feel as though this gallows type humour is still acceptable, when it is in a public space it is far from appropriate. Accordingly, there are increasing calls for the social work curriculum to actively include teaching about humour which can be a useful tool for working with service users. The 4Ps (see page 64) may be a useful framework for considering the use of humour in practice.

Debbie Greaves and Jim McGrath are social workers who perform a stand up comedy act.

Siobhan has seen them perform on a number of occasions and finds their humour both entertaining and thought provoking

The following stakeholder voice is written by Stephen Jordan, a former social worker, now Head of Social Work at Essex University. Stephen was so interested in the issue of humour and social work, he wrote his Professional Doctorate in Social Work on the topic (Jordan, 2015).

STAKEHOLDER VOICE
STEPHEN JORDAN

Stephen Jordan is the Head of Social Work at Essex University

In my work as a social worker there were lots of instances when colleagues came back into the office to share their humourous anecdotes. On one occasion Julia came back from a visit where she had been asked to assess a young man with a history of mental health issues. She knocked on the door of a semi in the middle of the housing estate where most families were familiar with the social work team. As she stood waiting for the door to be answered a dog came up, sat beside her and looked up at her. The dog seemed friendly enough and she took this as a good sign for her assessment. The young man answered the door and after Julia had introduced herself, showed her in to the living room. The dog followed her in and sat beside her, as Julia perched on the settee and conducted her assessment. About half way through the assessment, the dog walked over to the armchair where the young man was seated, cocked its leg and began urinating. The young man looked at Julia and Julia smiled at the young man, and thought: 'he has different standards from me, I won't comment on it at this visit, but ask him about hygiene on the next visit.' The young man said nothing. Bringing the interview to a close ten minutes later Julia stood up and went to the door. Just a she was about to leave the house, the young man asked her plaintively 'Aren't you going to take your dog with you?'

These times became the high points of my life at work, and despite all the lows there were times when service users would share jokes with me and together with my colleagues' anecdotes, this seemed to make the roller-coaster of social work life survivable.

The use of humour by social workers and their colleagues are cited as one of their most common coping mechanisms (Moran and Hughes, 2006) and several studies found that humour and the sharing of humour can build resilience in social work teams e.g. Siporin, (1984); Witkin (1999); Sullivan (2000); Moran and Hughes (2006) and Gilgun and Sharma (2011). Gilgun and Sharma's (2011) study found social workers in their study used humour to regulate anxiety, frustration and shock, and positive aspects of humour use, including emotion regulation, and creative problem solving and social workers in their study often used humour to express liking of service users

However humour not always been seen so positively - Kadushin and Kadushin (1997) and Hill and O'Brien (2004) have warned that the use humour should never be used at the service user's expense, as this conveys a degree of lack of empathy of insensitivity. Humour is common to all humans (Apte, 1983; Holt, 2008), and it is possible that humour has a unique potential for demonstrating particular characteristics of a social worker when applied sensitively and appropriately it could be a useful tool to enable social workers to help service users manage their own emotions, as Howe (1998) argued that if poor relationships are where psychosocial competences go awry, then good relationships are where they are likely to recover (Howe, 1998).

Social work is a risky endeavour, fraught with anxiety and complexities, and the practice of social work one could argue is primarily about risk taking. What could be the value to a social worker in using humour and taking such a risky course of action?

The answer lies in what humour communicates about the teller to the recipient, as humour is a universal human characteristic conveys a person's 'normality' to others and communicates their humanity, because it is founded in our earliest attachment experiences. In this sense humour has unique power to convey a particular characteristic about a social worker, and that is why I suggest some social workers take the risk of using humour, as the opposite, a lack of humour, conveys a lack of humanity.

Service users can themselves teach social workers the importance of finding the humour, irony and absurdity in their situations, and whilst it is unethical to laugh at people and their problems, it may be helpful to laugh with them as they describe the humourous aspects of their experiences (Frost, 1992).

The social worker who uses humour is also a more resilient social worker. Furnivall (2011) includes, amongst other attributes which build resilience in children in care, a sense of humour, particularly the capacity to laugh at one-self, and the same applies to building resilient social work practitioners.

So humour is something that cannot be avoided, and instead social workers have to engage with humour, either as the object of humour or as active participants. Humour is necessary for successful relationships, but is also a risky undertaking and social workers ignore humour at their peril, as humour is key to social life, but it remains an often unexamined component in explaining and understanding relationships. Attachment is crucial to establishing and maintaining relationships and humour helps social workers create and maintain attachments with others, at the same time as helping social workers managing their own emotions and the emotions of others. Social workers fear not being taken seriously, but conversely use humour and jokes, which can help social workers manage their unhappiness at work, to cope with the stress of the work and to have successful relationships with their service users.

So after all that, what's my favourite joke about social work?

A social worker is facing a mugger with a gun. 'Your money or your life!' says the mugger. 'I'm sorry,' the social worker answers, 'I am a social worker, so I have no money and no life.'

But I am always keen to hear more so feel free to email me with yours at sjordan@essex.ac.uk

© Stephen Jordan

What we hear in social work: The importance of feedback

Feedback is vitally important and is often viewed as one of the main catalysts for change. As a profession which seeks to support change there is an irony here in that the value of feedback is rarely recognised in social work. Very often people report a lack of feedback in a range of ways, for example social work managers seem to take a 'no news is good news' approach and so practitioners report feeling that they only get feedback on things that are not going well. Service users often report that they do not receive feedback from social workers or that the feedback they do receive lacks balance.

The value of feedback is widely recognised in relating to other aspects of social work practice. For example, Anseel, Lievens and Schollaert (2009) researched the impact of reflection on employee development. They found that reflection based on, or combined with, feedback significantly enhanced work performance - whilst reflection without feedback did not lead to measurable performance improvement. Ensuring that regular feedback on practice is central to supervision is therefore vitally important both in terms of ensuring the quality of social work services and promoting reflective practice and professional development. However, feedback is not just important for practitioners, service users need to be able to give and receive feedback, as do other professionals. This section will therefore explore the importance of feedback from a range of stakeholder perspectives.

Feedback can be either positive (reinforcing good practice) or negative (feedback on poor performance). Both positive and negative feedback can be constructive. Where feedback is constructive it will enable the receiver to develop and change. The main differences between constructive and destructive feedback are outlined in the following table.

Constructive feedback	Destructive feedback
Solves problems	Intensifies problems
Concentrates on behaviour or performance	Concentrates on personality
Strengthens relationships	Damages relationships
Builds trust	Destroys trust
Is a shared (two way) process	Is a one-way process
Reduces stress and tension	Adds to stress and increases tension
Helps in managing conflict	Creates conflict
Supports change	Creates resistance to change
Is assertive	Is aggressive

In our experience, social work training does not give due attention to the importance of feedback and to the skills of giving and receiving feedback, although this is being addressed to some extent within some of the teaching partnerships in England, where this has been highlighted as an issue. It is often only when social workers undertake practice educator training that they are given the space to consider the provision of feedback. However, being able to provide feedback constructively is a key skill for social workers at every level of their career, not least because feedback is often a catalyst for change and can be a key element of motivational support.

Constructive feedback should be:

Positive: Feedback should always start and finish with a positive. This is often referred to as the positive sandwich. The content of the sandwich gives the recipient something to work on, whilst the 'bread' is the positive aspects. In this way, the esteem and motivation of the person receiving feedback will be built on.

Specific: Deal clearly with particular instances and behaviour rather than making vague or sweeping statements.

Descriptive: Feedback should use descriptive rather than evaluative terms, or should at least start with a description to evidence the evaluation, so for example, "what I have seen and heard is.. this leads me to think that...".

Actionable: Feedback should be directed towards behaviour that can be changed.

Prioritised: Concentrate on the two or three key areas for improvement, preferably including those where the recipient can see a quick return. Break down a major problem into smaller, step-by-step goals. (This is the 'content' of the positive sandwich).

Facilitative: Rather than prescribing behaviour, feedback should help the recipient question their behaviour and consider how others might see it.

Clear: Avoid jargon wherever possible and ensure that your communication is clear. Always check feedback to ensure that the other person understands you.

Well Timed: The most useful feedback is given when the person is receptive to it and it is sufficiently close to the event to be fresh in their mind.

Always think about the timing when giving feedback

So, giving feedback is an important skill for everyone in social work. Being able to receive feedback is also a key skill, and one which is rarely considered. The SHARE model can assist with thinking through the skills of both giving and receiving feedback, as follows:

Think about SHARE when providing or receiving feedback:

	Giving feedback	Receiving feedback
SEE:	Think about your body language when providing feedback. Has anyone ever given you some feedback whilst wagging their finger for example? How did that feel?	What does the person giving you feedback see? Is your body language open and relaxed - are you indicating an openness to feedback through your body language?
HEAR:	What words are you using? How are you speaking? How will the person 'hear' what you are saying?	Are you employing active listening skills? Try to really hear what the person giving you feedback is saying. Don't become defensive.
ACT:	Think about how you approach the feedback conversation; what will you do? What action do you expect as a result of the feedback? How will you respond?	It's not unusual for people receiving feedback to experience a range of emotions. Think about how you can contain those emotions so that they don't impact on your behaviour at the time. For example, you may feel angry or upset by the feedback, but it is unlikely to be appropriate for you to cry at that time.
READ:	Have you written the feedback down so that the person can have it in writing? This might enable them to reflect more deeply on what you are saying at a later stage.	Try to write the feedback down to see how you understand it. If possible and appropriate ask the person providing feedback to give you a record of their thoughts for you to read again later. Reading feedback back at a later stage can help with reflecting on the feedback.
EVALUATE:	Be aware of the dangers of evaluation in feedback. Describe what you see, not what you think you see. If you feel the need to provide some evaluation in the feedback then be clear that you are commenting on the way you see something. For example, say "you are looking out of the window" rather than saying "You are not listening to me", or say "You are looking out of the window which gives me the impression that you are not listening to me."	Keep in touch with your feelings. If you find yourself feeling defensive about a piece of feedback, you need to remind yourself that the reality is that a defensive reaction to feedback generally results from it being accurate!

There is a clear need to ensure service users have the chance to give meaningful feedback to social workers and other professionals, without it being tokenistic. Social work students are often required to use service user and carer feedback in their placement portfolios and the use of feedback from people who have used social work services is a requirement in the ASYE in England. All of us encourage students to use creative and meaningful ways to receive feedback and not just rely on a tick box pro forma which can feel impersonal and rarely elicits useful feedback. It is also useful to remember that some service users and carers will have only ever received negative feedback from family as well as professionals. Often the best portfolios that we have read (for qualifications across the whole continuum) involve the practitioner drawing on feedback from the people they have worked with as a central thread through the whole portfolio.

The SHARE model aims to support practitioners to recognise that feedback is a two-way process, service users and carers must be given a real opportunity to provide feedback to social workers and social workers must develop their skills in both providing and receiving constructive balanced feedback.

STAKEHOLDER VOICE
LAURA NEWMAN & CLARE SKELSON

Laura Newman is a qualified social worker with practice experience in children's services and Claire Skelson is a Social Work Practice and Development Co-ordinator with extensive experience working within adults social work.

We are very committed to ensuring that service users are widely consulted about social work services but feel that often service user feedback is approached in a tokenistic way. So, when we had the opportunity to work together recently we used our experiences to collectively develop tools for gathering service user and family feedback and tools for reflection on the feedback.

We wanted to develop tools that would not only support social work students to gather feedback and reflect but that could also support service users and families to be able to provide honest feedback. We recognised that not only do most individuals want to say positive things but when we are working with individuals and groups who have suffered oppression and discrimination we need to recognise those individuals may not recognise poor practice.

Early into developing the tools we recognised the importance of being creative and visual and also tailoring the feedback tools to the individual. Feedback needs to be person centred or child centred dependent on the service user group. Social work professionals should be required to adapt the way in which they gather feedback when ascertaining views and wishes of service users within their daily practice. We acknowledge that the timing of asking for feedback needs to be carefully considered, for example it would not be appropriate to ask for feedback when an individual is showing signs of distress.

After creating the tools and consulting widely about the usefulness of the tools we concluded that we had included a lot of jargon, which could potentially make the use of the tool with service users and students more difficult, and less effective. We reflected that the use of jargon can result in service users feeling oppressed, which was the opposite desired result of the tools. Wanting to support service users to give their point of view and feedback with honesty, we adapted the tools to address the issue of jargon.

We are of the opinion that formal and informal feedback is equally as important. However, with all methods of feedback we believe that student social workers and qualified social workers should be reflecting on the feedback and identifying what the feedback actually means in relation to their development using the Professional Capability Framework and the Knowledge and Skills statements. For example, a service user might say that they felt that the 'social worker listened and responded with empathy'. Upon reflection the professional might identify this to be within the 'relationships and effective direct work' section of the Knowledge and Skills statement for children's. We have found that it can be useful for social work students or professionals to ask others (managers or practice educators for example) to seek feedback on their behalf to encourage objectivity, the added advantage to this is that the student can then reflect with their practice educator on the feedback to enable a more reflexive approach.

We will be developing new tools in the future.

© Laura Newman and Clare Skelson

Any musician reading this book will know that acoustic feedback occurs when the amplified sound from any loudspeaker re-enters the sound system through any open microphone and is amplified again and again and again. The sound made can vary from a low rumble to a piercing screech. It is the result of a loop in the sound system. Feedback being created *from* a loop in musical terms is interesting in that in social work the feedback should create the loop – each person 'in the loop' needs to provide feedback such that it is a two-way shared process.

A final word about SHARE in feedback

People are often concerned about providing feedback, how will the person receiving it see the feedback? If feedback is not a regular aspect of the relationship then getting started with a feedback 'culture' can be difficult. The SHARE model offers a really helpful framework for this. So, for example, in supervision with students Siobhan regularly has feedback on the supervision agenda. In this both Siobhan and the student SHARE feedback with the other. This will be about:

SEE:
Something that they have observed in the other person. So feedback might be shared in relation to direct observations - formal or informal.

HEAR:
Something about what they have heard from (or about) the other person. This might involve feedback about something one party had said which had prompted the other person to reflect.

ACT:
Something that the other person has done. Here feedback could relate to practice or general actions.

READ:
This often involves feedback about something that one party has written and the other has read.

EVALUATE:
The feedback given in each of the above will be descriptive and then both Siobhan and the student will evaluate what this might mean and what action might be helpful.
Once people have become familiar with the SHARE model this can provide a helpful way of ensuring fully rounded, well evidenced two-way feedback.

Using the term 'share feedback' as an agenda item has a range of benefits:
- It ensures that feedback is seen as a two-way process.
- It creates a supervision culture built around the importance of feedback.
- It helps both supervisor and supervisee become familiar with the SHARE model such that they are able to use it in other areas of practice.
- It ensures that feedback is provided on a range of areas drawn from the components of the model.
- Where there is something that one party is finding difficult to approach it can help prompt them to provide the feedback.

Use this page to record feedback you receive.

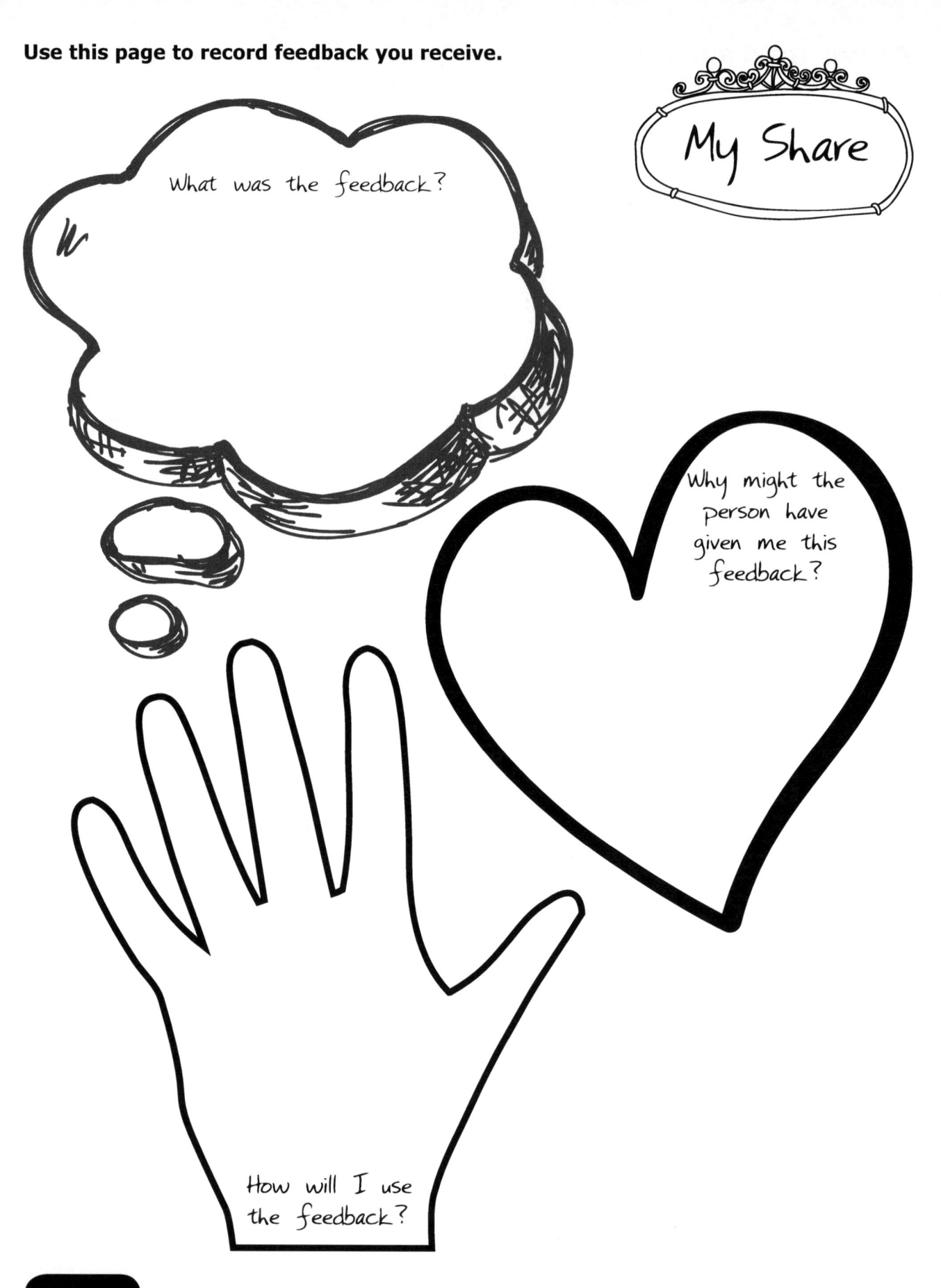

My Share

What was the feedback?

Why might the person have given me this feedback?

How will I use the feedback?

Conversational practice

The importance of conversations has long been widely recognised in social work. For example, Welbourne (2012:72) asserts *"If social work has a defining characteristic, it is perhaps the intensely conversational aspect of the work. What is done in 'doing social work is largely having purposeful conversations."* However, concerns have been raised recently that care management processes have undermined conversational practice in social work in favour of interviews and assessments; a series of questions that are asked to formulate a plan of action. Rob's stakeholder voice illustrates this very clearly.

STAKEHOLDER VOICE — ROB MITCHELL

Rob is the Principal Social Worker for Adults at City of Bradford Metropolitan District Council. He is presently co-chair of the Adult PSW National Network.

I received my social work qualification in the post just two days before I started my first ever social work post. New social workers, in the days before we defined Newly Qualified Social Workers, were just called a new social worker. The fact that you were newly qualified was never discussed. I was a social worker. I bought a new shirt for the occasion of my first ever day in the profession. It would have been ironed had one of the children not delayed me by being sick in one of my wedding (now work) shoes.

I met my first line manager in the first hour of the first day. She talked a lot and I was to listen. In fact, she even passed me a notepad and pen as she commented that she was surprised I was not noting some of the things she was telling me. In truth, I won't have been listening. I can't listen when people give me instructions. If I get lost and ask people for directions I never listen to a word they helpfully try and give me. As much as I need their assistance I instead find myself concentrating on the kindly direction giver's accent or slight whistle when they pronounce anything with an 's' in it or I notice the expression of their passenger's face. Whilst nodding and saying "yes, turn right" after they've said it to give the impression I am listening I am wondering where they going themselves or where they have been. Now that I would listen to. But directions and instructions far less so. I expect my new superior was telling me about fire alarms that probably wouldn't go off and the ritual of car parking or maybe even how to pay into the tea fund. I smiled and nodded and I remember noting something down in the pad she had given me. It is likely to have been the last word I heard her say in order that it looked like I was listening. My guess is that it said something like "ok". It may as well have said "turn right, yes".

I remember my first ever social work client from that day. She was called Jean. She talked and I listened because she was talking about herself, her life, her ambitions, her present situation and her desires. Jean spent a lot of time talking about her cat. There were no instructions attached to Jean's talking, and so I just listened. I asked questions from time to time, but crucially I listened and Jean just spoke. On my lap I had a Community Care Assessment. This, my boss explained, was where we wrote down relevant points about peoples' lives to do 'The Assessment'. I had heard a lot about assessments in my first morning as a social worker. They were described as the cornerstone, the purpose and the focus of our role. In truth, I hadn't had much in the way of training on assessments at university. There was some mention of Care Assessments and Care Plans but in three years of training, 24 separate 3,000 word assignments and two 8,000 word portfolios based on two practice placements I rarely mentioned assessments. My training was about our approach, our understanding of people, relationships, the dynamics of relationships, empowerment, advocacy and rights. Maybe I was off sick on the day they did 'assessments'? Either way, assessments were a form and forms came with instructions. I wouldn't have listened.

Half way through week one the boss was clear that my work with Jean needed reviewing. I was invited in to the meeting room and asked to explain where the discharge planning was up to. With my paperwork in hand I began talking about Jean. I had completed the assessment through recording what I had heard Jean say. So, half reading from the assessment document and half through memory I talked about my conversations with Jean. I talked about her background and her family, I talked about her husband Bob and his job and how when he retired he died shortly after robbing Jean of the retirement that they planned. I talked about how Bob had helped choose the new carpet that she had tripped on, causing the fracture that led to her fall and how she laughed at the thought that he was getting his own back. I talked about the grandchildren in Australia and how the letters and photographs kept Jean going as well as the 3am phone calls from her granddaughter Laura due to the time difference and how excited Jean felt when she was due a 3am call. I talked about Jean's cat and how when Bob had died and her daughter had gone to Australia it was the main focus of Jean's life. I had listened to Jean talking about the life that Jean once had, the life she was planning to have and the life she had now. After I had talked about Jean I waited for the boss to speak. There was a long pause and then she spoke. "You may have well as assessed the bloody cat". She went on to explain that what I needed to assess was the support Jean needed, not Jean herself and certainly not her long lost husband, far flung daughter and bloody cat. I needed to listen to how many times she needed the toilet during the night. I needed to hear if she now thought she needed to be in a residential home. I needed to hear how the care package was going to get her back home. I needed to listen out for who manages her finances and how much money she has. I was genuinely perplexed. I wasn't trained to do that sort of listening. I didn't like that sort of listening. That wasn't the social work I was educated in and in truth I didn't even recognise that it was social work. But this was my job.

I didn't speak to Jean again or get the chance to listen to her. Our conversation was converted into an assessment by an experienced social worker. Apparently with a half decent nursing report and a functional assessment from the OT we could just about throw together an assessment that would help Jean be discharged as quickly as possible. The assessment documented that Jean needed four calls of home care a day. The calls would start anytime between 7am and 11am. Lunch was between 12 and 3. Tea from 3.30 to 7 and bed every night by 10pm. No mention of Bob or little Laura in Sydney or even Audrey next door. On the box that documented whether or not Jean had got any pets it said in bold capital letters NONE.

Now as a Principal Social Worker I reflect on that experience with both a tinge of sadness and also frustration about I how dealt with the situation. Although the approach of the manager was poor I do think I could have better reflected the situation. Crucially my approach to Jean was exactly what I had been taught to do and it was the approach that I hope I now support social workers to undertake. However, I was unprepared for the power dynamics involved in terms of my relationship with my manager and moreover I had no real tactics for dealing with it. University had given me a good social work education but it hadn't necessarily taught me the prerequisite skills of office politics and how to survive. Since my experience with Jean things have changed in adult social work and whilst power dynamics are still often very evident it is important that social workers are supported to tackle this. In terms of the assessment with Jean I feel that we now have a wider legal context that enables us to undertake the social work we were trained to do regardless of the setting and the pressures of being a new member of the social work team. As the PSW supporting a Newly Qualified Social Worker in a similar situation now I would emphasise the legal context of assessment, rather than merely relying on a conversational approach to relay the details of the assessment. For example, couching the assessment in terms of the Principles of the Care Act would have given me a degree of professional gravitas that I lacked at the time. The assessment with Jean was conversational in style but the outcomes addressed things that we are legally obliged to cover, such as judging wellbeing, ensuring prevention through participations and upholding wishes, feelings and beliefs. Articulating our work in these terms often disarms those who may be seeking to unnecessarily or harshly critique our work. The social work role is multifaceted. Whilst providing Jean with a relaxed environment and conversational style to ensure I understood the outcomes she wanted it was as important to be able to describe those outcomes in a way that my fellow professionals could understand and respect. Listening to the person you are working with is at the heart of person centred working. Ensuring you are listened to by fellow professionals so that you advocate for the person you are working with is often equally as important.

© Rob Mitchell

Conversations: The five Cs

There is a great deal written about different types of conversation (Mager 2017), and a number of models have been developed to explore the importance of conversations, these tend to fall into the following three Cs:

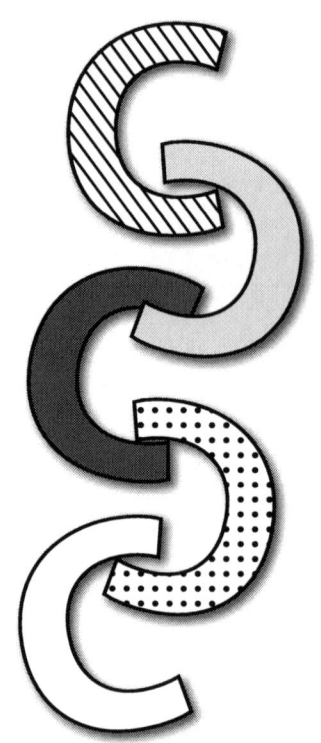

Crucial Conversations: Crucial conversations are widely referred to in terms of leadership models. The concept was developed by Patterson et al (2012) and refers to conversations where the stakes are high and those where there are opposing opinions and strong emotions.

Coaching Conversations: Coaching conversations centre on the delivery of feedback in a conversational style to support individual learning and development (deHaan and Stewart 2008).

Courageous Conversations: The notion of 'Courageous Conversation' was developed by Beddoe and Davys (2016) in relation to supervision practice. It is helpful nonetheless, in considering conversational practice more widely. Some conversations are avoided, because we know that they will possibly cause hurt, conflict, and a range of other difficult emotions, namely shame, anger and anxiety, in both oneself and the receiver. According to Beddoe and Davys (2016) there is a need to be courageous in starting these conversations.

We would add two further Cs to conversations in social work:

Constructive conversations: We have already discussed the importance of feedback in social work and keeping this constructive to enable learning. The issue of keeping things constructive and useful is important in social work. Sometimes people become concerned that conversational practice may take the social worker away from the importance of assessment and process and procedures (see Rob's voice page 161). However skilled conversational practice means that discussions remains constructive and helpful to all involved, in a range of ways.

Complex Conversations in social work: The four Cs above, come together in social work in what we would term complex conversations. Social workers have complex conversations with users of services as well as colleagues, managers and other professionals. Conversations become complex when:

- The stakes are high
- There is significant conflict about the issue under discussion
- There are a range of emotions involved
- There are a range of compounding barriers to communication
- There are significant issues about power and its use

The development of the three conversations model and subsequent discussions about the success of the model in a range of adult social care services (Kirin 2016 and Cole 2016) demonstrates the resurgence in interest in the art of conversations in social work.

The SHARE model recognises the value of conversations. People have conversations *with* people, as such they become restorative, supporting the development of relationships. Where service users have worked with a practitioner who is skilled in conversational practice then they feel that they have connected with the person and worked together with someone, rather than feeling that they have had something done to them.

The SHARE model promotes therefore, the importance of meaningful conversations, considering not just what each person shares in the conversion, but also each person's SHARE. What does each person involved in the conversation see, hear and do in the conversation, how do they evaluate the conversation and if it is written about, does what each person reads reflect their experience of the conversation?

Quality conversations connect the components of SHARE, since they are about 'doing' and what you see and hear as part of the act of conversation, how they are written up and how people evaluate these conversations adds the complexity to conversational practice. Social workers must never underestimate the professional artistry of conversational practice.

This book is in itself a collection of complex conversations, reflecting the complexity of social work. The conversations that we need to engage in, to practice effectively, can only reflect this complexity.

My Share

- How would I rate my skills in conversational practice?
- What could I do to improve in this area?

One of the objects in Mark Doel's Social Work in 40 Objects project was mouth-piece (see page 108). Simon Cauvain worked in child social work for many years and is now a principal lecturer at Nottingham Trent University in England. Simon's proposed object is the mouth-piece to a French horn. Simon's object reminds us of the importance of giving voice to people who are often silenced, and to really hearing what people have to say. He chose mouth-piece for very personal reasons:

"The horn was one of many instruments my birth father played; his favourite. We were estranged after he and my mum divorced when I was young. I learned only recently that during this process we had a social worker who communicated with all involved … I don't remember any of this.

I wondered about my birth father and whether he ever thought of me. I never longed for him, but felt curious - it was a gap, but not one that troubled me. Mum was open about him, shared photos, told me his strengths as well as the rest. He was a proud army band member and wrote musical scores for the range of instruments. He and his sister were adopted, but he was badly abused by his adopters. He was violent towards my mum and had problems with alcohol and drugs. She left him in order to protect my brother and me.

I decided to find him. It happened quickly; we communicated by letter and eventually met at his home. I learned of two sisters I didn't know existed. We arranged to meet again and exchanged texts.

Thirteen weeks after this, he died unexpectedly. The house was burgled the evening his body was removed. My brother and I cleared his cluttered rooms and prepared for the funeral. I got to know him more through his belongings, his Objects, ones he'd never have wanted me to see. He'd had a rough time, struggling with alcohol and poverty and he'd been in prison.

He'd sold his beloved horn for cash, but the mouth-piece was something he kept and that I retrieved. It represents our respective journeys that at one seemingly insignificant point involved a social worker. It's a lasting personal reminder that 'service user' is not a negative term. Service users are fellow human beings who need to be heard not just listened to.

The mouthpiece is a metaphorical voice; the opportunity to play one's own tune rather than dance to that of another; it represents that something special that good social workers manage to find. Despite the clutter." (Doel 2017)

The importance of having a voice

One of the most important things to us in developing the SHARE model has been really hearing all key stakeholders in social work. This reflects the fact that social workers must truly listen to the voices that surround them. Some voices are louder than others and as a result some are more likely to be heard. It is important that social workers actively ensure that they are hearing every voice in a situation, with a recognition that the service user's voice is the most important.

A child's right to be heard is enshrined in UK law and policy confirming the importance of this. The 1989 United Nations Convention of the Rights of the Child (UNCRC) asserts that children have a right to be heard when important decisions about their lives are being made. Children having a voice which is really listened to is even more important when the child is in contact with social work services. When children do not have a voice they can become entrapped in 'lethal silence' (Freeman, 1999:52) and Hillman (2006) argues that children who are denied the opportunity to contribute to decision making may find it difficult to make decisions in their adult life. Children who have the opportunity to share their views have also been found to have increased self-esteem and confidence (McLeod 2008).

We can therefore apply the same logic to adults, many of whom have had their voices suppressed and have not been heard, or indeed, have not expected to be heard. Having, a voice therefore, is not just about being heard it is also about learning and growth. For example, Campbell (2017) reported that *"getting involved in consultation about services when I was in care helped me to understand the care system more clearly."*

STAKEHOLDER VOICE — PAUL 'YUSUF' McCORMACK

Paul 'Yusuf' McCormack is an adopter and foster carer who experienced his first 18 years in care.

Until my late 30's I had refused to acknowledge, think or talk about my earlier childhood experiences. When I started to do so, I struggled to cope, so I locked away those feelings and carried on with life. At aged 40 I decided to write about my past. I got so far and found that the impact of my words was detrimental to me, my sleep and mental state became a concern for me and so again I shoved my thoughts away...would I ever be ready to explore my childhood?

I recognised that the person I am had been shaped by my childhood experiences but I didn't want to be dictated to by my past, I wanted to choose the person I wanted to be and so in November 2015 I wrote a verse titled 'A butterfly's heartbeat', in which I tried to articulate how I felt as a child of 5, following a particular incident. The ironic aspect of this particular beating, was that it took place in a 'work room' where repairs were made to clothing, not children. The cane was used indiscriminately as were the names screamed at me. After the punishment I was placed in the 'cloister', a dark corridor and made to kneel and pray to God for forgiveness...... I struggled with my own internal feelings, desperately seeking some peace. I used the quiet to give me the strength to carry on.

I sat back and I looked at the words I'd written and from nowhere tears came, and a noise, a strange noise, a wail, emitted from the very depth of my body. It left me shaking uncontrollably and I cried and cried.

My tears were painful, my body ached and I clung on to me desperately... I hadn't cried since I was 6 years old, (my vow of silence broken), I couldn't stop.. and something in me 'let-go'. I needed to write and words just poured out from me, describing the horrors of incidents, events, violence and abuse gifted to me as a child. Smells, visions, memories, words, incidents, violence, pain and hurt all came flooding back and I began to relive these experiences.

I spoke about feelings, my view of the world...I allowed the child within me a voice, something which I had been denied and had also denied to myself.

As my words gathered depth and clarity, reliving my past, I, too, found my voice. With each verse I cried writing the words.

I cried when I read each piece quietly and then I forced myself to read each verse aloud...I needed to hear the 'little boy' speak out and share his words, his feelings, and we cried together.

Writing about these experiences has allowed me to examine myself and see just how far I, the man, has come. I am today. I survived and that is massive. I don't blame myself...things shouldn't have happened, I know I should have been protected.

I have given myself permission to talk and tell my story. I try not to do this with blame or anger, even though there are threads within some of the verses / writings with the belief that, should people choose to listen, they may reconsider their own approaches and the use of their words and actions. Perhaps to take a step back and actually make a difference.

...and as for me, I have gained peace of mind. I have learned to sleep, smile, relax. I dream now, I don't wake with a start, I no longer carry the anxiety and torment I once did. I have been lucky to find my way to help 'heal' me...the only sadness is that it took so long. So, as a 'parent' and 'foster carer', I strive (and I make loads of mistakes still...but at least I apologise), to ensure that these experiences are never visited on the children in my care. That they get to be heard, listened to and believed but mostly that they feel like they belong.

© Paul 'Yusuf' McCormack

We are fortunate that Paul has allowed us to print here one of his spoken verses. Read it aloud - really HEAR it.

I felt quite euphoric when I wrote this. To release 'stuff' and not feel guilty about it was a whole new experience for me. To feel lighter as a result knowing you're not at fault and never were. No need to blame myself anymore..... I was a child. The importance of these feelings haven't escaped me and its relevance today, the need for children, young people to be heard, allowed to speak without disbelief, to be heard, especially for those things that aren't always said.

Let it all go

The relief, the heaviness...lifted

I've let go.......

my tears flow, pouring out

for my lost childhood

My body jerks in fits and starts,

heaving, trembling, shaking

it wails for

my innocence,

my deep sadness.

Mournful, melodic in it's rhythm.

Carrying such a burden

crippled emotionally by it's weight

given to me...a just deserve

A birth right for one who has more sin.

A strength is flowing through me,

filling my veins, giving life

my voice is given a public release

ejecting my torment

eradicating the disease that festered,

the disgust,

the consequence

of growing up in care

Look at me now!! ...I'm smiling

The importance of all stakeholders having a voice, and social workers ensuring that people who may be in a powerless position are supported to have their voices heard, isn't simply about practice. It is important that all stakeholders have a voice in relation to all issues surrounding social work. So, for example, it is vital that the voices of people who have experienced social work and care are heard in social work education and training. When research and new theories and models are being developed the widest possible range of voices should be included and the vital expertise of people who have received care and support and social work must be recognised. Andrew's stakeholder voice illustrates this very clearly.

STAKEHOLDER VOICE — ANDREW RICHARDSON

Andrew Richardson is an educator and researcher in Social Work (at the Tavistock Centre, London).

In Social Work research, methods based on principles of 'co-production' - an approach rooted in the notion of sharing power more equally between people who use services, carers and professionals, are likely to be more congruent with the rights based, anti-oppressive commitment of contemporary Social Work. Approaches based on principles of co-production often recognise a 'service user' as an 'Expert by Experience'. This is an important conceptual shift in terminology which seeks to value 'lived experience' and place this on a more equal footing with practitioner's practice-based experience. Such an approach is likely therefore to strengthen the 'voice' of service users and carers, whose invaluable experiences and insights might otherwise be muted in the research.

While it is right to embrace co-production in Social Work practice and research and to recognise and affirm the strengths of the people we work with as Social Workers we also need to be able to hear, bear and digest some more painful aspects of people's lives. Experiences of psychological and emotional pain, violence, discrimination and injustice and feelings of despair are hard to hear and can be demanding for practitioners and researchers. Yet, Social Work research and practice is limited, our assessments and our findings lacking if not unethical, if we are unable to hear the authentic, sometimes painful and sometimes challenging voices of people who use Social Work services. In this context, developing and supporting practitioners and researcher's capacity for 'containment' is, it would seem, an important concomitant alongside a commitment to 'co-production'. Put briefly, 'containment' is a concept developed by renowned British psychoanalyst Wilfred Bion that refers to the capacity to process raw emotions and returning them in more digestible states (Bower 2005).

I applied this combined approach to researching personalisation in Adult Social Care. Co-production guided me in collaborating with a group of 'Experts by Experience' who played a central role in research design, data analysis and quality assurance. In addition, qualitative interviews were undertaken with people who use services using an approach which required me to be sensitive to and capable of 'containing' participants raw emotions associated with various experiences including those associated with physical and psychological pain, stigma and discrimination.

Co-designing and co-producing with Experts by Experience entails taking time to hear what they have to say. This is not always easy. At times, the work can be very painful. Yet, the rewards can be immense. In terms of research it can enhance validity of research findings and can help to remain focused on what is most relevant and important to people who have direct lived experience of services. It should also be self-evident that the ethical credentials of the research are markedly enhanced by 'researching with people' rather than 'on people'. An approach to Social Work research based on both co-production and containment might just provide the best opportunity for the voices of people who use services to be strengthened and heard. I certainly feel that to be the case based on my research in the area of personalisation.

© Andrew Richardson

Speaking up as social workers

The debate around whether social work is a true or 'proper' profession, coupled alongside the negative public and political perception of social work, can lead to some social workers feeling that they, like the people they work with and for, lack a voice. Speaking up however, is a decisive way to take us to the next component of the SHARE model - that of action. It is important that individual social workers work hard to develop their 'voice' and that they share this with others, such that as a profession we can have a 'shared voice'. Indeed, if we as individual social workers, do not develop a professional and confident voice - how can we encourage those who use social work services to become empowered and develop a voice?

The importance of social work having a voice in the current political climate is widely recognised and is beginning to bring together a wide range of stakeholders. For example, as we are working on the very final parts of this book the British Association of Social Workers is arranging events with politicians at the various political party conferences to share the voices of social workers.

In many ways the need for a shared voice is also bringing practitioners and academics together, so for example Graeme Simpson presented information about the research project 'The Social Worker's Voice: An exploration of the experiences of being a social worker in times of austerity' asking for practitioners to become involved at a BASW supported seminar in October 2017.

One way of achieving a voice (and hopefully professional recognition) is to join a professional association, as Ruth's stakeholder voice explores:

STAKEHOLDER VOICE — RUTH ALLEN

Ruth Allen is the CEO of the British Association of Social Workers.

Being opinionated and outspoken is part of our shared social work identity and purpose. Social work that makes a real difference often requires a degree of rebellion, courage and persistence - to support the greater courage and persistence so often demonstrated by the citizens we work with.

This is a distinctive and defining thing - and an ethical necessity. Whether through advocating for a person's rights and entitlements in the face of discrimination or exclusion, or enabling a young person to speak for themselves when others want to speak for them, or challenging a deficit approach to mental health so a person can define their own journey of recovery - social workers dig deep and speak out with confidence and hope every day.

Despite this being part of our shared culture and identity, this can feel like a lonely place in practice. Challenge and professional assertion are not always welcome in organisational cultures that still too often expect practitioner conformity rather than informed professional opinion and autonomous decision making.

Eileen Munro captured this last point well in 2011 in her influential systemic review of child protection social work. She described how proceduralism and managerial dictat undermine social work professionalism and ultimately undermine our ability to meet children's (and adults') needs and wishes. She wrote of the importance of moving from a 'doing things right' compliance culture to 'doing the right things', requiring greater autonomy and confidence across the profession.

Implementation of Munro's recommendations and the development of new cultures across social work in the UK have been slow and very patchy - perhaps inevitably because 'slow' is the nature of culture change in organisational systems, but perhaps more because of subsequent contrary governmental policies and deep austerity cuts to services and welfare. These have increased crises and demand, raised thresholds for help (in adults and children's services) and hugely reduced the ecosystem of support options in our communities. The pay and support to social workers themselves has also been hard hit and recruitment, retention and forward workforce planning are in a more uncertain state than in 2011. Not an obvious good seed bed for the flowering of better social work and more fulfilling job roles across the system.

Hindsight is a wonderful thing and Munro produced a powerful and important report that in many ways has stood the test of time. But rereading it now, what also strikes me is how much stronger it might have been, and how many more implementation opportunities may have opened, if there had been an unequivocal emphasis on the importance of social workers building our own stronger culture of professional autonomy and unity through ensuring effective peer support and fulsome encouragement of an independent professional body.

The report is an excellent example of a well-argued case for change in national policy. But it envisages implementation through government, organisational leadership and educationalists shaping and facilitating change in the grassroots - but not really from the grassroots.

Social work operates in highly politicised and contested spaces. While all public professions are shaped by the churn and fickleness of governmental policies - and politicians playing to the gallery - as social workers we are often even more exposed because we embody society's unwanted, messy dilemmas and we shine a light on the injustice of marginalisation and exclusion of fellow citizens. We deal in the uncomfortable stuff and we need to be really organised as a profession, and to tell our own stories of how we use our skills and our values, to make positive difference.

Within the British Association of Social Workers (BASW), like scores of similar national associations across the globe, we have long believed that a strong profession requires a unified and independent platform from which our collective voice can be heard - loud, clear and authoritative. Our 2020 Vision for BASW is to be the Strong, Independent Voice of Social Work and Social Workers. This is essential if the profession is to thrive and grow, through tough times and good in public policy and funding. To be sustainable and have enduring integrity, it must be driven by the energy and expertise of social workers in practice, education, research, leadership and management. It needs to be founded on energetic connectivity and engagement between social workers, debating, building our positive professional discourse, allowing diverse views but with shared purpose to improve services and improve the profession, creating profession-led policy and campaigns, creating platforms to share our ideas within and outside the profession, creating new and better continuous professional development opportunities and learning from the evidence of practice as well as practising in evidence-informed ways.

Our strength and credibility as a profession grows through being stronger together as social workers, but also through our partnerships with others. That is why BASW partners with the Social Workers' Union which offers bespoke, affordable support for practitioners in employment and regulatory contexts with a shared commitment to social work ethics and values. We work alongside other trades unions too and with other professional bodies and colleges who share our vision values in the public, health and care sectors, complementing each other's roles and perspectives.

Of course, a key partnership is with those who use or may use our services. Social work is as good as the experiences and outcomes for those we have the privilege of working alongside for a while. If we are authoritative in our knowledge and capabilities, we are so only in as much as we share what we know and make it available to those who may find it useful. If we are strong in advocating for human rights and social justice we do it in alliance with those most affected and those in other organisations with shared views. Together we can have the influence on building the humane society that our values and ethics promote.

Join and be part of your national association, for better social work, a better society and a great profession.

© Ruth Allen

Whistle-blowing

Whistle-blowing is the phrase used to describe raising concerns about malpractice or other concerns in services and organisations. The Public Interest Disclosure Act (1998) in brief, provides legal protection for staff who whistle-blow, (i.e. make a disclosure). The Act defines the following as grounds for disclosure if the worker has reasonable grounds to believe:

(a) that a criminal offence has been committed, is being committed or is likely to be committed,

(b) that a person has failed, is failing or is likely to fail to comply with any legal obligation to which he is subject,

(c) that a miscarriage of justice has occurred, is occurring or is likely to occur,

(d) that the health or safety of any individual has been, is being or is likely to be endangered,

(e) that the environment has been, is being or is likely to be damaged, or

(f) that information tending to show any matter falling within any one of the preceding paragraphs has been, is being or is likely to be deliberately concealed.

(Part IVA, 43B, Public Interest Disclosure Act, 1998)

The Act gives significant statutory protection to employees who disclose malpractice reasonably and responsibly in the public interest and are victimised as a result. If an employee is victimised or dismissed for this disclosure he / she can make a claim for compensation to an employment tribunal. There is no cap to the amount that can be awarded. Whilst it is not a statutory requirement there is an expectation that organisations will establish their own whistle blowing policy and guidelines.

These guidelines should:

- Clearly indicate how staff can raise concerns about malpractice.
- Make a clear organisational commitment to take concerns seriously and to protect people from victimisation.
- Designate a senior manager with specific responsibility for addressing concerns in confidence which need to be handled outside the usual management-chain. Staff receive the full protection of the Act if they seek to disclose malpractice responsibly, for example, by following the organisation's whistle-blowing policy / guidelines.

Whistle-blowing however is not easy, in 2015, The Telegraph, for example, reported the stories of nine health care professionals who received terrible and sometimes illegal treatment for whistle-blowing in their places of work (Sawyer and Donnelly, 2015). Such was the concern, coupled alongside other scandals, such as that of Mid Staffordshire Hospital, where it is estimated that between 400 and 1,200 patients died because of poor health care over a 50-month period (Campbell, 2013) that Sir Robert Francis chaired an independent review in 2015, of whistle-blowing policies, practices and procedures in the NHS (Francis, 2015).

In the social work and social care fields, there have been some high-profile whistle-blowing incidences. In the Rochdale child abuse scandal, for example, a sexual health worker, Sara Rowbotham, repeatedly raised concerns about gangs of men sexually abusing vulnerable young girls. Margaret Humphreys was a social worker who brought public attention to the British government programme of 'Home Children', which involved forcibly relocating poor British children to other Commonwealth countries (where it was cheaper), the children were often used as child labour and systematically abused.

My Share

Am I familiar with the whistle-blowing guidelines that relate to my practice?

Key points

- Hearing is the second component of the SHARE model.
- The concept of hearing is useful in understanding the complex interplay of communication and relationships.
- There are a range of barriers to really 'hearing' in social work and it is important to explore these with a clear consideration of power dynamics.
- Holistic listening takes account of the other components of the SHARE model and seeks to address the potential barriers to hearing.
- The hearing component can be used to consider and address a number of important issues in social work. We have used this component to consider the use of language, humour and the importance of feedback.
- It is important that social workers seek to ensure that everyone has a voice in society.
- It takes courage to speak up but it is essential that social workers speak up about what they see and hear in their practice.

Reflective Questions

What do you hear in your practice?

What do people hear from you?

What stands out the most for you from this chapter? Why is that?

How do you use your voice in social work? In what ways could you build on this?

Chapter 7: ACTION

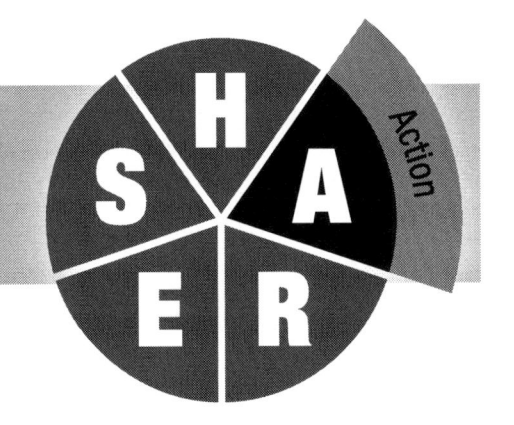

This chapter highlights the centrality of 'action' in the SHARE model. It uses a What? Why? How? framework to consider social work, including discussions on the profession's earliest origins, potential social work role models, the politics of social work policy and practice and examples of activism in contemporary social work. Finally, the chapter concludes with an exploration of stress and burnout in social work and acts of self-care.

SHARE: The centrality of action

It is not an accident that action is the central component of the SHARE model, because we hope that this model will be seen as very much about practice and action is at the heart of the model, so for example:

- What we see and hear will impact on what we do
- What we do impacts on what we see and hear
- What we read will impact on what we do
- What we do will impact on what we record and what we look to read
- We evaluate our action (practice) in light of what we have seen, heard, and read

The way that the other components connect around practice is potentially endless and the fact that action is the central component of the SHARE model illustrates the importance of interconnections in social work.

The connections between action and the other components of the SHARE model are well illustrated by the following proverb, attributed to Confucius, an ancient Chinese Philosopher:

> I hear, I forget
> I see, I remember
> I do, I understand

This proverb is often drawn in terms of adult learning, particularly in relation to experiential learning.

What? Why? How?

In many ways, these three questions form the basis of social work (Maclean 2017). When a social worker first meets a service user they are looking at:

- What is happening for this person?
- Why has this situation come about?
- How can we work together to bring about more positive outcomes?

The problem is that social workers have very busy working lives, sometimes unmanageable caseloads and very tight deadlines. The temptation then is for the social worker to go out to see someone taking the approach of:

- What is happening?
- How can I deal with it?

The *why* question falls off the agenda all too readily. However, the *why* question is vital for professional practice, it is where evaluation comes into play as we discuss in more detail in Chapter 10. Herein lies critical reflection and social work theory. When the why question is missing then practice becomes proceduralised or managerialist. In many ways it also becomes medicalised: After all the medical model is all about what and how without the why (What's the diagnosis? How is it to be treated?)

Action without a consideration of the other aspects of SHARE, or action without a consideration of the why question is potentially dangerous. The importance of the why question is widely acknowledged in terms of effective leadership. For example, Simon Sinek's book 'Start with Why: How Great Leaders Inspire Everyone to Take Action' is an international bestseller and Sinek's work on the why question is widely referred to in leadership training. One of the reasons that each of us finds working with students so refreshing is that they bring the 'why?' question to practice, regularly requiring social workers and managers to think about why they do something in a particular way.

The What? Why? How? framework can be used in a whole range of ways in social work practice. For example, when undertaking a piece of work, it can be used as an evaluation framework, to think about:

- What am I doing?
- Why am I doing it?
- How is it impacting on the situation?

In this chapter, we will use the framework to consider the whole act of social work itself, by exploring the following key questions:

- What is social work?
- Why am I a social worker?
- How do we do social work?

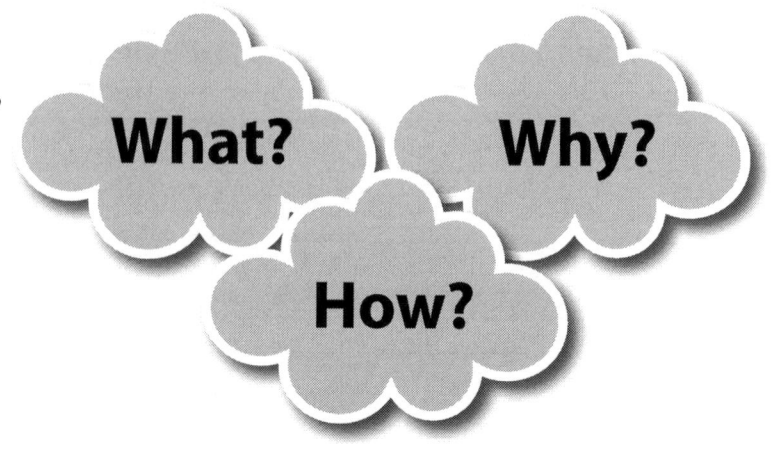

What is social work?

Social work is a contested profession (Finch, 2017) such that a shared understanding of the profession isn't universally agreed. However, how social workers describe what they do is very important in terms of:

- Developing a sense of professional identity
- Sharing with colleagues
- Multi-professional working
- Clarity about role with service users

In our work, we often ask people how they would complete the following sentence:

Social work is...

The answers vary considerably, and we can often tell how long a social worker has been in practice and how they are feeling about their role from the way that they complete the sentence. We have noticed that people are often invited to complete this sentence on social media through the use of hashtags, for example #socialworkis. Again, the responses are very diverse and further illustrate the contested nature of what social workers actually do.

Early in this book we referred to the international definition of social work (see page 22) which starts with 'social work is'. This definition of social work is acknowledged around the world and is in fact enshrined in statute in a number of countries. However, there are consistent challenges to the international definition of social work in contemporary practice, in England at least. So, for example, the first draft of the Health and Social Care Bill put before Westminster Parliament in 2011 completed the phrase as: 'Social work is what social workers do.' In the lead up to this, Jacqui Smith, former Minister of Social Care (quoted in Singh and Cowden 2009: 4) said: *"Social work is a very practical job. It is about protecting people and changing their lives, not about being able to give a fluent and theoretical explanation about why they got into difficulties in the first place."*

More recently the social work apprentice trailblazer group reportedly rejected the international definition when they had to produce the 'apprenticeship standard' (Woodham et al 2017). Given the limited word count for the standard this is understandable. However, the very fact that the newest route into the social work profession is based on a definition agreed between a small group of employers and academics rather than an internationally agreed definition is of concern.

Singh and Cowden (2009) argue that contemporary definitions of social work, such as that articulated by Jacqui Smith assume that 'thinking' and 'doing' are separate activities, whilst in fact social work is an intellectual profession which synthesises theoretical and practical, bringing the thinking and doing together.

There has long been a debate about whether social work is an art or science. We see it as both. Hence, we have referred to drawing from both the arts and science in developing the SHARE model.

Thinking about the history of social work

Understanding what social work is about can be helped greatly by exploring the history of social work and social welfare, as both are closely connected and intertwined. In all societies in history, there have always been those who have, and those who do not have. Many societies and religions have therefore long promoted charity, aid or the giving of alms. In the UK, there has been a long history of state regulated welfare. A key piece of legislation was the Elizabethan Poor Law Act (1601) which provided 'relief' for those in need (Payne, 2005). State funded 'welfare' and social work was not something that just came about post 1945. Indeed, social work as an activity and profession, had its early roots in Victorian philanthropy and charity.

The Victorian era saw rapid industrialisation and a move away from a more rural society to an urban society. This had implications for the types of work people did, and could do. It also led to people moving from the countryside to the cities in search of rapidly changing types of work. The plight of the poor, hidden from the view of richer Victorians, became increasingly visible through what we would now consider to be the anthropological works of Henry Mayhew (1861) and Seebolm Rowntree (1901). Mayhew's book documented the lives of ordinary peoples' precarious employment and poverty in London and Rowntree documented the situation of many people living in poverty in York.

During the Victorian era, more and more protective legislation was passed, due initially in part to poor working conditions in factories, later extending to the protection of children in employment and beyond. This period also saw the emergence of unionists, Charterists and friendly societies. Given the amount of uncoordinated charity and philanthropic work going on, The Charitable Organisation Society (COS) came into existence in 1869 with the purpose of organising relief as well as adopting so called scientific methods to explore the causes of poverty (Smith, 2002). The COS volunteers, were middle or upper-class women, with the task of determining who was eligible, (deserving or non-deserving) of charitable support (Dickens, 2010). These volunteers are often seen as the forerunners of social workers, and it would be nice to think social work has changed for the better, but it is important to think about the lasting legacy of the Victorian era on contemporary social work practice, both positive and negative.

For example, the image of a middle class 'do-gooder' social worker, the practice of putting people into 'asylums' still remains with us and the deserving and non-deserving narratives persist today. On the more positive side, the practice of needing specific knowledge and theory to undertake the role of a COS caseworker, then, was also established, with the first COS volunteers undertaking courses at what became the London School of Economics in 1903 (Finch, 2017).

Felix Biestek was ordained a catholic priest in 1945. He went on to study sociology and gained a social work qualification is the 1950s, becoming a professor of social work. In 1961, Biestek defined seven principles underpinning a positive relationship between a social worker and a service user (in his terms, a client). These are often considered to be the foundations of the professional value base in social work:

1. Individualisation: the service user being treated as an individual.
2. Purposeful expression of feelings: the service user having the opportunity to express feelings.
3. Controlled emotional involvement: the service user should have a sympathetic response from an interested professional who adopts a certain level of emotional involvement.
4. Acceptance: the service user should be seen as a person of worth.
5. Non-judgemental attitude: the service user should not be judged by the worker.
6. Self-determination: the service user should make choices and decisions.
7. Confidentiality: the service user has a right to professional confidentiality.

Biestek's work holds significant bearing for contemporary social work education and practice. So, how do we demonstrate acceptance, non-judgmental attitude, client self-determination and the other principles he proposed? This relates to the 'how' of social work practice and the way that values impact on action.

My Share

How do I demonstrate Biestek's seven principles in my practice?

Social work is considered a relatively new profession compared with older professions like medicine or law. As early as 1915, Flexner, asked the question as to whether social work could be considered a profession. These debates continued and it was labelled a semi-profession at the end of the 1960s by Etzioni (1969) and Toren (1972) because it was felt that it did not conform to the attribute model of professionalism adopted at that time by writers such as Greenwood (1958), who suggested five criteria to distinguish a profession from an occupation. These were:

1) a systematic body of knowledge
2) a professional authority recognised by the public
3) community sanction
4) a regulatory code of ethics
5) a professional culture sustained by formal professional associations

Later writers however (for example, Johnson, 1972 and Cullen, 1978) were more influenced by sociological approaches to the consideration of what is a profession, and utilised theories of power to understand the development of particular professions, and indeed the hierarchies of professions. As such, Weiss-Gal and Welbourne (2008) have combined both approaches in their international study that explored the professionalisation of social work.

They concluded that a profession should be typified by:

> "i) public recognition of professional status; (ii) professional monopoly over specific types of work; (iii) professional autonomy of action; (iv) possession of a distinctive knowledge base; (v) professional education regulated by members of the profession; (vi) an effective professional organisation; (vii) codified ethical standards; and (viii) prestige and remuneration reflecting professional standing"
>
> Weiss-Gal and Welbourne (2008, page unknown)

What are my feelings about the professionalisation of social work?

Social work role models

In Chapter 4 we explored the importance of role models in terms of social learning. The role models that social workers have are important in terms of how they approach social work. We have made some reference to a number of different people who we feel can be seen as role models in social work practice in this book; Martin Luther King, Nelson Mandela, Maya Angelou and Jo Cox to name a few.

In some countries, social work education focuses more on what we can learn from social work role models. However, in our experience this is rarely discussed on social work training in the UK. Although it actually pre-dates him, Isaac Newton popularised the phrase 'we stand on the shoulders of giants'. The idea being that if we learn from those that came before us we can see farther ahead. Here the importance of understanding the history of social work and having social work role models comes together.

Ask yourself can you name a famous nurse? No doubt you will be able to. In fact, it is a requirement of the National Curriculum in England that children are able to do so. The famous nurse you can name is probably Florence Nightingale, or maybe Mary Seacole. Generally, they are seen as very positive role models.

Now, ask yourself can you name a famous social worker? People are less able to do so. Even social workers struggle with this question. Often where they are able to name a 'famous' social worker then it is someone who has become known because of a perceived 'failure'.

We are not in any way seeking to claim that social workers should be famous, nor do we want to promote the social workers as superheroes narrative that has been playing out on social media in recent years, as we recognise the dangers of this. However, the fact that there are very few social work role models referred to in social work training concerns us. We have therefore taken the opportunity to share the story of one inspirational social worker in this chapter, as follows:

Social workers are not superheroes

Irene Sendlerowa (nee Krzyzanowska), widely known as Irena Sendler, was born about 15 miles outside of Warsaw, Poland in 1910. She was the daughter of one of the first Polish socialists. Her father was a doctor and Irena said that she got a profound sense of the importance of social justice and human rights growing up with him. At age 17 Irena expressed a desire to do something around social care. At that time, however, there were no options to study a degree in social care or social work so Irena began a course in law. She transferred to a degree in humanities with a course in social pedagogy during her time at University. When she graduated she worked as a social worker in a mother and child service in Warsaw, progressing to working as a senior social worker in the Warsaw Social Welfare Department.

In 1939 Germany invaded Poland. The Nazi party herded thousands of Jewish people into the Warsaw Ghetto. Disease, starvation and squalor were common place. Irena saw many of the families that she and her team worked with forced into the Ghetto, indeed some of her colleagues were also pushed into the Ghetto. At first Irena and her team colleagues went into the Ghetto to take in food and other supplies. However, the Nazis soon banned social workers from going into the Ghetto, seeing them as potentially political activists who were resistant to the Nazi occupation. They still allowed nurses and medical staff to go into the Ghetto as they were so concerned about the spread of diseases such as typhoid and cholera. Irena dressed as a nurse and was able to get a pass from the epidemic control department which allowed her to continue to get into the Ghetto along with some of her colleagues.

Irena heard stories of the 'death camps' and with her colleagues she began to develop a plan. Recognising the significant threat to the families living in the Ghetto, who could be sent off to the camps at any time, Irena persuaded reluctant Jewish parents to allow her to take their children and place them outside the Ghetto with Christian families so that they could be kept safe until the end of the War. Irena asked local families to take the children in and raise them as their own. It says a great deal about Irena's powers of persuasion in that she reported no one she asked refused to help, even though at that time it was punishable by death to help a Jewish person. There are many stories about how Irena got children out of the Ghetto, in a range of creative ways, some in body bags and some through the sewers system. Working with a number of colleagues and the Polish resistance movement ultimately Irena rescued 2,500 children from the Warsaw Ghetto.

This in itself is a fabulous story of courage and bravery and collaborative practice. However, many people saved Jewish people in the war, we know for example the stories of Kinder transport and Oscar Schindler. What is totally unique about Irena's story is that she took a social worker's perspective. She recognised that she was removing childrens' identity and faith from them as they had to pass themselves off as Christian children. She also recognised that she had severed a number of important ties – for example, she tried not to place siblings together in case they gave each other away by speaking to each other in Hebrew. Irena recorded information about the identity of each of the children she placed, in a code form. This information contained details about the child's identity, their family, their siblings and where they were placed etc. Irena placed all of this information in jars and buried the jars underneath an apple tree near to where she lived.

Irena paid a very significant price for her work. She was arrested by the Gestapo in 1942. They tortured Irena to try and get her to give them information about the children she had placed and the people who had helped. Irena refused to give any information. She reported that every morning a secret police officer came into the cells and read out a list of names. Those people were taken away and never came back and she knew that they had been taken to be killed. One day, Irena's name appeared on the list and she was taken to the firing line in the woods. The resistance movement bribed the guards and Irena was not killed. She was however, beaten very badly and left in the woods for dead. The resistance movement rescued Irena and kept her safe for the rest of the war.

After the war, Irena was able to dig up the jars and give the children back their identities. It took many years to trace all of the children since in times of war and crisis people move around a great deal. Over the years Irena was helped in her quest to give people back their identities by Jewish organisations.

From the 1960s onwards Irena's work was recognised, she was for example recognised by the Yad Vashem in 1965. However, in communist Poland her work was buried for many years. In 1999 a group of students in Kansas, America uncovered Irena's story as part of their work on a history project. They developed a short play about Irena's story which they called 'Life in a Jar'. This became a significant project with the play shown in many countries around the world. It remains a thriving project, with lots of information available on the internet with a simple google of 'life in a jar'.

Whilst Irena's story can be seen as a part of history, understanding Irena's story can help us to explore contemporary practice in a range of ways. What do social workers do when their employer is asking them to do something that they feel very uncomfortable about? What do social workers do to promote social cohesion? What do social workers do in times of crisis? What skills do we need to draw on? Irena's work also demonstrates the importance of recording and in many ways, is the birth of life story practice for social workers. Irena's story is essentially one that all social workers should know.

Irena died on 12 May 2008 at the age of 98 in a Warsaw Nursing Home cared for by one of the children that she smuggled out of the ghetto. She had three children, two sons who both died, and a daughter.

If you are interested in Irena's story and would like to know more, there is a film entitled 'The Courageous Heart of Irena Sendler'. Her memoirs are also available in a range of forms.

STAKEHOLDER VOICE
DONNA PEACH

Donna Peach has 30 years experience in social work with children and families. She now works as an academic and researcher. She is also a member of BASW Council.

Social work is situated at the heart of the struggle between policies which maintain social injustice and those who exist under its oppressive shadow. In practice, many of the functions social workers fulfil represent the Government amid the ever-decreasing provision for those who rely on its welfare. However, without a dedicated government minister social work is fragmented across parliamentarian portfolios leading the whole of our profession to be viewed as less than the sum of its parts. Thus, our capacity to respond well to the needs of people and to ensure they are treated fairly is inadequately supported. The failure of the profession to consistently perform to good enough standards are met with criticism and fast-track training models emerged instead of enduring social investment. Against this world view, social work and those it supports are often vulnerably positioned as damaged and dysfunctional. Simultaneously, social work thrives when engaged with people whose resilience is inspiring, who lift others as well as themselves, who know the meaning of survival. At its best social work understands the need to negotiate these conflicting narratives and is courageous enough to know its strength comes from recognising the contributory value of those we work with. Social work should not be something we do to others, it is about a way of being with people. For social work to be successful there has to be social justice which include a fair distribution of wealth and support for equable wellbeing. Therefore, for social work to perform in a consistently outstanding way it needs to challenge oppressive legislation and social policies, which results in biting the hand that sustains us. This dilemma is not new, but as the 21st Century progresses we can choose what we want the future of social work to be. As social workers we should feel secure in our values but recognise that while we position ourselves as above the adults, children and families we work with, we accentuate the division of people and the State. There is a need for our profession to be bold and to uphold our convictions of co-producing the future so we fully enable everyone to feel entitled to the experience of fairness. I'm reminded of the moment one abseils off a cliff edge, until you fully commit the rope is slack and you fear it will not hold you. Our professional values are the rope and they will sustain us into a future that we cannot predict, but one which we support being co-produced in the pursuit of social justice.

© Donna Peach

The politics of social work

Given the profession's early roots in Victorian philanthropy and charity, often tied up in a moralising Christian discourse, alongside the legislative base of social work, there is a strong political dimension to social work. Social work cannot ever be considered a neutral activity - not least because of our value base, with its very clear commitment and directive to tackle social injustice and inequality, coupled with the scope of practice being laid down in legislation and social policy directives. Social work therefore occupies a unique, but challenging space, between the populace and the government, and the care versus control inherent in social work, is always present. How can social workers be both agents of change as well as agents of the state? How can we really live our social work values, in a society that does not respect such approaches or view of the world? This is becoming increasingly important in a neoliberal world, particularly as new 'social problems' emerge that require a social work response, or indeed, legislation dictates a social work response to something.

Most recently, we can see this political dimension in action, particularly in terms of counter-terrorism work in the UK, that requires many professionals, not just social workers, to actively participate in counter-terrorism work and preventative activities of the state (McKendrick and Finch, 2016). The Counter Terrorism and Security Act (2015) implemented in the UK in the summer of 2015, requires a specified range of front line professionals, including teachers, social workers and medical staff to work within the PREVENT agenda - a policy emanating from Britain's overall counter-terrorism policy, CONTEST (Finch and McKendrick, 2015). The PREVENT agenda thus aims to prevent people being drawn into terrorism and extremism. Given this is new area of practice, one that McKendrick and Finch (2017) argue is being cynically sold by the government as a straightforward (and so non-controversial or problematic) matter of safeguarding. It is also clear, therefore, that there is a practice and a research vacuum. The SHARE model can help social workers and other professionals make sense of this complex issue (and indeed other political issues and concerns).

My Share

How well do I understand the politics of social work?

What impact does this have on my work?

Radicalisation, Extremism and Terrorism

SEE: What do you see on the news? What images are portrayed about terrorism, either abroad or in the UK? How were the recent Manchester and London Bridge / Borough market terrorist attacks reported? What key themes or messages do you see about extremism, radicalisation and terrorism? Is it always associated with so called Islamic terrorism? Do you see right wing extremists portrayed in the same way?

HEAR: What do you hear from different people about the issues? Do you hear viewpoints that are challenging? What have you heard when you attend compulsory PREVENT training? What have you heard about social work's role in countering radicalisation and extremism? Why are social workers involved in this work?

ACT: How far have the recent terror attacks in the UK changed your behaviour? Do you worry more? Why do you worry more? Are you avoiding going into cities or crowded spaces? Do you worry when you see a Muslim man wearing a backpack? Do you challenge Islamophobia when you hear it? What will you do if you work with an individual or family where there are extremist concerns? Is this something social workers should be involved with?

READ: What have you read about extremism or radicalisation? Is it from newspapers or government research? Do you read the associated policy documents? Do you read policy critiques? What do you need to do to become better informed? Why do you need to become better informed?

EVALUATE: What do you know about radicalisation and extremism? Is it something you may encounter in your professional role? How does it impact on you personally? Do you have concerns about it? If so what are your concerns?

You may have noted, the use of what, why and how questions. In this newly emerging field, there tend to be more what and why questions, then how.

STAKEHOLDER VOICE — YASMIN

Yasmin is a Prevent Engagement officer, who trained as a social worker. Yasmin is employed by a local authority which leads on Prevent in her area.

As a Muslim, I think the early stages of Prevent did appear to target Muslim communities. However, lessons have since been learnt and Prevent in the current form focuses on all forms of radicalisation and extremism – far right and Islamist. I have worked as a Prevent Officer for two years, building on the social work training which I undertook many years ago. The Prevent agenda has not been without its challenges and those who oppose Prevent have made it difficult at times to role the mandatory duty out beyond statutory bodies, labelling Prevent as a toxic brand and taking their anti-Prevent stance to social media, posting negative messages on Twitter, WhatsApp, Facebook, Instagram and Telegram. However, this has not hindered my commitment to drive forward the Prevent agenda and plan locally. I have successfully engaged diverse communities through Prevent project work, workshops and case work, breaking down barriers and Prevent myths, creating spaces for community members to meet and discuss radicalisation, extremism and other safeguarding strands such as CSE, Human Trafficking, FGM, Forced Marriages, Gangs and Hate crime.

I have found the opportunity to engage in preventative programmes with the local community a really liberating way of working. Much of this draws upon taking an educational approach to support learning and promote change and I have begun to recognise how important this is for everyone working in social work and social care.

I see the SHARE model as potentially helpful in my work in a variety of ways. For example, vulnerable young people are often radicalised by what they hear, this generally gives people a distorted view of doctrines, so I work to link people at risk of radicalisation with others in their local community so that they can hear different messages about their faith or beliefs. One of the criticisms of Prevent is that it shuts down conversations when in fact what we seek to do is promote an open transparent dialogue which can help people to see things differently. What people see and hear certainly impacts on what they do and one of the key things I seek to do is promote critical thinking, conversations and debate. The impact of fake news on people is also a major concern and part of my work involves supporting people to think analytically about what they are reading. A key element of working in contemporary safeguarding areas such as Prevent is being digitally competent and understanding sharing in this context is important.

© Yasmin

Social Work as a Human Rights profession

We all share human rights. Human Right are the rights and freedoms that belong to all individuals regardless of nationality and citizenship. Those rights that are inherent in our nature and without which we cannot live as human beings.

The centrality of human rights in social work is recognised in the international definition of social work (see page 22) and reiterated by Ruth Stark, the President of the International Federation of Social Workers who describes social work as *"a human rights discipline. It's not just an element of it - it is the core principle."* (Schraer 2014)

Social workers should be interested not only in the causes of peoples' problems, difficulties and undesirable circumstances, but they must also ensure that any strategies or interventions planned serve to reinforce human rights values and principles. Segal (2011) proposed the term 'social empathy' which is defined as the ability to perceive and experience people's life situations in order to gain awareness and insight about inequalities and disparities. Social empathy therefore has a social justice and human rights leaning.

Rights: the legislative background

The Universal Declaration of Human Rights was adopted in 1948 by the United Nations General Assembly and represents the first international agreement of the principles of human rights and fundamental freedoms. It forms the foundation for UK laws in relation to Human Rights. Its preamble states that:

> *"recognition of the inherent dignity and of the equal and inalienable rights of all members of the human family is the foundation of freedom, justice and peace in the world.*
>
> *Human Rights and fundamental freedoms allow us to fully develop and use our human qualities, our intelligence, our talents and our conscience and to satisfy our spiritual and other needs"* (United Nations 1987)

The Human Rights Act 1998 came into force in the UK in 2000 and protects everyone in the UK, without exception. All public authorities (the NHS, local authorities, prisons, and central government) have a duty to respect and promote the human rights of people it comes into contact with during the course of their work.

Whilst there is no hierarchy of rights, there are some Articles that are more frequently cited and referred to in social work than others. For example, we often hear Article 8 'the right to respect for private and family life' quoted in cases around immigration or separation. Also, Article 10 (Freedom of expression) is regularly cited in relation to the freedom to express one's opinions and speech.

In the wake of the 'war against terror' and global insecurity, much of the world has taken a cynical view towards human rights. Questions have been asked in the media about how human rights could possibly be a consideration for people who have committed atrocities. This view became topical political discourse when earlier in 2017, Prime Minister Theresa May said *"The European Convention on Human Rights can bind the hands of parliament, adds nothing to our prosperity, makes us less secure by preventing the deportation of dangerous foreign nationals and does nothing to change the attitude of governments like Russia's when it comes to human rights"*. As the provisions of the Human Rights Act are often contested, this has resulted in the UK government consulting on withdrawing the Human Rights Act 1998 from UK law. If the legislation that supports human rights in the UK can be revoked because of political pressure this again reinforces the issues of the politics of social work.

In addition to the Human Rights Act 1998, the United Nations Convention on the Rights of the Child (UNCRC) came into effect in 1989 and outlines human rights specifically for children. The Convention has 54 articles that cover all aspects of a child's life and set out the civil, political, economic, social and cultural rights that all children everywhere are entitled to. It also explains how adults and governments must work together to make sure all children can enjoy all their rights.

The Equality Act 2010 sought to bring together several separate pieces of legislation with a focus on protecting people from discrimination in the workplace and in society in general. The Act identified nine characteristics which made its bearers more vulnerable to discrimination than others. The Act therefore makes it an offence to discriminate (directly or indirectly) against the bearers of the nine protected characteristics of age, race, disability, gender reassignment, sex, sexual orientation, pregnancy and maternity, religion and belief and marriage and civil partnership.

Human rights and SHARE

The SHARE model mirrors core human rights principles and values as has already been mentioned throughout this book, however we ask readers to think about a case of domestic abuse and consider how they might apply human rights values and principles using the SHARE model.

Questions that must be at the fore of a social workers mind include:
- What am seeing? (pain, bruising, hurt, trauma, injury, fear)
- What am I hearing about the experiences of the victims and perpetrators?
- What will I do and what can I empower and support the victim to achieve?
- What do I know about domestic abuse and what have I learnt from this specific intervention? Is there any case law which might support or undermine my case?
- How might I make sense of the information, resulting in intervention or future action?

A social worker will need to consider the following articles contained in the Human Rights Act 1998 in relation to a case involving domestic abuse.

Article 2 Right to Life
Article 3 Freedom from torture, inhumane or degrading treatment
Article 4 Freedom from slavery and forced labour
Article 5 The right to liberty and security
Article 8 Respect for private and family life, home and correspondence
Article 14 Protection from discrimination

More specifically for children, a social worker might wish to refer to the following under the UNCRC:

Article 16 The right to privacy
Article 19 The right to be protected from all forms of harm, neglect and abuse
Article 24 The right to the highest attainable standards of health and health care
Article 31 The right to play, rest and leisure
Article 39 The right of the child to counselling and support if they have experienced abuse, harm and neglect

The list above is not exhaustive and social workers must remember there will be the need to understand the range of legal rules which apply to a particular service user or family.

Getting down to the WHY question - Why am I a social worker?

Research by Grant and Kinman (2015) indicates that social workers who have a strong 'core' can 'survive' the stresses of practice, creating social workers who can fly after their first year in practice. Understanding why we do things can be really helpful in terms of developing this strong core. Indeed, Korthagen and Vasalos (2009) suggest that the deepest 'layer' of criticality in reflection is that of 'mission' promoting a clear core for practice.

Often people coming into social work as a career think about the 'why' question regularly, certainly a great deal of work is carried out within social work education to help students explore why they want to be a social worker. However, consideration of this often lessens when a worker has been in practice for some time, in fact consideration about the 'mission' for practice is often the opposite. We hear social workers every day saying something like, "*this isn't why I became a social worker*". So, imagine the following conversation:

Think about it. 'I wanted to work with people' isn't enough is it? Hairdressers work with people, taxi drivers work with people, teachers work with people.... Why social work?

What happens is that over time social workers can become focused on 'this isn't why I became a social worker'. Social workers understand thinking processes. We know that when we focus on negatives, we find negatives; feelings, thoughts and actions are interconnected. If we focus on why we *didn't* become a social worker then we will find that every day in our practice. Conversely if we focus on why we *did* become a social worker we will find that every day in our practice. We have noted that a sure-fire way to reconnect with the 'why' we became a social worker, is to work with social work students, becoming a practice educator is really helpful in clarifying our overall professional 'mission'.

To avoid a potentially downward spiral which can pull a worker towards compassion fatigue or cynical practice, social workers need to recognise:

- The 'what we do' and 'why we do it' remain the same. They are our core.
- 'How we do it' and 'where we do it' might change. Certainly, the forms that we fill in will change constantly! This offers possibilities and opportunities as well as challenges.

How do we do social work?

If we tried to give a full answer to this question then this book would never end! However, we have included the question, since we do feel strongly that:

It's not what you do it's the way that you do it

And it's not just because this was a Bananarama song in our youth that we feel strongly about this. Whilst what we do as social workers is important, the way that we do it is perhaps even more so.

Maya Angelou, the well-known American poet and civil rights activist wrote the poem 'This is what I have learned'. The last line of the poem reads. *"I've learned that people will forget what you said, people will forget what you did, but people will never forget how you made them feel."* This line speaks to us, it has relevance for social workers. We are working with people when they are at their most vulnerable and the power that we have to make a real difference to a person's life just in the way that we act towards them must never be underestimated.

STAKEHOLDER VOICE — JAN BURNS

Jan Burns MBE, is a registered social worker. She is the chair of the National Dignity Council. She was awarded her MBE in 2016 for her dedication to the promotion of Dignity for all.

The role of the National Dignity Council is to promote dignity for all. It can only be successful in delivering this key aim by influencing the practice of a wide range of staff working with those using social care and social work services, and educating those who use services, and their carers and families, that they have a right to be treated with dignity at all times.

What do we mean by 'dignity'? This can be difficult to put into words but people are often very clear when they have not been treated with dignity. They reach this conclusion, consciously and unconsciously, by themselves assessing a wide range of factors - verbal and non-verbal - in terms of how staff look at them, speak to them, physically respond to them, the choices and opportunities they are offered, the decisions they are invited to make etcetera.

In this sense every human interaction has elements of assessment and critical reflection, albeit not in the professional, social work meaning.

Intervention in an individuals' life in the form of a social work assessment often occurs at a point of crisis - it can be invited and welcomed or enforced upon an unwilling subject. In either case, the individual and their wider networks are likely to be at their most vulnerable and least able to become involved as active and empowered participants in the assessment process. Dignity is as fundamental to social work as adherence to the law. Treating people with kindness, respect and compassion from the outset of the assessment process is the most critical component of building the humanistic relationships which underpin effective assessment.

The Care Act 2014 set out a clear vision of an assessment process that would deliver care that is built around the whole person, with the person concerned having control of their care and support, and care and support plans being developed that meet the needs and outcomes of the person, in ways that work best for them as an individual or family.

Person centred and person led assessments which effectively reflect a person's true wishes and feelings, their needs, values and aspirations and deliver outcomes which promote independence, choice and control can only be achieved by establishing relationships based upon kindness, respect and compassion along with a willingness to empathise with others. This will often require time and space to achieve, which poses questions more broadly about organisations and the potential conflict between the value base they espouse and the real-time implementation and operation of service delivery.

The Dignity in Care campaign has over 88,000 registered champions, its mission is - dignity in our hearts, minds and actions, translating as don't just feel it - don't just think it - take action to ensure that kindness, respect and compassion is afforded to everyone at all times. Just to imagine that if everyone was committed to operating and living this way what a massive difference we could make. We all know what it feels like to not be treated with dignity, so why not do something about it - after all an action as small as a smile costs nothing.

© Jan Burns

In Chapter 2, we outlined the importance of principles like kindness and compassion in our own approach to practice. The use of the word share for the model highlights the way we think social work should be undertaken, within a head, heart and hands framework.

Managerialism in social work

Much has been written about the rise of the managerialist approach in contemporary social work (see for example, Ferguson, 2007; Webb, 2007; Rogowski, 2010; Munro, 2011) which is characterised by case management, accountability, targets and evidence based practice. Managerialism, is seen as removing creativity and potentially the 'heart and soul' from practice.

New public management approaches came into particular prominence in the New Labour government era (1997-2010) although its early development was promoted by Thatcher's neoliberal position. Target setting, inspection regimes and public surveillance are all part of this move. Munro (2011) commented that the impact on social work of such approaches had not been positive, with a focus on meeting targets at the expense of a more intuitive, and responsive social work approach. The unintended consequences of new managerialism, was evidenced very starkly in a large ethnographic study by Broadhurst et al (2010) and White et al (2010) which revealed how performance indicators impacted adversely on initial referral decisions and how the integrated care system, a computerised system of tracking social work activity, also impacted negatively on social work.

Managerialism could be described as conveyor belt social work

My Share

In what ways could my practice be viewed as managerialist?

What could I do about this?

Radical social work

The word 'radical' has perhaps now become somewhat overshadowed by the term radicalisation and extremism. Nonetheless, as we saw in the brief discussion of the history of social work, some of the early pioneers in social work, were social reformers and would have been considered radical in their day, not least the female social reformers, who were certainly going against Victorian sensibilities about the role of women in society.

Radical social work emerged particularly strongly in the 1970s in the UK (Ferguson and Woodward, 2007). At its core, and still very much influential today in social work, were structural analyses and explanations for why people were in poverty, for example. Radical social work therefore had its roots in Marxist theory, feminism, social constructionism and counter culture (Turbett, 2014). A key text in the 1970s was the book 'Radical Social Work' published in 1975 and edited by Roy Bailey and Mike Brake (Lavalette, 2011). Radical social work emerged as an attempt to stem the worst effects of capitalism and within radical approaches, was an accompanying focus on consciousness raising. As Bailey and Brake (1975) remind us, radical social work should focus on understanding oppression in the context of social and economic structures, rather than an ideology of individual blame and pathology. A radical social worker's role should therefore be based on positive assistance, mutual respect, and locating the service user's problems within the wider social and political context. As it can be seen, such socio-political theories are influential today, as evidenced by the requirements for social workers to understand people in their wider social contexts. During the 1980s however, radical social work rather lost its way, given the turbulent political times and the emergence of neoliberalism and neoconservatism under the Thatcher government, and the massive changes wrought to social welfare and the unions.

In recent years, a new radicalism is growing in social work and it is interesting to note a significant amount of new writing in the field. Organisations such as SWAN: The Social Work Action Network are growing in strength and a range of international links are being made in this resurgence of radical social work.

Whilst we do not make the claim that the SHARE model is an essentially radical model, its underlying principles very much accord with some of the hopes of radical social work in the 1970s in the UK, namely that barriers are broken down between social workers and those who we serve, and that more humane ways of practice can emerge.

Radical social work is re-emerging

STAKEHOLDER VOICE
NORA DUCKETT

Nora is the social work course leader at University of Suffolk.

For social work to be radical is to act in ways that promote the values of the profession and oppose all forms of social injustice including abuse, oppression, inequality, disadvantage and discrimination. Vasilios Ioakimidis, (2016) a founding member of SWAN (Social Work Action Network) sees radical social work as historically referring to *"a political theory and practice that aims to understand the root causes of social problems as structurally caused"* and crucially as *"action that aims at social change"*.

SWAN sees social workers and people who use social work services as allies against violent and oppressive social structures which construct and maintain inequality; privileging the haves and demonising, even despising the have nots. This is most evident in current economic austerity measures that construct poverty as willful and a benefit class as a justified target of swinging public sector cuts. People's lives become the collateral damage of political ideology and despair is seen as inevitable.

Social workers are part of that construction if they are aware or not. Several years ago I attended a SWAN conference entitled 'We didn't come into social work for this!' and I found myself surrounded by people who were determined to act to bring about social change. In the speeches and conversations I had over the days of the conference I heard myself and others say what are SWAN doing about injustice wreaking havoc on peoples lives? I slowly realised that action to oppose oppression started with me. Subsequently I joined a collection of others and organised regional SWAN group meetings, seminars and a conference promoting social work voices. Being involved in these activities I began to see things differently and I found my voice in the conversations and in how I interacted with students, service users and others.

The scale of social inequality and oppression can feel overwhelming and leave us in a type of stunned inertia. Where do you start and what difference will it make? However each action to oppose social injustice is a step in a radical direction and part of an historical tradition. The community activist Saul Alinsky, likens an activist to an artist who spends a lifetime painting a tiny leaf

"what keeps him going is a blurred vision of a great mural where other artists – organisers – are painting their bits, and each piece is essential to the total" (1971:75).

© Nora Duckett

Social work has the X Factor: Praxis

In Chapter 2 we explored the concepts of complexity and reflexivity in social work practice. However, the X Factor that social work has, doesn't end there, as praxis is vitally important. This chapter could have also been called the praxis chapter, as in short, praxis means action or doing. Praxis sounds like a complicated notion, not least in that praxis has long been debated philosophically for many thousands of years, for example, Plato and Aristotle, had plenty to say about praxis.

The idea crosscuts a number of fields and disciplines, for example, education, medicine and philosophy to name but a few, and the meaning of praxis is subtly different in each area. We use the term to mean the process by which a theory, or a skill becomes embodied in action. It can also mean an act of engaging, applying, practising or realising practical ideas. In other words, it's the movement between reflection and thinking and doing. If we go back to Kolb's learning model for example (see page 80), this gives us a diagrammatic or pictorial way to think about the process, although of course we would caution that in the real world, it is not such a linear process. Freire, mentioned previously in Chapter 5, also used the concept of praxis in his book 'The Pedagogy of the Oppressed'. For Friere, praxis used in educational settings, meant going beyond dialogue between educatee and educator to aid understanding and deepen knowledge, in order to make a difference in the world through action.

Gramsci, an Italian political theorist and sociologist, who was imprisoned by Mussolini for his radical neoMarxist ideas, argued that praxis, was an action (or actions) related to changing society (Haralambos and Holborn, 2013). Gramsci coined the phrase the 'philosophy of praxis' which is the process of making philosophy and politics into one, so both thinking and acting (Gramsci 1973). Whilst coming from different disciplines, (Friere was primarily an educationalist and Gramsci a sociologist and political theorist), both called strongly for action, praxis, with the aim of changing society for the better: both theorists have a desire to make society better and fairer and to help those oppressed. We can see some resonance with social work practice, therefore, but it is important to note that praxis means more than just 'action' or 'doing', but thinking, reflecting and doing. The SHARE model therefore encourages such an inner Frierian dialogue (as well as dialogue with others) with an expectation of praxis.

We see praxis as connecting the components of the SHARE model with action. The following share from Prospera illustrates the way that she drew on all the components of SHARE in taking action to develop the MANDELA model.

I can sing, dance and play all at once. I've got the PraXis factor!

Praxis is the X Factor in social work. Thinking, reflecting and doing all at once.

Prospera Shares

My early years in social work education revealed a somewhat unequal outcome for students from Black African backgrounds and it appeared that practice learning experiences exacerbated these unequal outcomes. What became clear to me was that student voices had been heard but not necessary listened to across the country, and also abroad (Canada, USA, Australia). I observed student experiences and heard students' narratives. I had also been drawn to reading literature and research about their experiences in social work education and practice learning in particular. Having done this, I did not feel able to do nothing. I needed to take action.

I therefore developed the MANDELA model as a contribution to understanding the context of Black African student experiences and to provide a framework with which practice educators could understand the world of their Black African students in a much more empathic way.

In 2016, the MANDELA model was formally evaluated and the strengths and limitations were identified and highlighted (Tedam and Munowenyu 2016). A key outcome of the evaluation was the development of the MANDELA cards which are a practical tool to be used during practice supervision between students and their practice educators.

In linking the MANDELA model to the SHARE model, the parallels are around:

What is the practice educator seeing? What kind of student do they see? Conversely what image is the student seeing as their practice educator?

What is the practice educator hearing? Accents have been highlighted as resulting in unequal treatment and bias against black African students. Similarly, what does the student hear from their practice educator? Positive affirmation, negative, harsh and unwarranted criticism? Supportive and empowering feedback?

In terms of action what will the student do in the placement? What kinds of activities / learning opportunities will the student be involved in?

Has the practice educator read about the student and what they hope to get from the placement? Has the student read and understood the policies and procedures in relation to the agency / organisation?

How will the student evaluate their placement? What will the practice educator and on-site supervisor write about the student? Have they passed? Why? What are the areas of improvement required?

Making time to get to know a student should assist with the development of a healthy relationship. Understanding a student's needs and differences will help in formulating a plan which will be used to work with the student. The area of lived experiences is significant because a practice educator will need to know whether there are any areas of the student's life which mean certain cases or learning opportunities should be avoided at certain points in the placement until the practice educator has had the chance to work with the student to enable them undertake learning in this area.

Educational experiences are also important because we learn from previous education. It may be that the student has read and observed important things from previous education (formal or informal). The student may be able to evaluate their experiences of education which occurred in a country other than the one they are currently living in.

In using the MANDELA model, we are sharing ourselves with our students but with a clear purpose of initiating and hopefully maintaining relationships between students and their practice educators.

Activism

In many countries around the world, social workers are engaged in social, political and environmental activism. Swank and Fahs (2014) writing about USA, have suggested that social work pre-qualifying programmes should make every effort to motivate activism by highlighting the exploitation and discrimination faced by individuals. They further propose that social work educators promote activism through formal coursework and the provision of practice opportunities for social and political engagement as well as advocacy. One of the concerns we have about employer-led social work training is that by the very nature of being employer-led they will not address issues of radical practice and challenging the status quo.

There is a long history therefore of campaigning and activism, that whilst not always directly related to social work, nonetheless impacts. We can of course consider the early Victorian philanthropists, charities and pioneers of social work as activists. Some of those charities are still in existence today in the UK, the National Society for the Prevention of Cruelty to Others is now the NSPCC, The National Children's Homes, now Action for Children, the YMCA and the Coram Foundation. There were also many individual people whose names are familiar today, people, like Octavia Hill, who campaigned for social reform in education and housing, Elizabeth Fry who campaigned for prison reform, William Wilberforce who campaigned to abolish slavery and Florence Nightingale of course, who at the time, revolutionised nursing and medical practice. Activism is not something new in the history of social work, and we should consider activism as part and parcel of how we operationalise our values through our action, either in specific campaigns or specific issue groups, or in our day to day work, we might engage in activism on a micro level in terms of the individuals or families we are working with. Brian's stakeholder voice, discusses his long-standing work in a campaigning and support group for people impacted by child sexual abuse.

STAKEHOLDER VOICE
BRIAN DOUIEB

Brian is a social work academic.

Before I became a social worker I was a political and community activist concerned with social justice. I was involved in service user campaigns and the struggle in 1972 to keep the Paddington Day Hospital (PDH) open, which had been threatened with closure under the then Conservative Government cuts. PDH was a NHS therapeutic community which, had 'patients' co-managing the Unit and shunned the use of drugs (Spandler, 2006). Like RD Laing, the Unit's consultant (anti-)psychiatrist, Julian Goodburn believed medication 'replaced the bars of Bedlam' putting the locked doors inside the patient, arguing it didn't offer the solution to mental 'illness' (Laing 1965). Ken Loach's film Family Life encapsulated anti-psychiatry and how victim blaming serviced an unjust socio-economic system (Ryan 1970, Spandler 2006, Loach 1971).

I became a founder of the Mental Patients' Union (MPU) which emerged from PDH (Durkin and Douieb, 1975). Like the then Liberation / Rights movements, MPU fought for 'patients' rights and established a Declaration of Intent proclaiming the Rights of Mental 'Patients' (Roberts, 2017). It took direct action against oppressive 'treatments' and had nationwide branches, including in secure hospitals like Rampton and Broadmoor. Influenced by the theoretical perspectives of Friere (1972), Alinsky (1971) and aspects of Marxist thinking, it was a service user led and controlled organisation.

Involvement in MPU led to other community work outside of London. I organised an adventure playground with local families, established a crèche for a women's study group and set up alternative bookshops which served as base for other community campaigns, direct action and a local free press. A few years later in London, I was part of a collective which established the Archway Road Life Widening Scheme in North London. It involved the community squatting compulsory purchased buildings and creating a garden, women's centre welfare and legal rights service, café, bookshop and craft workshops.

I later qualified as a social worker and carried these ideas and experiences forward into my practice as a generic social worker. Community work was not included in my course however as a patch based generic social worker it was possible to incorporate these methods at a local level to address poverty and support residents of local council estates. I set up the Camden Clothing Exchange in a community centre, run and managed by service users, but subsidised by the Local Authority and utilising contributions from more wealthy areas (Davies 2016).

Projects like this were short-lived given cutbacks and the year-long Camden social work strike from 1991-2 when I was a NALGO shop steward and in which the overwhelming majority of practitioners took part (Martin 1991). The strike was in response to Camden's reneging on the national pay agreement in the context of increased legislative responsibilities conferred on social workers. When strikers became the target of sackings and redundancies I moved to another authority.

As a CSA survivor and social worker, I became acutely aware of the extent of child sexual abuse. In a children and families team, as an agency Guardian ad Litem and acting as an Independent Person (Children Act 1989), I began to investigate child sexual abuse in residential schools. It became increasingly clear that alleged perpetrators re-appeared across a range of child care resources and communities, indicating widespread organised abuse networks. My concern about organised abuse continued when I was a children's social work manager with responsibility for Unaccompanied Asylum Seeking Children, Looked After Children, Leaving Care / 16+ and the investigation of child abuse and child trafficking. Since leaving local authority, I have been active in exposing institutional abuse, perpetrators and those who facilitated the networks.

From 2000 I worked with the child abuse survivor movement including as a Trustee with the National Association of People Abused in Childhood which supports adult survivors and in establishing the WhiteFlowers Campaign. WhiteFlowers grew from the survivors calling for action and justice in the context of allegations against the Establishment (politicians, judiciary, etc.). It was inspired by the Belgian White March in 1996. Demonstrators marched in Brussels carrying white flowers to remember children abducted, abused and murdered by a paedophile ring involving members of the Belgian establishment. WhiteFlowers held vigils outside former children's homes and two large meetings in the House of Commons chaired and presented by survivors (islingtonsurvivors.co.uk/white-flowers). The campaign quickly spread nationwide, calling for the now established national inquiry.

At a time when social work is being privatised at an alarming pace for business gain and increasingly proceduralised as a form of state control of the population, it is more important than ever for social workers to actively campaign alongside survivors and others struggling against oppression, discrimination, inequality and abuse. This is the heart of social work practice, the reason I became a social worker and why I continue to be an activist for social justice and human rights.

© Brian Douieb

Of course, actions can be big or small *"Every little helps"* as the advert goes for a major supermarket. As we go on to explore in the next section, not feeling one has done enough can lead to feelings of stress, or concerns that we are not making a difference. But it's important to take conscious note of, and consider all the things we each do in terms of action, in both our professional and personal lives. We need to focus on the things we have achieved, and the actions we have taken, rather than on the things we have not done. In the following share, Jo discusses how she took a small action in a meeting.

Jo Shares

I worked in a charity that was contracted by two local authorities, to offer a range of children and families services, including parenting and family assessments, direct work with parents and carers, group work as well as play therapy with children. I was offering a series of play therapy sessions to a young boy of around 12. The family were experiencing some difficulties but I recall lots of professional hope around the boy and his mother but also some anxiety as the boy was not in mainstream school but in a pupil referral unit (PRU) and had been fire setting. I recall a review meeting with the professionals involved, his mum and the young man. I felt the professionals were somewhat focused on the negative aspects of his conduct and behaviour. I noticed the young man looked disengaged and crest fallen. In the play therapy sessions however, I had observed this young person's great imagination and story-telling abilities, as well as his ability to put on accents and mimic people, and so I fed that back to everyone in the meeting and suggested he might benefit from drama / acting lessons. This is not to say that the concerns noted by other professionals were not accurate, but I did feel his many positive qualities and clear talents had been overlooked. At that point in the meeting, I recalled he began to engage and said he would like to go to drama lessons.

I hoped that my 'action' did make a difference for this child and his mum, who had sat very quietly in the meeting, looking, I felt very sad. I hoped too that this simple action impacted on the professionals around this young man, to see him not as a problem to be solved, but as someone who had talents, skills and abilities.

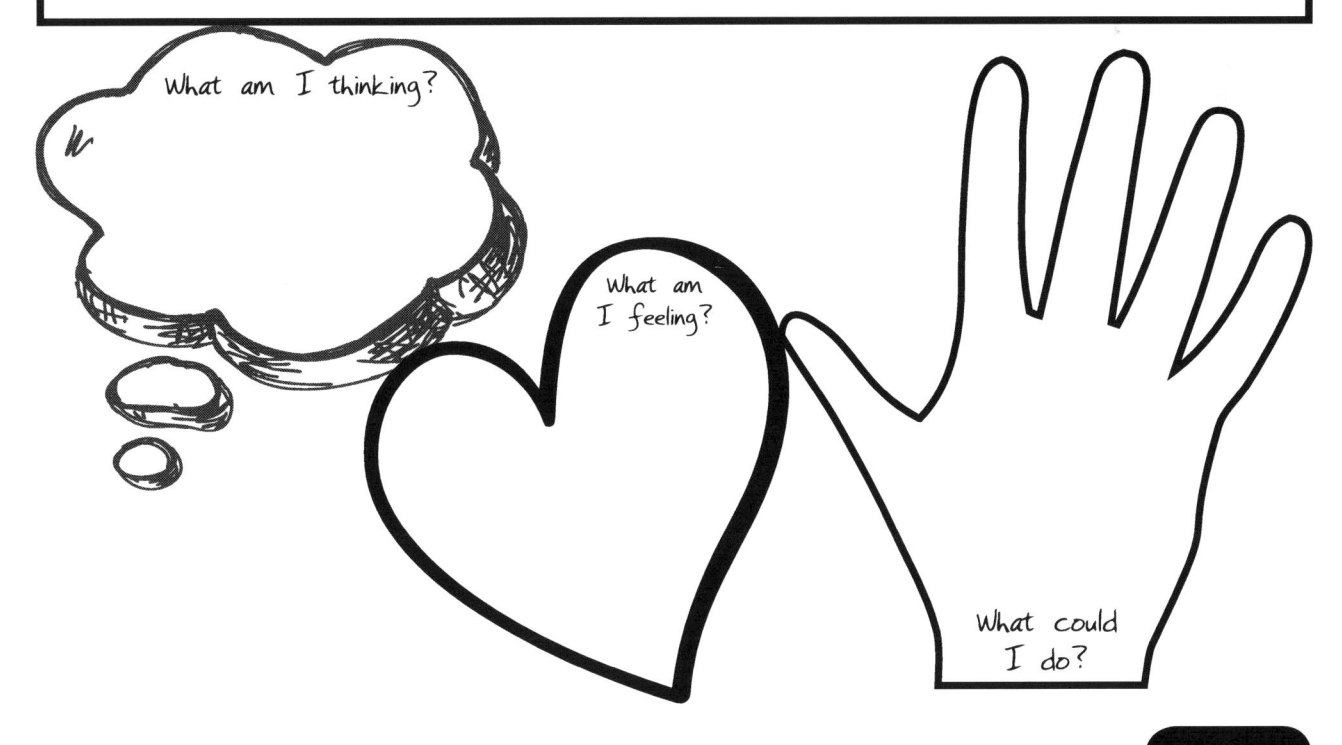

What am I thinking?

What am I feeling?

What could I do?

Boot Out Austerity

In England, a recent example of social work activism is Boot Out Austerity. We are fortunate that a group of the social workers involved in this action have written about their experiences, for inclusion in this chapter.

Reading can lead to doing, and the mention of a protest walk by a group of psychologists in an article by Psychologists Against Austerity inspired a group of social workers to don their walking boots to walk the 100 miles from Birmingham - the head office of the British Association of Social Workers (BASW) to be precise - to Liverpool - the venue for the 2017 BASW Conference and AGM. To issue the call to Boot Out Austerity!

Over 100 people joined the walk at some point, and at the core of this group were the '7-day walkers', eight people who walked the whole way together, sang together, visited austerity-embattled social care agencies together, and listened together to the testimony of service users who have borne the brunt of these devastating and all-too-unnecessary austerity measures.

Allison Hulmes, professional officer with BASW Cymru, was a 7-day walker and here she shares her thoughts:

As soon as I became aware of the Boot Out Austerity walk, I knew right away that I wanted to be part of it, because I am a social worker and I am angry.

I am a social worker and angry having seen the impact of continued austerity on the families and communities we support, and it is devastating. Use of food banks has become normalised for too many families, along with an acceptance that your home is temporary and not a place of sanctuary and refuge, where you and your children will experience stability, security and lay down life-long memories - too often benefit sanctions lead to a situation where you will lose your tenancy.

I am in a better position to reflect on the walk now that the blisters have healed! What strikes me most is the sense of comradeship and community that was formed along the way, not just amongst the 7-day walkers, but by all those who walked, even if just for half a day. I have thought about the reasons for this, and my conclusion is that we all witnessed the impact of austerity first-hand and we carried a shared belief that what we were doing was right and that we could make a difference. The conversations with ordinary people along the roadside affirmed this and were key to the success of our walk. Their stories and support gave us energy and hope. Having my Welsh flag on my rucksack throughout the walk, and then spotting another, made me think about how far people had come to take part - including Margaret from Exeter who had been trained by the Lady Almoners. We are one BASW.

Having backup, whether from our fellow walkers or our incredible drivers - Malcolm and Willie - was crucial. When times are difficult we all need to know that someone is standing alongside us, in our corner, willing us to do well. This is what we do as social workers - we stand alongside individuals, families and communities, looking for strengths, building capacity and co-producing solutions.

I am a social worker, and I have hope. I walked because I had no other choice. I will continue along with my social work family, to stand alongside those we support, to directly challenge the impact of austerity in all its manifestations.

As well as being a collective and physical action, Boot Out Austerity was full of creativity. Peter Unwin, social work lecturer at Worcester University, wrote the song Boot Out Austerity Blues for the walk, and as the self-styled Poet Austeriate wrote a daily poem recounting each day's events, which was recited at the next morning's rally before we set off on that day's walking. Angi Naylor, a retired social worker and member of the Social Workers Union Executive, brought her guitar and had us singing - in the words of The Who - Anyway, Anyhow, Anywhere! Here's Angi describing our arrival in Liverpool, singing the words of her song.

Never was I more proud nor more determined to do more and 'stand up for the Daniel Blakes' of this world than when I walked arm-in-arm towards the Pier Head with my fellow 7-day walkers, singing out loud:

'Rise Up, Rise Up and come with me, we'll march in solidarity,

Social workers one and all, listen to my rallying call...

From Birmingham to Liverpool in twenty seventeen,

We'll march for the rights of those who cannot fight, to Boot Out Austerity'.

Since arriving in Liverpool that late April day, the energy of the walk and the walkers has invigorated BASW's anti-austerity campaigning. We added our efforts to the campaign to encourage people to register to vote and use their vote in the General Election. We have been presenting and sharing our message around the UK - and beyond, as social workers around the world have been telling us how they have been inspired by the walk. We will continue, until there is social justice and the investment in public services needed to ensure the increased equality that will benefit us all. Boot Out Austerity marches on!

For more details visit:
www.boot-out-austerity.co.uk
and follow us on Twitter:
@BootAusterity

Days of action

Dedicating certain days to particular themes is fairly common in terms of promotions and campaigns. Whilst there can be criticism of this in that it can sideline issues to being of importance only on the allotted day, there is some value to bringing attention to topics through a day of action.

World Social Work Day

World Social Work Day was launched by the International Federation of Social Workers in 1983, originally as Social Work Action Day. Since it began other social work organisations such as the International Association of Schools of Social Work (IASSW) have joined as partners in the day. World Social Work Day is celebrated on the third Tuesday of March every year and the Global theme is agreed by IFSW and IASSW. The theme for 2019-2020 will be around promoting the importance of human relationships, which is a key aspect of the SHARE model.

Social Workers around the world take action on World Social Work Day, according to IFSW (2017) this involves social workers *"bringing messages to their governments, communities, and peer professional groups on the unique and significant contributions of the social work profession."*

One important aspect of World Social Work Day which some social workers do not hear about is the celebration of the day at the United Nations. There have been annual celebrations at the UN Headquarters in New York since 1983 and in Geneva since 2012. Sporadically World Social Work Day has also been celebrated at the United Nations in Vienna, Nairobi, and Santiago de Chile. In 2017 for the first time the day was celebrated at the UN in Bangkok. This connection with the United Nations is vitally important for social work as a profession where IFSW have special consultative status with the United Nations Economic and Social Council.

My Share

- What have I done to celebrate WSWD?
- What will I do next year?

Adult PSW Network activities

The Adult Principal Social Worker Network in England celebrate a range of action days. For example, they have supported Hospital Social Work Day, National AMHP day and most recently they celebrated the 10th birthday of the Mental Capacity Act. These days result in a range of activities in social work teams and organisations and a great deal of social media activity. As such key issues are promoted and discussed. Siobhan recently delivered some training where social workers were really keen to tell her about their activities to celebrate the birthday of the Mental Capacity Act. Siobhan reflected that the day had been successful in getting people to really talk to each other about what the Mental Capacity Act means for people. The sharing that these action days promote is really useful. The following stakeholder voice highlights what one AMHP thought about a day to mark the work of AMHPs organised by the Adult PSW Network this year:

STAKEHOLDER VOICE ASIFAMHP

AsifAMHP is a user of twitter. He describes himself as: AMHP, dad, rugby, beer & grumpy (with hope). Views are my own, unless I am instructed otherwise.   @asifamhp

AMHP - The P stands for Professional (by the way)

Most people have no idea what an AMHP is or what an AMHP does and that includes far too many people and professionals who really should know better.

The Approved Mental Health Professional is an almost invisible (mostly) Local Government Civil Servant, there are some nurse AMHPs and I am told that two psychologists have ventured from their consulting rooms to undertake the training.

The AMHPs are the ones who have actually studied and read the Mental Health Act (law) and the Code of Practice and probably the Reference Guide. When it comes to the law, they are the experts and they are the ones who have to make the law work in the real world.

The AMHPs are the people who "section" people, not the psychiatrist and more importantly, the AMHPs are the ones who do not "section" people, even when everyone else, including the psychiatrist, says that they should.

The state has invested in these AMHPs a huge amount of power, but not invested the resources to enable them to do the job expected of them. Far too often these AMHPs and the people and kids and families on the receiving end of what they do, are left up the proverbial creek, without paddle or indeed boat (think bed and ambo or alternative to admission).

People forget all too easily, that a Mental Health Act Assessment is actually a legal process and that it is the AMHP that is tasked with coordinating that process and the one that ultimately makes the decision.

People and other professionals and other organisations only tend to be interested in AMHPs when they need one and they only tend to think they need one when things have gotten past crisis point. Of course, they want an AMHP now and they want a nice compliant AMHP to rubber stamp their decision and to share risk. They are ever so disappointed when a grumpy and legally literate AMHP turns up and is all independently minded ;-)

We AMHPs should consider it a compliment that we are in such demand. But what we really need is to be more visible and supported better across agencies to do the job expected of us.

This Year, the Adult Principle Social Worker Network tried to do exactly that and on 29th June 2017 they promoted #AMHP17 and even this grumpy Luddite AMHP joined in.

The Network and the Co-chairs Rob Mitchell and Mark Harvey deserve great credit for, at least for one day, making AMHPs less invisible and raising the profile. The big cheese Lyn Romeo (Chief Social Worker for Adults – England) joined in and published a blog by a grumpy AMHP and we had the very lovely Ruth Allen (BASW CEO) visit and support us and an article published in Community Care and my friend @MentalHealthCop published a very good blog - AMHPs and AMHPing.

The Mental Health Act and AMHPs are it seems slowly making their way up the political agenda. It seems that ADASS are interested and that the Government wants to reform the MHA. Let us hope that they remember to actually invite AMHPs to contribute to the conversations and the MHA Review. Indeed we need to get ourselves invited in to the rooms and advocate for those on the receiving end of what we do.

PS Please remember, that ordering an AMHP is not like ordering a pizza ;-)

© AsifAMHP

Stress and burnout in social work

There is a significant amount of stress in social work, which is widely acknowledged in the profession. For example, the International Federation of Social Workers refers to the dangers of stress and burnout for social workers (ANAS 2010). We have been concerned though that this sometimes leads to a narrative about how difficult things are for social workers, without a recognition of how difficult things are for the people social work seeks to support. Indeed, the narrative about how 'hard the job is' has led to some very negative posts on social media that we see as adding to the oppression of vulnerable groups. In fact, high stress levels are not unique to people delivering social work services, the stress levels experienced by service users are incredibly high and social work must recognise this.

That said, we do feel that the SHARE model can be used to explore the importance of self-care in social work and not just for practitioners! As we explored in Chapter 2, we all share a common humanity and therefore we should all share responsibilities for self-care.

Forms of stress

Stress is not a bad thing in itself. We all need some level of stress to function. However, it can be helpful to understand the types of stress to think about our own stress levels and our response to these:

Acute Stress: This describes short term experiences of extreme stress. Small doses of stress can be thrilling and exhilarating. Some people seek out small amounts or short 'doses' of stress for the 'thrill of it'. Too much stress through can cause psychological distress and negative physical symptoms.

Some people seek out the thrill of acute stress. Chronic stress, however, is dangerous for health.

Chronic stress: This describes long term stress that grinds people down. Whilst people are well aware of acute stress, people can get used to chronic stress. They might miss the symptoms in the drama or crisis of the situation causing the stress. People can learn to live with chronic stress which actually makes it more dangerous for their long-term health.

There is a range of research that indicates social workers are vulnerable to work related stress. Indeed Eborall (2003) reports that stress in social work causes sickness absence and ultimately leads to a high staff turnover particularly in statutory social work. This leads to a shortage of staff which, in turn, leads to a reduced quality of care provided to service users. Additionally, Harrington and Dolgoff (2008) report that social workers who are stressed are less able to make effective and ethical critical decisions.

With the levels of stress in social work it is important that people recognise what they can do to manage their own stress levels. We can all take action which is positive in relation to stress and social work. The negative narrative that surrounds this area can lead towards a sense of helplessness and hopelessness so it is vital to maintain this sense that there is always something we can do. The next few pages will therefore address the concept of professional resilience and acts of self-care.

KEY MESSAGES FROM RESEARCH: STRESS IN SOCIAL WORK

Social workers vulnerability to work related stress has been a subject of research for some years (Gibson, McGrath and Reid 1989).

Various research studies (for example, Maslach and Leiter 1997, Milczarek, Schneider and Gonzalez 2009) suggest the characteristics of a job which are most commonly related to workplace stress are:
- Work intensification (this refers to the speed of work expected, the imposition of deadlines and the expectations that a worker should be able to do more with less over time).
- Long hours.
- Job insecurity.
- Poor work-life balance.
- Confusing, sometimes conflicting policies and procedures.
- Overloaded work schedule.
- Lack of support.
- Significant consequences when something goes wrong or mistakes are made.
- Conflict of values (particularly where a worker feels that they are being asked to do something which is unethical or against their professional values).

Writing about the role of approved mental health professionals (AMHP), Morriss (2015) identifies a range of stressors associated with the role. These stressors include being unable to fulfil the role due to a lack of resources such as beds, the emotional labour invested in working with a person with mental ill health and the reality of hospital wards not always being safe places to be.

Community Care surveyed more than 2,000 frontline staff and managers and found that 80% of respondents felt that stress levels were impacting on their ability to do their job. A third of social workers who responded to the survey were using alcohol and 17% were using prescription drugs such as anti-depressants to cope with stress. Almost all respondents (97%) said they were moderately or very stressed, but only 16% said they had received any training or guidance on how to deal with work-related stress (Schraer 2015).

Professional resilience

A whole industry has grown up around the concept of professional resilience. We are concerned that at times the idea is used in a pathologising and oppressive way. So that if, for example, a social worker comments about struggling with stress levels due their workload then they may be told that they need to be more 'resilient'. Social workers recognise the vital importance of a person-in-environment perspective and as such we must recognise that a worker's resilience must be viewed in context. How supportive is the organisation? Resilience is a shared responsibility and is effectively developed through a partnership between a supportive organisation and a committed practitioner.

Grant and Kinman (2015) define professional resilience as:

> "A positive attribute that can protect and enhance health and wellbeing. It is particularly important for helping professionals who face highly challenging and complex situations."

Professional resilience is generally seen in two main ways:

Adaptability	Bouncebackability
Professional resilience is often seen as being linked to a person's ability to adapt to what is going on around them. For example, Klohen (1996) described it as *"the general capacity for flexible and resourceful adaptation to external and internal stressors."*	Whilst this sounds like a completely made-up word, professional resilience is often described as the ability to 'bounce back' from challenges and negative emotional experiences' (Tugade and Frederikson 2004).

In the current climate there is the risk that resilience can become about a single-track issue incorporated into policy as checklists, rating scores and assessments of personality or behaviour. However, resilience is multi-faceted and complex. As individuals we may feel much more resilient at some points than others, we may be able to 'cope' with different levels of stress, differently at different times. Get the idea? It's all about diversity. One size does not fit all. Everyone needs to develop their own understanding about their stress levels and what works for them in terms of self-care at different times.

Siobhan Shares

I use a range of techniques drawn from the SHARE model in supporting social workers to think about their responses to the stressful nature of their work. Specifically, in workshops with newly qualified workers I introduced the idea of making 'resilience / self-care suitcases.' These are contextualised into the journey model of practice education (see page 116). I talk about how when you go on a journey you are asked if you packed your own bags and then introduce to the participants the idea of 'making' a suitcase, they write in the case whatever they want to, but generally something around how they know that their personal stress levels have got too high, what they will do when they feel this way, what acts of self-care they will commit to and so on.

The suitcase exercise illustrates the way that one short (half hour) activity connects a range of the components of the SHARE model:

Seeing: I provide a range of card, stickers, labels, luggage tags and felt pens so that this becomes a craft type activity. This draws on the benefits of visual arts and crafts in social work (see page 113). When participants walk into the venue and see the bright colours on the table they often comment on this and I have noted it provides a different 'feel' from the very start of the day.

Hearing: Participants generally talk to each other about what they are packing in their cases, often highlighting that they are not alone in their feelings and sharing ideas about self-care etc.

Action: The act of taking time out of the training to actually 'make' the suitcases is useful. It draws on actually doing something and aspects of experiential learning. Everyone is active since they are making individual suitcases.

Reading: I encourage participants to put things that they have written into the suitcase, so that they can read them again at a time when they need to. Specifically, one of the things that I ask them to complete is a sheet with the heading 'I am proud to be a social worker because...' they put that into the suitcase to pull out and read at different points in the journey. The act of actually writing down a commitment to self-care is also useful.

Evaluate: As part of the activity I encourage the participants to think about their feelings around self-care, and to evaluate the barriers that they face. They often conclude that the biggest barrier is themselves and recognise the need to take responsibility for their own self-care. Of course, evaluate can also relate to how participants evaluate the activity.

Generally, this activity is evaluated very well. With one group, I use this activity as part of one workshop. The participants attend six workshops across a twelve-month period. At the end, they write a short reflection about the workshop learning, what sticks out in their minds etc. The suitcase activity is regularly referred to; it really seems to link in with people's experiences and provides something useful after the training has concluded. Often people do comment that when the activity was introduced to them they were sceptical about its value - but that they really got a lot from creating their suitcase.

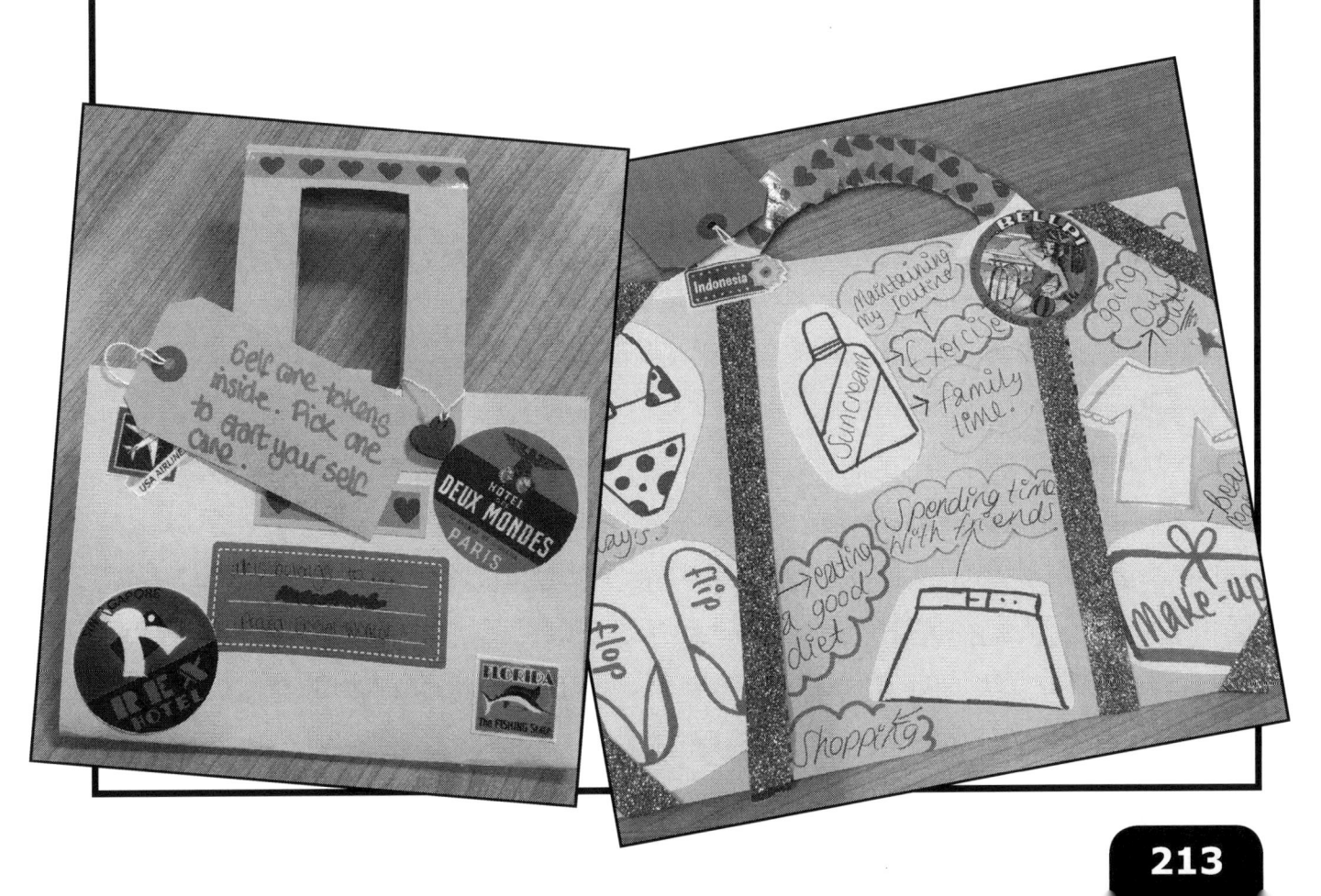

Acts of self-care in social work

Sometimes people view self-care as selfish or self-centred. However, it is really important that we each recognise the importance of taking care of ourselves. On page 48 we suggested that rather than seeing a glass as either half full or half empty we prefer to see it as refillable. It is impossible however to refill a glass when the jug is empty. Taking care of yourself is not selfish it is essential. Think about when you are on a flight and the safety information is being given – passengers are told that they must fix their own oxygen mask before seeking to help others to do so.

Self-care is not a one-time thing. We need to engage in acts of self-care on a regular basis, daily in fact. This doesn't need to be something huge, as we said on page 202 'every little helps'. Acts of self-care can be small and do not need to cost anything. If it is to be sustainable then self-care needs to be something that fits into every life. We find the website www.selfcarepsychology.com really useful in thinking about sustainable self-care. One of the recent blogs posted there by Kate Collier who is a social worker is entitled *"Self Care for Everyday People with Real Lives, Shit to do and No Magic Money Tree"* this illustrates the down to earth approach that the website takes.

Simple self-care activities are often the most helpful, but again there is the one size doesn't fit all rule. What works for some people won't work for others. You must get to know yourself and what works for you. Some of the acts of self-care that social workers we know have found useful include:

- Belting out a song at the top of their voices in the car
- Taking a brisk walk to get away from the desk at lunchtime
- Finding a particular spot on the drive home from work, where they actively commit to switching off from work issues
- Drinking extra water every day
- Using some hand cream or moisturiser kept in the car
- Taking a few minutes to concentrate on breathing in and out slowly
- Inhaling a positive smell – peppermint oil is said to be good
- Having fruit at the office – instead of snacking on those biscuits and cakes
- At home finding the time to take a bath before bed
- Listening to music
- Taking time off from social media and the smartphone generally

My Share

What acts of self-care do I find useful?

SELF CARE

	In social work	**Acts of self-care**
SEE:	Often what social workers see in practice can be disturbing to them. For example, they see poverty on a daily basis, and often see first-hand the impact of trauma, abuse and neglect. Chapter 5 explored some of the difficulties around what social workers might see in practice and the impact that this might have.	Catch sight of things. Really look at something simple in detail. Take time to look at the view on your way to work. It doesn't have to be a traditionally beautiful view, what about the wild flower growing on the edge of the road?
HEAR:	In Chapter 6 we explored the way that hearing about trauma can lead to compassion fatigue.	Think about the value of hearing positive stories. Share your positive stories about work with each other.
ACT:	As we have explored there are times where social workers may feel that they are not 'doing' what they thought they would. They are likely to be spending a great deal more time recording what they are doing rather than actually doing it (as we explore in Chapter 8), this can increase their feelings of stress.	Take a moment to do something for yourself each day. It doesn't need to be big. Just enjoy taking some time out to drink a cup of tea and savour the moment, rather than trying to do three things at once, leaving the tea to go cold by the time you get to it!
READ:	Social workers spend a great deal of time reading case files, recording, minutes of meetings, research and books (hopefully), social media posts etc. This calls for a particular kind of reading as we will cover in the next chapter.	What do you like to read? Sometimes social workers read so much at work that they switch themselves off from reading at other times - but losing yourself in a good novel can be a great act of self-care.
EVALUATE:	How we evaluate our experience of social work is very related to getting the balance with our own self-care. If you are not taking care of yourself then you are more likely to evaluate your practice in a cynical manner.	Do you recognise the importance of taking care of yourself - or are you always putting other people first? What are the barriers to you taking good care of yourself?

Key points

- Action is at the very heart of the SHARE model. It is central to the model.
- Actions can be big or small.
- Thinking through the what? and why? of social work can be helpful in supporting development in terms of how we practice.
- Understanding the history of social work and ensuring that we have positive social work role models is vitally important. We stand on the shoulders of giants.
- Social workers need to be in touch with the political context of practice, it influences practice in so many ways.
- Radical approaches to social work are gaining in popularity and there are a range of examples of social work activism that social workers can get involved in and learn a great deal from.
- Social work is stressful. Aspects of this are about the context and socio-political factors. However, everyone can take responsibility for their own self-care. This is one element of action that all people share in.

Reflective Questions

What stands out most for you from this chapter? Why?

What could you do as a result of reading this chapter?

If you had been writing a chapter on 'action' in social work what would you have included? Why?

Chapter 8: READING

This chapter covers the reading component of the SHARE model. Reading is considered from the perspective of a range of stakeholders and as such we cover what people read in social work, addressing literature, case files and the wider media. Recognising that reading is not always valued as it should be, we also address the importance of reading and the barriers to this. In developing the SHARE model, we have always tried to address all stakeholders' share in terms of social work and one of the most significant issues that has come up in terms of reading is the importance of what social workers record and how others (service users and managers) read this. This chapter therefore concludes with a consideration of the importance of record keeping in social work.

The importance of reading

Reading is important for everyone. It promotes growth and learning and opens up access to a wide range of information and services. Rates of adult literacy are often seen as a key indicator of a well-developed society. The importance of reading in social work is widely acknowledged and this is reflected in the fact that we received a large number of stakeholder voices in relation to this component (many of which were the first stakeholder voices we received).

As we have stated the components of the SHARE model must be explored in terms of the connecting factors. Reading connects with the other components of the model in many ways. For example:

- What people read will have an impact on how they 'see' social work.
- Reading information has been compared to experiencing it neurologically – so that when we read narratives of distress, trauma and abuse we empathise with people and our senses are often triggered.
- What we read can influence our actions.
- The knowledge that we have and how we evaluate things is vitally important – this is often influenced by what and how much we read.

In the following stakeholder voice, Peter explains from his perspective why reading is so important for social workers.

Reading is important but it must be linked to the other components. There is no purpose in being a walking encyclopaedia!

STAKEHOLDER VOICE
PETER SIMCOCK

Peter Simcock is a lecturer in social work

As a university student in the 1990s, I recall being asked by those I met, 'What are you reading?' The enquirers were not asking about a specific text, but rather the subject of my studies. I also recall being told in my first ever social work lecture that real social work wasn't about people; it was about being in the library reading books! Whilst I hope the lecturer was exaggerating to make a point, these recollections remind us of the importance of reading. At university you will be expected to read, perhaps in a way and to an extent you have not done before. The volume of reading expected may even feel overwhelming. However, it is key to achieving success in study at HE level and developing your reading skills will serve you well in practice. Social workers need to read case notes, court reports, assessments and correspondence from other professionals, and national and local policies and procedures. Failure to engage in such reading can have tragic outcomes; in her analysis of public inquiries into child deaths, Munro (1998) observes that in some cases, social workers had overlooked a history of previous child abuse in families, as they had failed to read their own case files.

Thompson and Thompson (2016) maintain that reading widely is essential if you are to get the most out of your social work studies. There are certainly many reasons why you should read widely. It is one of the key ways in which you gain knowledge (PCF Domain 5) and better prepares you for in class participation, resulting in deep rather than superficial learning. Our high cognitive functions are also developed through, amongst other things, reading; it helps develop critical thinking and critical reflection skills, which are essential to university study and social work practice (PCF Domain 6). Finally, reading is one of the best ways to improve your own academic writing. Engaging with a wide range of reading material will expose you to different writing styles and help you develop your own; it will also enhance your vocabulary, enabling you to better express your thoughts, reflections and analyses in academic assignments.

To be an effective reader, consider developing a reading strategy, making use of different reading styles depending on your purpose. For example, skim-reading and scanning can be useful when seeking to identify relevant materials, whilst use of the SQ3R technique (Survey, Question, Read, Recall, Review) can support critical reading and comprehension. Pay careful attention to reading lists provided by your tutors, but also make contact with your subject librarian to develop your own. Widen your reading by engaging with a range of material: core texts, academic journal articles, policy documents and research published by social welfare organisations, think tanks and charities. You should also explore material from other disciplines: papers by sociologists, psychologists, medics, nurses, educationalists, policy makers and economists will all be of interest to social workers.

Practice Educator Helen Bonnick encourages student social workers to read newspaper articles, particularly those concerned with politics and culture. She argues that this can 'help students to reflect on their own views and, by extension, their practice' (McGregor, 2012). Tice (1998) observes that social workers have often sought inspiration from novelists and playwrights, and echoes Paradise's (1932) suggestion that 'social workers read widely, because all good literature that interprets life is of professional value' (cited in Tice, 1998:62). In 2014, Amanda Taylor, social work lecturer at the University of Central Lancashire, developed a reading group, as a means to support and enhance learning. This is now a national project, with its own twitter account, enabling students and academics to discuss social work issues through reading both non-fiction and fiction. Get involved in such activities, and keep an eye on the Community Care Website, which periodically publishes book lists for social work students, containing the latest must read academic texts and novels.

To encourage students to move beyond the internet for their reading material, I sometimes show a Randy Glasbergen cartoon, which shows a teacher talking to her pupil as he questioningly holds up a text book: 'It's called 'reading'. It's how people install new software into their brains', she says. However, online resources do have much to offer, whether as a means to accessing e-books and e-journals, or blogs such as The Social Care Elf, which provides accessible summaries of peer-reviewed research publications.

The opportunities for wider reading are there. So, do read widely - your tutors, your grades, your future employers, your profession and, most importantly, your service-users will thank you for it!

© Peter Simcock

Peter refers to the social work book group. We would echo Peter's suggestion for people to get involved in this. Amanda Taylor, who instigated the book group, shares the background to this as follows:

STAKEHOLDER VOICE
AMANDA TAYLOR

Amanda Taylor is a senior lecturer in social work. She has a keen interest in the digitalisation of social work. She is also the founder of the social work book group.

Exploring what it means to be human is central to the whole notion of social work education. Creating spaces in which students can engage with, examine and experience not only the other but themselves the core business of a social work academic. The ways in which the curriculum is disseminated is largely bound by the requirements for practice. However, the majority of social work academics arrive to the educational environment from the practice milieu, a place which, amongst other things, requires the ability to innovate. Therefore modelling this skill, I believe significant to the professional socialisation of students in preparation for practice. This short 'story' outlines what can occur when responsibility meets creativity.

'How much reading' … [insert the emoticon that you think most fitting] to capture the look on the faces of a group of social work students at an induction event designed to outline the importance of engaging with literature relevant to social work education and practice. An introduction to a substantial body of knowledge that would assist them to understand, develop and apply that which is necessary for entry into the profession. However much I tried my efforts to romanticise reading and offer strategies for said reading did little to redress the visible manifestations associated with the magnitude of the task that lay ahead ahead. 'Experiencing' the students in this moment led me to consider how reading as an academic activity could be facilitated, in a way that would make this undertaking appear achievable.

Cue the idea of reading together. In an attempt to develop the reading habits of students I scheduled a series of reading type events, sessions that required students to come to the learning space having read an excerpt from a book relevant to their studies. The piece of fiction chosen was shared with student group, with an attached brief that simply required them to read the content from the text as if it were a practice referral. Applying the flipped classroom methodology provided students with an opportunity to apply learning from across the curriculum, and to identify and address knowledge gaps. In addition, this approach also meant that students were exposed to the way in which self-directed study can maximise the potential for learning gain within the classroom space. It was this initial idea and method of engaging students in the activity of reading that grew into what has now become widely known as Social Work Book Group.

What started out as four student social workers in a library has grown into what is an incredibly popular learning medium, with a membership that includes students, academics and practitioners. Book group events occur in physical and online spaces, synchronously and asynchronously, and are live streamed to increase engagement. The texts are carefully selected to ensure that the knowledge, values and skills of the profession can be applied, discussed and debated within the context of the overall story. In addition to this and in a bid to highlight the need for research mindedness literature relevant to the subject area is circulated using an online platform called Storify. This open access resource can be accessed through the following Google search 'The Use of Book Groups in Social Work Education and Practice'. The value of this type of reading experience has been described by students as 'engaging' 'thought-provoking' 'applied' and 'non-threatening' and by practitioners as 'challenging' 'enabling' 'supportive' and as 'powerful conversations that helped us to reflect'.

Social worker practitioners are surrounded by stories, including their own. They are required to engage with the story that the Government tells, become part of the story that their employing agency tells and understand the stories that service-users tell. A complex set of stories due to the very nature of the lived experience that often collide and conflict. Hence why it is that narrative analysis needs to be a more prominent feature of the social work curriculum and also weaved more explicitly throughout continuing professional development events. Recognising the importance of story and the skills required to navigate / read them is essential to effective practice and gained, in this instance, through analysing fictional tales. The characters, their environment and the circumstances they find themselves within all provide opportunities to develop and practice critical thinking.

© Amanda Taylor

As it can be seen from Peter's and Amanda's accounts, it is vital that social workers read a wide range of material for professional development but it is important to recognise that reading can also be therapeutic and relaxing. It might seem counter intuitive to recommend social work students read newspapers and fiction, surely they should be focusing on 'academic' texts after all? Well yes, of course, but we have found that for some social work students, often coming back to study after a break, academic texts can be off-putting. Reading a whole range of literature in addition to academic texts can help in understanding how complex arguments can be represented through written communication, so enhancing our own skills in producing well written reports and documentation.

What do we read in social work?

The answer to this question is, all kinds of things! Social workers spend a significant amount of their time reading about service users and their circumstances. They also read about services and methods, and they have to read and understand policies and procedures which assist them in reaching decisions. They also read academic writing and research articles.

What we read in social work: Literature

The learning to be gained from reading in social work is endless. Reading a range of literature (not just academic) has been useful to us in the various stages of our social work careers. For example, Jo was bought 'Fourth of July Creek' by Smith Henderson for Christmas, which tells the story of an American social worker, working in a mountainous town in Montana, USA. For Jo, the book whilst a good story in its own right, also raised issues about social work boundaries and roles in different countries. Siobhan recently read 'The Story of Beautiful Girl' by Rachel Simon, whilst an entirely fictional story it reminded her of her early career working with people in long stay hospitals and the barbarity of people with learning disabilities still being locked away in ATUs in the UK today. Prospera is currently reading 'I know why the caged bird sings' by Maya Angelou, a powerful autobiography about a strong-willed character who turns her experiences of trauma and racism into strengths, which enables her to challenge prejudice. As we finalise this book, we are all awaiting the publication of 'Justice for LB' by Sara Ryan. We very much want to read this book, although we see it as one which should never have needed writing (see Sara's voice on page 267).

Whilst a good book can stay with us and influence us individually in a range of ways literature can also have a significant impact on wider society, influencing culture and practice. Andrews (2012) identifies Charles Dickens as making a significant contribution to contemporary social work discourse and practice particularly around social justice, equality and poverty. Dickens is famous for writing about issues which many would have distanced themselves from at that time. Dickens writing illuminated elements of his experience as a child and within his family, further emphasising the need for the use of real life narratives which in contemporary discourse we refer to as service user perspectives. Charles was the oldest of six children and his father was imprisoned along with his wife and children for indebtedness in 1824. This indebtedness, Dickens described as arising from his father's borrowing to fund a lifestyle beyond his means. The trauma to the family was significant and Charles could no longer attend school. Charles surmised, at that early age that pathology or individual causes were not necessarily why a family would struggle. He concluded that environmental factors such as poverty and inequality contributed to a family's situation.

In Oliver Twist, Dickens portrays poverty in a different light. He sends a strong message about how people in poverty should attempt to challenge the status quo and not be accepting of anything that they are given without being assertive. So even creative writing that originates more than a hundred years ago has real resonance for social work today.

Amanda Taylor shared her thoughts about the development of the social work book group and here we return to her work around the importance of reading a range of literature:

> *"Books can draw the reader into spaces and places where all nature of thoughts, feelings, emotions and challenges are felt. They can confirm, and also confront, our ideas, ideals, values and beliefs; force us to question the world and how we fit within it. They replicate almost every aspect of life possible, with some even impossible to imagine, or so one might think. They allow us to feel, at times when our feelings are inaccessible, they keep us safe when we might need to escape; there is little that cannot be found within their covers."*
>
> (Taylor, 2016:168).

Literature then, in its broadest sense, can serve many functions. For those writing about difficult experiences, it can be cathartic and healing, and for the reader also cathartic in perhaps feeling that they are not alone with their difficult experiences. As Amanda states in the quote above, wide reading can challenge our very beliefs and the positions we hold about the world. So, challenge yourself with your reading, choose a book, a newspaper or an academic text, you might not normally choose - it doesn't have to even be specifically about social work, as it all helps with developing our knowledge of the world.

What we read in social work: Case files

Social workers often comment on the value of reading service user's files and electronic records more generally. So that when asked how they approach an assessment, social workers generally refer to reading any previous assessments and the referral and background information before meeting the service user. Whilst this is understandable it is important to recognise that reading something can mean that we pre-judge a situation. Sometimes the only power that a service user has is 'informational power' (Seabury, Seabury and Garvin 2011). The service user is the expert in what has happened to them, but this informational power base is often weakened when a social worker enters the situation after reading case files or referrals or consulting with others who already know the service user. Getting the balance between being prepared and pre-judging is really important.

It's that fine balance again!

The SHARE model encourages us to consider the different experiences of everyone involved. How people experience reading case files about themselves is vitally important to consider.

The first stakeholder voice we received when we started to write this book was from Lisa Cherry whose work on understanding trauma we value greatly. Lisa discusses her experiences of reading her files. Social workers create records and read files every day such that they often fail to recognise the value of these, Lisa's voice shows the importance of the records social workers keep incredibly powerfully:

STAKEHOLDER VOICE
LISA CHERRY

Lisa Cherry is a leading trainer and consultant, specialising in assisting education professionals and those in social care, to understand trauma, recovery and resilience for vulnerable children, young people and their families

If the place where the damage is done is within relationships, then it is within relationships that the healing can be done too. Relationships are the greatest therapeutic intervention that we have available to us and knowing this, gives us the power to create meaningful connections that are a worthwhile intervention.

It is with this in mind that I start to ponder the experience of reading my files; a collection of notes, allegedly a life recorded. I know full well it won't be my story prior to reading them, but rather the story of the people who were in my life during that time and their perceptions of what that looked like.

I look up at the clock anticipating a knock at the door and I repeat this clock watching motion several times before eventually it is time to go the door. Look up at the clock, anticipate a knock. Repeat.

I'm with a friend who rather cleverly thought that I might need someone with me. The fact it hadn't occurred to me to reach out for support during this part of the process when I had ensured so much support for after the process, suggested to me at the time that maybe I still had a little more work to do in understanding what I needed. As it turned out, her presence was hugely important.

Already I'd worked myself into an internal frenzy about who would be undertaking this piece of work with me, who would actually be on the other side of that knock at the door. I was mentally throwing out demands to my internal self that they had better be someone with lots of experience who can 'hold' the space. Someone who understands that this is a section of my life, of my past, that they would be bringing into my now, into my house, into my 'present.' Ultimately I wanted them to be a person who would not be judging me in any way.

My inner 14 year old, who was just about contained in the adult body of a 42 year old woman with two teenagers of her own, opens the door to the two social workers. They are clutching my files. My files from Social Services. My files from the 1980's. Endless scraps of paper, official letters, judgements of others, letters from my mother, breakdowns of placements, inadequate practice and lots of work that went on in the background by committed individuals who really really tried to make a difference. Faceless. Nameless. Committed.

After the usual pleasantries that we all feel befit this rather unusual event, that is the reading of a person's life which was recorded in all its glory through a traumatic adolescence, we have coffee. Once its' aroma is well and truly cascading around the room, we take a seat. Throughout the entire meeting I am every age between birth, 12, 26, 29, 42, repeat. Look at the clock and wait for the knock.

My friend and I along with the two social workers from the adoption team politely sit as if it were the 1970's and we'd been allowed to have this meeting in 'the front room,' the one for special guests, and then the unravelling of a life commences.

These two women, these two social workers, instinctively understand what I need; skilled and sensitive. In fact, they were just what I needed. Caroline was older and wiser than I and I valued that immensely. I could not have been so at ease at returning to my past with someone younger than I. I knew that. I knew that I needed someone older to do this with.

I'm certain she would have read through many files that would have made my life events pale into insignificance but she understood that this story was mine, she understood that I had been let down and that I had paid a high price for the actions of the adults around me and it was all of that that I needed to hear.

She gently talked through incidences using the correct names of the people as though she knew them, because she had taken the time to read through the file with a detail that afforded her the ability to sound familiar with it all, as if she had been somewhere in the background while it was all happening. Within a couple of hours, I was alone on my favourite chair with some blue files and a blanket.

*

Having decided that I wouldn't read this strange collection of papers in one sitting as it might be too much for me to process I proceeded, inevitably, to read them all in one sitting.

As I ploughed through, tears streaming down my face. Anger, hurt and despair boiling up inside my body simultaneously and separately all at once, I heard a voice. It was so real that I lifted my head up from the folder and almost looked round to see who it was. 'It wasn't your fault' said this voice. As I engaged in a rather surreal conversation with this 'person' that came from within and without all at once I replied, 'I know that.' But the voice persisted, repeating the sentence over and over again until I was weeping loudly repeating the same sentence over and over again to myself. It wasn't my fault. It wasn't my fault.

This woman, the woman I had become, who had journeyed through many years of recovery, acquiring a deep self-awareness, an all-embracing self-love, had written books and blogs and articles on healing and transformation from adversity, had carried around the quietest voice for the noisiest of stories of all. The story that probably underpinned many decisions that I had made as an adult, the story that had aided a sense of difference and isolation; the story that it was all somehow my fault. Why? Because that is one of the things that children do with childhood trauma.

Having waited so many years before I felt able to read my files, in an afternoon, they opened me up to a new story and this was swiftly added to the recovery adventure. The new narrative, created in part through the intervention of a healing relationship. That is the greatest knowledge of all, that a relationship can be a moment in time or across many years and everything in between. The most important thing is that it is used for the purpose of connection to enable healing and recovery to take place.

© Lisa Cherry

What we read in social work: The press

Social work is the subject of significant media scrutiny, but it feels as though this is rarely positive. In fact, Cunningham and Cunningham (2017) report that negativity in media reporting of social work is nothing new and has been around since the reporting of the death of Dennis O'Neill, a 12 year old child who died whilst in foster care in 1945. They refer to Greenland (1986:14) who described the "*peculiarly British sport of social worker baiting within the media*". Research has been unequivocal about the negative and damaging media coverage of social work, which usually intensifies when issues of child deaths occur. O'Neill (2002) and Seldon (2009) for example, highlight how the media promotes a lack of trust in social workers and a wide range of studies over a number of years, for example, Franklin and Parton (1991), Ayre (2001) and Braun and Robb (2010) have noted the intense hostility towards social workers in media reports. The negative media is damaging as it erodes public trust and confidence in the profession, which is harmful for all stakeholders.

There appear to be two key themes or narratives about social work in the press, the first that social workers have been over zealous and have removed children inappropriately. Indeed, one particular newspaper often portrays social workers as "baby snatchers" and one claimed in 2008 that "social services are paid bonuses to snatch children" (Reid, 2008). The other narrative is that social workers fail to remove children from parents or carers who go on to kill their children. All reporting therefore highlight 'failures' of social workers; basically, social workers are damned if they do and damned if they don't. This is however, nothing new. One of the first assignments Siobhan recalls writing in her social work training more than thirty years ago was titled: *Damned if you do, Damned if you don't. Discuss.*

During the writing of this book it was the 10-year anniversary of the death of Baby Peter Connelly (known as Baby P). The media reporting of the event was very salacious indeed, with the Sun calling for the sacking of the then Director of Haringey Social Services, Sharon Shoesmith, and the social workers involved in Peter's care. The famous headline 'Blood on their hands' was read by millions of people. All of the workers involved in the case, received death threats and had to leave their homes for their own safety. This media reporting had a very significant impact on the way that social work is perceived in British society.

It was interesting to note a recent article by Community Care magazine that asked social workers who qualified after the Baby P case came to the public's attention, how the case impacted on their decision (or not) to become social workers (Stevenson, 2017). The memory of Baby Peter and the so-called failings of the social workers rather than the failings of other organisations like the police or the health service, remain firmly in the public's attention. Indeed, when Sharon Shoesmith published her book in 2016, based on her PhD, she was again, subject to further media derision with several newspapers accusing her of "cashing in" on the child's death (Nicholl, 2016).

SEE: What do you remember seeing in the press at the time of 'Baby P's' death? Do you recall seeing the iconic photograph image of Baby Peter, wearing a blue jumper? Do you recall the leaked police image of a model of a child containing details of all the injuries he had received? What feelings did those images provoke, both then and now? Perhaps you recall watching the TV programme, 'Baby P: The Untold Story'.

HEAR: What do you recall hearing about the case at the time? What were your friends and colleagues saying about the case? What were you hearing about social work and its alleged failings in general and in relation to the London Borough of Haringey? What have you heard subsequently about the case and the aftermath?

ACT: If you were a social worker at the time, did it change your practice? We know for example, that care applications went up considerably, following the reporting of the death by the press when the criminal trial of the mother, stepfather and uncle was concluded. Did your organisation change at all in light of the Baby P case? Perhaps it became more risk averse and much more cautious in its approach to child protection.

READ: What did you read at the time, and since? What impact did this have on you?

EVALUATE: So now given the 10-year anniversary of Peter's death, how do you make sense of the events leading up to his death, and the subsequent treatment of Shoesmith and the two social workers involved in the case? What feelings might you hold towards the workers in this case, or indeed towards the adults who killed him? How does the death of Baby P, perhaps continue to impact on safeguarding practice in children and families settings, both in a positive and perhaps negative way? Does it for example, make for defensive social work practice?

KEY MESSAGES FROM RESEARCH: SOCIAL WORK IN THE PRESS

- As early as 1979, Mawby, Fisher and Parkin recognised that there were difficulties with the media portrayal of social work. They suggested that there was considerable diversity in the press coverage of social work. They identified press concentration on certain areas of social work practice (with children) and suggested that this may impact on public perceptions of the profession.

- Reid and Misener (2001) sampled the press in the USA and the UK (major 'dailies') for 20 weeks yielding 399 articles. Ratings of the image of social work in the press in the USA was largely positive whereas in the UK more stories had largely negative ratings rather than positive.

- Research into the media and social work in child protection highlights 'sustained negative media images' (Jones 2012).

- As part of their 'stand up for social work' campaign, Community Care reported that they had been monitoring media coverage of social work, describing the language used about social workers (predominantly staff working with children) as hostile, speculative and often pejorative. Lombard and Maier (2009) on behalf of Community Care asserted that frequently stories in the media show a lack of knowledge about the social work role and often break editorial guidelines in refusing to give a right of reply.

- The negative media portrayal of social work in the UK, was also noted by The Social Work Task Force (2010) and the Munro report (2011).

STAKEHOLDER VOICE
LOUISE TICKLE

Louise is an award-winning journalist who reports for the Guardian on education, social affairs and the family courts.

Social workers are wary of the media. I understand why - people have lost their careers due to intemperate media coverage that has scapegoated social workers, ignoring the responsibilities of other professionals. But I'd argue that battening down the hatches and failing to be transparent about wider social work practice and its impacts on vulnerable adults and children is not an adequate response to legitimate questions being asked in the public interest. All professions, particularly those funded by the public purse and whose purpose is to serve fellow human beings have an imperative to be open and accountable. But this is generally not what I find when it comes to children's services in particular.

It is reasonably easy, under normal circumstances, to interview a police officer, even a junior one. Same for teachers, doctors and lawyers. Trying to get access to a real life social worker however requires longwinded negotiations. On occasion I have managed it, but there is a nervousness there that does not imbue me with confidence in the robustness of the profession.

I am not suggesting that social workers individually go out on a limb and start talking to the press (though certainly professionals in other sectors will sometimes do this). But when I have been given access to speak to individual frontline social work professionals, I have tended to be hugely impressed. That's worth thinking about, because the best ambassadors for any profession are the people who do the job well and will talk about it honestly, not managers trying to tell journalists how it is.

It would be worth, I think, local authorities reconsidering their attitudes to media enquiries around social work, so that a more balanced picture can be drawn. This means being entirely transparent and actively helpful when something has gone badly wrong, as journalists try to work out how best to inform the public - I would cite Gloucestershire County Council recently as a great example of how to approach this, following its children's services Inadequate Ofsted rating. But building relationships with the media is not just about dealing with bad news: it also means volunteering interesting information about new initiatives that have started to gain traction and make a positive difference for families. Please tell us about your interesting new thinking and ways of working to solve traditionally intractable problems. We are not going to write 'good news' stories for their own sake, but where you are doing interesting work that could be of benefit to other local authorities and therefore the wider population, we might well cover it: an example might be the Guardian piece I did that featured Leeds City Council's approach to extending family group conferences way beyond children on the edge of care so that it progressively becomes an entitlement for all children in need of social services support.

© Louise Tickle

We are hopeful that the narrative about social work can change in the mainstream media. Indeed, Ray Jones, an Emeritus Professor of Social Work, engaged proactively with the media in an attempt to change the hysterical and quite frankly, dangerous narrative during the Baby P, media, public and political furore (Jones, 2012). Professor Jones subsequently went on to write an accessible and engaging book about the life and events leading up to Baby Peter's death, and the subsequent consequences (Jones, 2014) and also appeared in a BBC documentary, 'Baby P, The Untold Story'. Of course, due to confidentiality, social workers, and social services cannot speak to the press about their casework, or if they do, they need to be very guarded to ensure those they work with are not inadvertently identified.

Whilst we are hopeful of change, during the finalising of this book, The Times (on the 28th August) reported a very one-sided and irresponsible story about a white Christian 5-year-old, fostered by Muslim foster carers (Norfolk, 2017). It subsequently transpired that the accompanying picture used of a Muslim wearing a niqab and veil, holding the hand of a blond child, was from photo stock and the veil had been added (Grierson, 2017). So, the key message here is always be discerning about what you read in the media.

My Share

- What was the last story I read about social work in the press?
- What impact did it have on me?
- What impact did it have on the people I work with and for?

Barriers to reading

There are a number of significant barriers to reading in social work. In Chapter 6 we covered the barriers to hearing in terms of:

- Environmental barriers
- Clinical barriers
- Emotional barriers
- Attitudinal barriers
- Bureaucratic barriers
- Cultural barriers
- Organisational barriers

This categorisation was developed in health and social care qualification frameworks drawn from the work of the Royal College of Speech and Language Therapists, based on what they saw as the barriers to communication (Maclean and Harrison 2014). Reading is another aspect of communication, so it should come as no surprise that the barriers to reading could be grouped into similar areas. In this chapter, we have chosen to focus on the clinical, attitudinal and organisational barriers to reading, rather than looking at all the barriers in turn. However, it is important to recognise that the barriers to reading are all significant and can compound to create situations where reading is incredibly difficult.

My Share

What barriers to reading do I face?

Clinical barriers to reading

There are various clinical barriers to reading. We often take reading for granted, but many people have difficulties with reading in a range of ways. Where people have difficulties with reading this can invoke a range of difficult feelings for people; most notably denial and shame (Nielsen, 2011). We have worked with many students and colleagues who have had some difficulties with reading, indeed Siobhan's share as follows highlights the barriers which she has faced in reading.

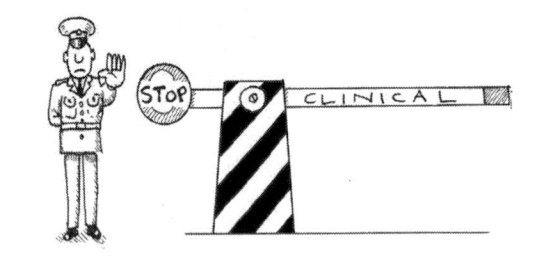

Siobhan Shares

Part of the impact of my stroke was that I lost the ability to read and write. I was very focused on re-learning this skill because it was essential for me to be able to return to work. The stroke team were more focused on me re-learning to 'independently mobilise' (their words not mine!) Reading was not a skill which was important in terms of discharge planning, and little value was placed on it in the rehab setting. It felt as though there was little shared understanding of priorities during my hospital stay. This really brought to life the concept of important to / important for, drawn from person centred planning. The focus of the hospital was on what they thought was important *for* me - to be able to walk. What was important *to* me was to be able to read and write again.

I did re-learn the skill of reading although I have been left with a form of acquired dyslexia and my reading ability is significantly affected if I am tired or stressed. This means that I much more likely to draw on the other parts of the SHARE model in my work. I very often see things visually rather than verbally.

I have always taken a strengths-based, hopeful, approach to my practice and I apply this in all aspects of my daily life too. So, I have been able to re-evaluate the way that I view my current reading skills in light of the fact that my visual skills have enhanced. As a result of needing to re-learn to read and subsequently understanding and valuing the different skills sets, I am now able to more readily recognise the interconnections between the various parts of what I have seen, heard, done and read, and as a result I can draw on each of these in my evaluation.

Whilst the barriers which Siobhan faced were acquired in adulthood, very often barriers to reading are lifelong. This means that when difficulties are encountered in adulthood, memories of oppression in childhood often come to the fore very quickly. It is vital that we recognise this, as barriers in reading and the resultant emotions can shape professional relationships in a range of ways. Neil's stakeholder voice illustrates this well.

STAKEHOLDER VOICE
NEIL HAMMOND

Neil is a social worker and practice educator, he has a diagnosis of dyslexia.

Dyslexia 'the devil on my shoulder' quietly whispering in my ear 'you're not good enough'. How I wish there was some physicality to this 'devil' so I could brush it away and never have to hear those words again. In using the analogy 'the devil on my shoulder' you may now be thinking there must be an 'angel', thus bringing an element of balance to my life. Indeed, there is and it quietly whispers, 'you can do it' and it has enabled me to achieve success. The 'devil on my shoulder' analogy, much loved by filmmakers and cartoonists alike to depict an inner conflict is not quite the same for me. My conflict did not start internally but externally. I may have been born with dyslexia but there was no 'devil', others helped to put him there and definitely gave him power. Indeed, my earliest memory of being taught was of being chastised for struggling to read and looking at the ceiling rather than the book. My recollection is of a reverberating boom as the teacher's hand hit the desk with such force that it startled everyone in the class. It was accompanied with a categorical "the answer isn't on the ceiling, look at the book!"

Now being diagnosed as dyslexic with accompanying Mears Irlen Syndrome, which affect the way the brain interprets visual information, I now know that looking at the ceiling, which was white, and at a distance, 'reset' my eyes and helped prevent the letters from moving on the page.

The answer isn't on the ceiling experience happened more than thirty years ago and yet it still holds strong in my memory today. This experience was genesis, the start of multiple similarly themed experiences of an educational and employment history marred by experiences of being labelled 'stupid', instances of bullying and a lack of understanding of dyslexia by peers and colleagues. All giving more and more power to that cruel voice saying 'you're not good enough.'

So if others put the 'devil' there where did the angel come from? Well others help place the angel on my shoulder also. This was through support and understanding and helping me to develop coping strategies to maximise my potential alongside reasonable adjustments and Access to Work assessments and funding. Although coping strategies are individual I have found the below to be of great benefit:

- Use of memory aids
- Robust preparation for tasks
- Prompt cards for theory
- Reflective practice prompt cards
- Tried and tested plans
- Maintaining positive influences in my life

- Further developing my understanding of dyslexia
- Sharing experiences with others
- Use of humour
- Doing a good job

The difference support and understanding of my dyslexia made to my career is almost beyond my own understanding. I went from leaving school and working in forestry where there was no expectation or requirement to be able to read or write proficiently. To completing a First Class (hons) degree in Sociology, Masters Degree in Social Work, becoming a Practice Educator, Line Manager in an Adults and Children's Services Team and publication of a number of academic pieces of work. However, the 'devil' is still there and has more power over me than colleagues and peers could ever imagine.

© Neil Hammond

As social work educators we have all worked with students whose experiences of compulsory education have not always been very positive. Some of these students often have undiagnosed specific learning difficulties and we are somewhat surprised, but disappointed that their teachers failed to pick this up earlier. Of course, not everyone is comfortable with a label but there is help and support out there.

Many people with specific reading and learning difficulties, such as dyslexia, develop creative coping mechanisms to address the issues that occur. It is important to recognise that most of these mechanisms are developed in an educational environment, sometimes these translate effectively into a practice environment and sometimes they don't. It's important to discuss what best meets the needs of people with dyslexia, and other forms of reading difficulties, with the person at an early stage and keep this under regular review. Remember what works for one person will not work for another.

Attitudinal barriers

Attitudinal barriers concerning the value of reading, and indeed books, can be very powerful indeed. Some of these attitudinal barriers may come from ourselves, perhaps based on the messages we were told at school about our reading abilities, or indeed our own families and the communities we live in. Reading books therefore, might be considered a waste of time, or not valuable in its own right. Many families and communities do not have the resources to buy books, and it is indeed a concern that today's cash strapped councils are choosing to shut libraries. It is important to reflect on such attitudinal barriers to reading, because these an impact on social work in many ways.

Research suggests that there is a gender divide in terms of reading, with girls at school engaging in reading more readily than boys. In 2012, The National Literacy Trust stated that 76% of schools in the UK reported that girls outperformed boys in literacy. They concluded that there were three reasons for this disparity between girls and boys literacy outcomes. Firstly, that girls were more likely to be brought books or supported to read by family, that teachers were not knowledgeable about texts that might be favoured by boys and lastly, that there may be a strong male identity that does not value books or reading or see literacy as success. Of course, being able to read well, and read widely, helps students access all other aspects of the curriculum. It's important to reflect therefore, to be aware of our own attitudes towards reading and the resistance to being labelled 'clever' or 'bookish'. Indeed, research into attitudes towards higher education in a London borough, where there had been low rates of progression into higher education, revealed this concern amongst young people (Finch, 2009). Some young people felt that they had had to hide being clever or interested in books, because it was just not considered very cool. Some young people suggested that if you were sporty and clever, then then proficiency at sport would hide the negativity associated with being clever and you could effectively 'get away with it'. This seems very sad indeed, that being clever or interested in learning is associated with some people in such a negative way. At times, we have noted similar attitudes in social work with students and practitioners taking an anti-intellectual stance. Sometimes a view is expressed that people who are academic can't possibly make good social workers.

We have noted, with some concern, a number of websites where very newly graduated social workers, sell their social work books. We can understand of course that for some newly qualified workers not yet employed, finances are likely to be in bad shape and this might be a much-needed quick source of income. We also acknowledge that there can be something quite therapeutic, about finishing a course, and wanting to clear all your papers and books away from your desk. We do wonder however, whether the need to sell books as soon as you finish the social work programme, might have something to do with the academy-field divide, something that has been covered elsewhere in this book. It might be presumed that there will be no need for academic books once one goes into the real world of social work. Books are not just for training, they are useful throughout your career, as the following stakeholder voice from Dave indicates.

STAKEHOLDER VOICE
DAVE ATHERTON

Dave is a social worker in a children and families team. When he wrote this he had been qualified for a year.

When I qualified last year, a wise old social worker told me, "Time to throw away your theory books sonny, you're in the real world now". How wrong he was. I am constantly amazed at how relevant social work theory is. Not a day goes by where I don't use it to shape my practice. Being a frontline social worker, we are regularly called upon to enter people's lives and try to make sense of the often chaotic and complex dynamics therein. This is achieved not through any innate personal wisdom, but by drawing on the theories that not only describe what we are seeing, but help us to predict what may happen next. In fact, I think perhaps the most profound thing I have noticed since qualifying is just how much of what I read and how much of the theory actually pans out in reality. As I have grown in experience, I find myself drawing on my reading and using knowledge of theory on an almost unconscious level. This knowledge helps me understand the service user's world, guides my decisions regarding a course of action and helps me appreciate the possible effects any of these actions may have.

© Dave Atherton

Dave's stakeholder voice demonstrates that the attitudinal barriers to reading may well not lie with the practitioner, but could come from other social workers or managers. When visiting the 'Experiencing Social Work' exhibition, Siobhan was struck by the commentary which went alongside Demi's work. This very clearly indicates the kind of barriers that Demi faced in relation to her reading around subjects to help her in her work. We are fortunate that Demi has allowed us to share her work in this book, as follows:

This piece is about moving towards professional autonomy and managing timescales in a more creative way. The boxes are processes and how I work around them to create positive relationships with families while trying to maintain professional competence.

I think as you gain the trust of managers and you gain the trust of your families, it's like an unfolding process for a newly qualified social worker: you become more competent throughout your profession and develop a sense of freedom. When you start you are fitting into a culture and for me it was a culture of you couldn't really express your ideas at the beginning.

I got told once in supervision that when I was reading books about the work that I was doing and talking about it, I was told that I'd learn more from reading Bella magazine or watching Jeremy Kyle… I even got told never to use the word passionate because it was like cheesy, but for me that was what kept getting me up of a morning and going to work and that wanting to improve things and wanting to learn different things and wanting to just step outside the box a bit, reading articles, keeping up [and] looking into new professional development.

Jo Shares

As I revealed in the introduction, I am a big reader and read fiction everyday before I go to sleep. This is my night time ritual, however tired I am, I will always read at least five pages of a novel. This is my down time, my way of switching off my brain before I go to sleep. I have always been an avid reader and as a child, could easily get lost in a book. I recall reading a book in school aged seven and getting so engrossed in it, that I failed to realise that my classmates had all gone out to play. Fiction, was and remains my escape from stress. In terms of my job, I am clearly required to read lots so I tend to distinguish 'work' reading, by reading articles or research reports online, whereas my 'personal reading', is always in the form of real books.

We acknowledge that academic texts and research reports are often written in a very inaccessible way, utilising long words where perhaps simple ones would do! These difficult to read texts and reports can perhaps subconsciously remind us of difficult learning experiences as a child. It is important to remember however that academia is a club with jargon and rules, that aims to exclude people. As long as you get the gist and main points of the article, book or report, then that is more than good enough. You do not have to understand every word, nor read every word (especially if you are reading an academic book). Read smart in other words, using the contents page or index to find the particular topic you are focused on and just read that particular section, focus on the main thrust or the arguments being presented and try to ignore the inaccessible and off-putting language! As an acknowledgement of this, we have tried to compose this book in a way that will facilitate 'smart' reading.

Organisational barriers

As we highlighted in Chapter 6 (hearing) there may be organisational barriers to overcome. For example, access to journals is prohibitively expensive for individuals. It is no wonder then, that practitioners rarely read journal articles due to access issues. Many organisations can no longer afford subscriptions to such journals. However, some universities we know of, enable access for practice educators to use their library facilities. As Finch (2017b) documents, there are some ways to get hold of new research or articles for free:

1) Use a well known search engine scholar function. Sometimes this turns up full copies of article.
2) If this fails, you might want to consider contacting the author directly and ask very politely for a copy, making sure they know you do not have access to a university library.
3) Researchgate is a useful tool for finding out what research there is on a particular topic and other people writing on that particular topic. You can use this as a guest so do not need to be a student or work in a university to access it. You can also use researchgate to contact the authors directly to ask for a copy of the paper.
4) Most universities have open access repositories, in which they collate their staffs' research articles, book chapters and other outputs. These will not be the published version but are the pre published version.

The reality is that there will always be situations you are confronted with in practice that require some research. We call this the Three R approach:

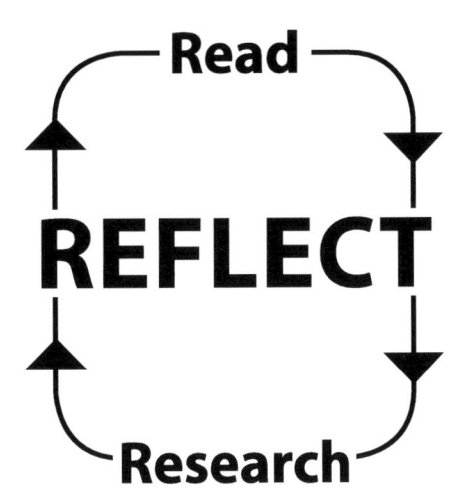

Read → REFLECT → Research (cyclical)

Do record what you read or research and think about how it helps with certain situations you are confronted with, and what you learnt and what you have now done differently. This record will also come in very handy should need to evidence your CPD to your professional body.

Recording in social work practice

The reading component of the SHARE model also covers recording (another r) in social work practice, since it is the recording that social workers do which is often read by other stakeholders (particularly service users).

In 1999, a manager quoted in an overview of inspections of case recording in Social Services said *"My staff are good at what they do, not what they write down"* (Goldsmith 1999). In response Ames (1999) identified recording as a central component in social Work, which was undermined due to practitioners being ill-equipped to undertake this robustly. Almost twenty years ago it may well have been acceptable to separate out 'recording' and 'doing'. However, it is now recognised that recording and reporting (writing down!) is an essential aspect of social work practice; in many ways it is the 'doing'.

A range of concerns about recording in social work practice have been raised in recent years. In Chapter 6 we outlined the concerns that were raised in Lord Laming's report into the death of Victoria Climbie about language and communication. In this report Lord Laming also highlighted a range of concerns in relation to reading and recording practices, as follows:

- Nobody in Haringey - not even [the social worker] - ever read Victoria's case file in its entirety. (p59)
- We cannot be certain what passed between the two because of the lack of recorded information - indeed in the case of the hospital there was none whatsoever (p177)
- It is unlikely that Ms R read any of this material because she said she found it illegible and 'could not read it'. (p185)
- Resolving this conflict of evidence has not been helped by Ms K's poor note taking. There is certainly no record of a telephone conversation between Ms A and Ms K in Ms A's contact notes on Victoria's case file. (p284)

Concerns such as these have led to a renewed focus on the importance of good record keeping in social work practice; linking the 'doing' and 'recording' more closely together within the realm of 'practice'. In fact, it is not unusual to hear the phrase *"if it's not written down then it didn't happen"* in social work teams (Grimwood 2016). We know that lots of social workers are irritated by this phrase. However, we do need to be clearer in our professional world about recording our actions and recognising the importance of this. Doing 'it' and recording 'it' are equally important in terms of social work practice.

In the 'Write Enough' online training programme, Walker, Shemmings and Cleaver (2003) identify a range of potential pitfalls in social work recording in terms of children and families social work:

- Case records are out of date.
- The child is missing from the record.
- Facts and professional judgments are not distinguished in the record.
- The size of the record makes it difficult to manage.
- There is no assessment on file.
- The record is not written for sharing.
- The record is not used as a tool for analysis.
- The record is disrespectful to the service user.

Although not updated for some time now, the Write Enough online package is a useful starting point for students and it also provides some useful refresher exercises for social workers. The Social Care Institute for Excellence (2017 online) also provide some useful information for those new to record keeping in social work and O'Rourke's (2010) book is highly accessible and useful.

It can sometimes feel like there is a forest of paperwork to get through.

Recording: Employer focus

Employers have regularly commented that social workers are not effectively equipped for the role by their training (see Mullan 2014). In our experience, the concerns that employers often have lie around the completion of agency documentation. Indeed, social work students have said to us "we haven't covered how to do assessments" (see Rob's stakeholder voice on page 161) when in fact what they mean is that they haven't covered how to complete specific assessment forms.

Understanding agency requirements in terms of recording and reporting is vitally important for social workers. In fact, Pritchard and Leslie (2011) introduce their work on recording in safeguarding adults with a questionnaire which starts with a range of questions about whether the practitioner knows about and understands their organisation's recording policy and whether they are confident about what and how the organisation expects them to record.

Of course writing for practice, is very different from writing essays, although we feel strongly that the skills used in essay writing (analysis, thinking about evidence, producing a structured document, writing for a particular audience) are the same skills used for writing practice. Rai (2014) notes the types of writing required in social work practice, for example, report writing, case recording, and writing letters, all of which require different approaches, but each of which draw on skills learnt through academic writing.

Perhaps the key difference between written communication and other methods of communication is that written communication is more permanent than any other form. Whilst what someone has said may be forgotten or confused what is written is permanent - it can be read time and time again perhaps for years! Written work remains 'on file' for years and can therefore influence future actions. Social workers must therefore recognise the vital importance of recording and ensure that they work to continually develop their skills in this area.

Recording: the 'wh' questions

We have used the What? Why? How? Framework regularly in this book. However, it is generally accepted that there are 6 'wh' questions, as follows:

- What?
- When?
- Why?
- Which?
- Where?
- Who?

The seventh key question simply includes the W and H in a different order:

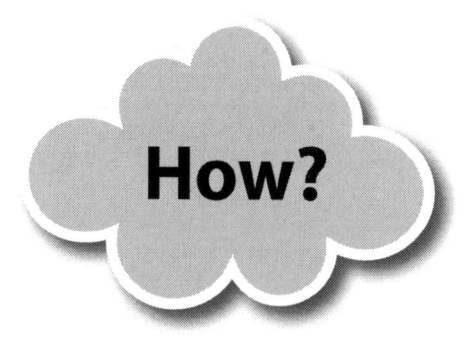

- How?

As we have explored in considering the What? Why? How? framework, often focus is given to the how? question. In terms of recording in social work this is no different, with the key question for consideration often being around 'how do I record? How do I fill this form in? and so on. In order to fully understand the *how* question though it is important to explore all six 'wh' questions, which we will address in the remainder of this chapter.

What to record

One of the difficulties in record keeping is that different people may choose to record different information. As we covered in Chapter 5, everyone sees things differently and so what one person sees as important another may not. Some people may record too much information and others too little.

Recording too much information is pointless, no one will have the time to read through reams of information just to pull out one or two key points. On the other hand it is important that sufficient information is recorded so that all relevant information is shared effectively.

It's that fine balance again!

One of the main problems with recording too little information is that the information given will usually focus on problems / difficulties, with little about strengths and what might be going well. This will result in the recording being very negative. Recording should always be balanced and respectful, but getting the balance right can be difficult and is a skill which needs to be developed.

Prospera Shares

Many years ago, I prepared a number of reports for court and asked if my supervisor would be so kind as to look through them and offer any advice or feedback. She agreed, but when I handed her the folder she made a disparaging remark along the lines of "I haven't got the time to read this thesis". The comment broke me. I wasn't entirely sure whether it was a joke to begin with, however when she proceeded to give it back to me, I understood that she meant what she had said. The implication here being there was too much to read.

I reflected on the source of the comment and immediately started to think about previous work given to her to review. I thought myself to be thorough in my writing. Did this feedback mean I had to stop being thorough and provide the bare minimum write up rather than a comprehensive overview? Did other colleagues in the team think similarly? Had she shared her views with them? Hang on, was this even feedback??

My experience of supervision on this occasion was not a positive one as I had felt let down by the manager employed to support me. I never took anything to her for review going forward however when an email from the local authority legal team complemented the quality and substance of my reports, the email went to this manager and copied to me. Whilst the email somewhat vindicated me, I wondered about how the person in the legal team had reached the decision to email my manager. The supervision session I perceive was not a conversation or dialogue. It was unidirectional and stopped me in my tracks. Supervision, formal or informal must be respectful and empowering. Areas for improvement can be given without reducing the supervisee to tears or despair.

STAKEHOLDER VOICE
MATT HUGHES

Matt Hughes is an independent Social Worker, Manager and the Director of One Stop Social which operates a website for social work and care professionals. Matt also provides supervision and support.
http://www.onestopsocial.co.uk/

In the world of Social Work, like it or not, we are an assessment led service. What I mean by this is the fact that our assessments dictate what interventions a service user or family may receive and at what level. Whether intervening to support a child in need, assessing risk or identifying capacity / support for vulnerable adults.

As a social work manager, I have been involved in inspecting and quality assuring a number of best practice thematic and external inspections relating to assessment skills within social work. In addition, I had my own work inspected as a practitioner focusing on quality of assessments and intervention delivery. Given my experiences, I am often asked for advice on the foundations of a good assessment and how this is recorded. So, what does it include?

In order to achieve the foundations of a good assessment, practitioners should have good self-awareness. They must understand and be confident in their ability to think critically through reflective practice and must have a good awareness of current evidence based work. When undertaking any assessments, you should consider the following:

- What do I know about people in this situation?
- Where does my knowledge base come from?
- What are my prejudices (positive and negative) and how does this inform my practice?
- What do I know / expect?
- What might surprise me and why?
- What are the overall goals for my involvement?

Sources of information

A good 'starter for 10' in any assessment is in the ability to collate a wealth of information from a variety of sources. This will strengthen the validity of the argument and will offer you a good foundation for exploring issues, themes or strengths. Remember, sources of information should be viewed as the descriptive element - the what, when, and where. With this you will be able to expand and find common trends.

Preparation for interview / assessment meeting

Being prepared prior to meeting with the service user / family is key. Remember, this is the starting point for gathering your information / evidence base. A significant number of 'unsatisfactory' assessments I have quality assured were not unsatisfactory as a result of their inability to write an assessment. It was their inability to conduct a 'good' interview / assessment meeting. You must not underestimate its importance.

Top tip: When I first started, I would not bring the assessment document with me - I found this disempowering for Service Users. Rather I completed a 'Buzz Word Sheet'. This was an A4 page that contained buzz words such as 'Family Dynamics', 'Attachments' 'Positive Role Models' etc. This prompted me to ask relevant questions and stay on track.

Assessment is not description

Again, every 'unsatisfactory' assessment I have quality assured were those that contained only a description of the event(s). It offered no analysis or break-down of the findings; the 'how and why'. My advice here is to view description as the narrative. The main body of an assessment is the analysis which should identify and highlight your understanding of the perceived situation. Remember, be confident in your ability, professional judgement and capabilities.

Clear theoretical base

Once you have gathered your evidence, you can now begin to assess and identify key themes, patterns, needs and risks (as well as positives). Make sure that you test different ways of understanding so as to offer you a holistic viewpoint on a particular situation.

Top Tip: Add a list of all the theories / legislation you are likely to use on your 'Buzz Word Sheet'.

Make defensible not defensive decisions

Given the significant negative media attention that social work attracts, we can be forgiven for making defensive rather than defensible decisions, with the starting point often being the assessment process.

What is the difference I hear you say? Well, defensive practice is reactional rather than preventative. It is responding through the need to 'cover one's back' rather than what the person may need. Whereas, defensible practice is where you have used your professional judgement (remember we are taught to think automatously) in highlighting areas of need. This is supported through evidence based practice and is identified within the sources of information.

Assessments should be SMART

Often practitioners believe that by writing pages of information it will equal a 'good' assessment. This is not the case. All assessments should be SMART.

- Specific: identify the reasons for involvement and concerns identified.
- Measurable: how and when we will know the circumstances for that service user / family have changed?
- Achievable: chunk and check. Focus on areas of strengths as well as weaknesses that are bite sized. Focus on short term change and identify longer term change.
- Realistic: are the areas of work / intervention realistic?
- Timely: we must identify, plan and review timely work.

Assessment is a fluid process

It is wrong to think that once an assessment has been completed, that's it. Remember, the assessment process is fluid and ever changing. There is rarely one straight and easy path. Assessments must be reviewed on a regular basis and be relevant to the 'here and now'. For me, a review should take place when 'circumstances change'. E.g. heightened or decreased vulnerability.

Conclusion must identify outcomes and plan

A 'good' assessment will identify what level of planning and intervention delivery is required within the conclusion element. The assessment should flow from the description, main body (analysis), to highlighting the overall plan and outcomes needed in order to promote change or safeguard. This should be reviewed and evaluated regularly.

Top tip: APIS - Assessment, Planning, Intervention and Supervision. Clearly identify what changes are needed imminently and what are the longer term objectives.

Use supervision to discuss findings

A good manager will offer you a sounding board so as you can discuss your findings or help you reflect on certain aspects of the case under assessment. Obviously, you will not be able to discuss every case in detail, but as a professional, you should be able to identify what needs to be prioritised. For me, the best staff I managed were those that presented an agenda during each supervision session. This resulted in a good reflective flow for both the supervisor and supervisee.

Use peer support

Every successful team I worked for had a strong sense of support for one another. During my newly qualified years, I benefitted from working with some fantastic social workers. I was able to shadow, observe and reflect in peer support group sessions both formal and informal. I believe this helped fast track my ability as a social worker as I was able to see first-hand what I considered as 'good' practice in action.

I hope this has offered some guidance in relation to what factors you must consider when undertaking an assessment. Remember, always evidence your work and the information you have gathered. This will strengthen your assessment, but it will also protect you in your decision making.

© Matt Hughes

Why record?

Pritchard and Leslie (2011) assert that social workers often do not understand the purpose of recording, resulting in them seeing recording as a chore. This means that they may not commit to the continuous development of their recording; they effectively create an attitudinal barrier to good record keeping.

It is easy to understand why this might be the case, as recording can be seem like part and parcel of defensive practice, perhaps justifying actions and decisions made in case of future concerns. It also takes away time from direct work with individuals and families. It is important though that the time spent on recording is recognised as valuable because, records serve to:

- Provide information to deliver the highest possible standard of service.
- Enable staff to assess intervention, plan, monitor and evaluate work with service users.
- Provide continuity of service when workers change.
- Communicate information.
- Enable managers to monitor the work of staff and give appropriate advice, support and direction.
- Provide a means of accountability, so that actions and decisions that have been taken can be understood and justified.
- Meet specific legislative requirements.
- Provide information that may be needed as evidence in court proceedings, judicial reviews, internal and external enquiries and complaint investigations.
- Enable information and data to be collected as a basis for evaluating service delivery, managing resources and future planning.
- Provide information to people about professional involvement if they wish to have access to their records.
- Support people to understand their life from a range of perspectives.

KEY MESSAGES FROM RESEARCH: SOCIAL WORK RECORDING

NIASW (2012) in a survey of members found that:

- 96% highlighted report writing as a specific difficulty that impacted on their ability to spend time in face to face work with clients.
- 90% highlighted recording in client files as a specific difficulty that impacted on their ability to spend time with clients.
- 73% identified entering information into computer systems as impacting on the time they can spend directly with clients.

White et al (2009) estimated that social workers spend between 60% and 80% of their time behind computers rather than in direct work with people.

You will notice that the other messages from research sections fill a page. We have really struggled to find up to date research in relation to recording in social work. We would invite your comments on this, so think through the following questions and tweet your responses; get them in the public domain. Let's work towards a shared voice here.

My Share

Why do you think there is such limited research in social work around recording?

What should be researched in this area?

When to record

It is vital to record as soon as possible after an event, even if only key points are captured at that time. One of the difficulties that we see on a regular basis is that social workers do not schedule time in their diaries for record keeping. Perhaps this relates to the fact that workers sometimes resent recording and see it as keeping them away from their 'real job.' What then happens is that practitioners get behind with their records - or they end up doing them at home out of their scheduled work. This has implications for confidentiality in relation to service users. So, one of our main tips for record keeping would be to plan time in your diary. Most practitioners have an electronic diary, don't use this just to schedule visits and meetings, a key part of your work is recording, so schedule this into your diary.

Where social workers get very behind with recording this can be overwhelming for them and can create a range of issues. Recording is a key part of the job and practitioners have a responsibility to keep on top of their recording. A social worker was struck off for asking a third party to type case records, thereby failing to protect the privacy and confidentiality of the service users and placing them at risk (Donovan, 2016).

Where to record

Organisational requirements vary significantly when it comes to recording practice and one of the most crucial things a social worker new to an organisation will have to do is get to grips with recording protocols.

Recording in contemporary social work is almost exclusively computerised. Some local authorities have trialled the use of mobile tablets which social workers take along on home visits and type directly onto. The system is used in Nottinghamshire where they found that laptops and other mobile equipment were not as efficient as they wanted, consequently they shifted to ipads which social workers report is saving on travel time and making recording much more robust. There are concerns however about how secure and confidential these devices are in that they store service user information and sensitive details. Managers in Nottinghamshire have confirmed that the necessary precautions have been taken and the ipads have strong security (Donovan, 2014). Whilst many organisations have now provided equipment such as this to assist in recording, there are issues around the way that these can create barriers for some service users. They may, for example, get in the way of conversational practice. Certainly, Maxine's voice (see page 140) is critical of the use of a tablet device and the sound that this makes when she is playing with her children.

Many of the assessments undertaken by social workers will have proformas or templates which should be expandable to enable practitioners to write as much as required. However, not all online proformas can be expanded and in some cases there is a word or character limit. This requires the social worker to use their skills of synthesis and summarising to ensure that only relevant information is captured on the form or in the assessment template.

Who will read the record?

A wide range of people will read the recording that social workers keep. For example, managers will access records on a regular basis to ensure quality, other professionals may have access to case records as part of information sharing. Service users and possibly family members also have rights of access to records.

Recording must be written with the 'audience' in mind. Participants in a study by Gannon (2005) found that in the area of birth records counselling in adoption, there were often artifacts such as photos with no names or identifying information which made it difficult for the current social worker to work with and even more difficult for the person wanting access to their records. Adult adoptees can ask to view their birth records and other relevant information and so it is crucial that the adoption social worker understand the protocols required for selection and access to particular types of information and records. The study by Gannon (2005) concluded that adoption social workers took the decision about how much and what to share guided by their agency's legal team. It is simply insensitive for a person to be given records about their birth, early years and adoption which are stigmatising, disrespectful and / or untrue. According to Gannon (2005) one adoptee found that a statement about their birth mother being 'pitiful and pathetic' (p60) was highly subjective and did little to enhance her sense of self. Other examples of subjective recording included descriptions of children as 'not particularly pretty' and with 'big ears' (p 60). Conversely, Archer and Burnell (2003) found that in trying to minimise the impact on an adoptee, some social workers would purposely leave out information which they felt was unhelpful and could cause distress.

We raised a point in Chapter 6 about avoiding the use of jargon and acronyms. It is really important not to use abbreviations or acronyms in records, as these will some become obsolete in the ever-changing acronym world of social work. Indeed, we note a family court Judge's criticism of a social worker's report in 2015 (Silman, 2015). The Judge was highly critical of the jargon used in the report, and commented that the assessment of a Grandmother for a Special Guardianship order, "*might just as well have been written in a foreign language*" (Ibid, no page number). For the Judge this raised concerns about how far the social worker had been able to communicate and work effectively with the family. The Judge highlighted one particular obtuse paragraph, which read as follows:

> "*I do not intend to address the couple's relationship suffice it to say it is imbued with ambivalence: both having many commonalities emanating from their histories that create what could be a long lasting connection or alternative relationship that are a reflection of this. Such is this connection they may collude to undermine the placement.*" (Ibid)

This makes no sense whatsoever and we feel the Judge was right to comment.

Write records to share them

Think about:

Use of jargon (will it mean anything to the reader?)

Respect: what you would want to read about yourself?

Organisation and clarity: does the record reflect a professional approach? What impression will it leave the reader with?

The which question

In working through all of the key questions and relating these to recording we must admit to being uncertain about the which question. What should we cover? This could include a range of things that a social worker needs to consider, but in using which to start a question in terms of record keeping most social workers would think about 'which form do I need to fill in?' and clearly that can't be addressed in a book of this kind. However, one 'which' issue that is often avoided but is in fact essential is to consider that there are often many versions of a record and there may be errors in bringing these together. Which record do we work from?

There may be multiple records in relation to a family or situation, it is crucial that these are synthesised into a single version for use by the agency or practitioner. Version control may become necessary when, for example, a social worker takes handwritten notes, drafts, types onto a blank document with possible annotations and also has a completed assessment proforma. In the absence of the particular social worker, it may be difficult to know which information to work with. Version control should therefore come with dates to enable readers identify earlier and later additions to a particular record.

Multi-agency work may also result in the emphasis on different elements of a service user's life and circumstances and could lead to confusion about which records to use or rely on. For example, if the health visitor records neglect in relation to a particular family but this is not captured by the social worker from their observations and assessments, how might this be recorded so that it reflects the contribution from the health visitor?

It is also vital that names are spelt correctly and if more than one name used, to use all versions. This came to light in the case of Aliyah Ismail, a 13-year-old girl who died of a methadone overdose whilst in the care of Harrow Council in London. The serious case review, commented that she was known by three different surnames, and so the agencies that worked with her, often did not coordinate or share information, as no connection was made that it was the same person (Harrow ACPC, 1999).

How to record

In many ways the style of recording is as important as the content, so this is perhaps one of the most important questions of them all. 'How' questions are often answered through an exploration of the 6 'wh' questions so, of course, to some extent this question has been addressed by the discussion so far in this chapter; we have already stated that how you record should be respectful of service users, that it should be clear and without jargon for example. Other issues also need to be considered in relation to how.

Recording should be professional in terms of clarity. For social workers for who English is an additional language or for those who may have difficulties with professional English language, our advice is to read often and ensure the use of dictionaries and spell checking functions to minimise errors and punctuation difficulties which may distort the meaning of what has been recorded. For example, Prospera worked with a social worker who recorded, in relation to a child 'I asked him to go and play with himself', Prospera immediately considered that this might be direct translation and asked for clarification. The recording was changed to 'I asked him to go and play by himself'. It is easy to see how such a recording may have created significant difficulties.

Recording should distinguish between facts and interpretation or opinion.

Fact: A fact is something certainly known to have occurred or to be true.

Interpretation: An interpretation is the representation of a thing or event, according to one's conception of it.

Opinion: An opinion is a judgement or belief based on grounds short of absolute proof.

All of these may be required in a record but it is important to be absolutely clear when you are offering an opinion, or when something is a fact. Of course, in the messy world of social work, much may be interpretative so there must be clarity and honesty about this. This becomes even more essential when writing court or tribunal reports, where there is potential for every word written to be questioned. Indeed, Jo made the mistake of writing 'traumatised' in a court assessment report which led to a long series of questions being asked about her qualifications to be able to make a 'clinical' assessment. Of course, what Jo should have done, is describe the behaviours exhibited by the individual concerned and not made such a blunt assertion of 'trauma', and used descriptors like, 'cried when asked about the incident' instead.

Using the SHARE model in recording

The SHARE model encourages us to consider the perspective of each stakeholder in any given situation. As such, it is important to be aware of the way what you have written will be read. Indeed Dyke (2016) suggests that social workers should "*write for it to be read, not for it to be written*". The starting point for using SHARE to support the development of good recording is therefore to keep the 'reader' at the heart:

- What is the intended audience for this record?
- Is it accessible to the reader?
- Is it fully respectful of the service user and everyone involved (whilst remaining descriptive and honest)?

Sometimes when we review records, we note that they read like a story. All the information is included, but it lacks a clarity about where the information has come from and is often devoid of analysis. The SHARE model specifically addresses these issues in recording, as the social worker developing the record ensures that the record is clear about what they have seen, heard, done, read and how they have evaluated this. The need for recording to address more than story telling is outlined in the following stakeholder voice, from Alton.

Always keep the reader at the heart of your writing

STAKEHOLDER VOICE — ALTON

Alton is a team manger in a youth offending team.

As part of my work I read a large number of records and reports. In Youth Offending, AssetPlus is the assessment and planning tool which we use. This is designed to recognise the professional judgement of practitioners in order to promote more sharply focused intervention plans for children and young people. A number of the practitioners on my team (who come from a range of backgrounds) seem to struggle with making the AssetPlus more than a descriptive account. They sometimes seem fearful of 'getting things wrong'. I recognise that there is a perception about a blame culture but what I (and the courts) really value is the skills in analysis of a professional who is able to evidence a professional recommendation which leads into a defensible decision. The apparent fear about putting the word *I* into a professional document worries me greatly.

© Alton

Moving record keeping away from a story telling approach demonstrates the connections between the different components of the SHARE model. Recording is part of the action component for social workers and it draws on what they see and hear. The recording must take an analytical approach which brings us to the final component, covered in the next chapter, of evaluation.

Recording in social work is more than telling a story.

Key points

- Reading is a vital activity in social work. Social workers need to read a range of material in relation to their own practice but they must also engage in wider reading for their own professional development.
- There are known barriers to reading which social workers need to be aware of for themselves, their colleagues and the people they work with.
- Social work is not represented well in the media. This means that people may have negative views based on what they have read about social work.
- Social workers often feel that recording gets in the way of their work, but in many ways recording is a central component of that work.

Reflective Questions

What do you read about social work? How do you draw on this in your CPD?

What do you think of the way that social work is reflected in the press?

What stands out the most for you from this chapter? Why is that?

How might you be able to improve your recording practice?

Chapter 9: EVALUATION

In this chapter we focus on the final component of the SHARE model – that of evaluation. We explore the various meanings of evaluation and consider how reflection is a vital aspect of evaluation and indeed of social work. We have tried to take a very practical approach to exploring evaluation in this chapter, since it is often presented in an abstract and academic manner. We therefore address what evaluation in contemporary practice might be about and conclude with analysis, ending the chapter using the first component of the SHARE model (to again illustrate the connections) taking a visual approach to analytical skills.

What is evaluation?

Evaluation is a word that is commonly used in professional practice, and as such practitioners all have different ways of understanding the concept. In dictionary terms, the word evaluate is about determining or calculating the significance, worth or quality of something (Merriam-Webster online dictionary, 2017c).

In project management then evaluation is always against standards of some kind. The online evaluation toolbox defines evaluation as *"a structured process of assessing the success of a project in meeting its goals, to reflect on the lessons learned"* (Community Sustainability Engagement 2017).

The term evaluation, used in research contexts, refers to a specific research design or methodological approach that usually focuses on how well an intervention, or a program, delivers on a set of outcomes. This is often known in the US context as program evaluation. Evaluations can be used across the research spectrum, namely quantitative, qualitative or a mixed methods approach. All approaches aim however, at coming to some sort of evidence-based conclusion, about how far a specific intervention for example, has achieved (or not) a set of pre-defined, specific and measurable outcomes.

In terms of the SHARE model we see evaluation as being about developing an evidence-based conclusion which draws on other aspects of the model. So, in light of what you have seen, heard, done and read what conclusion do you draw and why? As we have discussed earlier in the book, why questions are really important but they can get overlooked or forgotten. So, the evaluation component of the SHARE model is very much about using the other components in a highly reflective way to thoroughly evaluate, and reach an evidence-based conclusion. Of course, in the real messy world of social work practice, evaluation and drawing conclusions are not easy processes. The SHARE model however, can aid considerably by breaking down the process into components which do not need to be addressed in a linear, limiting manner.

255

Reflective practice

As we have just acknowledged, evaluation and reflection very much go hand in hand in terms of social work practice. The importance of reflective practice and reflective supervision is widely recognised in social work (see for example Research in Practice 2014). Despite the fact that reflection is high on the professional agenda, it is not always clearly understood and in many ways there is little agreement on the concept of reflection, and defining it can be problematic. As a result, a range of models of reflection have been developed and employers have developed policies and systems to promote reflective supervision. Despite this, White (2009) suggests that social workers have been turned into 'unreflective processors' due to the increased bureaucracy in contemporary practice.

Stages of reflection

The widely acknowledged three stages of reflection first proposed by Schön (1983) and later added to by Killian and Todnem (1991), are:

Reflection *for* action: reflecting in preparation for action.

Reflection *in* action: reflecting as the work is taking place, whilst the 'action' is happening.

Reflection *on* action: reflecting later, after the event.

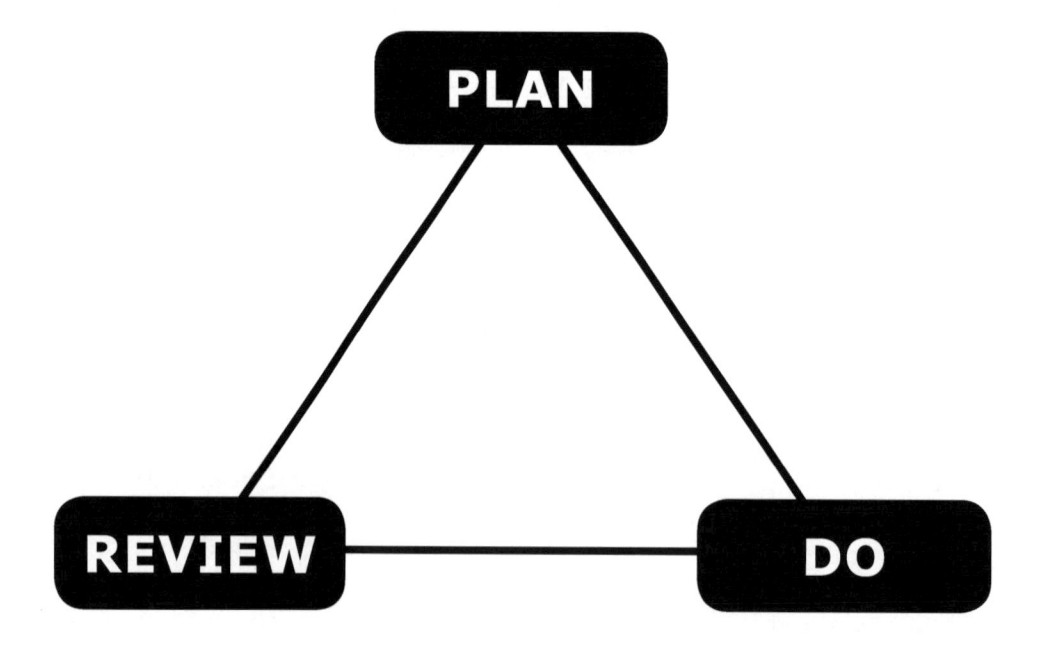

```
        PLAN
        /  \
       /    \
      /      \
   REVIEW —— DO
```

Spaces of reflection

Along with the three stages of reflection, there are what we would term three spaces of reflection (that is where social workers say they are most likely to reflect):

The car: social workers often describe reflecting on the journey between visits or on their way home.

The bathroom: often social workers identify that they reflect about work in the shower perhaps at the very start of their day getting ready for work, or in the bath unwinding at the end of the day.

Bed: social workers tell us that they often find themselves reflecting when going to sleep, or even waking up in the middle of the night. This is the most problematic (and may identify that there are issues of long term stress that need to be explored).

What this means is that social workers are likely to be alone when they are reflecting. As a consequence, their reflection is likely to be limited to their own thought process. Boud, Keogh and Walker (1985) were clear that there is a limit to reflection which is done in isolation and they highlighted the importance of mulling reflection over with others. Building on this idea that reflecting with others is important, the concept of critical friendships to promote deeper reflection is well established in some professional groups. For example, 'Critical Friendship Groups' are very widely used in education (Lyons 2010). The concept of critical friendships was first introduced by Stenhouse (1975) as a method to support action research and has more recently been developed as something which supports reflective practice. The idea is that the critical friend acts as an interested 'sounding board', listening and asking proactive questions which promote deeper thinking and encourage the practitioner to reflect on their work. Research into the use of critical friends in medical education indicates that whilst having a critical friend is useful, it might be even more advantageous for the person acting as the critical friend in terms of the development of reflective practice skills (Dahlgren et al 2006).

Whilst the focus on reflective practice in social work training often lies around the ideas of reflection in, on and for action, we would add a fourth to this: that of reflection with. The idea of reflection with is to promote the value of sharing reflections with others. It is also important though to recognise the importance of reflection with action - this illustrates the way that reflection and action are closely related. It is vital that reflection leads to action. Reflection 'with', links us back to the importance of knowledge sharing, discussed in Chapter 2.

Of course, in open plan offices and hotdesking environments reflection with colleagues becomes virtually impossible. Practices such as intervision (see page 123) can assist with this.

SHARE in reflection

Evaluation is therefore widely recognised as a key aspect of reflection, with references to the importance of evaluation in many models of reflection. For example, Gibbs (1988) developed six stages to reflective practice which make up a continuous cycle. Although developed as a framework for reflection on nursing practice, this model is very popular in social work training. Gibbs places evaluation right at the centre of his model of reflection, which reflects our view that evaluation lies at the very heart of reflective practice.

Where Gibbs sees reflection as a process to be worked through, we see reflection as much more dynamic. We take a component rather than process approach to reflection. The SHARE model recognises that what people see, hear, do and read will impact on their reflection and the conclusions they draw, or how they evaluate the evidence. The conclusion that they draw will then, in turn, influence what they do, see and hear in the future. This illustrates a circularity of understanding which builds on reflexivity in practice (see page 45).

Connecting the components of the SHARE model and recognising the relationships between each component can really enhance reflection in practice. We have used the SHARE model to evaluate experiences and contemporary news stories throughout this book: illustrating the way that the model can be used to reflect in, on and for practice. Sharing these reflections with others and using them to reconstruct future practice with a new outlook is what reflection *with* is all about.

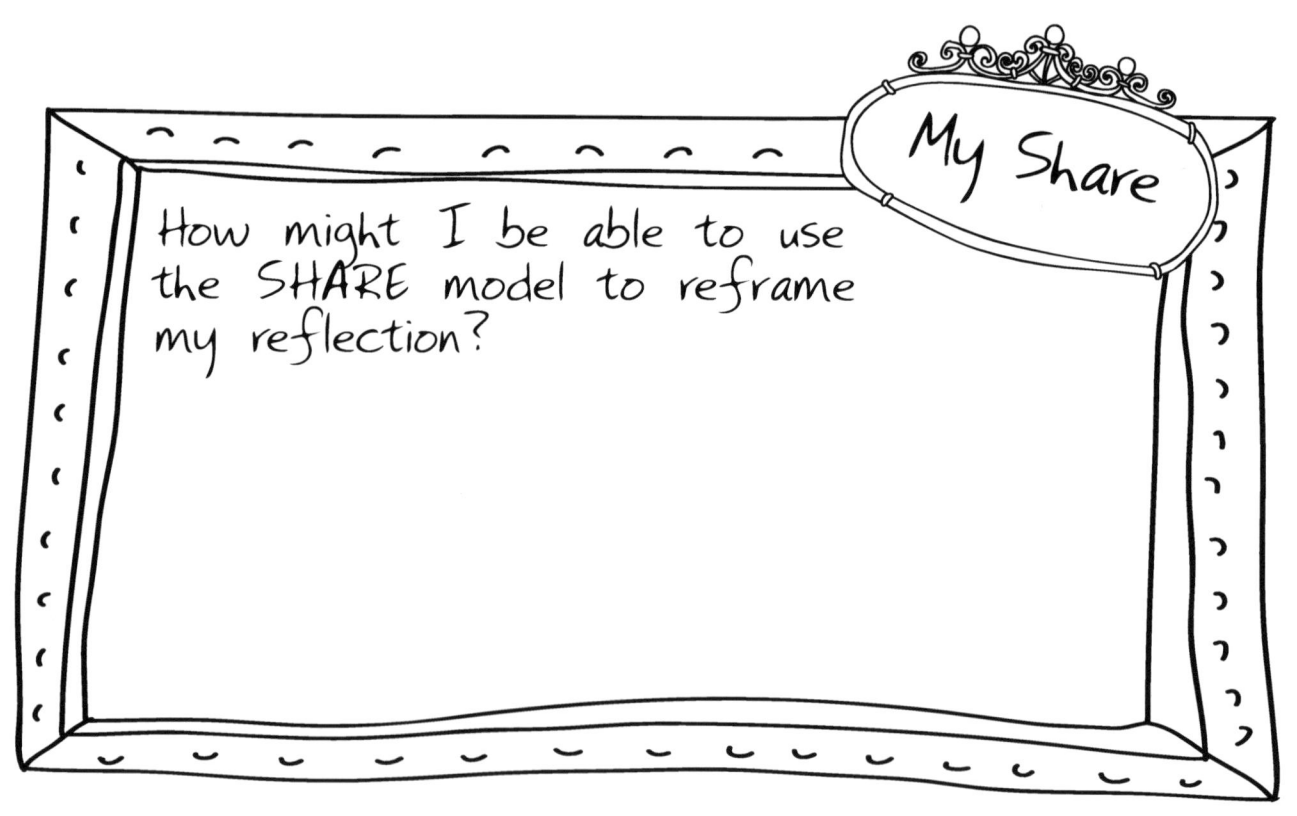

> **My Share**
>
> How might I be able to use the SHARE model to reframe my reflection?

Emotional intelligence and social work

In Chapter 1 we referred to the fact that we had extensive discussions about whether the E in the SHARE model should refer to emotions rather than evaluation. Ultimately, we concluded that evaluation would include a consideration of emotions as central to the model and indeed as we have developed this book, the word emotion appears in every chapter in one way or another.

Despite the fact that social workers are faced with emotional issues on a daily basis and the acknowledgement that social work is 'emotional work of a high order' (Howe 2008), social workers report a lack of support in dealing with emotions. For example, in a survey of social workers, 70% of respondents felt that the emotional issues arising from their work were not adequately addressed in supervision (BASW 2011). Hennessey (2011) argues that social workers who are encouraged to explore and reflect on the emotional aspects of their work are much more able to develop 'sound multi-dimensional practice' whilst Ingram (2013) believes that decision making is enhanced and is more transparent when emotions are shared in the context of the supervisory relationship.

Emotional intelligence was introduced as a term by Peter Salovey and John Mayer in 1990 and popularised by Dan Goleman in 1995. Emotional intelligence (sometimes referred to as EI or EQ) now has a whole 'industry' behind it - particularly in terms of business models and leadership consultants. As such there are a number of ways of looking at emotional intelligence, but generally speaking emotional intelligence includes the ability to identify, understand, manage and use emotions. Many of the skills which we promote as part of the SHARE model, such as empathy and self-awareness are therefore key to emotional intelligence.

Emotional intelligence is about practitioners recognising emotions in themselves and others (therefore, recognising all the stakeholders' SHAREs). Using this recognition helps practitioners to connect, engage and build relationships. Emotional intelligence promotes collaboration and reduces the negative impact of conflict. It also aids thinking and perceptions and supports the management of emotions - thus promoting professional resilience. Reflective supervision can support social workers to become more emotionally aware and can enhance practitioners' emotional intelligence.

A relationships-based approach to social work is underpinned by psychoanalytical theories. In brief, social workers should reflect on their emotions during and after interactions with others. This may inform them about the other person's emotional state. As Andrew Richardson comments, on page 170, social workers need to be able to understand and contain other peoples' emotions. This is a key aspect of emotional intelligence.

Emotional intelligence and reflection go hand in hand: it's difficult to be reflective without being emotionally intelligent and you can't be emotionally intelligent without being reflective. Certainly, in terms of the SHARE model we see a consideration of emotions as a key part of evaluation.

Emotions and evaluation frameworks

It can be very helpful to use frameworks in the evaluation process and of course there are many potential frameworks. Most of the frameworks which are useful in social work are clear about the impact of emotions on the evluation process. For example:

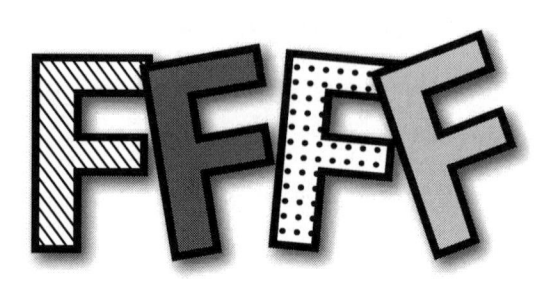

The 4Fs: This framework was developed by Roger Greenaway (2014) as a review framework. It is often referred to as an active reviewing cycle. It is commonly used in relation to outdoor activity centres and youth work activities with young people. However, it has been brought into social work by social pedagogues who, in many ways, straddle the fields of education and social work in the UK. The framework is based on the 4Fs of Facts, Feelings, Findings, and Futures.

The Mum test: This is a phrase commonly referred to by the Care Quality Commission (CQC) in their inspection of adult social care services. Essentially the mum test refers to *"inspectors considering whether these are services that they would be happy for someone they love and care for to use."* (Merrill 2014) The concept of the mum test was brought into the CQC by Andrea Sutcliffe who reported wanting to personalise the inspection framework.

SAFE: Jan Burns, whose stakeholder voice appears on page 193, offered us her personal framework for evaluation, which demonstrates the central importance of feelings for reflection and professional intuition. This involves looking at the following based around the acronym of SAFE:

    See: What do I see?

    Atmosphere: What is the atmosphere like?

    Feelings: how do I feel?

    Evidence: Where is my evidence?

Turning knowledge into understanding

Evaluation is essentially about understanding. Practitioners who take a critically reflective stance are constantly evaluating the knowledge that they have - turning knowledge into understanding.

Whilst a range of knowledge may be taught on social work training and knowledge can be kept up to date through reading and continual development activities, it is only really through evaluation that knowledge can be applied to, and used in, practice. Pawson et al (2003) developed a classification of knowledge for the Social Care Institute for Excellence based on five different sources of social care knowledge, as follows:

- Organisational knowledge
- Practitioner knowledge
- User knowledge
- Research knowledge
- Policy community knowledge

The sharing of knowledge (see pages 34-35) will lead to a further development of knowledge in each of these areas.

The importance of practice wisdom (referred to by Cameron and Boddy in 2006 as tacit knowledge) has long been recognised in social work. DeRoos (1990) argued that although practice wisdom has long been a basic concept in social work, what it is and how it is developed remain insufficiently understood. Essentially practice wisdom can be seen as the way that practitioners use the knowledge that they develop through their careers. In many ways, practice wisdom can only be developed through critical reflection following experiences. The experience itself is not enough to develop practice wisdom - there are lots of people who have made the same mistakes over and over again. Wisdom develops from evaluating and sharing experiences.

The other components of the SHARE model help to develop knowledge, for example, you learn things from what you see, hear, read and do. However, it is only through evaluation that this knowledge is developed into understanding or what could be seen as practice wisdom. Taking a critical stance to evaluating knowledge is a vital aspect of social work practice.

Knowledge is fixed and can create limitations to the way that we see things. Suspending knowledge to explore 'outside the box' is a key aspect of reflection. Knowledge is time, context and societally and culturally specific. Such that, what people know now is different to what people used to 'know', and it may well be different to what people in other countries 'know'.

People used to believe the earth was flat. Whilst this seems entertaining to us now, it clearly illustrates the way that knowledge changes over time. Evaluation helps us to explore this changing knowledge and where it comes from, helping us to explore knowledge and develop our understanding.

Fook argues that reflective processes can potentially unearth assumptions suggesting that *"some crucial but hitherto deeply hidden assumptions may be uncovered"* (Fook 2004: 59.) However, issues such as bias and perception, power structures, existing knowledge frameworks and dominant discourses (which we have explored in chapters covering the other components of the SHARE model) will all have an impact on an individual's evaluation of something. So, assumptions are not always unearthed - sometimes things are hidden and become buried. Exploring the development of our knowledge and understanding about child sexual abuse illustrates this well.

In 1896 Sigmund Freud stated that:

"Almost all of my women patients told me that they had been seduced by their father."

However, by 1933 he concluded:

"I was driven to recognise in the end that these reports were untrue and so came to understand that these hysterical symptoms are derived from phantasies and not from real occurrences......"

Clearly when Freud evaluated what he had heard, he buried the issue of sexual abuse. There could be a number of reasons for this, for example he may have been complicit in covering up what was happening. However, we think it is very likely that Freud's conclusions were based on the fact that the knowledge and practice that surrounded him at that time indicated that child sexual abuse just did not happen. The dominant discourse of the day was that this was not an issue for discussion or consideration. Freud went on to reflect on what he had heard and evaluated that differently as a result:

"....It was only later that I was able to recognise in this phantasy of being seduced by the father the expression of the typical Oedipus complex in women." (Freud 1933 in Steiner 2003)

Freud's theories about what he termed, the psycho-sexual phases of develoment are still very popular today. Indeed, Freud's denial of the possibilities of sexual abuse, would be later termed as one of many ways humans defend against anxiety. A psychoanalytic view therefore, is that when humans are confronted with issues or concerns that are deeply disturbing, and indeed may cause psychological harm they engage in a myriad of defensive behaviours, these might include splitting, introjection, projection, denial, idealisation, repression, acting out and regression to name but a few (Trevithick, 2011).

By 1982, Judith Herman picked up that the issue of childhood sexual abuse *"has been repeatedly unearthed in the past hundred years, and just as repeatedly buried… The information was simply too threatening to be maintained in public consciousness"* (Herman 1982:7.) Even following Judith Herman's work in the early 1980s it could be argued that knowledge about child sexual abuse was buried again. Press coverage about Jimmy Saville and Operation Yewtree illustrates very clearly the way that knowledge about child abuse and societal values around the safeguarding of children have changed significantly in the recent past.

On the following page, Siobhan shares an incident from her early career – which if it occurred now would have certainly prompted a different evaluation.

Siobhan Shares

There are some situations and people that you work with that remain with you through your professional careers. One of the most vivid recollections from my very early career lie around my work with a young woman, who I will call Jodie. As I write this I can still see Jodie in my mind's eye. Whilst I still see her as a 14 year old young woman, she will now be in her 40s. I had worked with Jodie for a few months and I felt that we had a good working relationship. There were a number of issues for Jodie living at home and as she moved into local authority care I remember driving her to the residential service about an hour away from her home environment and settling her in that evening. I visited her a couple of times over the next week and very quickly our relationship changed: Jodie refused to see me and was often out of the service setting when she knew I was visiting.

Over the next few weeks Jodie was seen getting into taxis; she went missing for days at a time and returned to the service simply to shower and change, leaving again when any staff tried to have conversations with her.

Reading this story now any social workers will recognise the key signs of child trafficking and sexual exploitation. At the time, I was really concerned and had various discussions about Jodie with residential staff and my manager. I was told that Jodie had made a 'lifestyle choice' and that she was now a child prostitute. I was advised to prioritise my time differently and not to spend so much time on trying to engage with Jodie ("*I know it's difficult - but it's best just give up on her. Move on to others that you can make a difference for.*") Even writing that now angers and upsets me. At the time, there was little or no language that I could draw on to help me to challenge the dominant discourse within the organisation. I challenged at every level I could. As a result, I was told that I had a training need and was sent on a training course run by one of the large National Voluntary Organisations which supports children. The course was entitled Child Prostitution.

I recall how uncomfortable I felt about the fact that I had been involved in supporting Jodie to move into local authority care which had now chosen to label her in such a way. Shortly after this I left the post, largely because I felt so uncomfortable in the role.

I want to share this to demonstrate that now it is impossible for us to look at stories of young people like Jodie and not understand that she was being abused, trafficked and exploited. However, less than 30 years ago social workers had no framework for understanding this. It was not part of either the public or professional consciousness. I often wonder what happened to Jodie and probably always will.

Evaluation in contemporary practice

A key aspect of good social work practice, is being aware of what is 'simply too threatening to be maintained in the public consciousness' (Herman 1982). The evaluation component of the SHARE model is all about thinking through every possibility in terms of what you see, hear, do and read and ensuring a fully reflexive response. In many ways, social workers work on the very edges of society we see and hear the things that most of society do not want to hold in their consciousness. It is vital that we are open to these issues and that we give full consideration to what we see, hear, do and read and that we evaluate this to develop our knowledge and understanding. We must also explore what others are seeing, hearing, doing and reading (and writing) to be fully reflexive.

It is easy for us now to look back at practice in the past and think 'how could social workers not recognise that or do something about it?' but being reflexive involves us giving a real consideration to contemporary practice issues and exploring what is currently 'too threatening to be maintained in the public consciousness'? What is it that social workers keep on uncovering and society (often specifically Governments) keep on burying? On the following pages, we explore some of the issues we see and think about regularly.

Witchcraft labelling

The labelling of children as witches has been raised as a concerning issue for some time, but keeps on being buried again. In its contemporary form witchraft labelling as an abuse of children is growing in many communities around the world and in the UK. Some have argued that immigration and the importation of traditional values and systems into the UK has resulted in more previously unknown forms of abuse (Tedam and Adjoa 2017). Social workers have more than enough to focus on, whilst still needing to keep abreast with different and emerging forms of child maltreatment and abuse.

The labelling of children as witches requires social workers to become familiar with this form of abuse, the risk factors and appropriate models of intervention. This form of abuse is not only specific to children but also adults. The murder of Naila Mumtaz in Birmingham, who was 21 years old and pregnant is a case in point. Naila's husband and members of his family were found guilty of her murder as they sought to drive out what they term a 'harmful djinn spirit'.

A social worker who is allocated a family to work with where there has been an allegation of abuse linked to witchcraft and spirit possession should think through the following:

See: What are the indicators of abuse in relation to this child? What can you see, what has the child seen?
Hear: What is the family telling you? What are professionals saying and importantly, what is the child or young person saying?
Act: What can you do about what you have heard and seen? what will your next course of action be in relation to safeguarding this child? Also think about what action other stakeholders are taking.
Read: As the social worker, have you engaged with any reading in the area of witchcraft related abuse? What did you read?
Evaluate: How might you reach conclusions about the line of action to take? What might be the ethical debates and considerations?

Prospera Shares

In 2015 I was approached by an adult who had experienced witchcraft labelling and its related abuse during her childhood in the UK and who wanted to share her experiences in order to create awareness. We agreed that she would document her narrative and I would attempt to provide some analyses in order to make it relevant to a range of child care professionals. The book 'Witchcraft labelling and child safeguarding in social work practice' challenged me in the sense that I had to draw on a range of skills particularly my analytical skills. Analysing information is not an easy activity and requires practice in order to become competent at it. It becomes even more complicated because for every idea, issue or experience, there can be multiple interpretations. Writing analytically relies on critical thinking as well as considering other components of the SHARE model such as reading extensively around the subject matter and hearing the narrative.

Modern day slavery

Often used interchangeably with trafficking, modern slavery continues to occur with the powerful enslavery of less powerful people and groups, through the threat of violence, domestic, religious, domestic and sexual servitude (Androff, 2010). The International Labour Organisation estimates that there are 21million people around the world in slavery and it has been estimated that around 13,000 people were victims of modern slavery in the UK (Independent Antislavery Commissioner 2017).

Anti-Slavery International (2017) asserts that the most common form of modern day slavery is debt bondage or bonded labour. This involves a person borrowing money which they cannot repay being required to work off the debt and losing control of the conditions of both their employment and the debt. They identify other forms of modern day slavery as:

- Forced labour
- Human trafficking
- Descent-based slavery
- Child slavery
- Forced and early marriage

Contemporary social work has some of the structures and processes to deal with the growing menace of modern slavery. However, in common with many of the other issues we have raised here the problem of modern day slavery has been raised many times but it soon falls off the agenda, perhaps because the people who enslave others are powerful. For social workers who are unfamiliar with this form of abuse, the Modern Slavery Act 2015 may be a useful starting point to understand the nature and extent of this within the UK. However, even this is a disappointment for social workers in many ways: for example, a Child Guardianship Scheme is included in the Act but the implementation of this is being put back to as late as 2019.

Witchcraft and modern day slavery can also be interlinked. Indeed, a Guardian Newspaper article reported how women of African origin trafficked into prostitution in Italy have often undergone 'religious' ceremonies in their countries of origin, whereby curses or 'ju-ju' are placed on them. This binds women into continuing sex work (Tondo and Kelly 2017).

As a very basic starting point, we would ask social workers to consider whether they are having their cars washed or their nails painted by modern day slaves. If they are not able to recognise modern slavery in their everyday lives how are social workers considering it in their professional practice?

'Death-making'

This phrase was first introduced in the United States a number of years ago in relation to adults with learning disabilities who had been placed in long-term institutionalised hospital care (Wolfensberger 1983). It was used as a phrase to describe the fact that people with learning disabilities were dying prematurely because of poor care and institutionalised practices. The phrase isn't commonly used in contemporary Britain, however, the process of death-making is still very prominent.

Essentially some lives are more valued than others, which is seen in a range of ways in social work, from references to 'do not resuscitate' to the premature deaths of people living in poverty, and the significant numbers of preventable deaths of people with learning disabilities and mental health problems. There is extensive research (as follows) which indicates that the processes which surround 'death-making' are still very much alive today. For example, there have been several calls for more rigorous explanations of deaths such as those of the four men who died in a six-month period on Grafton ward at St Andrew's hospital (Doward 2013). In America, the recent 'Black Lives Matter' movement has clearly illustrated the fact that some lives are more valued than others. The recent events surrounding the fire at Grenfell Tower, and the issues that are coming to light as a result, demonstrate perhaps more sharply than ever the process of death-making (some lives being valued more than others) and the consequences of social workers and others not speaking out about what they see or those in positions of power not listening to what they hear.

Make sure you know about Connor's death and do everything you can to ensure no one else dies a needless, preventable death. Also ensure that you know about Connor's life and the future he was denied.

The following stakeholder voice from Sara Ryan highlights the impact of Connor's death, and the vital importance of social workers developing their awareness of death-making processes.

STAKEHOLDER VOICE

SARA RYAN

Sara is the mother of Connor Sparrowhawk and a sociologist.

Connor, also known as Laughing Boy or LB, was a central part of our extended family. We all loved the socks off him and there are few family photos without one of his brothers or sister touching him; an arm around the shoulder, head leaning in or full on hugs. He was fun, quirky, generous and loving. He was also diagnosed with autism, epilepsy and learning disabilities. It is impossible to describe the devastation we experienced when one hot July morning he was left to drown in the bath, aged 18, in a specialist NHS unit. The NHS Trust, in response, wrote a briefing document about my blog - http://mydaftlife.com - the following day and circulated it to several people. This briefing focused on the potential reputational damage to the Trust. Our son, our beloved son, was simply discounted as a human being. A few weeks later the Trust, commenting on Connor's death in their board minutes, wrote the 'post-mortem indicates the user died of natural causes', an argument they were to later use to try to prevent Connor having a jury at his inquest. This argument failed when the Coroner instantly said that drowning was never a 'natural cause' of death. The jury found that Connor's preventable death was due to neglect and serious failings. The response to Connor's death by the various bodies involved - the Trust, the local authority, the clinical commissioning group - all demonstrate how Connor was not perceived to be fully human. This response was also reflected in the media which was largely silent about him for 9 months or so. This is in stark contrast to the instant national headline news generated by the death of a young gap year student. Connor was always the star of my blog as his commentary on everyday life was hilarious. It generated a strong following of a diverse range of people; self-advocates, families, carers, academics, disability and human rights activists, health and social care professionals and students. The **#JusticeforLB** campaign emerged to fight for accountability for Connor's death and to raise awareness about the limited life chances and increased mortality rates of learning disabled people. I feel a strong sadness that it is health and social care professionals who seem incapable of understanding just how human Connor, and other people like him, are, while people with no connection to learning disability simply get it. The erasing of humanity in this way is really a fast track to poor services and impoverished, or worse, futures.

© Sara Ryan

KEY MESSAGES FROM RESEARCH: DEATH MAKING

- Adults with learning disabilities around the world experience premature mortality and over-representation of potentially avoidable deaths (Trollor et al 2017).

- Nearly 90 people a month die after their claim for employment and support allowance (ESA) ended because a work capability assessment (WCA) found they were found fit for work. During the period December 2011 and February 2014, 2,380 people died after being declared fit for work. (Department for Work and Pensions 2015).

- Buck and Maguire (2015) looked at life expectancy in England from 1999 to 2003 and 2006 to 2010 for the Kings Fund. They found that the majority of areas with persistently low life expectancy during this time also had a high proportion of people earning low or no wages. They also found that the reverse was largely true.

- Early death and ill health are linked to low socioeconomic status (SES) - research coordinated from Imperial College London, revealed that low SES had almost the same impact on health as smoking or a sedentary lifestyle, and was associated with reduced life expectancy of 2.1 years, similar to being inactive (2.4 years) (Brogan 2017).

- The independent review of deaths of people with a learning disability or mental health problem in Southern Health NHS Foundation Trust across a four-year period uncovered major concerns in relation to the reporting and investigations of deaths. There was insufficient transparency around investigations into deaths; investigations and subsequent reports were very poor quality, 64% of investigations did not involve family and the Trust failed to use the data that it had to understand issues surrounding the deaths of service users (Mazars LLP 2015).

Connecting components: Looking deeper

A key aspect of the evaluation component is looking deeper at what is in front of you. Really explore what you face in practice, by drawing on all of the components of the SHARE model: what similarities and differences are there between what you see and hear? What are you and others doing? What have you read and have you fully recorded the issues? It is only in connecting all the components of the SHARE model that you can develop an evidence-based evaluation. This can lead to clearer recommendations and more defensible decisions in practice. Use of the SHARE model certainly supports a practitioner to develop their critical thinking skills.

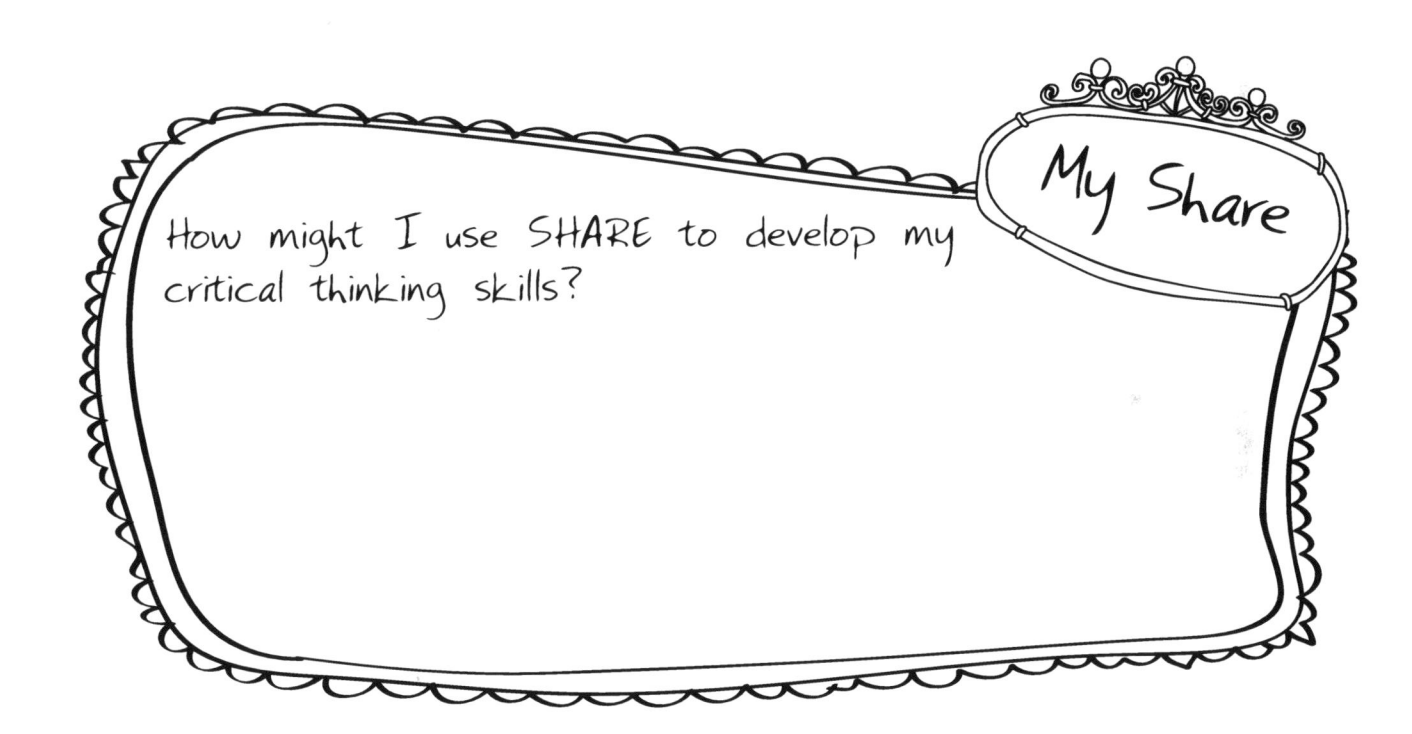

My Share

How might I use SHARE to develop my critical thinking skills?

Critical thinking

We believe that critical thinking is vital in social work practice. However, there can be a lack of clarity around what this really means. Students often report getting feedback on their writing which suggests that they need to take a more critical approach to their reflective writing. This is essentially about the need for the writing to illustrate a more critically reflective stance.

Often social workers and students understand critical reflection to involve self-criticism or to be about looking back at something that didn't go well. This probably comes from the inclusion of the word critical - the dictionary definition of which is 'expressing adverse or disapproving comments or judgements' (Oxford Dictionaries online 2014). Quinn (2000) recognises this and argues that once the word critical is introduced, it's hard to put a positive spin on reflection.

Essentially though, critical reflection in social work is about the bringing together of reflection and critical theory. So, in terms of social work, critical reflection involves adding a consideration of power and questioning the wider socio-political context of practice. This is one of the main reasons that we have included specific consideration of power issues throughout this book.

Being critically reflective involves not only considering where power lies but also:

- How is the power being used?
- Why is the power dynamic like this?
- How does the experience of powerlessness impact?
- What aspects of my practice are empowering? What aspects of my practice are disempowering?

In a specific incident, it might be helpful to think through:

- In what ways was the service user powerful?
- In what ways were they powerless?
- In what ways were they disempowered?
- How did they feel about me coming into their life?
- How would I feel if our roles were reversed?
- How did I communicate their expertise on their own needs, what their rights are and what options they have?
- Did we both understand these things in the same way?

(Maclean and Harrison 2011)

'Ermintrude' blogs and tweets about social work, social care, mental health and cats; in her stakeholder voice she explains the importance of evaluating information, which is the starting point for analysis.

STAKEHOLDER VOICE — ERMINTRUDE

Ermintrude is a social worker, blogger and user of social media
@Ermintrude2

In a world where we consume information from an increasing number of sources, the need to evaluate the information we are presented with grows. Strong social work communities are growing on social media with Twitter, Facebook, blogs and forums - we have more access to the voices of social workers and those who use social work across the country, across divides and across the globe as well as opportunities to share social work perspectives across disciplines.

Information can mesmerise, enchant, inform and engage. Our voices are able to reach places we could never have imagined and can fight through hierarchies and professional status. This is the true value of the increasingly diffuse ways of communication. But with more information comes the responsibility and the need to evaluate. Having a voice does not mean that all voices have an equal and equivalent value. Having followers or friends in a virtual space is no indication of quality or veracity. Followers can be bought, friends can be people who like to mock, numbers mean nothing. So the need to evaluate the worth and quality of information is much stronger.

We see the cry of 'fake news' and confirmation biases through our choices of who to follow and by default, who to listen to. We are, more than ever, able to choose what we want to recognise as true. The need to make judgements is more critical than it has ever been and critical evaluation of information sources is a key social work skill. We need to make our judgements based on our skill, of the value of the information which is presented to us. Does this voice have an authenticity beyond the name of the persona who claims to be behind it? Are they saying things that add value to my knowledge, learning and understanding as a social worker - either because they are someone who has experienced social work services and have a message I can learn from or because they are a social worker who reflects the kind of practitioner or student I want to be? It is easy to find voices and diverse views, but it through our skills of evaluation that we find the voices which increase our understanding and reflect the values we need to represent.

© Ermintrude

Analytical skills

In just the same way that students tell us that they have been advised to take a more critically reflective approach to their writing, we know that many social workers (particularly those who are newly qualified) want to develop their analytical skills. The SHARE model supports the development of analysis by encouraging a worker to explore what they have seen, heard and read and how they evaluate before planning future action.

In the context of social work, analysis is described as *"examining the elements [of an issue]; gaining an understanding of it and then selecting a course of action"* (Wilkins and Boahen 2013:2).

Essentially analysis is about breaking down information, exploring its meaning and restructuring what is known into a professional judgement or recommendation. It goes beyond the presentation of information by exploring it's meaning and relevance.

Good quality reports and assessments take an analytical view which draws on the way that information might be interpreted, clarifying the basis for professional judgement. To develop analysis, think through the what? why? how? framework which underpins the SHARE model. Don't just gather information but think through:

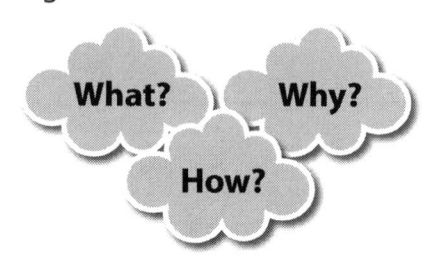

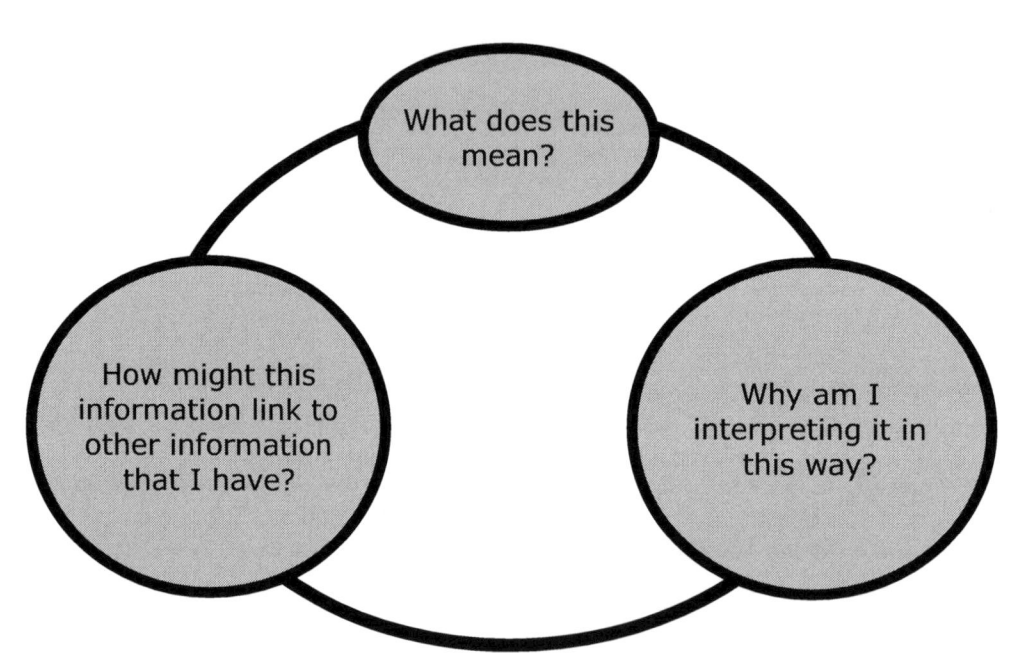

- What does this mean?
- Why am I interpreting it in this way?
- How might this information link to other information that I have?

Following this consideration, develop a conclusion and recommendation and base this on a range of evidence drawn from: seeing, hearing, action, reading and evaluation.

In the next stakeholder voice Caitlin discusses further the challenges of analysis in practice.

STAKEHOLDER VOICE
CAITLIN BURROWS

Caitlin is a newly qualified social worker in child protection.

As a newly qualified social worker, I have found evaluation to be one of the hardest aspects of the profession and one which I have particularly struggled to be confident in when completing assessments. With all the evidence in front of me, I must analyse and evaluate the situation in order to make important recommendations, such as whether the concerns I have meet the threshold for a child protection plan or initiating care proceedings.

The importance of practical experience in a statutory placement was pivotal for me. During these placements as a social work student, I was able to see, hear, act, read and evaluate a range of aspects of frontline social work. However, no number of placements can fully prepare you for writing your first Single Assessment for a family as a qualified social worker.

In order to make a holistic evaluation, it is vital to consider each of the components covered in this book. When asked to consider my analysis at work, I always look at the bigger picture. I think about what I have seen in my observations in the child's home, and in the parents' and child's presentation, what I have heard when listening to the parents' and professionals' concerns and what I have heard when listening to the child's voice. I look at what support has already been put in place and what changes this support has made, if any. I read and review all documents relating to previous involvement from social work professionals in order to formulate my analysis. Ultimately, I explore what I can do to promote positive change for the family, and the child.

Analysis is one of the most crucial skills in social work and I admit it has taken some time to develop confidence in. It has been challenging to fully understand my responsibilities as a social worker and as a professional and how I can take accountability for these. To support the development of my analytical and evaluation skills, I have been quick to recognise the importance of working alongside experienced social workers and discussing ideas and concerns with colleagues and managers. Time in supervision has been essential in the development of my analytical skills, and also my self-confidence.

Social work is a profession of continuous learning and development. The ability to evaluate from a holistic perspective is not excluded from this. No case, family or child is the same. One evaluation does not fit all. This is part of the challenge - to be able to constantly develop your analytical skills and use all five components in doing so: see, hear, act, read and evaluate. By collating evidence from each of these practice skills, I am now able to provide a complete analysis and am confident in my evaluation of cases.

© Caitlin Burrows

Jo Shares

In the last couple of years, as part of a research team, we have undertaken evaluations of a number of suicide prevention programmes and services (see for example, Briggs et al, 2016). In research terms, undertaking programme evaluation is a distinct methodological approach, yet shares many of the processes that have been explored in this chapter. As stated before, I am very much a visual thinker, and I see the process of programme evaluation like a tapestry, collecting all the different coloured threads of evidence, then sewing them all together into a clearly recognisable picture. Evidence therefore may be tangible threads, but might also include the threads created by reflection and thinking. When all the threads are together, one may see that particular threads might dominate (or be particularly brightly coloured in this particular visual image) so we should ask why? Why are these threads more brightly coloured than other threads? Are there paler threads that we need to ensure do not get over shadowed by the brighter threads?

As it can be seen, sorting out all these threads and deciding what picture they might best form, and then doing the tapestry itself can be time consuming. Sometimes we might have false starts and as someone who did used to do tapestry many years ago, used to feel frustrated when I had to undo my handy work due to an error. Evaluation in social work therefore has to be as accurate as we can make it, using many coloured and sometimes competing 'threads' of evidence.

The SHARE model can help to provide a golden thread through the tapestry of evaluation.

In our work with students we have found that they sometimes struggle to understand the difference between writing critically and analytically and writing descriptively. In many ways writing descriptively is the what and the how and writing critically and analytically is the why. On page 178 we addressed the way that the why question can all too quickly fall off the agenda for practice. In many ways this reflects the reason that the why question is so important in writing for academic purposes.

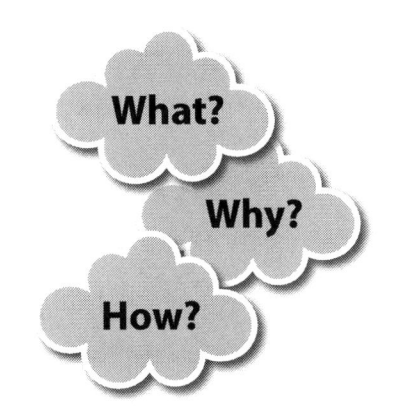

We have found Cottrell's (2013) distinction of the difference between descriptive writing and analytical writing useful:

Descriptive	Analytical
States what happened	Identifies the significance
States what something is like	Evaluates strengths and weaknesses
Gives the story so far	Weighs one piece of information against another
States the order in which things happened	Makes reasoned judgments (refers to evidence)
Says how to do something	Argues a case according to evidence
Explains what a theory does	Shows why something is relevant or significant
Explains how something works	Indicates why something will work
Notes the method used	Identifies why the timing will work
Says when something has occurred	Weighs up the importance of component tasks
States the different components	Gives reasons for selecting options
States opinion	Evaluates the relative significance of details
Lists details	Structures information in order of importance
Lists in any order	Shows relevant links between pieces of information
States links between items	Relates to social work practice
Gives information	Draws conclusions

Both descriptive and analytical styles of writing are important, as descriptive writing is required to give essential context and background information whilst critical and analytical writing is needed for evaluation. These reminders serve as a useful check list to consider what goes into a holistic evaluation. Descriptive and analytical writing come together in the SHARE model, in that the descriptive elements are the seeing, hearing, action and reading components and the evaluation component encourages analytical aspects.

The A - Z of Evaluation

- A is for analysis: it's all about active inquiry.
- B is for beliefs: they must be thought through.
- C is for complexity: which is always there.
- D is for depth: so vital.
- E is for emotions: they must be explored.
- F is for feedback: always helpful to consider.
- G is for gut: sometimes instinct is the starting point.
- H is for hypothesis: what are your thoughts?
- I is for ideas: you will generate many.
- J is for judgement: professional judgement is key.
- K is for knowledge: this must be explored.
- L is for learning: so much of this occurs.

- M is for meaning: things will become clearer.
- N is for need: we really must do it.
- O is for observation: always draw on what you see.
- P is for power: it is everywhere but often not addressed.
- Q is for questioning: dynamic textured questioning.
- R is for research: helpful to use.
- S is for skills: one of the most valued.
- T is for transformative: it can alter your views.
- U is for understanding: this will be developed.
- V is for values: is their impact clear?
- W is for when: and what, why, which, who and where!
- X marks the spot: think about the environment.
- Y is for you: developing self-awareness.
- Z is for zealous: do it with passion.

Key points

- Evaluation is a key component of the SHARE model
- Often evaluation will come after one or more of the other components as a social worker evaluates what they have seen or heard, what action they have taken or what they have read.
- Evaluation is further linked to the other components since evaluation may change the way that a social worker sees something, it might impact on what they hear, how they act or what they record and so on.
- Evaluating what social workers and service users see and hear on a daily basis should help to develop the social work knowledge base and consequently literature and practice.
- A key part of evaluation is the development of emotional intelligence.
- Evaluation frameworks can be helpful particularly in terms of locating feelings at the heart of evaluation.
- It is important for social workers to develop their skills in critical reflection and analysis.
- A key aspect of evaluation in social work is about exploring contemporary practice and thinking about what might be being missed.

Reflective Questions

What does evaluation mean to you?

How might you improve your evaluation skills?

What stands out the most for you from this chapter? Why is that?

What is happening is your practice that you are 'missing'? (There is something).

Chapter 10: APPLICATIONS OF THE SHARE MODEL

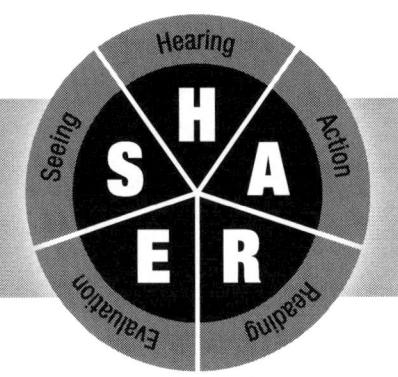

The SHARE model has a wide-ranging application to practice. In this chapter, we briefly outline some of the ways in which the model can be used. However, what we have covered is only a beginning for the model. The SHARE model is designed to promote creativity and since it is a dynamic model we hope that all stakeholders in the profession will find new and exciting ways to use the model. Our initial discussions with practitioners and managers about the model indicate that it can be applied in a range of ways to an even wider range of circumstances. We hope to be able to report on these uses of the model in the future.

Lopez (2011) explains that theory is typically taught in a way which presents theories as 'recipes' whilst students rarely have the opportunity to be creative and they may not be taught to cook. We hope that everyone reading this book will look at the possibilities for the SHARE model and get cooking with it.

In Chapters 1 and 4 we outlined our hope that the SHARE model would provide a bridge between social work practice and social work education. We have therefore included examples of using SHARE both in social work practice and in social work education. This reflects what we covered in Chapters 3 and 4 where we explored theory in relation to both social work practice and social work education. The SHARE model can be used as an extension to the theory base in either area.

We have tried to select a range of applications suited to the potentially wide audience reading this book. So that, for example, there is something for students, for practitioners (including those who are newly qualified), for practice educators, trainers, lecturers and managers.

The applications covered in this chapter are as follows:

1. Assessment in social work practice
2. Risk assessment and defensible decision making
3. Collaborative working
4. Continual Professional Development
5. Assessed and Supported Year in Employment
6. Induction for new staff
7. Supervision
8. Designing and delivering teaching sessions / training
9. Planning placement learning
10. Assessing a student in practice

The model is designed to be dynamic and adaptable. As such it can be used in a wide range of ways. You should not feel limited to the applications we discuss in this chapter. You should also recognise that we have simply provided some key suggestion points in each area - since there could be a whole book on each of the applications covered in this chapter. We want the model to be very practical and usable and have therefore remained focused on things that social workers 'do'. That said, we are very committed to a reflective approach to practice, and value the importance of the stages of reflection as covered in Chapter 9. As such we see that there are three stages to everything a social worker might 'do':

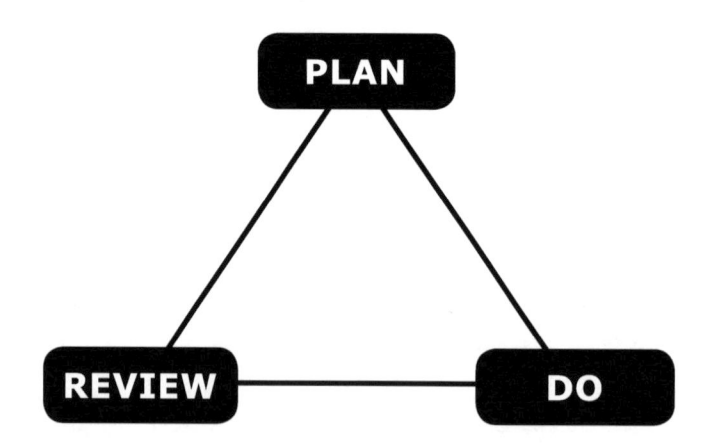

```
        PLAN
        /  \
       /    \
      /      \
  REVIEW────DO
```

This plan, do, review framework could apply to everything that we have covered in this chapter. For example, when undertaking an assessment, a social worker needs to plan how they will go about completing their assessment, then they need to do it and review it. The SHARE model can (and should, for the best results) be used at each of these stages. However, in order to demonstrate the wide applicability of the model in just one chapter we have highlighted only certain parts of the plan, do, review framework in each area.

Assessment

Traditionally, assessment is seen as the beginning of a social work process. Traditional process models of assessment in social work include:

Sutton's (1999) ASPIRE model:	Thompson's (2005) ASIRT model:
AS - assessment **P** - planning **I** - intervention **RE** - review	**AS** - assessment **I** - intervention **R** - review **T** - termination

One of the problems with this kind of process model is that they take a very linear approach, suggesting that things are done to a person in a logical order, whereas we see assessment as being about working through a process with a service user.

In the early 1990s, social work changed considerably following the implementation of the Children Act 1989 and the NHS and Community Care Act 1990; it was against this backdrop that Smale et al (1993) undertook research into assessments in social work, out of which they developed three main models of assessment, which are still widely referred to (at least in social work qualifying training) today:

Questioning model: Here the professional is seen as holding the expertise. They devise a series of questions which they ask the service user, processing the answers to form a professional opinion. The use of this model means that the assessment largely reflects the worker's agenda.

Procedural model: Here the professional gathers a range of information from a variety of sources to make a judgment about whether the service user meets the criteria for service provision. It is likely that a range of checklists will be used to help clarify judgments. The use of this model means that the assessment will largely reflect the agency's agenda.

Exchange model: Here the worker views the service user as the expert in their own situation. The professional follows what people are saying, rather than interpreting what they think is meant. The worker tries to help the service user to identify internal resources and potential. In this way, the practitioner can consider how best to help service users mobilise their own resources in order to reach goals which they identify for themselves. The use of this model means that the assessment and the process should reflect the service user's agenda.

Smale et al (1993) make it clear that the exchange model of assessment is their preferred model. However, it takes a great deal of skill to employ the exchange model of assessment, and in the current financial climate, practitioners often report feeling pushed more towards a procedural model of assessment, as organisations introduce increasingly proceduralised measures in order to manage financial constraints.

Each of these three models of assessment identify that a different stakeholder's agenda is being addressed. It is our view that everyone has a stake in the provision of a good quality assessment. Essentially, a good quality assessment should recognise the expertise of the service user in terms of their situation and the resources that they could draw on; the expertise of the practitioner in terms of problem solving and the navigation of difficult systems alongside the expertise within the organisation in terms of the difficult management of resources in a legally literate manner, so an approach which combines aspects of each of the three models may need to be used.

In considering assessment in social work, Milner and O'Byrne (2009) developed a five-stage process:

Stage 1: Preparation - which might include deciding who to see, what the purpose of the assessment is, what information will be needed etc.

Stage 2: Data collection - the worker gathers the necessary information.

Stage 3: Weighing up the data - the worker weighs up the information to reach an answer to the key question 'is there a problem and is it serious?'

Stage 4: Analysing the data - the information is interpreted to gain a fuller understanding so that ideas for intervention can be developed.

Stage 5: Utilising the data - this stage is used to finalise judgements. The data will be used to evidence judgements and recommendations for intervention.

The SHARE model can be used to support assessment at any of the five stages. In the following pages, we will consider the use of SHARE at the assessment planning stages. As this chapter explores other applications of the model you will be able to see how SHARE could be used in undertaking an assessment, whilst the way that SHARE can be used to write up an assessment is explored in Chapter 8.

So, the SHARE model in assessment is about:

- Drawing on the five components (seeing, hearing, action, reading and evaluation) at each stage of the assessment process (see following page for example at the planning stage).
- Recognising each stakeholder's share in the assessment (see page 284 for example).
- Writing up an assessment in a way which can be easily shared.
- Information sharing as appropriate.
- Demonstrating the share(d) values we covered in Chapter 2.

When planning your assessment think about:

SEE:
Who do you need to see?
What do you need to see?
What might you see and how will you respond?

HEAR:
Who do you want to talk to?
Who do you need to hear from?
How will you make sure everyone's voice is reflected in your assessment?

ACT:
What do you need to do?
What do you need others to do?

READ:
What is already 'on file' that you may be able to read?
How will this impact on your assessment?
What other information do you want to read?
Are you familiar with, and confident about, the documentation you need to complete in relation to the assessment?

EVALUATE:
How will you evaluate all of the information you gather, to pull together your assessment?
Are there any particular frameworks you need to use as part of your assessment?

Taking the time to plan something well can feel like a luxury when pushed for time, but good planning prevents poor practice and effectively slows us down to speed us up.

I'm Late, I'm Late!

Rushing often means you get less done.

Exploring the service user's share

The SHARE model highlights the importance of considering all stakeholders' experiences, so in terms of assessment it is vital to think about how the person being assessed experiences this. This can be explored by thinking about their SHARE in the assessment as follows:

Consider the experience of the person being assessed by exploring:

SEE:

Who and what does the person see as part of the assessment process? (for example, think about how you present yourself).
How do they view this?
What impact does this have? (for example, on how they view the assessment experience).

HEAR:

What does the person hear in the assessment process? (what is said, what questions are asked etc.)
What impact does this have?
Does the person feel fully 'heard' in the assessment? How do you know?

ACT:

What does the person do to become actively involved in the process?
What do people around them do to support the person to be as involved as fully as possible?
How is what the person does during the assessment viewed by the people around them? (for example, what labels are attached to the person's behaviour?)

READ:

Has the individual been given anything to read about the assessment process?
Will the person be given a copy of what is written about them as part of the assessment process?
What impact does this have?
Does what is recorded for people to read fully reflect the service user's experiences? How do you know?

EVALUATE:

How does the person evaluate their experience of being assessed?
How do you know?
What impact will their evaluation have on their view of social work and on their future involvement?

STAKEHOLDER VOICE — IAN

Ian is a social work manager @positivesimply.

I woke up as a father, husband, manager, Social Worker, not criminal or mad! I ended the day having been taken from my home by at least eight police officers and placed on section 2 of the Mental Health Act.

In a moment, I had become mentally disordered, in acute crisis, hospitalised and medicated. I had obtained additional labels and my life had imploded. This is a very big deal and I was scared but without knowing why! I understand, in hindsight, why certain decisions were reached but I feel the methods were fundamentally flawed.

Throughout the assessment process the questions asked of me were proforma and medicalised, this did not take my humanity in to account. Therefore, as a result my actual experience is left largely unexplored and the written words on the page do not sound anything like me. I don't question the outcome as I was unwell however in my view the assessment makes many false assumptions based upon second hand information.

In my first week of detention I was restrained on more than one occasion, however no one has sought to understand why I was behaving in such a way and the story beneath. I was clearly distressed but the response was to medicate me rather than to seek to understand the root causes.

For me the most important elements of real assessment were missing; being validated as a human being, being listened to and actually heard, to be made to feel there is hope and someone to take an interest in my individuality. I firmly believe that you cannot trick instinct and as a result I will know if you are genuinely interested in me or not. This requires unconditional positive regard for me, not a judgement based upon your view of how I am behaving in a moment of time!

My assessments are many words without much meaning or real value to me. They effectively serve the purpose of evidencing why certain things have happened but not much else! What was important to me was little things, simple compassion and to have my hand held when I was unable to know myself. Perhaps real assessment cannot always be written?

What is sure is that what the assessment decided cannot be undecided and as a result I now have to live with the multiple consequences and enduring pain.

© Ian

Risk assessment and defensible decision making

Risk assessment is a key aspect of all social work practice. Risk assessment is generally carried out in terms of two areas:

- The risks a person poses to others (dangerousness).
- The risks a person is subject to (vulnerability).

These two issues are often assessed concurrently because social workers are involved in complex situations which include issues of both dangerousness and vulnerability.

Whatever the focus of the assessment, the purpose is generally for the assessment to inform plans about intervention. This intervention generally focuses on risk management.

In recognition of the fact that risk assessment is a highly fallible process, with no guarantee of certainty, Carson (1996) introduced the concept of defensible decision making. Carson argued that the key skill is to arrive at decisions in a manner that a reasonable body of co-professionals would also have followed. This makes the decision defensible if brought to account. One of the key aspects of a defensible decision is clarity about the evidence which is being drawn on in the assessment.

The importance of shared decision making in relation to risk has been recognised for some time, with a range of safeguards and benefits for stakeholders being recognised within this discussion. For example, Stevenson (2005) claims that the element of supervision which social workers value most is the concept of shared decision making. According to Stevenson, shared decision making involves six main safeguards and benefits:

1. Peer review of professional decisions.
2. Protection of civil liberties: ensuring that no service user's liberty is affected without scrutiny of that decision.
3. Protection of service users: service users are not left in unacceptable risks on the basis of an individual's assessment or actions.
4. Protection of staff: ensuring that professionals are not put in positions where situations may exceed their knowledge, skills or experience or where they have to deal with very stressful situations.
5. Protection of the agency: shared decision making ensures a fail-safe element and confirms that the agency has taken the importance of scrutiny seriously.
6. It encourages openness and collective responsibility and creates a climate where professionals are open about their decision and can explore the reasons for this. A culture should be created where practitioners are prepared to jointly take responsibility for key decisions and to challenge each other in the interests of the service user and indeed the agency.

Shared decision making in supervision ensures more defensible decision making and enhances a practitioner's ability to develop more autonomous practice whilst recognising the need for accountability.

The SHARE model can be particularly helpful in considering risk assessment and defensible decision making. Essentially it is about creating a shared understanding of risk and reaching shared decisions about acceptable levels of risk and risk management strategies. The starting point is therefore involving all key stakeholders, as the SHARE model promotes, then using the SHARE components to ensure that the risk assessment draws on all the necessary evidence.

In undertaking a risk assessment think about:

SEE:

What have you seen? Be specific. At this stage, be descriptive about what you have seen rather than evaluative (what have you observed rather than what this might mean). This provides a clear evidence base for your ultimate evaluation of risk.
What haven't you seen? Does this impact on your ability to draw a conclusion?
How do you see risk in this situation? Do others see it in the same way?

HEAR:

What have you heard?
From who? (you must consider the validity of feedback and what you hear from others: what position are they coming from?)
Who haven't you heard? Why?
What do others need to hear from you?

ACT:

What have you done?
What have others done?
What impact has this had on the identified risk?
What have people done to try and manage the risks? What impact has this had?

READ:

What have you read?
What have you recorded for others to read?

EVALUATE:

What conclusions have you drawn from the above?
Why are you drawing these conclusions?
Are other stakeholders drawing the same conclusions? How do you know?

It is widely acknowledged that in undertaking any risk assessment social workers need to frame their decision around a clear understanding of the service user's world (Taylor 2017b). A recurring theme throughout this book is the value of using the SHARE model to understand this, so the SHARE model could be used specifically to consider each person's share in a situation in order to complete a holistic risk assessment (see page 284 for an example of this.

Collaborative working

Collaborative working is vital in social work practice. Working with the range of people that surround an individual in ways which uphold the vital importance of those relationships in the person's life is a key element of a person centred, holistic approach. The importance of collaborative working in social work is highlighted in all social work literature and in legal frameworks. For example, Working Together To Safeguard Children provides statutory guidance on inter-agency working and how all professionals must work together collaboratively in order to safeguard children.

Many social workers now work in integrated teams, which brings them together with a range of other professionals, often from health but also from education and the police. Some areas have started to integrate children's and adult's social workers, especially around teams like MASH (Multi-agency Safeguarding Hubs).

Collaborative working is not just about working with other professionals. It is also about working collaboratively with service users, carers and families in restorative ways to create and further develop relationships.

The development of this model and the production of this book are the outcomes of collaborative working among the authors. We have used tools such as google docs to facilitate the collaborative process and to ensure we could develop our work in a progressive and coherent way enabling access to the document at any time and from any location. A whatsapp forum enabled us keep in touch when were out and about, reminding each other about deadlines, sharing information and generally checking in with each other. Collaborative working involves working as part of a team, listening to each other alongside being each other's 'critical friend'. The stakeholder voices added value, making the finished product a real collaboration.

We have recognised the SHARE principles in our own collaboration and acknowledge the importance of seeing our stakeholders as equal partners in this endeavour, hearing and listening to each other's points of view, reading, analysing and evaluating information we've read. The point has already been made about the value of collaboration in social work practice and by modelling collaboration in our production of this book; we hope we have demonstrated its importance.

Starting off any multi-professional meetings with a 'share' from everyone can be very helpful in promoting collaborative practice. So, for example, in any discussions about a service user, everyone in the meeting should be encouraged to share with those present what they have seen, heard, done, and read since the last meeting and how they have evaluated this. This will provide a clear evidence base for discussions about any differences of opinion. It is really important that everyone's 'share' is listened to and that service users are fully supported to share their views perhaps through the use of an advocate if necessary.

STAKEHOLDER VOICE — AGNES

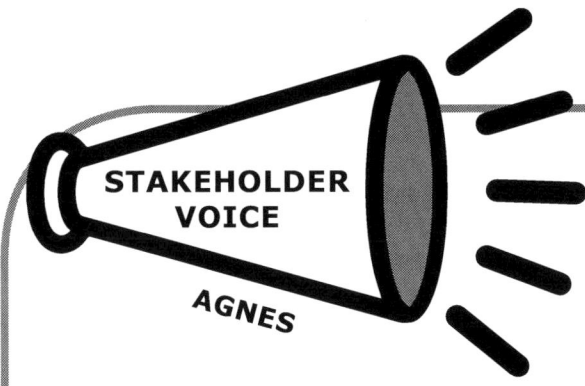

Agnes is a social worker in a children's safeguarding team.

I regularly get telephone calls from health visitors, midwives, teachers and other professionals sharing concerns with me about families that I am working with. When I ask them if they have shared their concerns with the family they nearly always say that they haven't because they don't want to 'ruin the relationship' they have with the parents, so they say they are 'just passing it on so that you can address it.' It makes me so cross. The implication seems to be that I don't have any relationship with the family and that I can just act as the police, judge and jury in relation to any concerns people want to make. However tenuous or lacking in evidence the concerns are the expectation is that I will do something. Even worse is when they attend a core group or case conference and with the family there they say that things seem to be going well or something similar. Then later they tell me they have lots of concerns that they want me to deal with.

I have started to be much firmer about the sharing of concerns now. In core groups, I have found using SHARE has worked really well at making sure concerns are shared in an open and honest way and that the evidence of concerns is considered, rather than other professionals raising concerns based on prejudice or personal values. This has given parents more opportunity to say when they feel the professionals have got it wrong. If feels like everything is just more open and transparent.

© Agnes

Continual Professional Development

In recent years, the vital importance of continual professional development (often referred to as CPD) has received increasing attention in social work. The connection between CPD and quality practice and care has also been highlighted in a range of UK Government reports, Regulatory Body documents and Serious Case Reviews and Inquiry Reports (BASW 2012b).

Changes to the regulation of social workers has led to a move towards an output model of CPD. It is no longer about inputs (what training have I done?) but is much more about the outcomes of a wide range of professional development activities (what have I learnt?)

CPD tends to go on the back burner when practitioners are busy (when aren't they?) Perhaps social workers are still maintaining the thought that if they are required to present evidence about how they meet the regulator's CPD requirements they will have a quick look through their diaries and write up what training they've done. With the changes to CPD requirements, this simply won't work.

There is a clear process to professional development:

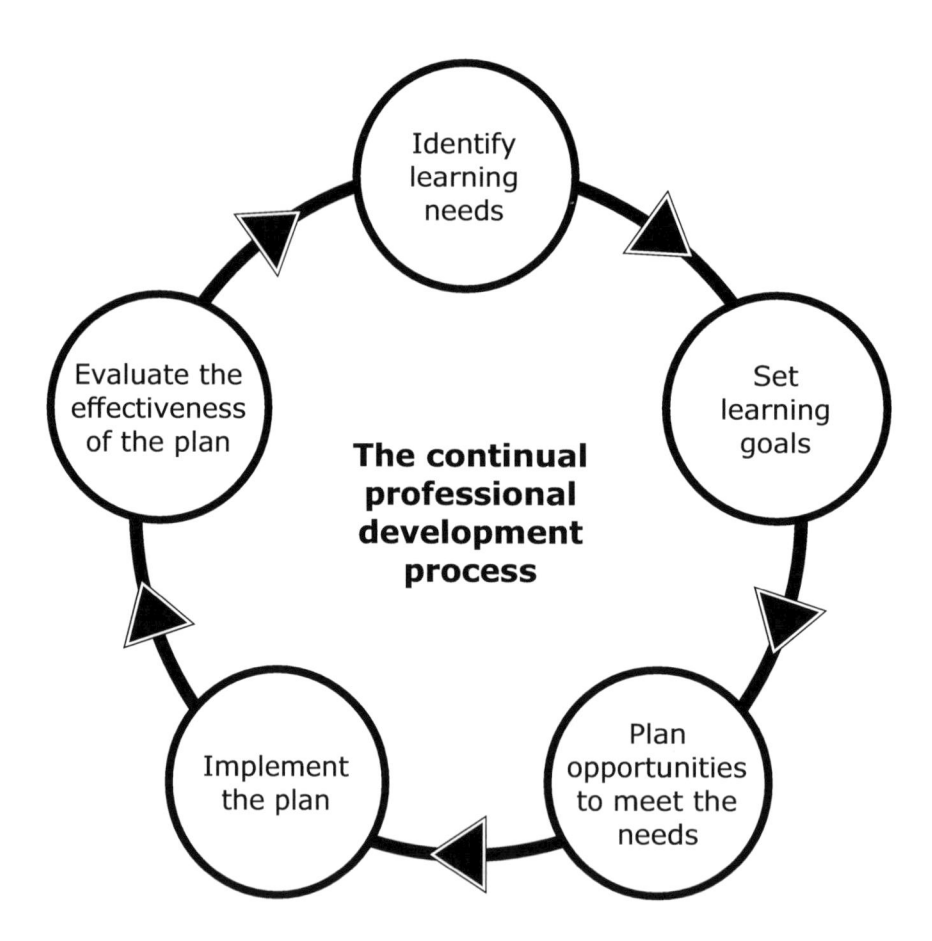

```
         Identify
         learning
          needs

Evaluate the                Set
effectiveness              learning
 of the plan   The continual  goals
              professional
              development
                process

    Implement           Plan
    the plan        opportunities
                    to meet the
                       needs
```

This process again reflects the plan, do, review framework. Essentially, the CPD process is about planning your learning, doing the learning and then reviewing and recording it. The SHARE model can be used at any stage. As examples, we have applied SHARE to thinking about learning needs and to recording CPD:

In considering your learning needs think about:

SEE:

What do you see at work?
Are there things that you regularly see at work, which perhaps you don't feel confident about?
Maybe you have observed other workers doing things that you would like to explore further...

HEAR:

What have you heard?
Think about what feedback you have had on your practice. What does that tell you about what skills you might need to develop further?
What have you heard about that you would like to know more about?

ACT:

What do you do?
What is the scope of your role? Are there areas that you feel less confident about?
What other things would you like to be able to do?
Looking ahead, what might you be required to do in the future? What implications does this have for your CPD?

READ:

What have you read?
What would you like to take the time to read more about?
Are you reading a wide enough variety of material?

EVALUATE:

What conclusions can you draw?
Drawing on the first four components, what conclusions can you draw about your learning needs?
How will you action your learning?
How will you know when your learning needs have been met?

Sometimes professional development plans or learning needs statements read more like a shopping list of training courses that people want to do. Using SHARE can help a practitioner to develop a more individual, textured framework for learning.

When recording your CPD think about:

SEE:

What do you see at work?
You may have observed someone else's practice and learnt a great deal from this.
Perhaps you have watched a documentary.
You may have seen a visual image that you have learnt from.
Could you record or capture any of your learning in a visual way?

HEAR:

What have you heard?
Think about what feedback you have had on your practice.
Maybe what debates you have heard or been involved in.
You may have listened to something on the radio that you have been able to reflect on.
Discussions in the team room, in supervision or in group sessions can be used to evidence your CPD.

ACT:

What do you do?
Think widely don't just focus CPD on training. Taking the right kind of approach means that you will learn from everything you do. Try to draw on a different kind of activity each time you consider your CPD.

READ:

What have you read?
Reading is an important part of learning, but think widely:
What books, journal articles, online content etc have you read?
What have you read in terms of feedback from others?
Have you read any of your colleagues recording? What have you learnt from this?

EVALUATE:

What conclusions can you draw?
How is your CPD going?
Do you have a good balance of activities in the first four components? Which ones might you be able to focus your learning on in the next few months? Which of the four components has supported your learning the most?

Assessed and Supported Year in Employment

Known as ASYE, this is specific to the English context. However, many other countries have a similar or equivalent process for supporting social workers in the early stages of their career. For example, Wales has a formal first year in practice programme, followed by CPEL. What is written here about the ASYE can be adapted for use with equivalent processes or indeed it can be used to support candidates on other programmes of study.

The ASYE (and its equivalents in other countries) recognises the need to support qualifying social workers make the transition into professional practice. Effectively bridging the gap between education and practice in relation to one individual. Many other allied professions have a similar scheme of support and assessment in the early stages of a professional career (for example, in nursing there is a preceptorship).

In England, the ASYE recognises that a number of people have a 'share' in the development of the newly qualified worker and promotes their involvement in the programme. So, for example the social worker needs to seek feedback from other professionals and from service users. The importance of feedback from people who use social work services is highlighted in all of the documentation which supports the ASYE.

As the title of the programme suggests the ASYE is about supporting the new social worker in their development as they transition into the professional role and it is also about assessing their ability.

The SHARE model can be used to support the ASYE in a range of ways:

- The plan to support a newly qualified worker can be drawn up using SHARE (what will they see, hear, do and read and how will they evaluate this?)
- The newly qualified worker can be provided with feedback based around the SHARE model to enhance their practice (see page 159).
- The assessor can use SHARE to assess the worker and make a robust recommendation about their practice (see page 313).
- At each review meeting where the worker's progress is reviewed each person at the meeting can SHARE what they have seen, heard, done and read and how they have evaluated this.

On the following pages we have used the SHARE model to consider the perspectives of both the assessor and the newly qualified worker.

The assessor's 'share' covers:

SEE:

What is the assessor seeing?
This covers observations of the worker's practice (both formal and informal).

HEAR:

What is the assessor hearing?
This is about the feedback that they are receiving about the social worker (from service users and other professionals). The ASYE has a requirement that feedback from service users and feedback from other professionals is drawn on in assessing the worker.

ACT:

What does the assessor need to do?
This could be about what action might be required to support the new worker. It could be about the development of action plans where there are concerns about the development of the worker and their ability to meet the requirements of the ASYE.

READ:

What is the assessor reading?
The ASYE has a requirement that assessors read and feedback on two essential aspects:
- The quality of the candidate's professional recording
- The candidate's reflective log

Essentially, this means that the assessor is reading about the worker's practice (their recording) and their thinking behind the practice (their reflective writing)

EVALUATE:

Drawing on the first four components what conclusions can the assessor draw about the newly qualified worker?
The use of the word evaluation rather than assessment is actually really important in the ASYE, because this is not about simply assessing whether someone meets a standard or not - it is also about ensuring that a person has developed over time. Every newly qualified worker will have a different starting point in terms of their previous experiences etc and the ASYE should explore how the worker has progressed.

The newly qualified worker's 'share' covers:

SEE:

What are they seeing?
This is about whether the new worker is being given sufficient opportunity to observe and be shadowed by more experienced practitioners. We often develop our social work skills from watching others in action.
What are they seeing in their practice? Are they having sufficient opportunity to talk about this and seek support if they need it?

HEAR:

What is the new worker hearing?
This can relate to what feedback the worker is receiving on their practice: is this sufficiently constructive to enable them to reflect on their practice and develop this?
It should also be used to consider what the worker is hearing from other workers and what impact this is having on them. New social workers often report hearing very cynical comments from more experienced workers ('if I had my time over again I wouldn't do social work...' 'This isn't why I became a social worker...') This can create a negative culture which impacts significantly on a new worker's sense of professional identity and hopefulness.

ACT:

What is the worker doing?
The ASYE in England carries with it a recognition of the importance of new social workers having a 'protected' caseload with specific time allocated for learning and professional development activities within the workload.
What does this look like for the worker? What are they doing? Is the work commensurate with their status as a newly qualified practitioner?

READ:

What are they reading?
Is the new worker being supported to read a range of case recording to enable them to develop their own skills in recording? Are they still encouraged to read a range of literature relating to social work? Are they being given the space to record their own reflective journal?

EVALUATE:

What conclusions is the new worker drawing from their experiences?
Are they being encouraged to reflect on the various issues covered above? Are they being given the space to discuss their reflections in supervision and with team colleagues? Do they get the opportunity to meet with other newly qualified workers to explore their evaluation of their experiences?

Thinking about both the new worker's share and the assessor's share can help to plan and evaluate the ASYE experience to ensure that it provides an effective supportive experience for the candidate, whilst their capabilities for social work practice are accurately assessed.

The ASYE involves regular review meetings at key points during the year. These meetings bring together the assessor, the new worker and perhaps the line manager or a member of a learning and development team. Using the SHARE model in these meetings - so that each person present discusses their 'share' (what they have seen, heard, done and read and how they have evaluated this since the last meeting) can promote a transparent, evidence based discussion and a clear structure to the sharing of information within the meeting.

The journey model (see page 116) is often helpful in the ASYE too. Considering the year as a journey and understanding that the portfolio is made up of a range of material to support the journey is helpful:

- The professional development plan is like a map – what is the worker going to do on the journey? How is the journey planned out? What does the destination look like?
- Reflective accounts are like a travel journal – how is the journey going?
- The observations indicate that someone else checked in with the worker on the journey and shared aspects of their experiences with them. What is their view of the progress that the worker has made?
- The feedback is about how other people think the journey is going.

The final portfolio should illustrate the whole journey that the worker has been on – it is not just about the destination, but more about the starting point, the experiences along the way, how the worker adapted to any challenges on the journey and so on.

The very concept of sharing is also important for newly qualified workers. For example, they often learn from other, more experienced workers, sharing their perspectives and they generally enjoy sharing learning with other newly qualified workers. To promote this 'sharing', Siobhan uses an activity in workshops with newly qualified workers which works really well:

Each worker is given two pieces of card, on one they are invited to write down their most burning question to other social workers and on the other they are asked to write down one piece of advice that they would share with other workers. The cards are pinned on the wall – one space for questions and one space for advice. Across break times the workshop participants are encouraged to look at the walls and use the content to prompt discussion. At the end of the workshop participants are invited to take one question and one piece of advice off the wall (not their own). Siobhan then asks the participants to try to follow the piece of advice that they have for at least one month (often until the next workshop), they are also directed to ask the question that they have to at least three other social workers jotting down their answers on the back of the card. The workers feed back on how this went at the next workshop. This activity has been very popular with newly qualified workers and has really encouraged a 'shared' approach to learning in a range of ways. Siobhan has occasionally posted the questions and advice on twitter, and at times other practitioners have offered answers to the questions, encouraging newly qualified social workers to recognise that we are part of a shared profession and that appropriate sharing on social media can be helpful.

Put your own question and piece of advice in the centre.

KEY MESSAGES FROM RESEARCH: ASYE

- A quarter of social workers who responded a year after completing their ASYE felt that it had prepared them 'very well' for the transition from student to social worker whilst almost three fifths felt it had prepared them 'fairly well' (Skills for Care 2015).

- Two thirds of newly qualified social workers agreed with the statement 'my employer takes my professional development seriously' (Skills for Care 2011).

- The 'vast majority' of newly qualified workers stated that the supervision they received as part of the ASYE supported them in reflective practice either quite well or very well (Skills for Care 2013b).

- Moriarty and Manthorpe (2014) found that social work was late in establishing a link between registration and CPD in comparison with professions such as medicine and nursing.

- A Community Care Survey found patchy implementation of the ASYE with newly qualified social workers facing unprotected caseloads in some local authorities. In total, 40% of the 208 social workers responding to Community Care's survey said their caseload was not protected or capped during their ASYE (Schraer 2016).

- Bailey and Sach (2015) reported on a programme evaluation at the University of East Anglia using a mixed method approach with participants who had completed an academically accredited ASYE. Results from the social work practice questionnaires showed that NQSWs were most positive about their ability to show care and compassion and to consult with service users, and to be able to explain to users what they were doing and why.

Induction for new staff and students

The importance of a good induction into a workplace is widely recognised in all human resources practice. For example, the Chartered Institute of Personnel and Development (2016) states that

> *"an employee's first impressions of an organisation have a significant impact on their integration within the team and their level of job satisfaction. For an employer, effective induction may also impact turnover, absenteeism and employer brand."*

The International Federation of Social Workers (Europe) recognise the importance of social workers receiving a good induction, linking this to retention and preventing burnout (IFSW Europe 2011).

Jack and Donnellan (2010) identify that there are three forms of induction:

Workplace induction: This covers the individual becoming familiar with the immediate working environment

Corporate induction: This addresses the individual feeling that they are a part of the wider organisation and therefore developing a sense of belonging

Role related induction: This covers a person becoming familiar with their specific role in the organisation

Inductions are important in social work for both new staff and students (the inductee). Understanding the different forms of induction is important in planning inductions because different people will need the focus to be on different forms of induction. For example, students will need more focus on the workplace and role induction rather than the corporate induction, whilst an experienced worker who is new to the organisation will need more focus on the corporate and workplace induction rather than the role induction.

SHARE can be used to think through and plan an induction (whatever the form) as the following few pages demonstrate.

What kind of induction did I have in my current role?

What impact that have?

My Share

Planning an Induction:

SEE:

What will the person need to see when they start in the organisation?
The inductee is likely to spend time on 'observational visits' - visiting other service providers or establishments and local resources during their induction. For students, it is useful if such visits continue through the whole placement, because it is likely that a student will find more meaningful learning in visiting a resource when it is particularly relevant to their practice. For example, if a student visits a day service when they are working with a service user and want to make a referral, they are likely to learn more than if they visit during their induction period when they have nothing to associate their experiences with.

HEAR:

What will the person hear in the early stages of their work or placement?
It is not unusual for people to say how much negativity they hear about social work during their induction. Students particularly refer to this as they often spend time shadowing a range of social workers in the first few weeks. If each of these social workers shares with the student what they find difficult about the job, which is common, then this can create a really negative starting point for the student.

It is important to think about whose voices the inductee will hear during their induction. Students have often reported that in their induction they have really valued listening to service users about their experiences of practice, whereas often arrangements are made for them to listen to other professionals more than service users. It is important to make sure that the student has the opportunity to hear from a wide range of voices relevant to the placement setting.

ACT:

What will the inductee do in the induction?
Students are often very keen to 'get on' with things in their induction. Sometimes induction experiences are very passive, with lots of observing and reading. Make sure that a student also has the opportunity to do things for themselves. Clearly what a student can 'do' at this stage will be limited, but doing something helps to ensure that a student feels a sense of their own responsibility and does not feel de-skilled.

If someone is new to a geographical area spending time walking or navigating public transport in the area can be a really helpful 'doing' activity which encourages learning about the local community. This is important on a range of levels for example, a strengths based approach calls for practitioners to really know the locality they are working in.

READ:

What will the inductee have to read during the induction?
Inductions often involve a great deal of reading with induction packs often turning out to be huge! Reading can be a passive activity and inductees will need the opportunity to discuss their reading to develop their learning. Use a range of techniques to follow up the learning - you can provide a 'quiz', ask the person to take notes to discuss with you or ask them to highlight the most relevant points. Whatever you do to try to bring the reading to life, always make sure that you discuss the reading and its relationship to practice in supervision. Otherwise inductees may feel they are being asked to read lots of material for no reason.

Practice educators and supervisors should be able to guide students towards useful reading material - this is likely to include reading agency documentation and policies and procedures. Some of this will take place during induction. However, the student is most likely to learn from reading material when it is specifically relevant to the work they are undertaking - so it is important to prioritise what must be read early in the placement and what can be read later on, as and when it applies to the student's practice.

EVALUATE:

Make sure that the individual evaluates the induction and that they are able to identify what they have learnt.
A key element of the induction process is ensuring that the inductee evaluates the induction process, identifying what they have learnt. This is essential before the person moves to the next stage of their work or their placement. Once you both understand what the person has learnt from the induction you can work together to plan ongoing learning.

Be careful about the size of an induction pack, too much reading can be off putting

Supervision

Despite the known importance of supervision in social work there is no universally agreed model for the provision of good quality reflective supervision and many commentators (Munson 2002, Dewane 2007, Social Work Policy Institute 2011) have pointed out that very often social workers who are given responsibility for supervising others are not effectively prepared for the role.

It is generally accepted that there are four main objectives to supervision (Morrison 2005):

1. Ensuring competent accountable practice
2. Encouraging continuing professional development
3. Offering personal support to practitioners
4. Engaging the individual practitioner with the organisation

The objectives of supervision are met through the main functions of supervision. Whilst different writers use different terms it is generally accepted that there are four main functions to social work supervision (which relate to the four objectives). These functions are often reflected in agency supervision policies.

Managerial function: This is also referred to as the accountability, administrative or normative function. This is all about supervisors ensuring that the supervisee is competent in their practice and about supervision being used to monitor the quality of service provision.

Developmental function: This is also referred to as the educative or formative function. Supervisors sometimes misunderstand the developmental function and think that asking a question like 'What training have you been on?' or 'What courses are you considering?' means they have covered the developmental function! However, supervision should be developmental in itself - it should enable a practitioner's learning by promoting adult learning processes and critically reflective practice. Supervisors should encourage practitioners to reflect on what they have learnt from their practice within all supervision discussion.

Supportive function: This is also referred to as the restorative or pastoral function. Supervision needs to provide a supportive forum where the supervisee can discuss their concerns and explore their emotional responses to their work.

Mediation function: This is also referred to as the negotiation function. This is the function of supervision which is least commonly written about. Many agency supervision policies reflect, or even specifically refer to, the first three functions of supervision, but most make little or no reference to the mediation function. Focused on engaging the worker with the organisation, Morrison (2005: 46) asserts that the mediation function is about:

- Negotiating and clarifying team roles and responsibilities.
- Briefing management about resource deficits or implications.
- Allocating resources in the most efficient way.
- Representing supervisees needs to higher management.
- Consulting and briefing staff about organisational developments or information.
- Mediating or advocating between workers, within the team or other parts of the agency or outside agencies.

SHARE provides a useful framework to promote a relationships-based reflective style of supervision, which addresses the functions of supervision. Recognising that supervision is *"not done by the supervisor but rather jointly by the supervisor and supervisee together"* (Hawkins 2008: 3) the SHARE model should be used to consider the supervision 'share' from the perspective of both supervisor and supervisee.

Since the Munro review of child protection was published in 2011 there has been a renewed focus on the need for reflective supervision for social workers. As such Research in Practice focused on the development of reflective practice as one of its 'Change Projects'. Ultimately it published a Resource pack to support reflective supervision (Earle, Fox, Webb and Bowyer 2017). This recognises the value of using a range of different tools (which would address different components of the SHARE model).

Reflective supervision is often misunderstood as being about allowing time for reflective discussion in supervision. However, it is about much more than that, it requires:

- A focus on relationships.
- Creative methods.
- A shared understanding of the what, why and how of reflection.
- Consideration of outcomes of practice.
- Discussions about evidence.
- A focus on feedback.
- Space for discussions about feelings, thoughts, values and the impact of these on actions.

The SHARE model can support this in a range of ways. For example, in supervision think about what might be shared and how this sharing can be encouraged. Jones (2011: 19) highlights that:

> "One of the requirements in the social work role is to stay close to, and empathic with, people at times of stress and pain. At times, all of this can be overwhelming... Supervision should provide a safe and secure space for these stresses and strains to be shared with the supervisor as well as reflected and acted upon."

Rather than being equally balanced around the SHARE model, very often supervision is based around two people having a conversation (which is often limited to managerial issues and casework) and one of them writing down what is said so that it can be read later, therefore just addressing the hearing and reading components of the model. Drawing on all the components of the SHARE model ensures a more holistic sensory experience for both supervisor and supervisee; some suggestions on this are provided over the next two pages.

In supervision

SEE:

There is often not much to 'see' in supervision. Specifically providing a visual experience in supervision can be very useful. Prompt cards for supervision such as reflective cards or other prompt cards (Maclean 2016 and Tedam 2016) or postcards (see page 116) add an extra dimension to supervision. When we have asked students about their supervision experiences on placement visual activities are often the first thing they recall.

HEAR:

Whilst supervision draws on conversation and discussion and in some ways therefore addresses the hearing component, there are other specific issues to be considered in relation to supervision:

Does the worker feel that they are being 'heard'? Do they feel able to be open and honest in what they say?

A wide range of issues can impact on the quality of listening in supervision. Rushton and Nathan (1996) quote a manager as saying *"If they tell you what they're feeling, what the hell can I do about it? Maybe some of my holding back (from the staff member) is because I think if they tell me all this, what can I do except say, well, you've got to carry on. Hold on."*

Is the service user's voice fully heard in the session? Is feedback from the service user central to the session?

Is the supervisor sharing clear constructive feedback in the session?

ACT:

Supervision can feel like a passive activity. Bringing in an element of 'action' in some way can be useful. For example, the use of prompt cards and postcards (seeing) provides not only a visual but also a tactile experience. Drawing up 'mind-maps' or using some other form of action in supervision adds to the multi-sensory experience which can create a more reflective session.

Use of social work theory cards in group supervision

Use of Mandela Model cards in supervision

READ:

Social workers make consistent reference to the importance of the recording of supervision (Maclean 2012). Increasingly, supervision is recorded electronically. Supervisors will need to be aware of the way that this can create barriers to the supervisory relationship. If the supervisor is concentrating on typing and looking at a computer screen, this will have an impact on the supervisee's feelings of being listened to and being valued.

Agency requirements for recording should be discussed with the supervisee and agreed as part of the initial negotiations around supervision.

It might be worth considering sharing responsibilities for recording - for example, the supervisor might record the information which relates to service users, whilst the supervisee might record the information which relates to them. It is important to be clear that supervisees should have a copy of any records which relate to them. Since practitioners may make use of these in a range of ways, for example, to demonstrate their professional capability or their development; these should not contain any information which can identify service users.

EVALUATE:

One of the most important aspects of reflective supervision is providing space for the worker to discuss their thoughts and feelings in relation to their work. They need to explore the impact they have on the work and the impact that the work has on them. They need to experience supportive reflective questioning which encourages them to see things differently. Supervision must provide the supervisee with the opportunity to evaluate their mission for work, their experiences, their growth and development and their changing sense of self.

My Share

Do I make the most of the supervision I receive?

What is positive about my supervision experiences? How can I build on this?

Designing and delivering teaching sessions / training

The importance of drawing on a range of techniques is widely recognised in teaching and the days of writing on a board (or 'chalk and talk' style teaching) should be over. However, sometimes the new technology which can be used to make learning so exciting and vibrant is used in old traditional ways and 'death by powerpoint' is a phrase that you often hear people use about training they have been on.

We have known people describing even a fairly short workshop presentation as interactive, this was a very large audience and individuals couldn't really 'interact' in any traditional way, but specific comments were made about the use of visual and auditory methods, as well as the fact that people were asked to stand up and sit down (comments heard during presentation on integrated working at Community Care Live event Manchester 2017).

When one of our children was young, they talked about the new 'attractive' whiteboard that had been installed in their classroom. In fact, the whiteboard was interactive but this being a new word to them they had heard it as attractive. In many ways, this is just what interactivity in training and learning should be, attractive to everyone involved.

Lessons which are based on simple 'chalk and talk' techniques only draw on the hearing and the reading components of SHARE. Thinking through all of the components of the model can help to create a multi-sensory learning experience, promoting the idea of learning being shared. Of course the SHARE model is not simply about thinking through the components of the model. It is also important to think about the word share and the underpinning principles behind the model.

On page 297 we outlined an activity which Siobhan uses in working with newly qualified workers. In training, one of the activities which Siobhan uses to promote the value of creativity is to ask social workers to 'do something' creative around exploring what social work is. She is vague in starting off the groupwork and often people struggle at first, but some really good things develop out of these group sessions. Participants need to share ideas and be creative about what they can use. Siobhan provides pens and flipchart paper of course, she also provides a basic kit of scissors and tape, a few pieces of card and a few other bits of craft equipment. This activity is always commented on positively, people often start off saying that they don't like creative activities on training, but the working together and the sense of producing something shared is valuable. It prompts discussion about the value of creativity in social work, as well as direct work and the whole nature of the profession, how we deal with the inherent lack of resources in social work and so on...

At a workshop in September 2017 this 'apple art' was produced by the following group of newly qualified social workers. It represents the diversity of roles that a social worker has and of course the central importance of a social worker developing their core in practice: Laura Brown, Kerry Clifft, Jade Houston, Sarah-Jane Patton and Rachel Timms.

In planning training

SEE:

Think about what the participants will see:
Can you use any video?
Do you have powerpoint? (is it full of text or do you have some visual content?)
How can you make the environment visually exciting?

HEAR:

Who will the 'audience' listen to?
Whose voices will they hear?
How can you encourage people to share their views?

ACT:

What will participants 'do' in the session?
What groupwork will you draw on?
What specific movement based activities can they do? (sometimes getting a group moving around in an activity can aid in learning and breaking down any barriers)

READ:

What reading will you refer people to?
Will you provide any handout material?

EVALUATE:

How will you make sure that the training is fully and effectively evaluated? Sometimes training evaluation reflects whether the chairs were comfortable and whether there were biscuits provided rather than the important aspects about how the training will impact on a person's future practice. How will you make sure that the evaluation is meaningful?

Think about how you can make the learning environment visually stimulating

STAKEHOLDER VOICE
ANGELA PYE

Angela is a senior social worker with children and families. She qualified in 2009 and have has worked in the voluntary sector since then.

As a Practising Social Worker for the last 9 years, one of the scariest moments of my career was returning to University in order to train as a Practice Educator. For me this was a whole new direction.

On my first day of training I recalled feeling anxious, nervous and excited. My worst fear was sitting in lectures again and being 'lectured' to from a PowerPoint. I recalled many instances during my Social Work training where I had fallen asleep at the tone of a lecturer reading word for word from a powerpoint presentation. I was prepared, I had drunk coffee and had copious amounts of change for the coffee machine. To my surprise as I entered the classroom there were sweets on the desk, coloured pens, handouts, and other articles on the lecturer's desk clearly ready for an interactive lecture. I found myself engaged. Yes there was a powerpoint but it was flicked through here and there, there were activities, discussions, group work. I was being taught rather than lectured and this was what I wanted, this was how I would deliver group work to my future students.

During my training I learnt how to approach different methods of teaching taking into consideration the way that students learn. All of the sessions during my training were clearly planned to meet the different needs of diverse learners and it was these sessions that gave me the knowledge and motivation to ensure that any group work and supervision I delivered would meet the learning needs of my students. I learnt how to SHARE a session and the biggest example of this took place within my own learning; visual aids in the form of diagrams, group work for the talkers, handouts to read, and music to listen to in order to help the learners to associate songs with the subjects and enable this to remain imbedded in our memory. I prepared for my first group teaching session and had a plan! I knew I needed a PowerPoint but had every intention of using it as a reminder, not to be read from word for word. I used Case studies to promote an active style of learning (action), from the case studies we created mind maps Genograms and family trees to satisfy the visual learners (seeing). In order to address 'hearing' I made sure the group were all given the opportunity to discuss their findings and present it to the group and the PowerPoint presentation with the handouts to make notes on gave enough information for the 'reading'. My students gave amazing feedback on the session describing it as being 'engaging' which helped them to remember what they had learned in comparison to being lectured 'at.'

© Angela Pye

Planning placement learning

The main 'education' role of the practice educator is to ensure, as far as possible, that the learning opportunities offered to the student are matched to their learning needs. This is often done through the devising of a learning curriculum. Whilst developing a written learning curriculum is not essential within most social work programmes, it is considered good practice (Maclean and Caffrey 2014).

To understand the concept of a learning curriculum in social work practice, it is helpful to 'see' the meaning of the word in a general sense. The word curriculum has its roots in Latin, where the word curricle refers to an open, two-wheeled carriage pulled by two horses side by side and 'currere' means to run a course with a racing chariot. So, taken literally the word curriculum could mean running a course. Since the early roots of the word it is generally only used in education. However, the development of a learning curriculum by a practice educator can help the bridge between practice and education.

In social work, learning curriculums, sometimes known as practice learning plans, are simply what they say they are. They are a written statement of the individual student's learning needs and a plan of how these will be addressed through the practice learning opportunity. The actual style of the document is not important. However, the curriculum should detail the student's learning needs, the learning methods and materials to be used, the learning opportunities that will be sought and possibly some expected outcomes.

There are various advantages to the use of learning curriculums:

- The drafting of a curriculum will lead to meaningful negotiation with students, leading to a shared ownership of the learning plan.

- The curriculum will give some focus to the practice learning opportunity. It should also structure the learning process, though clearly there should still be flexibility. This is important since placements can seem very short considering the amount of work there is to do. The use of a learning curriculum and the regular review process, will ensure that nothing is missed out or taken over by other issues.

- The use of a learning curriculum will ensure that every student has a unique learning experience, tailored to their specific needs.

- The use of a learning curriculum should help to focus the choice of work the student undertakes, ensuring that this meets their learning needs.

A traditional approach to a learning curriculum is as follows:

Learning needs	Opportunities	Responsibility	Review	Outcomes	Notes
Here the learning needs will be detailed one by one. Some simply list assessment requirements here (for example in England, the PCF requirements) some put student's individual needs, others write a combination of the two.	Detail is provided here about the specific learning opportunities which will meet each need.	Who is responsible for ensuring that the opportunity is provided will be recorded here.	When the need will be reviewed is recorded here.	How will you know when the learning need has been met?	Any ongoing notes can be recorded here.
Further development of assessment skills	1. Shadowing team members carrying out various forms of assessments. 2. Review of assessment documentation and reading assessment policy / procedures / agency standards 3. Carrying out an assessment with a co-worker 4. Undertake low level need assessments 5. Produce some notes on theories around assessment practice Etc............	1. Team colleagues and student 2. Student – practice educator to provide information 3. Student and co-worker 4. Student 5. Student	7th August 12th August 21st August by 15th September 11th September	1. Student to complete shadowing forms 2. Discussion in supervision: student to demonstrate understanding 3. Completed assessment documentation 4. Completed assessment documentation 5. Notes to be discussed in supervision	Student found shadowing useful: would like additional opportunity to shadow carers assessment worker. Student now feels confident to undertake assessments Etc............

Whilst this kind of curriculum is helpful it can lead to a one-dimensional approach to learning and can limit the opportunities that are made available to the student. It does tend to focus on what the student will 'do', sometimes limiting the learning that can come from other sources and effectively widening the gap between the academic side of learning and the placement. A SHARE approach to a learning curriculum considers each of the components of the SHARE model in planning the learning experience with a student:

Learning need	SEE:	HEAR:	ACT:	READ:	EVALUATE:
Development of assessment skills.	Observe other workers undertaking assessment.	Talk to service users about their experiences of assessment.	Begin to ask some questions when shadowing other workers, working towards taking the lead on some assessments - shadowed by the other worker. When confident carry out assessments independently (if appropriate).	Read assessments undertaken by other workers. Write up assessment documentation based on observations of other practitioners and compare with what they have written up. Read around assessment practice in the organisation. Write assessments and seek feedback on these - from service users, colleagues and managers.	Evaluate learning. Undertake self-evaluation of assessment skills. Discuss the learning experiences in supervision throughout the placement: keeping these under review.
Responsibility					
Date for review					

This kind of learning curriculum is much more holistic, it encourages the student to engage in a wide range of activities involving something from each of the components of the SHARE model. It can help the student to develop their understanding of the SHARE model and can therefore enable them to understand that taking a full account of SHARE in assessments of service users (see pages 281-287) can be useful.

STAKEHOLDER VOICE — MONIKA

Monika is a final year social work student.

My first placement was in a domestic violence refuge. I was keen to get into the placement, but wasn't sure how I could meet the requirements of the PCF or what I should be doing. There were no social workers in the refuge - although some did visit and many of the children in the refuge had social work involvement. When I met with my practice educator we agreed a learning curriculum in conjunction with the refuge manager, who was acting as an on-site supervisor. This really helped me out. I was clear about what was going to happen after my induction and I understood (in principle at least) how I could address the PCF domains I was being assessed against.

What the practice educator brought to the discussions was suggestions about a wider variety of learning experiences for me. The on-site supervisor was focused on what I would be 'doing' in the refuge during the placement, whereas the practice educator helped me to think about what I could read, what observations I could carry out by visiting other local agencies, and how I could draw on all my senses in approaching the placement learning. In a way, I had the best of both worlds - I was clear about what I was going to be doing in the refuge, but I was also clear about how I could make sure that I learnt from this.

© Monika

Assessing a student in practice

This chapter has outlined a range of applications of the SHARE model. We have started and ended with assessment because this is such a core aspect of the social work role and perhaps one which offers a starting point for bridging the gap between social work practice and social work education.

An essential aspect of the practice educator role is to assess whether the student has developed professional capability in the practice learning environment. New practice educators often find the assessment aspect of the role very challenging - perhaps because it carries with it a great deal of responsibility and is where the power differentials are most notable. However, social workers should have an expertise in assessment and can draw on this in their assessment of students. The consideration of the SHARE model in relation to assessment (pages 281-285) will be helpful to illustrate how the model can be used in planning a student assessment.

Finch (2017a) argues that the framework for assessing students in practice must be clear and transparent. Using the SHARE model to plan the assessment helps to provide such a framework.

In using the SHARE model as part of their assessment of students, practice educators must be sure to take account of everyone's 'share' in the assessment process. There are three key stakeholders in the assessment process: the student, the practice educator and service users. The practice educator needs to promote partnership between all the stakeholders in order to ensure effective assessment practice. As (Williams and Rutter 2007:121) explained:

> *"The learning that can be achieved through service user and carer involvement in assessment is not just important for the development of individuals but also for the development of a culture in which whole organisations 'learn' to understand and be more responsive to the needs and wishes of its service users."*

Understanding the difference between formative and summative assessment can be helpful for those new to practice education:

Formative assessment: describes the assessment activities that take place on an ongoing basis throughout the placement. These activities involve partnership between the student and practice educator. As such, formative assessments also have intrinsic learning value.

Summative assessment: describes the 'final' stage of an assessment process. Summative assessments take a snapshot approach - indicating where a student is at the point of assessment. Focusing entirely on using summative assessment therefore leads to a lack of opportunities for learning.

Formative assessments influence the summative assessment - so that nothing comes as a surprise but the summative assessment is where the professional judgement is made, recorded and ultimately 'processed'.

Each component of the SHARE model can provide a formative assessment (for example something that the practice educator sees or hears) but in making a judgment about the overall capability of the student's capability then an overview of the whole SHARE will need to be considered as follows:

Essentially, the plan, do and review framework is key in the assessment of social work practice. So, the student and practice educator should work together to plan the assessment as a whole and to plan specific assessment activities. The assessment activities are then 'done' and the practice educator and student work together in evaluating the activities. Ultimately the practice educator is then responsible for making a clear recommendation about the student's practice. Have they passed or failed the placement? This is a significant responsibility and a range of methods have been developed to support practice educators with this aspect of their role.

One traditional strategy used in the assessment of students lies around the importance of triangulation. This is essentially about drawing on three sources of evidence in coming to a recommendation about a student's practice:

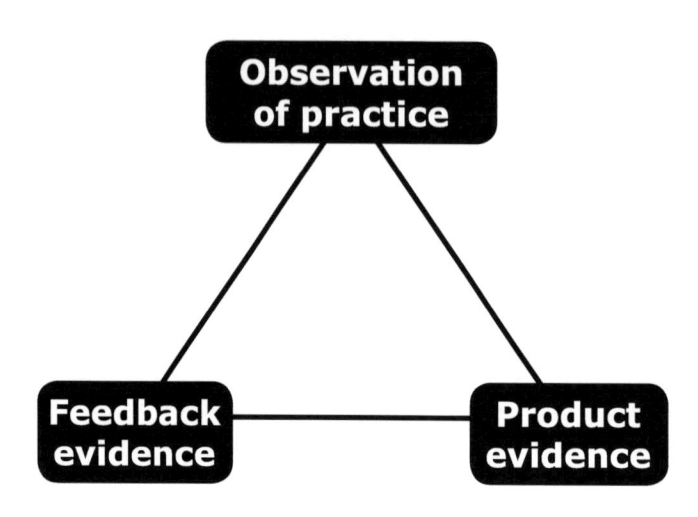

```
              Observation
              of practice
              /         \
             /           \
            /             \
    Feedback ———————— Product
    evidence           evidence
```

Triangulating evidence can help to ensure a rounded picture is obtained. It can also help to avoid error in the assessment decision and we have all drawn on this approach in our work with students. More recently, as we have been developing the SHARE model we have found that for new practice educators working on an assessment 'share' is easier to remember than thinking through triangulation.

In assessing a student

SEE:

What observations has the practice educator undertaken of the student's practice (both formal and informal)?

HEAR:

What feedback has the practice educator received about the student's practice?
What has the student told the practice educator about their practice?

ACT:

What has the student done on placement?
How does their action demonstrate that they have made progress across the period of the placement?

READ:

Practice educators will have examples of the student's written work to read. This will assist in making a decision about the suitability of the student towards progression. The reading will fall into two main areas:

- the student's practice (reading agency recording)
- the student's reflection (reading reflective writing and academic assignments)

Where there are concerns about the quality of a student's writing, every effort must be made by the practice educator to provide feedback in a timely manner to enable the student work on areas and difficulties highlighted.

EVALUATE:

Holistic assessments need to be evidence based and textured with a variety of evidence. A practice educator should draw on evidence drawn from the first four components of the model (as covered above). In evaluating the evidence, practice educators should look for consistency in the evidence. Does the evidence from the different components complement each other? If not, why not?
What recommendation does the evidence from the assessment 'share' lead to?

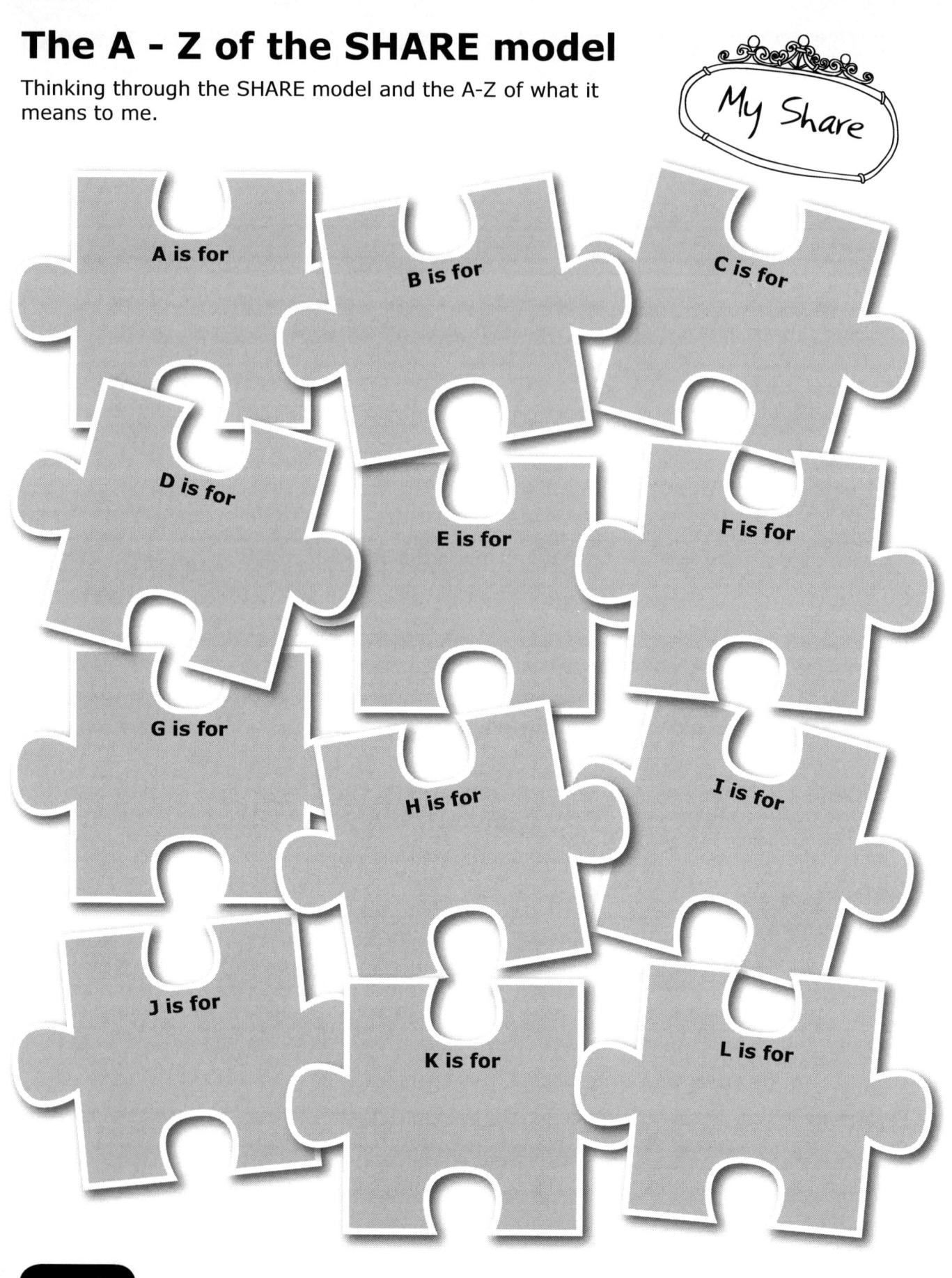

The A - Z of the SHARE model

Thinking through the SHARE model and the A-Z of what it means to me.

My Share

A is for

B is for

C is for

D is for

E is for

F is for

G is for

H is for

I is for

J is for

K is for

L is for

#socialworkSHARE

M is for

N is for

O is for

P is for

Q is for

R is for

S is for

T is for

U is for

V is for

W is for

X is for

Y is for

Z is for

Key points

- The SHARE model can be used in a range of ways. In fact, we have been able to think of a way that the SHARE model can help in relation to any social work task or issue we have considered.

- In this chapter we have tried to illustrate the use of the SHARE model in some specific situations, drawing on social work tasks that will be useful for people in a variety of social work roles.

- We would like you as a reader to think about other ways that the SHARE model can be used and develop your own A to Z of the model.

Reflective Questions

Which application of the SHARE model covered in this chapter stands out most for you? Why?

What other application would you have liked to see included?

Chapter 11: Conclusion

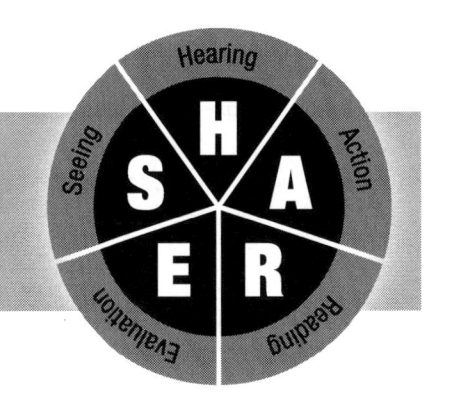

We are now at the final chapter, which should ideally practice what we have preached in terms of the E in SHARE. A concluding chapter of course, is an evaluation of sorts. At this point, we can confess that all three of us find writing conclusions the hardest part of writing a book or an article. This is because sometimes we have rather run out of steam, or have reached a deadline and need to do it quickly, and at other times, because a simple repetition of the main points of the book or a short summary of an article, can feel somewhat meaningless. There is something, however, that connects evaluation, or a conclusion or summary to the issue of two further 'Es', namely endings and emotions. We have therefore all invested emotionally in this book, you the reader, us the authors and of course our generous stakeholders who willingly contributed their voices and stories. Some of our stories were humorous, some were incredibly sad, angry and full of injustice and some were full of passion, joy and hope. Many of the stories, revealed a range of emotional states and we thank the stakeholders who had the courage to write with such honesty.

As authors, we 'shared' our experiences and our thoughts throughout the book, which at times, felt a little exposing. Namely sharing personal and professional stories or issues that illuminated or illustrated further the points we were making. This is however, a good example of use of self for the purposes of supporting readers to make links between theory and practice. This is perhaps an unusual approach in an academic textbook on social work in particular, but we felt strongly that we could not ask stakeholders to share if we ourselves were not prepared to do it. When we think about practice however, we ask service users, and indeed expect them to share their stories.

The origins of the model and this book were fuelled by our concern about the growing divide between service users, academics, practitioners, managers and employers, but also a need for something new and fresh, which came from a broader, multicultural and international perspective. As we commented, whilst we embrace social media and can see much good in its use, we remain concerned about how the social work profession is being so negatively portrayed by those both inside and outside of the profession. One of the challenges we faced in writing this book was the need to have some structure and plan, but trusting that the book would develop organically – depending in part on what people chose to share with us, and how these shares would emphasise and highlight the points being made. What we found however, was that the stakeholder voices directed us in our writing. The book therefore does feel very congruent with our aim to engage in a creative shared endeavour.

The book developed organically

So in terms of a more traditional conclusion, the book began of course, with an introduction to the SHARE model, a new model for social work practice. We outlined our reasons for the development of the new approach, not least our concerns about an urgent need to reinvigorate social work practice. As we outlined at the start of this book, we were very concerned about the field-academy divide, not helped, we argued by new approaches to social work education that possibly emphasised employers needs over that of social justice needs. The SHARE model tries to bridge this gap, by emphasising the commonality between anyone who has an interest and a stake in social work practice and education.

We also emphasised that the 'seeing' and 'hearing' aspects were not necessarily about the physicality of seeing or hearing, as we recognise many people have visual or hearing impairments but more so, the seeing and hearing of those 'under the surface' aspects of human functioning, the unconscious, the non-verbal and thinking about emotional states. The approach is both complex and straightforward at the same time, it is not a linear model but a dynamic, interconnected model. It is a both a practical and reflective model that can be applied to all social work contexts and issues. This may seem a bold claim perhaps, but our long-standing concern has been a growing divide between adult social work and children and family social work in England. We see social work as a generic profession and this is a generic model that can be applied in a range of social work contexts. We also made an earlier claim that this is also a model that could easily and very readily be applied in other caring professions. As we saw in Chapter 10, the model has wide applicability in practice learning and many areas of social work practice.

We encourage readers to engage with the suggested reading, both fiction and non-fiction, to inform their academic writing and enhance their practice. A great deal of 'reading' and research has gone into the production of this model and the book and our aim was to share the collective knowledge of a wide range of people.

We surmised that the model would appeal to an international audience; consequently we have kept references concerning social work policy which is only relevant to the English context, such as the Professionals Capabilities Framework (PCF) The Practice Educator Professional Standards (PEPS) and Standards of Proficiency (SoPs) to the minimum. This allows readers from all parts of the world to make the necessary links to their localised frameworks as they feel appropriate. Written for people in the social work and social care professions, SHARE may be able to offer other professionals (healthcare and education) opportunities for application to their own professions. We encourage social work educators to include this model in their teaching and delivery of social work education and call upon students to draw upon the framework in their work with service users.

We have also highlighted the important contribution SHARE makes to advancing anti-oppression in the academic and practice parts of the social work curriculum. A focus on reflection and reflective practice, respecting and acknowledging stakeholder contributions and ensuring we draw upon all evidence available when undertaking assessments, empathic listening, minimising and reducing the barriers to listening, to mention a few are areas where students and social workers can actively work to dismantle oppression and discrimination.

We know that the model does what it proposes primarily because we have tested it out in training with social work students and qualified practitioners during the writing of this book. We would like to thank those for the helpful comments made about the model, as this informed the book as well. It is essential that people who engage with this model strive to enhance and improve their practice at all times. We have concluded that SHARE is here to stay. It will contribute significantly to current practice and will also add value to the training and development of future social workers.

The last major challenge we faced in completing this book in a timely fashion, was quite simply knowing when to stop, not least when to stop editing and adding additional text, and when of course to stop adding stakeholder voices. We acknowledge therefore that a social work book in particular can never really be finished, because of the way social work constantly changes and adapts to new situations or new legislation. There is always more that can be written about social work, and more research to know about. The plans for SHARE here on in, will be to produce a series of smaller books (as an organic process this book did end up longer than we had originally anticipated!) which will focus on the application of the model to particular issues in social work practice and education, so if you have an idea about what the SHARE series could focus on, please do get in touch - enquiries@kirwinmaclean.com or #socialworkSHARE. We also intend to disseminate the model via conferences and training sessions, using creative methods we so strongly advocated for in the book! So, whilst the book has been completed, rather than an ending, we see it as a start of a long and interesting journey and we look forward to seeing how the journey unfolds.

The best part of any journey is who you get to share it with. Will you get on board with the SHARE model?

References

Aked, J., Marks, N., Cordon, C. and Thompson, S. (2014) *Five Ways to Wellbeing.* The new economics foundation centre for wellbeing. Available online at www.neweconomics.org/projects/entry/five-ways-to-well-being. Accessed 3.3.15.

Alinsky, S. (1971) *Rules for Radicals.* New York: Random House

Allen, A. (2017) *DON'T Consider Employees' Learning Styles When Developing Training.* Available online at https://www.saba.com/uk/blogs/2017/03/07/dont-consider-learning-styles-when-developing-training/ Accessed 16.8.17

Ames, N. (1999) *Social Work Recording: A New Look at An Old Issue.* Journal of Social Work Education. 35 (2)227-238.

ANAS (2010) *Proposition de recommendation IFSW sur le burn out.* Available online at www.ifsw.org/p38002013.html. Accessed 2.11.10.

Andrews, A.B. (2012) *Charles Dickens, Social Worker in his time.* Social Work, 57(4). 297-307

Andrews, J., Robinson, D. and Hutchinson, J. (2017) *Closing the Gap? Trends in educational attainment and disadvantage.* (London) Education Policy Institute.

Androff, D.K. (2010) *The Problem of Contemporary slavery: An International Human Rights Challenge for Social Work.* International Social Work 54(2) 209-222.

Anka, A, and Taylor, I. (2016) *Assessment as the Site of Power: A Bourdieusian Interrogation of Service User and Carer Involvement in the Assessments of Social Work Students.* Social Work Education, 35:2, 172-185, DOI: 10.1080/02615479.2015.1129397

Anti-Slavery International (2017) *What is Modern Slavery?* Available from https://www.antislavery.org/slavery-today/ Accessed 6.11.17

Briggs, S., Finch, J. and Firth, R. (2016) *Evaluation of a non-statutory 'Place of Calm' ,a service which provides support after a suicidal crisis to inform future commissioning intentions.* Centre for Social Work Research, University of East London http://recovery-partners.co.uk/mailouts/Anna/PlaceofCalmFinalReport.pdf

Anseel, F., Lievens F. and Schollaert, E. (2009) *Reflection as a strategy to enhance task performance after feedback.* Organizational Behavior and Human Decision Processes, 110 (10). 23-35

Apte, M.L (1983) *Humour research, methodology and theory in anthropology.* In Goldstein, J.H. and McGhee, P.E. (1983) Handbook of Humour Research. (New York) Springer-Verlag.

Archer, C. and Burnell, A. (eds) (2003) *Trauma, Attachment and Family Permanence: Fear can stop you loving.* (London) Jessica Kingsley Publishers

Ayre, P. (2001) *Child protection and the media: lessons from the last three decades.* British Journal of Social Work, 31 (6) 887-901.

Backwith, D. (2015) *Social workers must work with service users to tackle brutal poverty of austerity.* Guardian social care network. Available online at https://www.theguardian.com/social-care-network/social-life-blog/2015/may/06/social-work-poverty-austerity-welfare Accessed 3.7.17

Bailey, R. and Blake, M. (1975) *Radical Social Work.* (London) Hodder and Stoughton Educational.

Ballatt, J. and Campling, P. (2011) *Intelligent Kindness: Reforming the Culture of Healthcare.* (London) Royal College of Psychiatrists.

Bandura, A. (1977) *Social Learning Theory.* (Englewood Cliffs, New Jersey) Prentice Hall.

Barbe, W B; Swassing, R H. and Milone, M N. (1979) *Teaching through modality strengths: concepts and practices.* (Columbus, Ohio) Zaner-Bloser.

BASW (2012a) *Code of Ethics for Social Workers.* Available from http://cdn.basw.co.uk/upload/basw_95243-9.pdf Accessed 11.7.14

BASW (2012b) *BASW Continuing Professional Development (CPD) Policy.* (Birmingham) BASW.

Beckett, C. (2003) *The Language of Siege: Military Metaphors in the Spoken Language of Social Work.* British Journal of Social Work, 33 (5)625-639.

Beddoe, L. and Davys A. (2016) *Challenges in Professional Supervision.* (London) Jessica Kingsley Publishers.

Belshaw, D.A.J. (2011) *What is 'digital literacy'?* Dissertation for Doctor of Education, Durham University. Online at https://dmlcentral.net/wp-content/uploads/files/doug-belshaw-edd-thesis-final.pdf

Bengtsson, E., Chamberlain, C., Crimmens, D. and Stanley, J. (2008) *Introducing social pedagogy into residential child care in England: An evaluation of a project commissioned by the Social Education Trust (SET).* (London) NCB/NCERCC.

Beresford, P. (2017) *The Big Questions.* BBC Broadcast 12 February 2017.

Berra, Y. (2008) *You Can Observe a Lot By Watching: What I've learned about teamwork from the Yankees and life.* (New Jersey) John Wiley and Sons.

Betancourt, J.R. (2006) *Cultural competency: Providing quality care to diverse populations.* Consult Pharm 21(12) 988–995.

Bichard, M. (2004) *The Bichard Inquiry Report.* The Stationery Office, London. Available from http://dera.ioe.ac.uk/6394/1/report.pdf Accessed 9.8.17.

Biestek, F. (1961) *The Casework Relationship.* (London) George Allen and Unwin.

Bingham, J. (2013) *'Colour blind' social workers couldn't see glaring racial clues to Rochdale sex abuse.* The Telegraph. Available at http://www.telegraph.co.uk/news/uknews/crime/10529794/Colour-blind-social-workers-couldnt-see-glaring-racial-clues-to-Rochdale-sex-abuse.html Accessed 20.8.17

Blom-Cooper, L. J. (1995) *A Child in Trust: The Report of the Panel of Enquiry into the Circumstances Surrounding the Death of Jasmine Beckford.* London Borough of Brent, London.

Borton, T. (1970) *Reach, Teach and Touch.* (London) McGraw Hill.

Boud, D., Keogh, R. and Walker, D. (1985) *Reflection: Turning Experience into Learning.* (London) Kogan Page.,

Bower, M (Ed.) (2005) *Psychoanalytic Theory for Social Work Practice: Thinking Under Fire.* (Oxfordshire) Routledge.

British Association of Social Workers (2011) *BASW / CoSW England Research on supervision in social work, with particular reference to supervision practice in multi-disciplinary teams.* (Birmingham) BASW.

Brandon, J. and Davies, M. (1979) *The Limits of Competence in Social Work; The Assessment of Marginal Students in Social Work Education.* British Journal of Social Work, pp:295-347

Braun, D. and Robb, B. (2010) *Developing the College of Social Work.* Research, Policy and Planning, 28 (2) 129-137

Broadhurst, K., Wastell, D. White, S., Hall, C. Peckover, C. Thompson, K., Pithouse, A. and Davey, D. (2010) *Performing 'Initial Assessment': Identifying the Latent Conditions for Error at the Front-Door of Local Authority Children's Services.* British Journal of Social Work, 40(2), 352-370.

Brogan, C. (2015) *Early death and ill health linked to low socioeconomic status.* Imperial College London available online at http://www3.imperial.ac.uk/newsandeventspggrp/imperialcollege/newssummary/news_31-1-2017-13-35-54 Accessed 2.8.17

Bronfenbrenner, U. (1994) *Ecological Models of Human Development.* Available online at http://www.psy.cmu.edu/~siegler/35bronfebrenner94.pdf Accessed 22.12.10.

Brown, J.S., Collins, A. and Duguid, S. (1989) *Situated Cognition and the Culture of Learning.* Educational Researcher, 18(1) 32-42.

Brown, M. J. E. and Hatton, C (2017) *A Trade in People: The inpatient healthcare economy for people with learning disabilities and/or Autism Spectrum Disorder.* (Lancaster) Centre for Disability Research.

Brown, S.D., Reavey, P. and Brookfield, H. (2014) *Spectral objects: Material links to difficult pasts for adoptive families. In P. Harvey et al. (Eds). Objects and materials: A Routledge companion.* (pp.173-182). Abingdon, Oxon: Routledge.

Bryman, A. (1998) *Quantity and Quality in Social Research.* (London) Routledge.

Buck, D. and Maguire, D. (2015) *Inequalities in Life Expectancy: Changes over time and implications for policy.* Kings Fund. Available online at https://www.kingsfund.org.uk/sites/files/kf/field/field_publication_file/inequalities-in-life-expectancy-kings-fund-aug15.pdf#page=26 Accessed 1.8.17

Burns, R. (1995) *The Adult Learner at Work.* (Sydney) Business and Professional Publishers.

Busch, B. (2016) *Four neuromyths that are still prevalent in schools – debunked.* Available online at https://www.theguardian.com/teacher-network/2016/feb/24/four-neuromyths-still-prevalent-in-schools-debunked Accessed 20.8.17

Butler, P. (2017) *Child Poverty at its Highest Figure since 2010, official statistics show.* The Guardian Newspaper, available from https://www.theguardian.com/society/2017/mar/16/child-poverty-in-uk-at-highest-level-since-2010-official-figures-show Accessed 14.5.17

Cade, B., and O'Hanlon, W. H. (1993) *A brief guide to brief therapy.* (New York) W W Norton & Co.

Cameron, C. and Boddy, J. (2006) *Knowledge and education for care workers: What do they need to know.* In Boddy, J., Cameron, C. and Moss, P. (Eds) Care Work: Present and Future. (London) Routledge.

Campbell, D. (2013) *Mid Staffs hospital scandal: the essential guide.* Guardian online, available from https://www.theguardian.com/society/2013/feb/06/mid-staffs-hospital-scandal-guide Accessed 5.9.17

Campbell, M. (2017) *Views of People Who Use Services.* Presentation at Resilience in Times of Austerity. Joint PSW Conference. 21 July 2017, Kings College London.

Carpenter, J. Webb, C. and Bostock, L. (2013) *The Surprisingly weak evidence base for supervision.* Children and Youth Services Review, 35 (1) 1843-1853

Carson, D. (1996) *Risking Legal Repercussions.* In Kemshall, H. and Pritchard, J, (ed) Good Practice in Risk Assessment and Risk Management (Volume 1). (London) Jessica Kingsley Publishing.

Chadborn, N. (2017) *Time to unite.* blogpost available from https://idea.nottingham.ac.uk/blogs/posts/time-unite Accessed 1.9.17

Chambers, A, and Hickey, G. (date unknown) *Service user involvement in the design and delivery of education and training programmes leading to registration with the Health Professions Council.* Available from http://www.hpc-uk.org/assets/documents/10003A08Serviceuserinvolvementinthedesignanddeliveryofapprovedprogrammes.pdf

Chartered Institute of Personnel and Development (2016) *Induction.* Available online at https://www.cipd.co.uk/knowledge/fundamentals/people/recruitment/induction-factsheet Accessed 6.7.17

Chetwynd, H. and Pona, I. (2017) *Making Connections: Understanding how local agencies can better keep missing children safe.* The Children's Society. Available online at https://www.childrenssociety.org.uk/sites/default/files/making-connections-how-local-agencies-can-keep-missing-children-safe.pdf Accessed 1.10.17

Christensen, T. M., and Kline, W. B. (2000) *A qualitative investigation of the process of group supervision with group counselors.* The Journal for Specialists in Group Work, 25(4), 376–393.

Clark, E. (2012) *Social workers are holders of hope.* NASW News 57, 3.

Clark, E. (2017) *10 essentials social workers must know about hope.* Available online at http://www.socialworker.com/feature-articles/practice/10-essentials-social-workers-must-know-about-hope/ Accessed 18.8.17.

Clark, E.J. and Hoffler, E.F. (Eds) (2014) *Hope Matters: The Power of Social Work.* (New York) NASW Press.

Cole, A. (2016) *The 'three conversations' model: turning away from long-term care.* Available at https://www.theguardian.com/social-care-network/2016/nov/01/the-three-conversations-model-turning-away-from-long-term-care Accessed 1.9.17

College of Social Work (2012) *Understanding what is meant by holistic assessment.* Available online at http://cdn.basw.co.uk/upload/basw_121554-1.pdf Accessed 18.8.17

Community Sustainability Engagement (2017) *What is Evaluation?* Available at http://evaluationtoolbox.net.au/index.php?option=com_content&view=article&id=11&Itemid=17 Accessed 1.1.17

Cottrell, S. (2013) *The Study Skills Handbook* (4th edition) (Basingstoke) Palgrave.

Council on Social Work Education (2013) *Educational policy and accreditation standards.* Available from http://www.cswe.org/File.aspx?id=41861 Accessed 11.7.16

Covey, S. (1999) *The Seven Habits of Highly Effective People.* (London) Simon and Schuster.

Craig, G. (2013) *Invisibilizing 'race' in public policy.* Critical Social Policy, 33 (4) 712-720.

Cree, V. (Ed) (2011) *Social Work: A Reader.* (Oxon) Routledge.

Cullen, J. (1978) *The structure of professionalism: A quantitative examination.* New York, Petrocelli.

Cunningham, J. and Cunningham, S. (2017) *Social Policy and Social Work. An Introduction.* 2nd edition. (London) Sage Learning Matters.

Dahlgren, L.O., Eriksson, B.E., Gyllenhammar, H., Korkeila, M., and Saaf-Rothoff, A. (2006) *To be and to have a critical friend in medical teaching.* Journal of Medical Education, 40(1) pp. 5-6.

Danbury, H. (1994) *Teaching Practical Social Work.* (Aldershot) Arena. Ashgate Publishing Ltd.

David Binder Research and MTV (2014) *MTV Bias Survey Final Results.* Available at http://d1fqdnmgwphrky.cloudfront.net/studies/000/000/002/DBR_MTV_Bias_Survey_Full_Report_I.pdf?1398858309 Accessed 1.10.17

Davies, L (2015) *Speech to the House of Commons* http://islingtonsurvivors.co.uk/

Davies, L (2016) *Community Work – protecting children* Available at https://lizdavies.net/2016/09/11/community-work-protecting-children/ Accessed 31.08.17

De Beauvoir, S. (1972) *The Second Sex.* (London) Penguin.

De Bono, E. (2015) Simplicity is not easy. (London) Penguin Life.

de Haan, E. and Stewart, S. (translator) (2008) *Relational Coaching; Journeys towards mastering one to one learning.* (London) John Wiley.

Dekker, S., Lee, N.C., Howard-Jones, P. and Jolles, J. (2012) *Neuromyths in Education: Prevalence and Predictors of Misconceptions among Teachers.* Front. Psychol., 18 October 2012 https://doi.org/10.3389/fpsyg.2012.00429

DeRoos, Y.S. (1990) *The development of practice-wisdom through human problem-solving processes.* Social Service Review, 64(2) pp. 276-287.

Department for Children, Families and Schools (2009) *The protection of children in England – action plan: the government's response to Lord Laming.* London: TSO, available from https://www.gov.uk/government/uploads/system/uploads/attachment_data/file/327238/The_protection_of_children_in_England_-_action_plan.pdf Accessed 9.8.17

Department for Work and Pensions (2015) *Mortality Statistics: Employment and Support Allowance, Incapacity Benefit or Severe Disablement Allowance.* Available online at https://www.gov.uk/government/uploads/system/uploads/attachment_data/file/459106/mortality-statistics-esa-ib-sda.pdf Accessed 1.8.17

Department of Health (2015) *Culture Change in the NHS: Applying the lessons of the Francis Inquiries.* (London) The Stationery Office.

Department of Health (2017) *Strengths-based social work practice with adults: Roundtable report.* (London) HMSO. Available at https://www.gov.uk/government/uploads/system/uploads/attachment_data/file/652773/Strengths-based_social_work_practice_with_adults.pdf Accessed 21.10.17

Dessau, B (2012) *Beyond a Joke: Inside the dark minds of stand-up comedians.* (London) Arrow.

Dewane, C.J. (2007) *Supervisor Beware: Ethical Dangers in Supervision.* Social Work Today 7(4) 34.

Dewey, J. (1933) How We Think. In Boydston, J.A. (2008) *The Later Works 1925-1953. Volume 8. Essays and How We Think. The Collected Works of John Dewey.* (Illinois) Southern Illinois University.

Dickens, C. (1859) *Hunted Down.* (London) JC Hotten.

Dickens, J. (2010) *Social work and Social Policy: An introduction.* (London) Routledge.

Dingwall, E., Eekelaar, J. and Murray, T. (1983) *The Protection of Children: State Intervention and Family Life.* (Oxford) Basil Blackwell.

Doel, M. (2017) *Social Work in 42 Objects (and more).* (Lichfield) Kirwin Maclean Associates.

Doel, M., Sawdon, C. and Morrison, D. (2012) *Learning, practice and assessment: signposting the portfolio.* (London) Jessica Kingsley.

Dominelli, L. (2017) *Keynote presentation: Marginalization and Social Work in a Changing Society.* IFSW European Conference 2017. Reyjavik, Iceland.

Donovan, T. (2014) *Case work on the go: How iPads are shaking up social work practice in Nottinghamshire.* Community Care online, available from http://www.communitycare.co.uk/2014/06/27/case-work-go-ipads-shaking-social-work-practice-nottinghamshire/ Accessed 1.9.17.

Donovan, T. (2016) *Social worker struck off after disclosing case details.* Community care online, available from http://www.communitycare.co.uk/2016/04/27/social-worker-struck-disclosing-details-families-using-personal-laptop/ Accessed 1.9.17.

Donzelot, J. (1977) *The Policing of Families.* (Maryland) John Hopkins University Press.

Doward, J. (2013) *Call for inquiry into deaths of four men at psychiatric hospital.* The Guardian. Available online at https://www.theguardian.com/society/2013/jul/07/call-inquiry-deaths-psychiatric-hospital Accessed 2.8.17

Doyle, T. and Zakrajsek, T. (2013) *The New Science of Learning: How to Learn in Harmony with Your Brain.* (Virginia) Stylus.

Drakeford, J.W. (1967) *The Awesome Power of the Listening Ear.* (Waco) World Books.

Durkin, L. and Douieb, B. (1975) *The mental patients union.* In D. Jones and M. Mayo Community Work Two. London: Routledge and Kegan Paul

Dyke,C. (2016) *Writing Analytical Assessments in Social Work (Critical Skills for Social Work).* St Albans. Critical Publishing

Earle, F., Fox, J., Webb, C. and Bowyer, S. (2017) *Reflective Supervision Resource Pack.* Available at https://www.rip.org.uk/~ftp_user/Reflective_supervision_Resource_Pack/files/assets/basic-html/page1.html Accessed 1.11.17

Eborall, C. (2003) *Modernising the Social Care Workforce: progress on delivery Volume 2 of the first Annual Report of the Topss England Workforce Intelligence Unit.* Topss England, available from http://www.skillsforcare.org.uk/Document-library/NMDS-SC,-workforce-intelligence-and-innovation/Research/Research-Reports/social-care-workforce-report/2003-Vol-2.pdf Accessed 1.9.17

Egan, G. (2002) *The skilled helper.* (Pacific Grove, CA) Brooks/Cole.

Etzioni A (1969). *The semi-professions and their organization.* (New York) Free Press.

Fairtlough, A. (2017) *Professional Leadership for Social Work Practitioners and Educators.* (Oxon) Routledge.

Fairtlough, A., Barnard, C., Fletcher, J., Ahmet, A. (2014) *Black social Work Students Experiences of practice learning; understanding differential progression rates,* Journal of Social Work, Vol 14 (6) 605-624

Ferguson, H. (2016) *How Children Become Invisible in Child Protection Work: Findings from Research into Day-to-Day Social Work Practice.* British Journal of Social Work, Vol 47 Issue 4, pp:1007–1023

Ferguson, H. (2017a) *Why are social workers so reluctant to celebrate their achievements?* Guardian Social Care. Available at https://www.theguardian.com/social-care-network/2017/mar/20/social- workers-reluctant-celebrate-achievements Accessed 19.8.17

Ferguson, H. (2017b) *What makes a good home visit?* Presentation as part of Coventry Practice Development Week. Coventry City Council.

Ferguson, I. (2007) *Increasing User Choice or Privatizing Risk? The Antinomies of Personalization*. British Journal of Social Work V7 (3) 387-403.

Ferguson, I. and Woodward, R. (2009) *Radical social work in practice: Making a Difference (Social Work in Practice)*. Bristol, Policy Press

Finch, J (2009) *Communities and Widening Participation in Higher Education in the London Borough of Barking and Dagenham.* Higher Education Funding Council of England/University of East London, London. DOI: 10.13140/RG.2.1.5113.9602

Finch, J. (2010) *Can't Fail, Wont Fail: Can't fail - why practice assessors find it difficult to fail social work students: a qualitative study of practice assessors' experiences of assessing marginal or failing social work students.* Falmer, Sussex University Doctoral Thesis, available from http://sro.sussex.ac.uk/2370/ Accessed 11.7.17

Finch, J. (2016) *"…it's just very hard to fail a student…" Decision making and defences against anxiety – an ethnographic and practice-near study of practice assessment panels.* Journal of Social Work Practice, 32 (1) pp51-65 doi: 10.1080/02650533.2016.1158156

Finch, J. (2017a) *Supporting Struggling Students on Placement. A Practical Guide.* Bristol. Policy Press.

Finch, J. (2017b) *Don't Throw Your Books Away: The importance of research-mindedness in social work practice (and how to get your hands on research)*, http://www.scopt.co.uk/archives/3255 Scottish Organisation of Practice Educators 16.5.17.

Finch, J. and McKendrick, D. (2015) *The Non-Linear War on Social Work in the UK: Extremism, Radicalisation, Troubled Families and the recasting of "safeguarding"* http://www.reimaginingsocialwork.nz/2015/07/the-non-linear-war-on-social-work-in-the-uk-extremism-radicalisation-troubled-families-and-the-recasting-of-safeguarding/ Reimagining Social Work Blog (New Zealand).

Finch, J. and Schaub, J. (2015) *Projective Identification as an Unconscious Defence: Social Work, Practice Education and the Fear of Failure.* In Armstrong, D. & Rustin, M.(eds) Social Defences against Anxiety: Explorations in the Paradigm, (London) Karnac.

Flynn, M. (2007) *The Murder of Steven Hoskin A Serious Case Review Executive Summary.* Cornwall Adult Protection Committee, available from: http://www.cornwall.gov.uk/media/3630284/a_e_SCR_Executive_Summary1_Dec_2007_.pdf Accessed 9.8.17.

Fook, J., Collington, V., Ross, F., Ruch, G. and West, L. (Eds) (2016) *Researching Critical Reflection: Multi-disciplinary Perspectives.* (Oxon) Routledge.

Foucault, M. (1972) *The Archaeology of Knowledge: And the Discourse on Language.* (New York) Pantheon Books.

Francis, R. (2013) *Report of the Mid Staffordshire NHS Foundation Trust Public Enquiry.* (London) The Stationery Office.

Francis, R. (2015) *The Freedom to Speak up: An independent review into creating an open and honest reporting culture.* Available from http://freedomtospeakup.org.uk/wp-content/uploads/2014/07/F2SU_web.pdf Accessed 5.9.17

Franklin, B. and Parton, N. (1991) *Media Reporting of Social Work: A Framework for Analysis.* In Franklin, B and Parton, N. (Eds) Social Work, The Media and Public relations, (London) Routledge.

Freeman, M. (1999) *The right to be heard.* Adoption & Fostering 22(4) 50–59.

Freire, P. (1994) *Pedagogy of Hope: Reliving 'Pedagogy of the Oppressed'.* (New York) Continuum Books.

Frost, C. (1992) *Having fun in social work.* Middle Tennessee State University paper accessed on line http://capone.mtsu.edu/cfrost/soc/thera/HUMOR.htm

Fryberg, S. M. (2010) *When the World Is Colorblind, American Indians Are Invisible: A Diversity Science Approach.* Psychological Inquiry, 21(2), 115-119.

Furnivall, J. (2011) *Guide to developing and maintaining resilience in residential child care* Community Care Inform article http://www.ccinform.co.uk/articles/2011/11/07/6507/guide+to+developing+and+maintaining+resilience+in+residential+child.html?

Gannon, J. (2005) *Holding and Sharing Memories: The Significance of Social Work Recording for Birth Record Counselling.* Adoption and Fostering, Vol 26 (4) 57-67

Gauci, J. and Kent, S. (2015) *Social Work Action Research: Transformative Community Practice.* Presentation at Social Work Partnerships in Europe. IFSW European Conference 2015 Edinburgh.

Gibbs, G. (1988) *Learning by Doing: A Guide to Teaching and Learning Methods.* (Oxford) Further Education Unit Oxford Polytechnic.

Gibson, F., McGrath, A. and Reid, N. (1989) *Occupational stress in social work.* British Journal of Social Work, 19, 1-18.

Gilgun, J.F. and Sharma, A. (2011) *The Uses of Humour in Case Management with High-Risk Children and their Families.* British Journal of Social Work (2011) 1–18.

Goldsmith, L. (1999) *Recording with Care: Inspection of Case Recording in Social Services Departments.* (London) SSI and DoH.

Gramsci, A. (1973) *Selections from the Prison Notebooks.* Edited and Translated by Hoare, Q. and Nowell-Smith, G. Lawrence and Wishart, London available from https://archive.org/stream/AntonioGramsciSelectionsFromThePrisonNotebooks/Antonio-Gramsci-Selections-from-the-Prison-Notebooks_djvu.txt Accessed 23.4.17

Grant, L. and Kinman, G. (2015) *Guide to Developing Emotional Resilience.* Available online at: www.ccinform.co.uk/guides/guide-todeveloping-social-workers-emotional-resilience. Accessed 15.9.15

Greenaway, R. (2014) *Doing Reviewing.* Available online at: http://reviewing.co.uk/articles/reviewing_outdoorsx3.htm. Accessed 25.8.14.

Greenwood E (1957). *Attributes of a profession*. Social Work 2: 5–45.

Guardian Letter (2017) *No evidence to back idea of learning styles.* Available online at https://www.theguardian.com/education/2017/mar/12/no-evidence-to-back-idea-of-learning-styles Accessed 19.8.17

Guo, S. (2013) *Economic Integration of Recent Chinese Immigrants in Canada's Second-Tier Cities: The Triple Glass Effect and Immigrants' Downward Social Mobility.* Canadian Ethnic Studies 45 (3): 95–115.

Gutteridge, R. and Dobbins, K. (2010) *Service user and carer involvement in learning and teaching: A faculty of health staff perspective.* Nurse Education Today, Vol 30, (6) pp509-514

H M Government (2015) *Information sharing Advice for practitioners providing safeguarding services to children, young people, parents and carers.* Available at https://www.gov.uk/government/uploads/system/uploads/attachment_data/file/419628/Information_sharing_advice_safeguarding_practitioners.pdf Accessed 1.11.17

Hafford-Letchfield, T., Lambley, S., Spolander, G. and Cocker, C. with Daly, N. (2014) *Inclusive Leadership in Social Work and Social Care.* (Bristol) Policy Press.

Haralambos, M. and Holborn, M. (2013) *Sociology Themes and Perspectives* (8th edition). Collins Educational

Haringey Local Safeguarding Children Board (2017) *Learning from SCRs.* Available online at http://www.haringeylscb.org/serious-case-reviews/learning-scrs#seen Accessed 12.8.17

Harrington, D. and Dolgoff, R. (2008) *Hierarchies of Ethical Principles for Ethical Decision Making in Social Work.* Ethics and Social Welfare 2 (2) 183-196

Harrison, G. and Ip, R. (2013) *Extending the terrain of inclusive education in the classroom to the field: International students on placement.* Social Work Education, 32, 2, 230–243.

Harrow ACPC (1999) *Part 8 Review Summary Report*. Available from https://www.whatdotheyknow.com/request/193815/response/474398/attach/2/739763%20Response.pdf Accessed 1.9.17

Hartley, N. and Payne, M. (2008) *The Creative Arts in Palliative Care.* (London) Jessica Kingsley Publishers.

Hawkins, P. (2008) *Foreword to Passionate Supervision*. Edited by Shohet, R. (London) Jessica Kingsley Publishers.

HEFCE (2016) *Higher Education in England: Key Facts.* Available from: Keyhttp://www.hefce.ac.uk/media/HEFCE,2014/Content/Pubs/2016/201620/HEFCE2016_20.pdf Accessed 12.12.16

Helg, A. (1995) *Our Rightful Share: The Afro-Cuban Struggle for Equality, 1886-1912.* (London) Chapel Hill.

Hennessey, R. (2011) *Relationship Skills in Social Work.* (London) Sage.

Hill, C. E. and O'Brien, K. M. (2004) *Helping skills: Facilitating exploration, insight and action.* Washington American Psychological Association.

Hillen, P. and Levy, S. (2015) *Framing the experiences of BME social work students within a narrative of Educating for a Culturally Diverse Workforce.* Social Work Education, Vol 34 (7) 785-798

Hillman, M. (2006) *Children's rights and adults' wrongs.* Children's Geographies 4(1) 61–7.

Hinson, S. and Healey, R. (2003) *Building Political Power.* Prepared for the State Strategies Fund Convening. Grassroots Policy Project.

Hofstede, G. (2001) *Culture's Consequences: Comparing Values, Behaviours, Institutions, and Organizations across Nations.* Second Edition. (Thousand Oaks, CA) Sage.

Holt, J. (2008) *Stop me if you've heard this before: A history and philosophy of jokes.* (London) Profile Books.

Honey, P. and Mumford, A. (1982) *Manual of Learning Styles.* Peter Honey Publications.

Houston, S. (2015) *Enabling Others in Social Work: Reflexivity and the Theory of Social Domains.* Critical and Radical Social Work, 3(2), 245-26

Howe, D. (1998) *Relationship-based thinking and practice in social work.* Journal of Social Work Practice: Psychotherapeutic Approaches in Health, Welfare and the Community, 12:1, 45-56.

Howe, D. (2008) *The Emotionally Intelligent Social Worker.* (Basingstoke) Palgrave Macmillan.

Howe, D. (2011) *Attachment Across the Life Course: A Brief Introduction.* (Palgrave) Basingstoke.

Hussein, S., Moriarty, J., Manthorpe, J. and Huxley, P. (2008) *Diversity and progression among students starting social work qualifying programmes in England between 1995 and 1998: a quantitative study.* British Journal of Social Work, Vol 38 (8) 1588-609.

IFSW Europe (2011) *Charter of Rights for Social Workers.* (Berlin) IFSW Europe.

Independent Anti-Slavery Commissioner (2017) *Home page.* Available from http://www.antislaverycommissioner.co.uk/, Accessed 1.9.17

Independent Anti-slavery commissioner (2017) *What is modern day slavery?* Available from http://www.antislaverycommissioner.co.uk/ Accessed 3.11.17

Ingram, R. (2013) *Emotions, Social Work Practice and Supervision: An Uneasy Alliance.* Journal of Social Work Practice. 27(1) pp. 5-19.

International Federation of Social Workers (2014) *Global Definition of Social Work.* Available from http://ifsw.org/policies/definition-of-social-work/ Accessed 10.7.17

International Federation of Social Workers (2017) *World Social Work Day.* Available at http://cdn.ifsw.org/assets/ifsw_85801-10.pdf Accessed 18.8.17

International Federation of Social Workers (2017a) *Closing the Gaps Between Social Work Practice and Education.* Available at http://ifsw.org/news/closing-the-gaps-between-social-work-practice-and-education/ Accessed 20.10.17

Ioakimidis, V. (2016) *A guide to radical social work.* The Guardian Social Care Network https://www.theguardian.com/social-care-network/2016/may/24/radical-social-work-quick-guide-change-poverty-inequality Accessed 7.9.17

Islam, N. (2011) *Top Five Skills in a Social Worker's Professional Toolkit.* Available online at https://msw.usc.edu/mswusc-blog/top-five-skills-in-a-social-workers-professional-toolkit/ Accessed 20.8.17

Jack, G. and Donnellan, H. (2010) *Recognising the person within the developing professional: tracking the early careers of newly qualified child care social workers in three local authorities in England.* Social work education., 29 (3) 305-318.

Jensen, S.Q. (2011) *Othering, identity formation and agency.* Qualitative Studies, 2(2): 63-78. available from https://tidsskrift.dk/index.php/qual/article/view/5510 Accessed 10.7.17

Jersild, A.T. and Meigs, M. F. (1939) *Direct Observation as a Research Method.* Review of Educational Research 9(5) Methods of Research in Education (December 1939), 472-482

Johnson, N. (2011) *Simply Complexity: A Clear Guide to Complexity Theory.* (Oxford) Oneworld Publications.

Johnson, T. (1972) *Professions and power.* (London) Macmillan.

Jones, R. (2011) *The Glue that Binds.* Professional Social Work. February 2011. pp. 18-20.

Jones, R. (2012) *Child protection, social work and the media: doing as well as being done to.* Research, Policy and Planning 29 (2) 83-94.

Jones, R. (2014) *The Story of Baby P: Setting the Record Straight.* (Bristol) Policy Press.

Jordan, S. (2015) *That Joke Isn't Funny Anymore: Humour, Jokes and Their Relationship to Social Work.* Professional doctorate thesis, University of East London. Available from http://roar.uel.ac.uk/4591/ accessed 1.9.17.

Jozwiak, G. (2017) *G4S completes sale of children's homes for £11m.* Children and Young People Now. Available online at https://www.cypnow.co.uk/cyp/news/2003769/g4s-completes-sale-of-childrens-homes-for-gbp11m Accessed 1.11.17

Kadushin, A. (1992) *Supervision in Social Work.* (3rd Ed) (New York) Columbia University Press.

Kadushin, A. and Harkness, D. (2002) *Supervision in Social Work.* (4th Edition) (New York) Columbia Press.

Kadushin, A. and Kadushin, G. (1997) *The social work interview.* (New York) Columbia University Press.

Kapoulitsas, M. and Corcoran, T. (2014) *Compassion fatigue and resilience: A qualitative analysis of social work practice.* Qualitative Social Work, 14(1), 86–101.

Kelly, J. (2016) *Poverty and Ethnicity: Key Messages from Scotland.* Joseph Rowntree Foundation, York, UK. Available from https://www.jrf.org.uk/report/poverty-and-ethnicity-key-messages-scotland Accessed 14.5.17

Kemp, N. (2017) *Six Stereotypes of women in advertising.* Available online at https://www.campaignlive.co.uk/article/six-stereotypes-women-advertising/1426391 Accessed 1.10.17

Kendal, L. and Reed, S. (2015) *Change or get out of the way.* Available at: http://www.progressonline.org.uk/2015/02/05/change-or-get-out-of-the-way/ Accessed 21.2.15

Kennedy, A.L .(2000) *Supervision for Practicing Genetic Counselors: An Overview of Models.* Journal of Genetic Counselling, Vol 9 (5) pp: 379-390

Killian, J. and Todnem, G. (1991) *Reflective judgment concepts of justification and their relationship to age and education.* Journal of Applied Developmental Psychology 2(2) pp. 89-116.

Kim,H., Sherman,D.K., Shelley,D.K., Taylor,E. (2006) *Pursuit of Comfort and Pursuit of Harmony: Culture, Relationships, and Social Support Seeking.* Personality and Social Psychology Bulletin. 1595-1607

Kirin, C. (2016) *How three conversations have changed the way we do social work.* Available at http://www.communitycare.co.uk/2016/05/03/three-conversations-changed-way-social-work/ Accessed 1.11.17

Klimek, A. and Atkisson, A. (2016) *Parachuting Cats into Borneo and other Lessons from the Change Café. A Toolkit of Proven Strategies and Practices for Building Capacity and Creating Transformation.* (Vermont) Chelsea Green Publishing.

Klohnen, E. C. (1996) *Conceptual analysis and measurement of the construct of ego-resiliency.* Journal of Personality and Social Psychology, 70(5), 1067-1079

Knowles, M. (1978) *The Adult Learner: A Negotiated Species.* 2nd edition (Houston) Gulf Publishing

Kolb, D.A. (1984) *Experiential Learning.* (Englewood Cliffs, NJ) Prentice Hall.

Korthagen, F. and Vasalos, A. (2009) *Going to the Core: Deepening Reflection by Connecting the Person to the Profession.* In Lyons, N. (ed) Handbook of Reflection and Reflective Inquiry: Mapping a Way of Knowing for Professional Reflective Inquiry, (Boston) Springer

Laing, R.D (1965) *The Divided Self.* (Harmondworth) Pelican

Laming, L. (2003) The Victoria Climbie An Inquiry. HMSO, London. Available from https://www.gov.uk/government/uploads/system/uploads/attachment_data/file/273183/5730.pdf Accessed 9.8.17.

Lavalette, M. (2011) *Introduction.* In Lavalette, M. (Ed) Radical Social Work Today: Social Work at the Crossroads (Bristol) Policy Press

Lave, J. and Wenger, E. (1990) *Situated Learning: Legitimate Peripheral Participation.* (Cambridge) Cambridge University Press.

Leahy, T. (2012) *Management in 10 Words.* (London) Random House.

Lenkeit, J. Caro, D. and Strand (2015) *Tackling the remaining attainment gap between students with and without immigrant background: an investigation into the equivalence of SES constructs, Educational Research and Evaluation,* Vol 21 (1) 2015, pp. 60-83(24)

Le Navenec, C. and Bridges, L. (Eds) (2005) *Creating Connections Between Nursing Care and The Creative Arts Therapies: Expanding the Concept of Holistic Care.* (Illinois) Charles C Thomas Publishers.

Le Riche, P. (1998) *The Dimensions of Observation. Objective Reality or Subjective Interpretation.* In Le Riche, P. and Tanner, K. (Eds) Observation and its Application to Social Work. (London) Jessica Kingsley.

Lester, S. (1999) *From map-reader to map-maker: approaches to moving beyond knowledge and competence.* In O'Reilly, D, Cunningham, L. and Lester, S. (Eds) Developing the Capable Practitioner. (London) Kogan Page.

Lloyd, A. (2016) *A restorative approach to working with adolescents.* Presentation at Association of Directors of Children's Services Conference. Relationships, Risk and Restorative Approaches: Doing Things Differently for Young People.

Loach, K (1971) *Family Life* http://www.imdb.com/title/tt0068569/

Lombard, D. and Maier, E. (2009) *Exclusive Survey: Media coverage of social work is mostly negative.* Community Care. Available online at http://www.communitycare.co.uk/2009/05/12/exclusive-survey-media-coverage-of-social-work-is-mostly-negative/ Accessed 18.8.17

Lopez, J.J. (2011) *Contemporary Sociological Theories.* Available online at: http://docs.google.com/viewer?a=v&q=cache:JdxbXU3vSGsJ:ssms.socialsciences.uottawa.ca/vfs/horde/offre_cours/0028710205. (Accessed 1.8.11)

Lucas, B. and Greany, T. (2000) *Schools in the Learning Age,* (London) Southgate Publishers,

Lum, D. (2007) *Culturally competent practice: A framework for understanding diverse groups and justice issues.* (Belmont, CA) Brooks/Cole.

Lyons, N. (Ed) (2010) *Handbook of Reflection and Reflective Inquiry: Mapping a Way of Knowing for Professional Reflective Inquiry*. (London) Springer.

Maclean, S. (2012) *The Social Work Pocket Guide to Effective Supervision.* (Lichfield) Kirwin Maclean Associates.

Maclean, S. (2015) *Social Work Theory Cards.* (Lichfield) Kirwin Maclean Associates.

Maclean, S. (2016) *Journeys through Change: Keep calm and keep on travelling.* Key note at Scottish Organisation of Practice Teaching Conference. Glasgow November 2016.

Maclean, S. (2016) *Reflective Practice Cards.* (Lichfield) Kirwin Maclean Associates.

Maclean, S. (2017) *My CPD Journal.* (Lichfield) Kirwin Maclean Associates.

Maclean, S. and Caffrey, B. (2014) *Developing a Practice Learning Curriculum.* (Lichfield) Kirwin Maclean Associates.

Maclean, S. and Harrison, R. (2011) *The Social Work Pocket Guide to Power and Empowerment.* (Lichfield) Kirwin Maclean Associates.

Maclean, S. and Harrison, R. (2014) *The City and Guilds Textbook Level 3 Diploma in Health and Social Care.* (London) City and Guilds.

MacLeod, D. and Clarke, N. (2009) *Engaging for Success: enhancing performance through employee engagement. A Report to Government.* (London) Department for Business, Innovation and Skills.

Mager, D. (2017) *How to have difficult conversations.* Psychology Today. Available online at https://www.psychologytoday.com/blog/some-assembly-required/201703/how-have-difficult-conversations Accessed 20.8.17

Martin, B (1991) *Forgotten Stories.* Social Work Today 19.9.91 p9

Maslach, C., and Leiter, M. P. (1997) *The Truth about Burnout: How Organizations Cause Personal Stress and What to do about It.* (San Francisco, CA) Jossey-Bass.

Mawby, R.I., Fisher, C.J. and Parkin, A. (1979) *Press Coverage of Social Work.* Policy and Politics 7 (4) 357-376.

Maxwell, N., Scourfield, J., Zhang, M.L., De Villiers, T., Hadfield, M., Kinnersley, P., Metcalf, L., Pithouse, A. and Tayyaba, S. (2016) *Independent evaluation of the Frontline Pilot.* Department of Education, London. Available from https://www.gov.uk/government/uploads/system/uploads/attachment_data/file/560885/Evaluation_of_Frontline_pilot.pdf Accessed 11.7.17

Mayhew, H. (1861) *London Labour and the London Poor.* Available from https://archive.org/details/londonlabourand01mayhgoog Accessed 1.11.17

Mazars LLP (2015) *Independent review of deaths of people with a Learning Disability or Mental Health problem in contact with Southern Health NHS Foundation Trust April 2011 to March 2015.* Available online at https://www.england.nhs.uk/south/wp-content/uploads/sites/6/2015/12/mazars-rep.pdf Accessed 1.8.17

McCaughan, S., Anderson, M. and Jones, W. (2013) *Social work education in the creative arts space.* Journal of Practice Teaching and Learning (Special Issue Creative Arts in the professions: Contributing to learning in practice) 12 (1) 34-52

McGregor, K. (2012) *Why social work students should read newspapers* [online] Available: http://www.communitycare.co.uk/blogs/social-work-blog/2012/09/why-social-work-students-shoul/ Accessed 6.5.17

McKendrick, D. and Finch, J. (2016) *Under Heavy Manners: Social Work, Radicalisation, Troubled Families and Non-linear War.* British Journal of Social Work. 47 (2): 308-324.

McKendrick, D. and Finch, J. (2017) *Downpressor man: securitsation, safeguarding and social work,* Critical and Radical Social Work, doi.org/10.1332/204986017X15029697482460

McLeod, A. (2008) *Listening to Children: A Practitioner's Guide.* (London) Jessica Kingsley.

McNab as cited in Tehrani, N. (Ed.) (2010) *Managing trauma in the workplace: Supporting workers and Organisations.* (New York) Routledge.

Menzies-Lyth, I. (1960) *Social systems as a defence against anxiety.* Human Relations, Vol 13, pp: 95-121.

Merriam-Webster online dictionary (2017a) *Reciprocity.* Available from https://www.merriam-webster.com/dictionary/reciprocity Accessed 18.7.17

Merriam-Webster (2017b) *Reciprocal* Available from https://www.merriam-webster.com/dictionary/reciprocal Accessed 18.7.17

Merriam-Webster (2017c) *Evaluate* Available from https://www.merriam-webster.com/dictionary/evaluate Accessed 9.8.17

Merrill, J. (2014) *Mum Test Will Help Inspectors Rate Care Homes.* Available at http://www.independent.co.uk/life-style/health-and-families/health-news/mum-test-will-help-inspectors-rate-care-homes-9783218.html Accessed 1.11.17

Milczarek, M., González, E.R. and Schneider, E. (2009) *OSH in figures: Stress at work-facts and figures.* Office for Official Publ. of the European Communities.

Milner, J. and O'Byrne, P. (2009) *Assessment in Social Work.* Third Edition. (Basingstoke) Palgrave MacMillan.

Montgomery, M. (2008) *An Introduction to Language and Society.* Third edition, (London) Routledge.

Moran, C.C. and Hughes, L.P. (2006) *Coping with Stress: Social Work Students and Humour.* Social Work Education, 25(5), 501-517.

Moriarty, J., Manthorpe, J., Chauhan, B., Jones, G. Wenman, H and Hussein, S. (2009) *Hanging on a Little Thin Line: Barriers to progression and retention.* Social Work Education, The International Journal, Vol 28 (4) 363-379

Morris, K. (2017) *Child Welfare Inequalities.* Keynote Presentation. Resilience in Times of Austerity. Joint PSW Conference. 21 July 2017, Kings College London.

Morrison, F. (2016) *Social workers' communication with children and young people in practice: Iriss Insight 34.* Available online at https://www.iriss.org.uk/resources/insights/social-workers-communication-children-and-young-people-practice Accessed 9.8.17

Morrison, T. (2005) *Staff Supervision in Social Care: Making a Real Difference for Staff and Service Users.* (Brighton) Pavilion.

Morriss, L. (2017) *Multisensorality and social work research.* Qualitative Social Work 16(3) 291 – 299.

Moss, B. (2017) *Communication Skills in Health and Social Care.* (London) Sage Learning Matters.

Mountford-Zimdars, A., Sabri, D, Moore, J., Sanders, J., Jones, S. and Higham, L. (2015) *Causes of Differences in Student Outcomes.* Higher Education Funding Council England, London. Available from http://dera.ioe.ac.uk/23653/1/HEFCE2015_diffout.pdf Accessed 11.7.17

Mullan, R. (2014) *Training should produce social workers well-acquainted with the sector.* In Guardian online, available from https://www.theguardian.com/social-care-network/2014/feb/18/martin-neary-social-workers-education Accessed 1.9.17

Munro, E. (1998) *Improving Social Workers Knowledge Base in Child Protection Work.* British Journal of Social Work. 28: 89-105

Munro, E. (2010) *The Munro Review of child protection – Part one: A systems analysis.* (London) Department for Education.

Munro, E. (2011) *Munro Review of child protection: Final report – A child-centred system.* (London) Department for Education.

Munson, C.E. (2002) *Handbook of Clinical Social Work Supervision.* Third Edition (Binghampton) Haworth Social Work Press

NASW (2010) *How would you complete this sentence? Social work is...* National Association of Social Workers (America) World Social Work Day DVD 2010.

NASW (2017) *Standards and Indicators for Cultural Competence in Social Work Practice.* Available at https://www.socialworkers.org/LinkClick.aspx?fileticket=7dVckZAYUmk%3D&portalid=0 Accessed 1.11.17

National Audit Office (2103) *The role of major contractors in the delivery of public services* (London) The Stationery Office.

National Literacy Trust (2012) *Boys Reading Commission, The report of the All-Party Parliamentary Literacy Group Commission.* Report compiled by the National Literacy Trust. Boys' Reading Commission available from https://literacytrust.org.uk/policy-and-campaigns/all-party-parliamentary-group-literacy/boys-reading-commission/ accessed 1.10.17

Neilson, C. (2011) *The Most Important Thing: Students with Reading and Writing Difficulties Talk About their Experiences of Teachers' Treatment and Guidance.* Scandinavian Journal of Educational Research, Vol 55 (5) pp: 551-565

New Policy Institute (2017) *Disability and Poverty.* Available from http://www.npi.org.uk/files/7414/7087/2444/Disability_and_poverty_SUMMARY_REPORT_FINAL.pdf Accessed 14.5.17

Newberry-Koroluk, A. (2014) *Hitting the ground running: New-conservatism and first year Canadian social work.* Critical Social Work, 14(1), pp. 42–55.

Norfolk, A. (2017) *Christian child forced into Muslim foster care: Concern for girl who 'had cross removed and was encouraged to learn Arabic'* The Times Newspaper, August 2017, available from https://www.thetimes.co.uk/article/christian-child-forced-into-muslim-foster-care-by-tower-hamlets-council-3gcp6l8cs Accessed 1.9.17.

NIASW (2012) *NIASW Consultation.* Available online at https://www.basw.co.uk/resource/?id=1004 Accessed 1.10.17

Nicholl, A. (2016) *Sharon Shoesmith on Baby P, blame and social work's climate of fear.* Community Care online, available from http://www.communitycare.co.uk/2016/08/25/sharon-shoesmith-baby-p-blame-social-works-climate-fear/ Accessed 1.10.17

NSPCC (2016) *Summary of Case Reviews Published in 2016.* Available from https://www.nspcc.org.uk/preventing-abuse/child-protection-system/case-reviews/2016/ Accessed 13.6.17

Nzira, V. (2010) *Social Care with African Families in the UK.* (London) Routledge.

O'Connor, E. (2017) *The [Re]Turn to Relationship-based Social Work.* The Irish Social Worker. (Dublin) IASW.

Office for National Statistics (2016) *Persistent Poverty in the UK and EU 2014.* Available from https://www.ons.gov.uk/peoplepopulationandcommunity/personalandhouseholdfinances/incomeandwealth/articles/persistentpovertyintheukandeu/2014 Accessed 14.5.17

O'Loughlin, M. and O'Loughlin, S. (Eds) (2014) *Effective Observation in Social Work Practice.* (London) Learning Matters Sage.

O'Neill, O. (2002) *A Question of Trust.* (Cambridge) Cambridge University Press.

O'Rourke, L. (2010) *Recording in Social Work: Not Just an Administrative Task.* (Bristol) policy Press

Ostafin, B.D. and Kassman, K.T. (2012) *Stepping out of history: Mindfulness improves insight problem solving.* Consciousness and Cognition 21 (2) pp.1031-1036.

Oxford Dictionaries Online (2014) *Critical.* Available online at: http://www.oxforddictionaries.com/definition/english/critical Accessed 24.10.14

Parkes, J. (2015) *Gender Violence in Poverty Contexts: The educational challenge.* (Oxon) Routledge.

Patterson, K., Grenny, J., McMillan, R., Switzler, A. (2102) *Crucial Conversations: Tools for talking when stakes are high.* (London) McGraw Hill.

Pattoni, L. (2012) *Strengths-based approaches for working with individuals.* Iriss. Available online at https://www.iriss.org.uk/resources/insights/strengths-based-approaches-working-individuals Accessed 19.8.17

Pawson, R., Boaz, A., Grayson, L., Long, A. and Barnes, C. (2003) *Types and Quality of Knowledge in Social Work.* (London) Social Care Institute for Excellence.

Payne, M. (2005) *Modern Social Work Theory.* (Basingstoke) Palgrave.

Pellico, L.H., Friedlaender, and L., Fennie, K.P, (2005) *Looking is not Seeing: Using Art to Improve Observational Skills.* Journal of Nurse Education, 8 (11) 648-653

Philipson, A. (2013) *Woman who campaigned for Jane Austen bank note receives Twitter death threats.* Daily Telegraph (28/7/13) available from http://www.telegraph.co.uk/technology/10207231/Woman-who-campaigned-for-Jane-Austen-bank-note-receives-Twitter-death-threats.html Accessed 10.7.17

Pincus, A. and Minahan, A. (1973) *Social Work Practice: Model and Method.* (Itasca) Peacock.

Pink, S. (2015) *Doing Sensory Ethnography,* 2nd edn. London: Sage.

Pritchard, J, and Leslie, S. (2011) *Recording Skills in Safeguarding Adults: Best Practice and Evidential Requirements.* (London) Jessica Kingsley Publishers

Quinn, F.M. (2000) *The Principles and Practice of Nurse Education.* (4th Edition) (Cheltenham) Stanley Thorn.

Rai, L. (2014) *Effective writing for social work: making a difference.* (Bristol) Policy Press

Reid, S. (2008) *How social services are paid bonuses to snatch babies for adoption.* Daily Mail online, available from : http://www.dailymail.co.uk/news/article-511609/How-social-services-paid-bonuses-snatch-babies-adoption.html#ixzz4xdxnA6UF Accessed 1.11.17

Reid, W.J. and Misener, E. (2001) *Social Work in the Press: a cross national study.* International Journal of Social Welfare 10 (3) 194-201.

Research in Practice (2014) *Developing best practice in reflective supervision.* Available online at https://www.rip.org.uk/news-and-views/blog/developing-best-practice-in-reflective-supervision/. Accessed 2.9.15.

Richardson, S. and Asthana, S. (2006) *Inter-agency Information Sharing in Health and Social Care Services: The Role of Professional Culture.* The British Journal of Social Work, Volume 36, (4) pp 657–669

Roberts, A (2017) *Declaration of Intent* http://studymore.org.uk/mpuhtm accessed 31.08.17

Roberts, D.D., Roberts, L.M., O'Neill, R.M. and Blake-Beard, S.D. (2008) *The Invisible Work of Managing Visibility for Social Change. Insights from the Leadership of Reverend Dr Martin Luther King Jr.* Business and Society. 47(4) 425-456

Rogers, C. (1980) *Freedom to Learn for the 80s.* (New York) Free Press.

Rogers, M., Whitaker D., Edmondson, D. and Peach, D. (2017) *Developing Skills for Social Work Practice.* (London) Sage.

Rogowski, S. (2010) *Social Work: The Rise and Fall of a Profession.* (Bristol) The Policy Press

Romeo, L. (2017) *Think you know supervision? It's about to become a different animal...* Blog available at https://lynromeo.blog.gov.uk/2017/01/11/think-you-know-supervision-its-about-to-become-a-different-animal/ Accessed 3.9.17

Rothlisberger, F. J. and Dickson, W. J. (1939) *Management and the Worker.* (Cambridge) Harvard University Press.

Rowntree, S. (1901) *Poverty: A Study of Town Life* (London) Macmillan and Co, available from https://archive.org/details/povertyastudyto00rowngoog

Ruch, G. (2014) *Helping children is a human process: Researching the challenges social workers face in communicating with children.* British Journal of Social Work, 44, 8, 2145–62

Rushton, A. and Nathan, J. (1996) *The Supervision of Child Protection Work.* The British Journal of Social Work 26. 357-374.

Rustin, M. (2004) *Learning from the Victoria Climbié Inquiry.* Journal of Social Work Practice, 18(1), pp. 9-18.

Ryan, W (1970) *Blaming the Victim.* (New York) Pantheon Books

Said, E.W (1994) *Culture and Imperialism.* (London) Penguin Classics.

Said, E.W (2003) *Orientalism.* (London) Penguin Classics.

Saleebey, D. (1996) *The strengths perspective in social work practice: extensions and cautions.* Social Work 41, 296-305.

Sawyer, P. and Donnelly L. (2015) *Meet the NHS whistle-blowers who exposed the truth.* The Daily Telegraph on line, available from http://www.telegraph.co.uk/news/health/news/11398148/The-NHS-whistle-blowers-who-spoke-out-for-patients.html Accessed 5.9.17

SCIE (2010) *NQSW resource - Outcome statement 8. Recording and sharing information.* Available from http://www.scie.org.uk/publications/nqswtool/information/ Accessed 7.8.17

SCIE (2017) *What is a strengths-based approach to care?* Available online at http://www.scie.org.uk/care-act-2014/assessment-and-eligibility/strengths-based-approach/what-is-a-strengths-based-approach.asp Accessed 19.8.17

Schön, D. (1984) *The Reflective Practitioner: How professionals think in action.* (London) Temple Smith.

Schraer, R. (2014) *Social work is a human rights discipline: IFSW president speaks up for the profession.* Community Care online, available from http://www.communitycare.co.uk/2014/07/23/social-work-human-rights-discipline-ifsw-president-speaks-profession/ Accessed 1.9.17

Schraer, R. (2015) *Social workers too stressed to do their job according to survey.* Community Care online, available from http://www.communitycare.co.uk/2015/01/07/stress-stopping-job-social-workers-say/, accessed 1.9.17

Schwartz, R. H. Tiamiyu, F. and Dwyer, D.J. (2007) *Social worker hope and perceived burnout: the effects of age, years in practice, and setting.* Administration in Social Work, 31(4) 103-119.

Seabury, B.A., Seabury, B.H., & Garvin, C.D. (2011) *Foundations of Interpersonal Practice in Social Work: Promoting Competence in Generalist Practice.* (3rd ed.). Thousand Oaks, CA Sage Publications, Inc.

Segal, E. (2011) *Social Empathy: A Model Built on Empathy, Contextual Understanding, and Social Responsibility That Promotes Social Justice.* Journal of Social Service Research, Vol 37 (3) pp:266-277

Seldon, A. (2009) *Trust: How We Lost it and How to Get It Back.* (London) Biteback.

Shennan, G. (2017) *From Marginalization to community and environmental sustainability: Panel Discussion.* IFSW European Conference 2017. Reyjavik, Iceland.

Silman, J (2015) *Social worker criticised by judge for using jargon in court report.* Community Care Online. Available from http://www.communitycare.co.uk/2015/08/05/social-worker-criticised-judge-using-jargon-court-report/ Accessed 5.10.17.

Singh, G. and Cowden, S. (2009) *The Social Worker as Intellectual.* European Journal of Social Work. 12 (4) 479-453

Siporin, M. (1984) '*Have you heard the one about social work humor?'*, Social Casework: The Journal of Contemporary Social Work, 65, pp. 459–64.

Skills for Care (2011) *Getting a good start: Evaluation of the first year of the Newly Qualified Social Worker framework for adult services, 2009/10.* (Leeds) Skills for Care.

Skills for Care (2013a) *Social Work: Informing judgements and processes.* Available online at www.skillsforcare.org.uk. Accessed 21.3.13.

Skills for Care (2013) *Concept to reality: Implementation of the ASYE with social workers in adult services.* (Leeds) Skills for Care.

Skills for Care (2015) *ASYE longitudinal study report one – Social worker and supervisor surveys.* (Leeds) Skills for Care.

Skinner, B.F. (1973) *Beyond Freedom and Dignity.* (Hammondsworth) Penguin.

Smale, G., Tuson, G., Biehal, N. and Marsh, P. (1993) *Empowerment, Assessment, Care Management and the Skilled Worker.* (London) HMSO.

Smith, M. K. (2002) *Casework and the Charity Organisation Society*. the Encyclopaedia of informal education, www.infed.org/. Last update: July 08, 2014 available from http://www.infed.org/socialwork/charity_organisation_society.htm Accessed 28.8.17

Social Care Institute for Excellence (2004) *Leading Practice: A Development Programme for First Line Managers.* Available online at www.scie.org.uk/publications/leadingpractice/files/SCIE_Participant's_HB.pdf Accessed 1.11.06.

Social Care Institute for Excellence (2009) *Developing User Involvement in Social Work Education.* Available from http://www.scie.org.uk/publications/reports/report29.pdf Accessed 11.7.17

Social Care Institute of Excellence (2016) *Practice issues from Serious Case Reviews 8. Incomplete information-sharing by schools in child protection conferences.* SCIE, London, available from http://www.scie.org.uk/children/safeguarding/case-reviews/learning-from-case-reviews/08.pdf Accessed 9.8.17.

Social Platform (2010) *Briefing Number 33: Annual Theme 2010 on Care.* (Brussels) Social Platform.

Social Work Policy Institute (2011) *Supervision: The Safety Net for Front-Line Child Welfare Practice.* (Washington) National Association of Social Workers.

Social Work Task Force (SWTF) (2009) *Facing up to the Task—The Interim Report of the Social Work Taskforce.* Department of Health, Department for Children, Schools and Families, London.

Spandler, H (2006) *Asylum to Action. Paddington Day Hospital, Therapeutic Communities and beyond.* London, Jessica Kingsley

Spivak G. C. (1985) *The Rani of Sirmur: an essay in reading the archives.* History and Theory, 24(3) 247-272.

Staffordshire Safeguarding Children Board (2017) *Serious Case Review Child B Final Report.* Available online at https://www.staffsscb.org.uk/Professionals/Case-Studies-Case-Reviews/SCIE-SCR-Child-B-FINAL-Report-For-Publication.pdf Accessed 3.10.17

Staempli, A. Fairtlough, A. and Royes, J. (work in progress) *Evaluation of Pilot Implementation of Key Situation Model for Continuous Professional Development Reflective Learning,* available from https://www.researchgate.net/publication/320243898_Evaluation_of_Pilot_Implementation_of_Key_Situation_Model_for_Continuous_Professional_Development_Reflective_Learning accessed 1/9/17

Stanford, S.N. (2011) *Constructing Moral Responses to Risk: A Framework for Hopeful Social Work Practice.* British Journal of Social Work Online March 24, 2011.

Steele, W. and Malchiodi, C.A. (2012) *Trauma-informed Practices with Children and Adolescents.* (London) Routledge.

Steiner, R. (2003) *Unconscious Phantasy.* (London) H Karnac Ltd.

Stenhouse, L. (1975) *An Introduction to Curriculum Research and Development.* (London) Heinemann.

Stevens, I. (2010) *Social Pedagogy and its links to Holding the Space.* Scottish Institute for Residential Care and Action for Children. Available at http://www.sppa-uk.org/wp-content/uploads/2016/10/holding_the_space_and_its_links_to_social_pedagogy.pdf Accessed 10.9.17.

Stevenson, J. (2005) *Professional Supervision in Social Work.* Available online at www.unison-edinburgh.org.uk/socialwork/supervision.html. Accessed 15.10.11.

Stevenson, L. (2017) *People tried to put me off: becoming a social worker after Baby P.* Guardian online available from www.communitycare.co.uk/2017/08/17/people-tried-put-becoming-social-worker-baby-p/ Accessed 10.10.17

Stone, C. and Harbin, F. (2016) *Transformative Learning for Social Work: Learning for and in practice* (London) Palgrave Macmillan.

Sullivan, E. (2000) *Gallows humour in social work practice: an issue for supervision and reflexivity Practice* 12:2 pp 45-54

Survation (2014) *Public Sector and Outsourcing Issues Poll.* Available online at http://survation.com/wp-content/uploads/2014/05/Public-Sector-and-Outsourcing-We-Own-It.pdf Accessed 23.5.17.

Sutton, C. (1999) *Helping Families with Troubled Children.* (London) Wiley.

Swank, E. and Fahs, B. (2014) *Predictors of Feminist Activism among Social Work Students in the United States.* Social Work Education, 33 (4) 519–532.

Taylor, A. (2016) *Books Groups and Fiction: A Novel Approach to teaching and Learning.* In Stone, C. and Harbin, F. (Eds) Transforming Learning for Social Work: Learning for and in Practice, (London) Palgrave Macmillan

Taylor, A. (2016) *'Researching the contribution of social work education to the digital socialisation of students in preparation for practice in the technological age'.* Paper presented to the Social Media for Learning in Higher Education Conference, Sheffield Hallam University, 16 December 2016. Online at https://blogs.shu.ac.uk/socmedhe/16-researching-the-contribution-of-social-work-education-to-the-digital-socialisation-of-students-in-preparation-for-practice-in-the-technological-age/

Taylor, A. (2017) *Social work and digitalisation: bridging the knowledge gaps.* Social Work Education, The International Journal. 36 (8) 869-879.

Taylor, B. J. (2017b) *Decision Making, Assessment and Risk in Social Work.* 3rd edition. (London) Sage Learning Matters.

Tedam, P. (2012) *Using Culturally relevant case studies to enhance students' learning: a reflective analysis of the benefits and challenges for social work students and academics.* Enhancing the Learner Experience in Higher Education. 4(1) 59-69

Tedam, P. and Adjoa, A. (2017) *The W Word: Witchcraft labelling and child safeguarding in social work practice.* (St Albans) Critical Publishing.

Tedam, P. and Munowenyu, M. (2016) *Keeping MANDELA alive: A qualitative evaluation of the MANDELA supervision framework four years on.* Journal of Practice Teaching and Learning. 14(1)

ThemPra Social Pedagogy Community Interest Society (2009) *Social Pedagogy: Theory meets Practice.* Available online at http://www.socialpedagogy.co.uk/concepts.htm Accessed 19.1.10.

Thorolfsdottir, H. (2017) *Keynote presentation: Marginalization and Social Work in a Changing Society.* IFSW European Conference 2017. Reyjavik, Iceland.

Thompson, N. (2005) *Understanding Social Work: Preparing for Practice.* (Basingstoke) Palgrave Macmillan.

Thompson, N. (2010) *Theorizing Social Work Practice.* (Basingstoke) Palgrave Macmillan.

Thompson, N. and Thompson, S. (2016) *The Social Work Companion.* Second edition. (London) Palgrave Macmillan.

Thompson, S. (2016) *Promoting Reciprocity in Old Age: A Social Work Challenge.* Practice, 28 (5) 341-355

Tice, J. W. (1998) *Tales of Wayward Girls and Immoral Women. Case Records and the Professionalization of Social Work.* (Chicago, IL) University of Illinois Press.

Tigervall, C. and Hubinette, T. (2010) *Adoption with complications: Conversations with adoptees and adoptive parents on everyday racism and ethnic identity.* International Social Work. 53(4) 489-509.

Tinson, A. Ayrton, C., Barker, C., Barry Born, T., Aldridge, H and Kenway, H. (2016) *Monitoring Poverty and Social Exclusion 2016.* Joseph Rowntree Foundation and New Policy Institute, available from https://moodle.chs.ac.uk/pluginfile.php/17640/block_html/content/2016_mpse_uk_report_3228_final_0.pdf Accessed 27/9/18

TLAP (2017) *Developing a wellbeing and strengths-based approach to social work Practice: Changing Culture.* Think Local Act Personal. Available online at https://www.thinklocalactpersonal.org.uk/_assets/Resources/TLAP/BCC/TLAPChangingSWCulture.pdf Accessed 3.7.17.

Tolan, J. (2017) *Skills in Person-centered Counselling and Psychotherapy.* (London) Sage.

Tondo, L. and Kelly, A. (2017) *The juju curse that binds trafficked Nigerian women into sex slavery.* The Guardian online, available from https://www.theguardian.com/global-development/2017/sep/02/juju-curse-binds-trafficked-nigerian-women-sex-slavery Accessed 1.10.17

Toren N (1972) *Social work: The case of a semi-profession.* Beverly Hills, Sage.

Trevithick, P. (2003) *Effective relationship-based practice: a theoretical exploration.* Journal of Social Work Practice, vol 17(2), pp. 163 - 176.

Trevithick, P. (2011) *Understanding defences and defensiveness in social work.* Journal of Social Work Practice vol. 25, no. 4, pp. 389–412.

Trollor, J., Srasuebkul, P., Xu, H., and Howlett, S. (2017) *Cause of death and potentially avoidable deaths in Australian adults with intellectual disability using retrospective linked data* BMJ Open 2017;7: e013489. doi: 10.1136/bmjopen-2016-013489

Turbett, C. (2014) *Doing Radical Social Work* (Reshaping Social Work) (Basingstoke) Palgrave.

Tugade, M. M., and Fredrickson, B. L. (2004) *Resilient Individuals Use Positive Emotions to Bounce Back From Negative Emotional Experiences. Journal of Personality and Social Psychology, 86(2), 320-333.*

Turner, F.J. and Rowe, W.S. (2013) *101 Social Work Clinical Techniques.* (New York) Oxford University Press.

Uehara, E. S. (1995) *Reciprocity Reconsidered: Gouldner's 'Moral Norm of Reciprocity' and Social Support.* Journal of Social and Personal Relationships 12 483–502.

Van der Haar, M. (2007) *Ma(r)king Differences in Dutch Social Work: Professional Discourse and ways of Relating to Clients in Context.* (Amsterdam) Dutch University Press.

Wachtel, T. (2016) *Defining Restorative. International Institute for Restorative Practices.* Available online at https://www.iirp.edu/images/pdf/Defining-Restorative_Nov-2016.pdf Accessed 19.8.17

Walker, S., Shemmings, D. and Cleaver, H. (2003) *Write Enough: Effective Recording in Children's Services.* Available at http://www.writeenough.org.uk/ Accessed 1.11.17

Wallcraft, J., Fleischmann, P., and Schofield, P. (2012) *The involvement of users and carers in social work education: A practice benchmarking study.* (London) Social Care Institute for Excellence.

Weade, G. and Evertson, C. M. (1991) *On what can be learned by observing teaching.* Theory into Practice 30 (1) pp. 37-45.

Webb, S. (2007) *Social Work in a Risk Society.* (Basingstoke) Palgrave

Welbourne, P. (2012) *Social Work with Children and Families: Developing advanced practice.* (Oxon) Routledge.

We Own It (2017) *What's the Problem with Outsourcing Companies?* Available at https://weownit.org.uk/privatisation-doesn%E2%80%99t-work/whats-problem-outsourcing-companies Accessed 22.5.17

Weiss-Gal, I and Welbourne, P. (2008) *The professionalisation of social work: a cross-national exploration,* International Journal of Social Welfare, Vol 17 (4) pp 281-290, available from http://onlinelibrary.wiley.com/doi/10.1111/j.1468-2397.2008.00574.x/full

White, S., Hall, C. and Peckover, S. (2009) *The Descriptive Tyranny of the Common Assessment Framework: Technologies of Categorization and Professional Practice in Child Welfare.* The British Journal of Social Work, Volume 39, Issue 7, 1 October 2009, Pages 1197–1217.

White, S., Wastell, D., Broadhurst, K. and Hall, C. (2010) *When policy o'erleaps itself: The 'tragic tale' of the Integrated Children's System,* Critical Social Policy, Vol 30 (3) pp:405-429

White, V. (2009) *Quiet Challenges: Professional Practice in Modernised Social Work.* In Harris, J. and White, V. (Eds) Modernising Social Work: Critical Considerations. (Bristol) Policy Press.

Wilkins, D. and Boahen, G. (2013) *Critical Analysis Skills for Social Workers.* (Berkshire) Open University Press.

Williams, A. (2013) *The Listening Organisation.* (Cardiff) 1000 Lives Plus.

Williams, S. and Rutter, L. (2007) T*he Practice Educator's Handbook*. (London) Sage Learning Matters.

Williams, S. and Rutter, L. (2015) *The Practice Educator's Handbook.* 2nd edition. (London) Sage Learning Matters.

Witkin, S. L. (1999) *'Taking humour seriously',* Social Work, 44(2) 101–4.

Woodham, G., Hanrahan, J. and Markley, K. (2017) *Social Work Apprenticeships.* Presentation at Joint PSW Conference. 21 July 2017, Kings College London.

Wolfensberger, W. (1983) *Social role valorisation: A proposed new term for the principle of normalisation.* Mental Retardation, 21, pp. 234-239.

Wright, A. and Pearson, S. (2017) *Dynamic Duos: Northumberland.* Presentation at Joint PSW Conference. 21 July 2017, Kings College London.

Zuchowski, I. Savage, D., Miles D. & Gair, S. (2013) Decolonising field education challenging Australian social work praxis. Advances in Social Welfare and Social Welfare Education, 15 (1) pp47-62